m S. Anderson

Why Horace?

A Collection of Interpretations

Bolchazy-Carducci Publishers, Inc.
Wauconda, Illinois

General Editor
Laurie K. Haight

Contributing Editors
Gaby Huebner
Georgia Irby-Massie

Cover Design and Typesetting
Charlene M. Hernandez

Lyre Graphic
Adapted from
Costumes of the Greeks and Romans
by Thomas Hope

© 1999 Bolchazy-Carducci Publishers, Inc.

Printed in the United States of America
1999
by BookCrafters

Bolchazy-Carducci Publishers, Inc.
1000 Brown Street
Wauconda, Illinois 60084 USA

http://www.bolchazy.com

Paperback: ISBN 0-86516-417-7
Hardbound: ISBN 0-86516-434-7

Library of Congress Cataloging-in-Publication Data

Why Horace? : a collection of interpretive essays / edited by William
S. Anderson
      p.   cm.
   Includes bibliographical references (p.).
   ISBN 0-86516-434-7 (paperback : alk. paper)
   1. Horace--Criticism and interpretation. 2. Laudatory poetry,
Latin--History and criticism. 3. Epistolary poetry, Latin--History
and criticism. 4. Verse satire, Latin--History and criticism.
5. Rome--In literature.   I. Anderson, William Scovil, 1927-
PA6411.W49 1998
874'.01--dc21   98-45905
                                                         CIP

Contents

Introduction

Horace: Odes I

Horace: Odes II

Horace: Odes III

Horace: Odes IV

Horace: Satire I.9

Bibliography

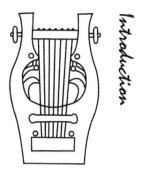

INTRODUCTION TO HORACE, ESPECIALLY THE ODES

The title of the volume might be read in a tone of complaint: Why do I or we have to read Horace of all people? That is obviously not the intention of those who have carefully chosen to add Horace to the subjects of Advance Placement and then have given considerable thought to the poems which students should read from his versatile output. Nor is it my intention as I have put together this volume: Horace is one of my favorite Latin poets, and I have worked with affection for all those who would benefit from exposure to him. Or we may think of the title rather as an answer to a question, addressing, we hope, the curiosity and interest of readers who perhaps know a little about Horace or have read some of his verse and, having done so, want to know more. The essays in this volume have a lot of enthusiastic answers.

Except for one, all the Horatian poems in this volume are odes, and all but one of them come from the collection which Horace published in 23 B.C. in three Books or book-rolls. Mainly, then, you are being asked to encounter a series of lyric poems that were written by a man of thirty going on to forty. What Horace did before he was thirty is very interesting and no doubt affected the ways he regarded Rome and the momentous changes it experienced while he was composing these odes; and it certainly influenced his view of poetry. Let us then briefly go back to the year of his birth, December in 65 B.C., and review the thirty-five years that take us to the approximate beginning of the Odes in 30.

Horace could not claim distinguished origins. He came from Apulia in the south of Italy; his father had been a slave, acquired his freedom, and as a *libertinus* worked his way into the middle class; of Horace's mother, we know nothing, so presumably she died when he was very young. Horace was unaware, we may assume, of the confused and menacing political events that wracked Rome when he was a child in Venusia: Cicero and Catiline; Crassus and Pompey; the rise of Julius Caesar. But early in the 50s, the ambitious father packed up, moved to Rome, and devoted every effort to seeing that his son Horace received the best education that money could buy and a father's constant attention could insure. He actually escorted the boy to and from his classes, acting as a humble pedagogue instead of the affluent man he was: it must have been embarrassing at the time, but an experience to which later the mature Horace would look back with pride and gratitude. So Horace was a schoolboy while Caesar formed and controlled the First Triumvirate and while Catullus was amazing literary Rome with his poems on Lesbia and Neoteric practices. He seems to have acquired the anti-Caesarian sentiments of his fellow students (sons of Senators) and the interest in Catullan innovations that a young man of talent would naturally feel. War broke out in 49, when Horace was in his sixteenth year, and Caesar passed the Rubicon to take all Italy, then crossed the Adriatic to defeat Pompey and his Senatorial army at Pharsalus. Horace stayed in Rome and finished his rhetorical training. Just before Rome settled down under Caesar's domination, Horace went to Athens, with other young men like Cicero's son, to receive the equivalent of a "university education" at that Center of Learning. That educational phase of his youth came to a drastic halt after the Ides of March of 44, when the assassination of Caesar ushered in a long period of political chaos and forced Horace, for a while, to act on his political beliefs.

He threw himself passionately into the cause of the Republican regicides, eagerly following Brutus after he addressed the Roman students in Athens. In the position of a junior officer he fought at Philippi in 42, where Brutus and Cassius and the Republican cause went down to defeat. (He later wrote Ode 2.7 about those days.) That seems to have been the end of Horace's active political engagement, certainly the end of his ardent support of Senatorial opposition to the ambitions of Octavian. He came back to Rome and started in a new direction.

Although his father was probably dead and much of his wealth in Apulia gone as a result of Octavian's confiscations for his soldiers, there was still enough money so that Horace could buy himself a lucrative position in the equivalent of our Civil Service. Using that as a basis of security, Horace lived prudently in the city and started to make friends among the writers and literary patrons of the time. He met Vergil, five years his senior, and they hit it off well, sharing ideas about poetry, with which by this time Horace was no doubt heavily engaged. Through Vergil, he met Maecenas, the right-hand man of Octavian in Rome and a highly intelligent and supportive patron of the arts. (To Maecenas, for example, Horace will dedicate his collection of Odes, as we shall see in Ode 1.1.) Horace became a frequent companion of Maecenas, which suggested to many Romans that this man was a political opportunist and warm supporter of Octavian's faction, a charge with which Horace deals as early as 35 B.C. in Satire 1.9. There, he implies that his relationship with Maecenas was based on friendship and common literary interests.

Living in Rome, then, he tried to avoid politics in spite of the oppressive frictions between Octavian and Antony, and he wrote a lot of poetry. By 35 B.C. he had his first collection ready for publication: ten Satires, which were informal moral discourses on life in Rome, a brilliant adaptation of the poetry of Lucilius a century earlier, in the light of the modern interests of the Neoterics and their Hellenistic model Callimachus. In the next five years, Horace worked on a second, even more innovative collection of Satires and on a set of lyrics, partially in the vitriolic style of the Greek poet Archilochus and partly along the playful amatory lines of his Neoteric predecessors. Book 2 of the Satires and the collection of seventeen Epodes were both published in 30, just after Augustus finished off Antony at Actium in 31 and then freed himself from the threat of his paramour and ally Cleopatra the next Spring. So at this point Horace was a successful and versatile poet, living in a peaceful Roman world that was about to embark on the long and fruitful Augustan Era. (In fact, Maecenas had given him a villa in the Sabine Hills, so Horace alternated his residence between the monumental urban center and the quiet rural landscape.)

Under these conditions and from this background, Horace at age thirty-five began to pour out the most famous of his long series of works, the three Books of Odes. What did he achieve, then, that makes it important for us to read and study him? First, we must recognize his own claim, that he introduced certain Greek meters into Latin. If you have been reading Vergilian hexameters and perhaps some of the poetry of Catullus, you will perhaps have some respect for hexameters, elegiac couplets, and hendecasyllables. You may even have read one or both Catullan experiments in the Sapphic stanza. But when you start on Horace, you are dazzled and daunted by his metrical variety and ingenuity, from the first poem in Book 1 of the Odes. The first four poems in our selection all have different metrical patterns. Horace, in fact, was so proud of his originality that he used nine different patterns in 1.1–9 and then added a tenth in 1.11. Horace polished what he considered the awkwardness of Catullan Sapphics, giving the stanza the finished shape that it used through the remainder of antiquity (in Seneca and later poets). He seems to have been the first to try the even more demanding Alcaic stanza and the five different patterns of Asclepiadeans. Sapphics, Alcaics, and Asclepiadeans: those are the predominant meters of the Odes. You will encounter only one other meter in this selection, namely, in 4.7, where the use of the hexameter and a shorter variant, for grand effect, should occasion you little difficulty. Horace uses all with the ease of a master, sensing the individual tonal possibilities of each pattern. It is to be hoped that your experience of Horace will make you able to enjoy his meters and to appreciate the ways in which they enhance his poetic themes.

This volume makes little effort to explain Horatian meter except as an element in the interpretation of the poems. Similarly, it leaves to other resources the all-important area of Horace's grammar and choice of words, his marvellous placing of them in an intricate pattern that a century ago Nietzsche compared to the tesserae of a mosaic. What these pages offer is a variety of interpretations of the individual odes selected and some guidance to the way the poet introduces and develops his favorite themes and situations. I might classify the odes here in four groups (some of them overlapping): (1) The poet and his vocation; (2) Love; (3) The importance of seizing the moment and enjoying it, in accordance with the injunction *carpe diem*; (4) The poet's response to the historical events of his lifetime and to Augustus, who was transforming Rome and the Roman world. Let me review these four groups for a while.

1. The Poet and his Lyric Vocation

The opening poem of the three books of Odes, 1.1, and the closing poem, 3.30, together the only examples of the particular Asclepiadean pattern employed, offer us significant insights into the way the poet wants us to regard him. In 1.1, as the essay by Pomeroy shows, he includes his own poetic concern along with the more common goals that people set for themselves in sports, politics, and business, but in the end expresses his desire to be associated with the great Greek lyric poets (such as Sappho and Alcaeus of Lesbos, line 34). The relative modesty of this opening poem can be contrasted with the strong confidence of 3.30, where Horace proclaims the immortality of his achievement (which includes his metrical originality, lines 13–14) and invites the Muse to crown him. Woodman, in his discussion, demonstrates how deftly the poet adapts and innovates on themes that poets before him have used to claim their own immortality.

In other poems, Horace develops what I may call a personal myth about his special providence as poet. He escaped death at the Battle of Philippi (Ode 2.7) because Mercury intervened and spirited him away (evidently so that, surviving, he could become the poet he is). He had a narrow escape from the ambitious bore in Satire 1.9, and that was because Apollo saved him (line 78) or, in more human terms, because he was thinking about poetry before the fellow's rude intrusion. Apollo, god of poetry, saved his poet. Ode 1.22 features another miraculous escape, when Horace, rapturously singing love poetry about Lalage, suddenly encountered a monstrous wolf near his Sabine Farm; and the beast turned tail without hurting our unarmed hero (line 12). In the case of this poem, however, as Davis' essay ingeniously argues, there is more than the familiar theme of the poet's special safety. Horace is also resolving a potential generic conflict in his poetic output, declaring, so to speak, as he routs the wolf, that he has finished with and now rejects the themes of the violent and wolfish iambic poets of Greece like Archilochus (inspiration for the earlier Epodes) and opts for the amatory themes that characterize poets like Sappho, Alcaeus, and Anacreon. It is no accident that 1.22 uses the Sapphic stanza.

Other essays reflect on Horace's active role as poet or his possible defects as a writer. Fitzgerald, for example, studies the final poem of Book 1, 1.38 (which is well recognized to have generic concerns) and the quite different 3.13, in order to show how the poet worked his way through his text to a sense of pleasure. Akbar Khan interprets 1.24 as Horace's criticism of what he believed a poor elegiac poem that Vergil supposedly wrote on the death of a close poet-friend, Quintilius Varus: Horace shows Vergil how he should have approached his theme. A. J. Woodman takes Horace to task for his uninspired reliance on clichés in 2.3. And in the first Roman Ode, 3.1, as Witke emphasizes, Horace ostentatiously announces his role as priest and prophet to the young people of Rome (lines 1–4) and then uses the main body of the poem to demonstrate his ethical integrity, free of the corrupting materialism of the times: he shrewdly avoids the moral dangers of the city of Rome, leading a modest life of contentment and poetic creativity in the Sabine countryside. Horace is preoccupied with all aspects of poetry throughout these Odes.

2. Horace as a Poet of Love

For those who believe that a love lyric should be the passionate declaration of a lover to his or her beloved, Horace's love poems are somewhat disappointing, at first. He was writing these in the heyday of the elegists Propertius and Tibullus, whose poems feature a male lover who registers the various degrees of his passion, especially his disappointment, anger, and frustration, to Cynthia, Delia, and the aptly-named Nemesis. Horace takes apart the elegiac situation of paired love and the elegiac monologue of the ardent lover and exposes it to his own and our ironic observation. Thus, he composes love poems that add a third person to the pair of would-be lovers and inject a note of practical realism into the artificial scheme of elegiac ardor. We come away from his love poetry smiling indulgently at the amusing behavior of lovers.

In the first such ode selected, 1.5, we meet a speaker who watches with imprecise emotion the passionate lovemaking of an obvious courtesan named Pyrrha and an inexperienced younger man (*puer*, 1) whose name is unknown to the speaker. Vessey gives us a detailed reading of the poem, line by line, and he is particularly good on the personality of Pyrrha that emerges in comparison with the naiveté of the "boy." He points out, for example, that Pyrrha has prepared for this assignation by makeup and dress and that she obviously plays a role with the boy as an eagerly responding lover. The speaker, the observant third person, has a role far more important than that of an objective reporter. He knows Pyrrha not only by name, but by personal experience from a time before this. Thus, although he affects to be merely concerned for the boy's future disappointments with Pyrrha, he proves more concerned with his own memories regarding this fascinating woman, memories which, in spite of his assertions, might be aroused again to another attempt. Horace, then, has taken an elegiac match and expanded it to a lover's triangle and given the speaker's role to the odd man out. With similar skill, he represents another triangle in 1.13, and Segal's essay has elegantly captured the complex of passion and comedy that we hear from the mouth of the third man who painfully watches the success of another *puer* (line 11), Telephus, with another woman, Lydia, who interests him very much.

That is one strategy of presenting love that Horace uses to query ironically the conventions of popular elegy. Another is to depict the lover wooing the girl, with familiar motifs from the elegiac repertoire, yet finally in a self-serving manner that exposes the egotism of elegiac love and the love that we know in our own experience and that the world has always known. Ancona's essay on 1.23 provides a fine reading of Horace's poetic strategy here. An older male addresses Chloe and compares her, with smiling disapproval, to a frightened doe. He teases out the comparison and tries to argue that, just as the fears of his fictional doe are imaginary, so Chloe's suspicions of him have no true basis. He does not intend to hurt her at all. She should act her age, then, which, according to him, is designed to please a man like himself. Ancona analyzes the ways in which Horace constructs male desire, correctly refusing to take sides with the lover's rhetoric of the speaker. We should resist him, too. I find a similar strategy but a more devious rhetoric in 1.25, so devious that it has fooled commentators more than it would its addressee Lydia. By artful use of tenses, the speaker turns the conventional threat of old age for the woman into a confident prediction, in the vain hope that she will open her door to him now. I have also reviewed the self-serving rhetoric of the speaker to Leuconoe in 1.11, as he perverts to his own use the normally altruistic Horatian advice of *carpe diem*. We will discuss that theme next. I have already mentioned above that 1.22 functions as a love story: it uses the elegiac topos that a true lover is safe no matter where he may be, because of his love. Davis, however, also demonstrates that Horace uses the poem to define his generic choice. So love can easily be combined by the poet with other themes.

An ingenious variation on the innovation of elegiac material is Ode 3.9, which Horace has cast as a genuine dialogue between former lovers that leads, it would appear, to their temporary reunion. Putnam examines the personalities and commitments of the man and woman; he is unnamed, but she is Lydia again. By the very arrangement of the conversation, with the male initiating proposals and Lydia disposing of them, we gather the power that she has in the relation now. He may have been the first to get restless and choose another woman, Chloe, but she quickly found herself a lover and aroused his jealousy and desire for reconciliation. We listen to this dialogue, biased for neither party, and we are led to reflect on the complex forms in which love operates and the curious ways lovers use words both to convey and conceal their feelings.

3. Carpe diem

I have mentioned that Horace combines a lover's wooing line with the theme of *carpe diem* in 1.11. In fact, the phrase *carpe diem* occurs in the final verse of the ode, used to urge Leuconoe to adapt her time, against her wiser inclinations, to the advantages of the wooer. The wooer in 1.23 made the same pitch in different words. When we translate the phrase as "seize the day or the moment," we should understand that the verb *carpe* implies a metaphor connected with agriculture: "plucking" or "picking the fruit." Thus, in English love-poetry, there arose a common equivalent that stated the metaphor as "Gather ye roses while ye may." In terms of fruit, it would be: "Pluck and enjoy the fruit while it is ripe."

Obviously, we should not need to limit such general advice to the sphere of amatory relations. All life is a struggle to achieve the means and determination to enjoy its wonderful opportunities. Ever since the fourth century B.C., the Classical world had become familiar with the philosophy of Epicurus, who recognized as the primary goal of human beings pleasure (*voluptas* for his Roman follower Lucretius, and Horace in many poems) and the need to educate the soul to a proper inclination for true pleasure and not simply for the unreliable goods of material affluence and political power. Horace uses *carpe diem* themes in all kinds of odes to older men of wealth and power, to young men who run the danger of uncritically imitating the mistaken model of their elders, and, as we have seen, to women who are prudently shying from an amatory commitment where they might be exploited. He is still urging the theme in the one poem from Book 4 that has been selected; and by then the poet was over fifty.

In the first relevant selection of the Odes, 1.9, the speaker is an older man encouraging a younger, Thaliarchus, to defy the threat of winter and old age while he can and to enjoy the opportunities of love and play in the Campus Martius with the faintly resisting courtesans. Rudd's essay nicely works out the system of contrasts by which Horace moves us from an opening scene of still snow on Mt. Soracte to the spring-time games of young men and women in Rome. In earlier poems of Book 1, Horace had first worked out the themes of *carpe diem* with older men of political eminence, namely, the consul Sestius of 23 B.C. and the soldier-politician Plancus, who, among other things had proposed in 27 B.C. that Octavian be hailed forever as Augustus. Now that the Civil Wars were over and the talents of these men were not in demand in a period of peaceful reconstruction, they needed to find new directions for their existence. They were middle-aged and comfortably rewarded with estates; what could they do with their time? In my essay on 1.11, I briefly review the arguments of *carpe diem*, especially as they have been defined in Gregson Davis' recent book on Horace, *Polyhymnia*; and I show how the succession of serious poems, 1.4, 7, and 9, allows Horace the opportunity to play off the ironies of 1.11 against that seriousness. His first and only use of the phrase *carpe diem*, then, assumes that we can smile at the perfunctory and selfish way that its speaker uses it on that occasion.

The three Odes selected from Book 2 are all *carpe diem* poems, each one significantly different from the others and each differently viewed by its essayist. In 2.3 Horace addresses another politician who made good in the wars up to Actium in 31 B.C., but has since then had no important role in the Augustan Era. He has his estate on the lower Tiber and all the comforts that the materialistic heart could crave. Dellius, as he was named, was not a very virtuous or principled politician, but he had been a determined opportunist and survivor. Now that he has survived, though, with maybe twenty more years to live, can he make life worthwhile? Woodman argues that this poem is so cliché-ridden, that it is a partial failure. But that is because he believes that Horace addresses a man who is already using every effort to exploit his opportunities for pleasure. I believe that Dellius stands for the many people of affluence who are regular topics of the Epicureans, because they do not know how to live happily and wrongly assume that lavish expense on villas, trips, yachts, and parties will automatically bring them peace of mind. So Horace's Dellius has not grasped the point of intelligent *carpe diem*. A quiet picnic in the country with a few friends can produce far more pleasure than another new villa on the seashore.

Postumus of 2.14 is probably a fictional character with a name that Horace has usefully appropriated, to emphasize his theme of time. Otherwise, he is evidently as affluent as Dellius. Varying the usual organization of *carpe diem*, the poet never does get to that injunction. He does, however, dwell on all the terrible misery that inevitably awaits Postumus after death and his pathetic deprivation from some wonderful wealth and family warmth that he now could and should be enjoying. Thus, the obvious, but unstated, conclusion of the poem is: *carpe diem*. The third poem, 2.7, blends *carpe diem* with political themes, which I shall next discuss. As the occasion for this ode, Horace has chosen the time soon after an old friend of his, usefully named Pompeius, has at last returned from his diehard resistance to Octavian during the Civil Wars. He was a contemporary of Horace and a soldier-comrade until the defeat at Philippi in 42 B.C. separated them: Horace stopped fighting and went home to Italy, whereas Pompeius continued fighting another decade, until Actium, always on the losing side. Now he has come home under amnesty. There have been changes beyond his and Horace's control, and the future surely menaces them with more change. In the present, however, they do have some power to affect the day they are living. Seize the day, then, says Horace; let us celebrate the renewal of our friendship, even with a certain crazy indulgence. Present friendship matters more than all those disappointing battles of the past fifteen years and whatever troubles the future years bring to us as we age.

The varying situations in which Horace proposes *carpe diem* and the varying ways he puts the argument mean that we find it in a vast number of his poems. He used it in Book 3, but the odes selected do not feature it. Only in 3.1 do we discover its muted message in the contrast between the anxious men of power and wealth who cannot sleep for worry and, on the other hand, the person who desires only what is enough (25), of whom the best example is the poet at the end, who prefers the peace and obscurity of his Sabine valley to riches that cost people so much trouble (*divitias operosiores* 48). And as I mentioned, *carpe diem* is the central theme of 4.7, to which Fredericksmeyer has devoted a favorable essay. It was A. E. Housman who once, in a moment of unexpected softness, declared 4.7 the "most beautiful poem in ancient literature." It has the basic themes, or clichés, if you prefer; but it has combined them, as Horace does elsewhere, with spectacular success.

4. Horace and the Politics of the Augustan Era

As I stated when giving biographical data on Horace, he was educated in Rome with sons of senators and probably adopted the political inclinations of their class against Julius Caesar. When Caesar was murdered in 44, then, he joined the ranks of the forces that defended the regicides and fought against Octavian, because he and his friends did not wish to see a continuation of Caesar's domination in the person of his adopted son. Therefore, if in the years before Actium he came to side with Octavian against Antony, it was because the Republican cause had failed, and he preferred Octavian to Antony (as most Italians did). It was also because Octavian went to great lengths to avoid being a clone of his adoptive father, Julius Caesar. He kept his wars away from Italy and worked to bring peace and gradual prosperity to a world that had been exhausted and ravaged by Civil Wars. That meant that it was possible and permissible for men like Horace, who had been on the losing side, to lead their lives without necessarily being co-opted by propaganda of the winner.

Horace wrote about Augustus and reflected on the political scene in Rome and the Empire in some odes from every book. Our selection gives us only a few of those. In the early Satire 1.9, written by 35 B.C., well before Actium, Horace represents the tension in his personality between his commitment to poetry and his disinterest in politics. This tension is epitomized in his attitude toward Maecenas: he regards Maecenas exclusively as an intellectual friend, a fellow admirer of literature, and he seems to be blind and deaf to the political importance of this dedicated and powerful supporter of Octavian, who regularly rules Rome and Italy during the many military absences of Octavian in this period. Thus, when he encounters an ambitious climber, who seeks to use Horace to worm his way into the power center near Maecenas, it becomes a "war" that the wretched poet wants no part of.

Then, in 1.37 we read the controversial ode that takes as its occasion the death of Cleopatra some nine months after Actium in 30 B.C. Horace does name Caesar in connection with the queen's flight from the naval battle (line 16), but he does so in poetic terms that divide our sympathies. At first, Caesar seems to function as a true Roman hero who reduces the arrogant Egyptian to proper humility and terror in defeat (13–15). When, however, the poet appends a simile to his description, he compares Caesar to a hawk or a pitiless hunter and Cleopatra to a dove or a rabbit, that is, to a harmless prey. And then he goes on to describe the suicide of the queen as an act of heroism, far beyond what one would expect of a decadent foreigner and a woman (*generosius, nec muliebriter*). At the least, it would seem that Cleopatra replaces Octavian in our admiration; at the worst, as Johnson brilliantly suggests, she serves to demonstrate the shallow inanity of Octavian's propaganda, a person too grand to be confined and grasped by his superficial political methods. Horace has certainly not let himself become a mere Augustan adherent.

In Book 2, two of the selected odes touch upon political concerns. As Moles argues in his essay on 2.7 (which we have discussed for its exemplification of *carpe diem*), the early part of the poem casts a jaundiced glance at the Battle of Philippi, where Horace and his friend Pompeius fought under Brutus hoping to defeat Octavian and Antony, with disastrous results. Brutus, it appears, was not an able general, only a man of approximate Stoic *virtus*, and he failed to discipline his army into an effective fighting force. Half the poem concentrates on the stages of the Republican debacle at Philippi, so that it is impossible for Horace or Pompeius to regard it as a noble defeat. And that means that Horace was right to give up the fight right then and there, but also that Pompeius, looking back at it now, has no reason to blame himself but rather the incompetent Brutus. Nowhere does Horace view the battle in terms of Augustan propaganda, which treated the Republicans as murderers (especially Brutus for his role on the Ides of March) and Octavian as the righteous avenger of his "father" Julius. He vowed a Temple to Mars, if he were victorious; and many years later that temple rose as the central focus of the magnificent Forum of Augustus. Horace, then, leaves out the political purposes of his conqueror at Philippi. Yet in a way he gives Augustus credit for bringing Pompeius back from his years of futile fighting, back to Rome and renewed friendship with his former comrade. The question that he asks at the start, "Who has given you back to Italy as a citizen?" gets no open answer in the ode. Nevertheless, it is Augustus who, by his general amnesty, has made life in Rome a safe possibility again for Pompeius. Horace thus puts implicit stress on the positive results of the Augustan Peace, which provide the ideal conditions for true Epicurean pleasure, for the realization of *carpe diem*.

The occasion of 2.10 could have been a signal opportunity for political commentary. It addresses Licinius, who is almost surely the elected consul of 23 B.C. who entered a still-obscure plot against Augustus, was quickly executed, and replaced. Licinius had been adopted by a prominent man named Terentius Varro, whose daughter Terentia was the wife of Maecenas. Of all these complex relationships and the purposes and developments of the planned assassination of Augustus, Horace says nothing. Instead, he addresses Licinius as though he were simply a representative of a politician at the outset of his career, capable of listening to some well-put truisms about moderation, about what Horace neatly epitomizes for posterity as the "Golden Mean." Reagan's essay takes the poetic themes of Horace as his exclusive topic and shows how the poet has built up his argument in terms of oxymoron. More than one commentator has expressed his disappointment, that Horace did not exhibit more political concern and help modern historians to understand better the facts of Licinius' conspiracy. But Horace didn't deal with burning political issues, anymore than Licinius listened to counsels of moderation.

In refusing opportunities to exploit current events and in muting the warlike achievements of Octavian-Augustus and the importance of military exploits, Horace stands apart from the warm supporters of Augustus and the Augustan program of moral and political reform. He is too much of an Epicurean to want to participate in the toil and anxieties of political activity. This distancing from the Augustan achievement shows up in the first Roman Ode, 3.1, where Horace turns political power into anxiety, epitomized in the Sword of Damocles (17–21) and in the frenzied efforts of the rich to buy happiness with new buildings and boats; where, then, he concludes by opting for a simple existence, free of anxiety, on his Sabine Farm. He will write poetry, not serve the Roman state; and he constantly attempts to lure Maecenas away from his responsibilities in Rome to some days of quiet enjoyment with him at the Farm. Even more insidious could be the implications of the final poem of Book 3, 3.30. As Woodman shows, Horace claims his poetry as his eternal Monument—Augustus had just completed his great funeral Monument or Mausoleum in the Campus Martius—and ranks himself, like Augustus, *princeps* (13), a leader who first planted a Greek colony (*deduxisse* 14) of Greek meters on Italian soil. Horace here appears to apply to his poetic career the language of Augustan politics, as if to suggest by metaphor that he, as poet, is on a par with, or superior to, the ruler of Rome, his former enemy.

To come back now to the question, Why Horace? I hope that I have sketched a life of considerable activity in a period of momentous changes in Rome and introduced a poet who was a supreme artist of meter, language, and lyric originality. Horace will not echo the transports of youth. He brings understanding, tolerant irony, and a strong sense of ethical independence to the Roman world he portrays. We are fortunate to have access to his poetic talents, so as to balance the elegiac enthusiasms of Propertius and Tibullus and the reluctant political dedication of Vergil. His is a unique voice that we need to hear.

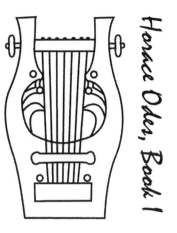

Horace Odes, Book 1

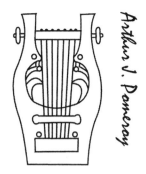

A MAN AT A SPRING: HORACE, ODES 1.1

Horace's first Ode functions as an introduction to the entire collection, and its emphasis falls on the role of the lyric poet in ancient society and Horace's self-consciousness as such a poet. He adopts a rhetorical form familiar to Greek poets and orators and to their Roman admirers: we call it today a "priamel." It lists a number of choice goals or occupations that three or more groups prefer, in order to lead up to the particular choice that the speaker wants to stress. Pomeroy gives a good example from Sappho on p. 11. Horace however creates perhaps the longest priamel in ancient literature: the choices of others occupy lines 3–28, and only at 29 with *me* do we come emphatically to the poet's enthusiastic version of being blessed by the Muses. Pomeroy reviews the special way that Horace employs the priamel, with irony about the objects of other men's ambitions, for example, the Olympic victors of the chariot race in 3–6 ("collecting dust" and "grazing the pole with their wheel") and the successful candidates in Roman elections in 7–8 ("exalted by the fickle citizens"), but also irony about his own ideal ("hitting the stars with his head" 36), and he suggests that the poem operates on two levels. Using the simple structure of the priamel, Horace seems to exalt the role of the lyric poet over all other human pursuits. But by complicating his material with irony and with "a man at a spring" at 19–22, who strikes us as a version of the poet enjoying his creative leisure, he invites us in his audience to correct the initial impression of the priamel. Horace is really not an exception to the one-sided way we all regard our chosen careers: he is, and he will show himself to be so in subsequent poems, a man of recognizably human proportions. (Ed.)

The first poem in a new poetry book is of paramount importance. As the first that a reader — or browser — would see, it acted as a virtual preface by giving some indication of the content and style of the whole collection. While the initial poems in books of elegies and satires have often enough been examined for their 'programmatic' content, the function of the first of Horace's odes is less clear.

In the main, scholars have not been particularly impressed by or interested in the first of Horace's odes. Fraenkel's remarks on the poem may be taken as representative:

This essay originally appeared in *Ramus* 9 (1980) 34–50 and is reprinted here by kind permission of Aureal Publications.

In the greater part of the ode Horace does not say anything especially original. What he wanted to put forward in this proem to
his new songs was a bold, though not arrogant, statement of his
own hopes and, preparatory to it, an elaborate variation of a theme
that had often been treated before.[1]

The 'meaning' is clear — the poem is an introduction to Horace the poet,
expressing 'the poet's desire to be included in the canon of classics.'[2] But in
order not to be too forthright in the statement of this desire, Horace delays
his wish by leading up to it through the familiar form of the priamel. Such
was the interpretation of Pseudo-Acro:

> exponit varia esse hominum ingenia et non unas voluptates, ne
> sit arrogantiae quod sibi poeticam vindicare videtur, cum singulos
> quosque rerum aliarum diversus amor habeat.[3]

> Horace explains that there are various natural inclinations among
> men and no single pleasure, in case it should be taken as a mark
> of arrogance that he seems to claim poetry for himself when dif-
> ferent desires for other things control each individual.

The poem is simple in structure, as in meter, then, and unpretentious in
tone and theme.[4] If this were really true, *Odes* 1.1 would indeed be a dull
poem, to be quickly read and passed over. Only the first two and last two
verses would matter — the rest would be mere expansion. Yet if the priamel
of lines 3–34 is taken as padding, it would be equally legitimate to excise
the introductory and final lines as extraneous. And this is what G. Hermann
did. Convinced that 1–2 and 35–36 were composed by someone who
thought that the first ode ought to be dedicated to Horace's patron Maecenas, he excised them as *inepta et ridicule*.[5] While few have followed
Hermann's lead, we should see in both modern criticisms and Hermann's
excision the recognition of an important problem — does *Odes* 1.1 have a
logical and artistic unity? Particularly troublesome is Horace's description
of himself as already in the grove of the Muses *before* his request to Maecenas for inclusion amongst the great lyric poets.[6]

To some degree, our reading of the poem has been caught in a trap
which denies this prefatory ode its proper status. For as Horace almost
certainly wrote 1.1 after most of the other odes included in Books 1–3, in
effect composing an epilogue rather than an initial statement, so the critic
reads the first ode not as an introduction, but as a statement about the
other poems and the poet himself. But by investigating the 'overture' in
the wider context of a Horatian poetics, the critic denies the rhetorical value
set on it by Horace as the introductory ode. Caught between aftersight and
a desire to capture the effect of the original reading, we do not distinguish
between Horace's methods of production and the effect of what he produces on his audience. So what exists is explained in terms of its existence,

not as a creation which continues to work in producing meaning as the initial statements are refined or corrected by new information, either as the poem progresses and 'explains' itself, or in terms of its relationship to the rest of the Horatian corpus. Perhaps it will be best to talk of the 'meaning' of the poem as consisting in the codes through which it is composed (in terms of references to ethical values, poetic norms, and social relationships, to name but a few of the possibilities). The 'significance' of the ode would need to be expressed in terms of other codes which link it to the rest of Horace's work. In each case the program of reading will remain open-ended as each reading will assign values to be examined in terms of a re-reading, just as the first ode is of dual significance as preface to *Odes* 1–3 and epilogue also.

As a critical strategy, it may be productive to attempt a 'naive' reading of this ode, a reading which will cooperate with the poet by accepting his vision of his methods in order to return to a critical re-examination of the text. In particular, this means an avoidance of any attempt to set up diagrammatic structures for the poem. Although there is no consensus on what the structure of the ode may have been,[7] I would not deny that Horace may well have had some plan in mind. But while the schemas which have been proposed could tell us something about the original method of constructing the poem, they do not correspond to the rhetorical processes of reading or listening. The process of reading (and, to a large extent, of writing too) is diachronic, not synchronic. New information continually revises the meaning of older information and so changes the 'meaning' of the poem as it is read. While earlier meanings are adjusted or erased, the reader is continually waiting for further information to complete the poem—a process which does not even stop at the end of the poem, but is merely in abeyance.

As *Odes* 1.1 begins, the first two lines define the recipient of the verse (Maecenas) in opposition to the speaker, the first person implied by *meum*. In contrast to epic, where the narrator is generally hidden and the audience unmentioned, the participants in the act of communication are immediately revealed and also the relationship between them: given the added expectations aroused by the Asclepiadean meter, *Odes* 1.1 can only be read in the lyric mode. Since it is such a regular feature of Horace's poetry to introduce a second participant in the ode, the addressee (for instance, Augustus in the second ode, Vergil in the third, Sestius in the fourth, etc.), we can quickly dismiss Hermann's scissors-wielding 'solution' to the problems of the poem. However, we should note that the recipient is not only Maecenas, but also the general listener. If in epic the listener remains permanently an onlooker, in lyric he becomes an active participant, not a mere eavesdropper. From Maecenas, we pass to the general second person (*numquam demoveas*, 13: 'one/you would never move') and by the end of the ode, the wish expressed by *inseres* is no longer confined to the stated addressee, but can be taken as the ideal second person singular of the future.[8] In this way the reader becomes the patron to allow the poem to achieve its goal — indeed the wish is stated as realized in *Odes* 4.3.13–15:

> Romae principis urbium
> > dignatur suboles inter amabilis
> vatum ponere me choros.

> The youth of Rome, the prince of cities, thinks it right to
> place me among the lovely choruses of bards.

In such a fashion, then, the poem revises its meaning as it progresses. If Maecenas is transformed into the general reader, this likewise must alter our reading. The reader becomes the defender of Horace's poetry by the very act of reading, but the meaning of *dulce decus* ('sweet glory') is altered too. Instead of Horace taking pleasure in the reflected glory of Maecenas, the man descended from Etruscan kings, it is the reader who becomes the source of glory for the obscurely-born Horace.[9] Although this may seem fanciful, the latter use of *praesidium* ('protection') and *decus* seems more natural. This is illustrated by Lucretius' account of the Great Mother teaching men to defend and so bring glory to their parents: *praesidioque parent decorique parentibus esse* (2.643: 'that they ready themselves to be a source of protection and bring glory to their parents'). Thus Horace's apparently simple language in line 2 is not as innocent as it appears, but almost 'overcharged' as he varies from his poetic model. Even the unpoetic *praesidium* can be taken as not merely defence, but livelihood (*praesidium vitae*) as well, to return to its more usual meaning later.[10] And while the poem begins with the proper names of Maecenas and a grandiloquent description of his descent and function in regard to Horace, at the end of the poem it is the signature *Horatius* inserted into the list of lyric bards which dominates.

If we have dwelt at length on the role of the reader in the production of meaning in this ode, it is because the relationship of author to reader is of the utmost importance in linking the narrative section of the poem (the priamel of 3–34) with its conclusion (35–6). It has long been recognized that the description of man's varied pursuits is a standard topos.[11] The various lives described by Horace seem to form a synecdoche for the inexpressible list of the occupations of mankind. But the rhetorical description here is not merely incomplete — there appears to be a logical difficulty in offering illustrative examples of man's pursuits in order to contrast the general with the specific pursuit of the poet. In what way is the poet removed or excluded from the generality of mankind? It is this question which must be faced before we can ask 'precisely in what ways does the delight of the poet surpass the delights of others?'[12] In a 'typical' example, from Libanius, the topos implies a union of mankind through the diversity of its interests: the speaker, the warrior, the farmer, the sailor, the miser, and the glory-hunter are all united by their singular obsession with their life to the exclusion of other pursuits.[13] Even when a Euripidean character contrasts his personal desires with those of others, he describes his hope as only one out of many possible.[14] Nor do the schemes of *bioi* ('life-styles') offered by the philosophers help us out of this difficulty. La Penna,[15] especially, has done good service in pointing out how the philosophical constructs may have influenced Horace. For instance, Lucretius 2.1–13, which contrasts the life of the philosopher with those of other men, is a fine parallel. But it is difficult to see a close connection between the usually tripartite schemes of lives offered by the philosophers and Horace's apparently irregular series of lives culminating in the description of himself.[16]

Closer to Horace's usage are the well-known lines of Sappho:

> Some say a force of horsemen, others of infantry, others
> of ships is the finest thing over the black earth; but I say it
> is whomever one loves.
>
> (fr. 16 LP 1–4)

While others take pleasure in the assemblage of horsemen, infantry, and ships, Sappho does not accept this male-oriented, collective delight. Rather, she sets up a personal definition of the most beautiful: the person whom each loves. There is no attempt to sympathize with the general view, but a lyric, personal statement of Sappho's own desire, reinforced by the mythological example of Helen.[17] Desire is not socially set, but considered as an individual phenomenon whose value must be fixed by each.

In the priamel of *Odes* 1.1, it is clear that the poet as master of words sets the values of his community. Although all may find pleasure in what they do, value is not assigned by the tokens of Olympic victory nor by the exchange of patronage between the political leader and the crowd (3–8). Poetic evaluation resides in the poet's description of these pursuits. Without this dual vision, provided by the poet's assessment of the activities in which men find pleasure *(iuvat)*, we would be left puzzled by the use of 'irony' or 'satire' in the poem, and perhaps forced to agree with Schönberger who denies that there is any real judgment by the poet on his characters because of the apparently 'unironic' pictures of the farmer and the man at the spring.[18] But once we accept the two different judgments at work, there is little difficulty with the method of description adopted by Horace.

Initially we are introduced to Olympic victors gathering clouds of dust in the race (*curriculo pulverem Olympicum/collegisse iuvat*, 3–4: 'some delight in raising the Olympic dust with their chariots') and in courting death as they brush the turning-post (*metaque fervidis/evitata rotis*, 4–5: 'the turning-post narrowly avoided by the fiery wheels'). In recognition of their achievements, the token of the palm carries these men off to the gods. Yet the palm is seen as a conventionally set (*nobilis*: 'renowned/noteworthy')[19] object which amusingly functions as a magical broomstick in carrying (*evehit*) its recipients on earth off to heaven. The uncertainty of this accomplishment is increased by line 6: *terrarum dominos evehit ad deos* ([The palm wreath] 'carries them off to the gods as masters of the lands,' or 'carries them off to the gods, the masters of the lands'). While the masters of the lands may be carried off to the gods, there is also the suggestion that these are no divinities of philosophical type, but ones who lord it over or on the earth.[20] The gods are then cast in the same mould as their emulators. The scene may recall Pindar, but there is no Pindar here to establish the permanent renown of the victor in the minds of men.

So too the politician does not control, but is the object of the fleeting attentions of the Roman populace. The *Quirites* ('Roman citizens') are not *nobiles* ('noble') but *mobiles* ('mobile') as they vie with one another to carry off the politician with 'triplet' honours (*certat tergeminis tollere honoribus*, 8). The connection between the picture of the charioteers and the politician is quite clear. Apart from the linking theme of contest, there is an excellent Roman parallel in Cicero, *Tusc.* 2.41: *sed quid hos, quibus Olympiorum victoria consulatus ille antiquus videtur?* ('But what about those men, to whom that consulship of old seemed like an Olympic victory?'). Horace is restating the theme of the first life in a revised form, substituting a Roman for a Greek example, but we should also note that this leads to a reassessment of the introductory lines. Maecenas is not merely Horace's patron, but a symbol of fixed values (*atavis edite regibus*, 1: 'offspring of ancestors who were kings') which can shield the poet. He is already on the way to becoming a fixed symbol of human beneficence to poets, a proper name with common significance.[21]

If the first two examples are rejected as unsatisfactory, the next portrait of the wealthy man who is not reliant on public recognition, but rejoices in making his own whatever comes his way (*[iuvat] illum si proprio condidit horreo/quidquid de Libycis verritur areis*, 9–10: 'that man rejoices if he stores in his own granary whatever is swept up from the Libyan threshing-floors'), is no improvement. He sets a personal valuation on his goods, but one which is limited to him alone and indiscriminate as he bursts his granary with heaps of wheat, and so it lacks true significance in a social context. The man is virtually burying (*condidit*) his wealth and, by hiding it, takes away its circulation and meaning. Indeed Horace makes his image explicit in a later ode (3. 16. 25–29):

> contemptae dominus splendidior rei
> quam si quidquid arat impiger Apulus
> occultare meis dicerer horreis,
>   magnas inter opes inops.

> I am prouder as the owner of a despised property than if I were said
> to be hiding in my granaries whatever the diligent Apulian produces
> with his plough—then I would be a poor man amid great riches.

The following two examples, syntactically linked by *gaudentem* (11: 'rejoicing') and *luctantem* (15: 'grappling'), develop the idea of commerce introduced with the wealthy man. But here we have private citizens. The farmer, labouring to cleave his native soil with his hoe (*gaudentem patrios findere/sarculo agros*, 11-12), can be taken as an archetype of the Roman yeoman, a humbler reflection of a M'. Curius Dentatus or a Gaius Fabricius. Yet while he is willing to split the earth with hard labour, he will not slice through the seas of adventure at any price. Even an inheritance such as accepted from Attalus by the Roman people will not induce him to venture sailing the ship of Venus (*trabe Cypria*)[22] and test the sea of Myrtilus (*Myrtoum...mare*).[23] He is rigidly attached to his ancestral soil and the life of the past. 'You would never separate him from this' (*numquam demoveas*, 13), Horace declares; given the imagery of cutting and cleaving in these lines, it is amusing that a number of the manuscripts give this as 'you would never split him away from his land' (*numquam dimoveas*), a reading which is undoubtedly incorrect but draws to our attention the possible punning quality of Horace's language.[24] In contrast, the merchant wavers in his desire for the homely life when caught by a southerly gale in the sea which received the body of the all-too-daring Icarus (*luctantem Icariis fluctibus Africum*, 16: 'the African wind grappling with the Icarian waves').[25] He may praise leisure (*otium et oppidi/laudat rura sui*, 16-17: 'he praises the leisure and countryside of his home town'), yet he also fears it. The initial reading *mercator metuens otium* ('the merchant fearing leisure') will be corrected by the reader to conform with syntactical necessity, but the impression remains: the merchant soon returns to his trade, a man who cannot be taught to endure the humble life (*indocilis pauperiem pati*, 18).[26] While the farmer doggedly clings to early Roman values and refuses Greek gifts, the merchant rejects the Roman values of *otium, oppidum* and *rus* ('leisure,' 'town,' 'countryside') for the Greek waters of the sea of Icarus.

By geographical selectivity, Horace has given the impression of not only portraying the social roles of great and small, but even showing them throughout the Roman world. We have passed around the Mediterranean, to Greece (*pulverem Olympicum*: 'Olympic dust'), Rome (*turba Quiritium*: 'the crowd of citizens'), Africa (*Libycis...areis*: 'Libyan threshing-floors'), Asia Minor (*Attalicis condicionibus*: 'the terms of an Attalus'), Cyprus (*Cypria trabe*: 'Cyprian ship') and the Greek seas (*Myrtoum...mare; Icariis fluctibus*: 'Myrtoan sea'; 'Icarian waves'). Although the mention of *otium* (16) provides a bridge to the next figure, the poem also seems to restart half-way through, since *est qui* (19: 'there is one') corresponds to the introductory *sunt quos* (3: 'there are those'). The three lives that follow can be characterized as extra-social; that is, they are marked off from the earlier types by their position outside the normal structure of society. The man at the stream enjoys his *otium* alone by a gently murmuring spring of sacred water (*ad aquae lene caput sacrae*, 22), while others enjoy the blare of clarion and trumpet (*lituo tubae/permixtus sonitus*, 24),[27] delighting in hated war (*bella...matribus detestata*, 24-5). The hunter's joy comes from the yelps of his young hounds chasing a doe or the destructive crash of a boar breaking his fine-woven nets (*teretes...plagas*, 28). Since he ignores the attractions of his comely wife, he is appropriately cold-shouldered by Jove (*sub Iove frigido*,

25: 'beneath a frigid Jove'/ 'under a cold sky'). These last two types particularly well demonstrate the poet's voice correcting their views of their
activities. The soldier rejoices in war, but Horace interposes *bella...matribus
detestata* ('warfare hated by mothers'). The huntsman's voice is heard in
the affectionate description of the *catuli fideles* ('faithful hounds').[28] In opposition to this, Horace sets a value more important to the lyric poet – the
man has mistakenly left unattended his *tenera coniunx* ('tender wife').

Horace appears to define his own role against these lives, both social
and extra-social. Twice in his description of the poetic *locus amoenus* Horace
emphasizes his uniqueness with emphatic *me* and in the concluding prayer
too he posits *quodsi me lyricis vatibus inseres* (35: 'but if you will enter me
among the lyric bards'). Initially we may suppose that the pleasance is the
embodiment of the poet's achievement.[29] Crowned with Bacchus' ivy, sig-
nifying his glory as a poet of the light lyric genre (*doctarum hederae praemia
frontium*, 29: 'ivy, the reward for learned brows'),[30] Horace is in the cool
grove of poetry, escaping the dusty heat of the chariot race. He is isolated
from the rest of mankind and under the patronage of the Muses. The scene
is undoubtedly inspired by Greek poetry and foreshadows Horace's 'future'
efforts – the odes which follow in his collection. Interestingly, the ancient
commentators took this scene as a type of metapoetry. Pseudo-Acro states
that Horace sets the very material of his poetry as an object of glory,[31] and
Porphyrio comments that Horace reveals he has obtained great glory
through his subject matter, since groves, fountains, and the like are the
staple of lyric.[32] While Horace's poetry is hardly as limited in subject-matter
as the commentators might have us believe, the scene is certainly replete
with images of poetic power. We are led to believe that poetry has the
ability through its metaphors to meditate on its own being, that Horace's
act of writing and its referent can be identical. So the scholiasts have their
point: composing poetry is glorious in itself.

Finally, the poet asks for something more – to be included amongst
the *lyrici vates* ('lyric bards'). Horace will join the select company of Greek
forerunners and also have a particular place in Roman society as a *vates*, an
oracular, shaman-like figure of mysterious magical power.[34] His *carmen* is
not merely a poem, but also an incantation.[35] According to this reading,
Horace has placed himself on a level with or even above his dedicatee by
creating his own ancestry. He has the glory of the charioteer or politician,
but owns it personally and independently. Rather than associating with
the divine lords of the earth, he is in a state of repose with the *di superi* ('the
gods above').[36] The poet enjoys an atemporal utopia where the music of
flute and lyre contrasts with the military uproar of trumpet and clarion or
the noise of the hunt. He is *doctus* ('learned'),[37] in contrast with the *indocilis*
('uneducable') merchant, and surrounded by fleet-footed (*leves*) nymphs,
not a fickle crowd of vying citizens (*mobilium turba Quiritium*, 7). The poet's
world is full and apparently lacking nothing, where, without being sought,
his pleasure is freely bestowed by the presiding divinities. The garden is
complete and self-contained.[38]

So we might initially read *Odes* 1.1. But the very emphasis on the uniqueness of the poet, stressed by the threefold *me*, raises suspicions. A reexamination of the carefully composed lines 19–22[39] calls into question the apparent simplicity of the ode:

> est qui nec veteris pocula Massici
> nec partem solido demere de die
> spernit, nunc viridi membra sub arbuto
> stratus, nunc ad aquae lene caput sacrae.

> There is one who does not spurn cups of vintage Massic,
> nor taking off part of the day, sometimes stretching his
> limbs under a green arbute, sometimes by a gentle spring
> of sacred water.

We may choose between the names attributed to the figure: *philēdonos*,[40] *l'epicureo*,[41] *otiosus*,[42] *Geniesser*,[43] lazy drinker,[44] idler,[45] gentleman,[46] or man of leisure ('he seems to be the owner of some shop [or shops]; at any rate, he is self-employed since he apparently can take time off from the business day').[47] Such a desire to denominate the actor shows an unwillingness on the part of the critic to accept Horace's rhetorical construct in this ode, where the emphasis is on the evaluation of the action, not its nominal agent. What is important is that the figure here in many ways resembles the poetic narrator in his attributes and activities.[48] The vintage Massic wine suggests Bacchic inspiration;[49] the *locus amoenus* of the arbute-tree and the gentle spring of sacred water recalls the repose and sacredness of poetic creation.[50] And the man's solitude (since *est qui* contrasts with the priamel's introductory *sunt quos*) indicates the internalized world of the poetic imagination. Furthermore, the position of the characterization is, on a rereading of the poem, found to be emphasized by its placement at the center of the ode.[51]

Of course it would be a matter of some concern to identify the man at the spring with Horace. How can the poet be part of his list of occupations and simultaneously external to it? So Nisbet and Hubbard attempt to dispel this view: 'the indolence will seem to some peculiarly Horatian...in fact the scene is sanctioned by poetical convention as well as the needs of a hot climate.'[52] But ordinary workers do not drink vintage Massic. While the water and shade are common enough in poetry, the addition of wine occurs only here and in Hesiod, *Works and Days* 592–596, where it is the reward in store during the summer for the farmer's earlier labours. An 'off-duty' Horace would fit the picture, and this is reinforced by *Epistles* 1.14.32–36, where Horace describes himself:

> quem tenues decuere togae nitidique capilli,
> quem scis immunem Cinarae placuisse rapaci,
> quem bibulum liquidi media de luce Falerni,

cena brevis iuvat et prope rivum somnus in herba.
nec lusisse pudet, sed non incidere iudum.

The man who you know was well-suited by togas and gleaming
hair, who was able to please greedy Cinara without any gifts, who
is drunk on pure Falernian at mid-day — he likes a snack and sleeping on the grass by the river bank. There's no shame in playing,
only in not stopping.

In particular, lines 34–35 are highly relevant, since Horace preserves the
ambiguity of the outsider's picture of himself — *scis bibulum esse* ('you know
I am drunk') is perhaps a more natural reading of the line than *scis bibulum
fuisse* ('you know that I used to be drunk'). So the poet's description of
himself and that of the man at the spring are very close.

The passage from the *Epistles* also gives a key to the meaning of *partem
solido demere de die* (*Odes* 1.1.20). Sample explanations of this are 'breaking
into the working day'[53] and, enigmatically, '*solido* i.e. *integro*.'[54] But we
should recognize a commercial metaphor as the oftcited parallel from Seneca, *Epistles* 83.3, shows:

hodiernus dies solidus est, nemo ex illo quicquam mihi eripuit;
totus inter stratum lectionemque divisus est; minimum
exercitationi corporis datum, et hoc nomine ago gratias senectuti:
non magno mihi constat.

Today is totalled up and no one has stolen any of it away from
me; it is columned into resting and reading. A tiny amount has
been expended on exercise, and I thank old age on this account: it
doesn't cost me much.

The man drinking Massic is willing to subtract (*demere*)[55] a part from the
sum total (the *solidus dies*).[56] So too in Seneca, the day's accounts are in
order, columned up into rest and reading without any entry subtracted for
an outsider. While the metaphor seems to have been perceived by past
translators,[57] its importance should be stressed. As *Epistles* 1.14.32–36 shows,
the pleasures of mid-day, where time seems to cease, are after all temporary. The temporal ordering of the lives is significant: the first examples
occur sometimes during the day; the man at the spring is in a mid-day
setting, as *Epistles* 1.14 and earlier examples of the topos indicate; the hunter
ends the list of lives, spending the night *sub Iove frigido*; and Horace's position in the grove of the Muses seems to be outside temporal references. So
not only is mid-day only apparently outside the changes of time, but the
impermanence of momentary joys at the spring is suggested by the emphatic *nunc...nunc* ('sometimes...at other times,' but literally 'now...now').
The description of the arbute as *viridis* ('green,' 'flourishing') is also suggestive of the fragility of this pleasance — the colour of the leaves will change

soon enough.'[58] Hence we can see that the man at the spring must soon balance his books and turn away from *otium* to *negotium*.

The poet's world too is vulnerable. Horace may enjoy the ethereal zones, marked off from the common crowd by the sign of the ivy wreath. Yet the *gelidum nemus* ('cool grove') is obtained at a cost of warmth and life[59]—not Horace, but only his poetic *persona* can inhabit this ambivalent pleasance. The poetic world of nymphs and amorous satyrs must invite in the poet. If Euterpe stops (*cohibet*) the pan-pipes or Polyhymnia does not tune the lyre to the correct high pitch, the poet will no longer be divine.[60] He will rejoin the rest of mankind striving continually toward the uncertain goal of glory and happiness.

This leaves the final prayer (35–6). Here Horace rejects the fantasy and even sterility of the unstable world of the imagination. If instead his reader places his name amongst those of the mystic writers of lyric, he will span heaven and earth and strike his head against the stars.[61] The use of the verb *feriam* ('strike') in an otherwise clichéd expression gives comic overtones to the wish.[62] The comic use does not deny the validity of Horace's aspirations, in the way that irony might function, but creates a meaning in between the positive and negative extremes. The desire for reputation remains, but Horace cannot pronounce on its complete accomplishment. That is in the hands of the reader who will judge *after* this poem ends and *after* reading the poetry that follows.

But by this concession to his reader, Horace has substantially changed the form of his priamel. So far the list has been considered as functioning synecdochally: each portrait seems to be part of a picture of mankind's desires, with each being erased and replaced by other exemplars. Yet this last item, the poet in the grove of Muses, cannot be totally independent from the rest of mankind. It too is a temporal phase. The portrait of the self-sufficient poet is undermined from within by Horace's indications of the vulnerability of the pleasance and finally contradicted by the poet's address to the reader. The synecdochal reading now fails because the portrait of the self-sufficient poet is at odds with the introduction of the audience—the last is not to be subsumed into the general picture of mankind so far drawn, but acts to evaluate the whole construct, including the poet, from outside the rhetorical frame. So we have turned away from types to the unexpressed judgement of the readers and this no longer fits our tropical construction for the ode.

In order to try to preserve a rhetorical logic in the poem (and surely that is what is meant by poetic 'unity'), we should consider treating the lives as metonymical, rather than read each item as synecdoche. That is, the list does not express a whole, but instead emphasizes the congruence of each item. To use a trivial analogy, this is the difference between a grocery bill (which can be totalled) and a shopping list (where the relationship is the existence of the series itself). Or perhaps a better example would be a writer's manuscript, where a succession of words may have been deleted before the final choice is made. The congruent feature in this list is the element of excess in the desires which is indicated throughout the descriptions. This allows each item to be successively replaced and culminates in the description of the poet. Rather than indicating a whole, the metonymy serves simply to unify the series. Yet the privileged portrait of the poet in the sacred grove does not simply erase the earlier pictures, but, because it owes its meaning to its relationship to the others, brings them back into play as alternate possibilities. Horace too longs for glory, the peace of his Sabine farm, or the pleasure of *otium* by a cool stream. The priamel is not merely illustrative of mankind (synecdoche) but, while aiming at a definition of the poet, links him with the other lives (metonymy).

The problem of the rhetorical form both aiding the poet's expression of his character and frustrating his desire for individuality can be seen as the reason for the final two lines. They should be taken as no mere addition, but the poet's acceptance that by himself he cannot create his own uniqueness. It is up to his partner in the act of communication to reply and assert that Horace really is a poet. Yet the order of the last two lines is significant. Horace expresses his desire to depend on his reader, then reminds that reader that he was the one who began the discussion in the first place. It is a serious matter — which should not be taken too seriously, Horace intimates. As understatement (the litotes of *nec spernit*) rescued the banal in the description of the man at the spring, so the exaggeration in the final line of short-statured Horace butting the stars with his head keeps the poem from becoming too self-important. The poet needs his audience, but it must remember that only he can express that need in poetry.

A further consideration of the ode may help to draw the threads of our analysis together. Fraenkel, noting the echoes in other odes of lines in 1.1, suggested that the poem was intended as the poetic equivalent of a musical overture.[63] That is questionable — we may wonder if the reader would recognize the parallels from the first ode when reading the later poems, and it is hard to see how many of the correspondences function in the fashion of musical themes. But Fraenkel was right in showing that 1.1 is virtually a sample of Horatian poetry. It may be duly retorted: 'What else could an Horatian poem be?' Yet the frequent echoes not only in the *Odes*, but also in the *Satires*,[64] the *Epistles*,[65] and the *Epodes*,[66] mark the opening ode as a very Horatian poem — Horace displaying how Horace the poet writes, not as an overture, but in an attempt to define Horace the author of the *Odes*.[67] It would be too large a task and too tangential to treat the problem of self-quotation that these echoes raise. Yet it seems reasonable to view such quotations as lending a monumental, fixed quality to the words, almost marking them as 'true' through their repetition. But, as we have seen, the 'truth' is very debatable in *Odes* 1.1: the repetitions instead reinforce the impression that the poet cannot define himself as producer of poetry, but only as a product of his own verse, as Horace the poet-figure, not Horace the poet.

This need to introduce an outside observer (the reader) into the poem to truly assess Horace's worth, accounts for the form of *Odes* 1.1. We do not have two pieces linked merely by their common denominator in Horace. The framing wish, setting forth the necessary relationship between the poet and reader, acts as a critique of the poetic wish to define and evaluate the world while somehow making the poet external to that world. To give a proper evaluation, the valuator must escape the system which he investigates. But Horace cannot escape his own rhetoric in his description of himself. The idea of externality is part of the poetic fantasy — as the desires of mankind are fragile and almost futile, so the poet's place outside that world is a fancy which cannot be maintained. Instead of being separate, Horace the poet is but another type with similar aspirations to those of the others in the priamel — and the very element of aspiration in the picture of the poet is what makes it impossible to separate that portrait from the others in the poem. Hence the Horatian appearance of the types that are chosen for the list. Horace's interesting novelty of emphasizing the relationship between the producer and consumer of poetry is what finally rescues the apparently archaic and naive form of the priamel and changes it into something fresh, complex, and ambiguous. The introduction of the reader does not reduce the poet's desire for permanence (as recognized by the very existence of a list of lyric bards), but its realization can only be in terms of what might be expressed, in further forms of the wish, not as a simple statement. Taking *Odes* 1.1 as the first of a line of poems which aim to produce Horace the lyric writer, culminating in *Odes* 3.30, we may see its ultimate role as introducing the possibility of writing poetry without as yet stating its achievement.[68]

Notes

[1]E. Fraenkel, *Horace* (Oxford 1957) 232.

[2]R. G. M. Nisbet, M. Hubbard, *A Commentary on Horace: Odes, Book I* (Oxford 1970) 1. Hereafter *N&H* with reference to comments *ad loc.* unless otherwise noted. The following discussions of *Odes* 1.1 will be cited by author's name only: J. V. Cody, *Horace and Callimachean Aesthetics* (Coll. Latomus 147, Brussels 1976) 45–71; H. Musurillo, 'The Poet's Apotheosis: Horace, *Odes* 1.1,' *TAPA* 93 (1962) 230–239; O. Schönberger, 'Horatius, carm. 1.1,' *Gymnasium* 73 (1966) 388–412; H. J. Shey, 'The Poet's Progress: Horace, *Odes* 1.1,' *Arethusa* 4 (1971) 185–196; H. P. Syndikus, *Die Lyrik des Horaz*, Band I (Darmstadt 1972) 23–27; K. Vretska, 'Horatius, Carm. 1, 1,' *Hermes* 99 (1971) 323–335.

[3]Ps. Acro *ad* 1.1. *N&H* 1: 'Horace [in expressing his aspirations] goes a long way with a description of other people's varied occupations.'

[4]*N&H* 3.

[5]G. Hermann, *De Horati primo carmine dissertatio* (Berlin 1842): reprinted in Hermann's *Opuscula* 8.395–401. Only Nauck followed Hermann's suggestion — and often received the blame for the former's idea (e.g. in T. E. Page, *Q. Horatii Flacci Carminum Libri IV* [London 1895] 131). Hermann's view is discussed at length and rejected in J. C. Orelli, *Q. Horatius Flaccus*, revised by J. G. Baiter and W. Hirschfelder (Berlin 1886) vol. 1, 12–13.

[6]Hermann would have a good point if it were fully correct to say 'as a poet Horace comes closest to the gods by his special contemplative vision of life...even

before Maecenas can pay him the honour of counting him among the great lyric poets of antiquity' (Musurillo 23).

[7] For such schemas see: N. E. Collinge, *The Structure of Horace's Odes* (London 1961) 108–9, who also records earlier structures; Musurillo 232–3; Schönberger 410 n. 61; Vretska 334–5; Shey 185; A. Ghiselli, 'Lettura dell' Ode 1, 1 di Orazio,' *Lingua e Stile* 7 (1972) 115–8.

[8] For this ideal second person singular future, see S. A. Handford, *The Latin Subjunctive* (London 1947) 109 n. 1. So too in English, 'you see' may be specific, referring to the addressee or a general audience ('one sees'). It is important to recognize this ideal type; for instance, in *Odes* 2.12.9–10, *latius regnes avidum domando/ spiritum*, it is unlikely that Horace is directly warning his recipient, Sallustius Crispus ('one rules more widely by taming one's greedy instinct'). This movement from specific address to the general reader is frequent in Horace's poetry. For example, *caelum ipsum petimus stultitia* (*Odes* 1.3.38: 'we seek heaven itself in our stupidity') clearly has wider significance than to Horace and Vergil alone.

[9] Ps. Acro: *decus – quia magna laus est placere meliori* ('because it is a great glory to win the approval of a superior'). But Maecenas can also glory in Horace (cf. *Odes* 1.32.13: *o decus Phoebi et dapibus supremi grata/testudo Iovis;* 'lyre, the glory of Phoebus and delight for the feasts of highest Jove'). For Horace's glory from his readers, see *Odes* 3.30 (the concluding ode of the collection), especially 7f.: *usque ego postera/crescam laude recens* ('I will eternally grow, renewed by the praise of posterity').

[10] For *praesidium* as 'unpoetic,' see B. Axelson, *Unpoetische Wörter* (Lund 1945) 98; the 'unpoetic' word is here introduced by the grandiloquent *o* to produce a typically Horatian *callida iunctura*. For *praesidium vitae* ('livelihood'): Petronius 116.4.

[11] For instance Solon 1.43ff. (Diehl); Pindar fr. 221; Bacchylides 10.38–45. Musurillo (235–7) has shown interesting Egyptian and Semitic parallels for the *topoi*. Yet there is no evidence that this was a Roman commonplace: Horace transforms the Greek *topoi* into Latin novelties.

[12] Shey 185.

[13] Libanius, *Decl.* 30.31 (Foerster).

[14] Euripides fr. 659 (Nauck) 1–10: 'We have all types of desires for our lives...Yet I do not want to obtain any of these, but would like to have a reputation for good repute.'

[15] A. La Penna, *Orazio e l'ideologia del principato* (Torino 1963) 203–224.

[16] The philosophical scheme of the lives first appears in Plato, *Rep.* 581c; the numerous variations thereafter are examined by La Penna. Yet we may do well to keep Fraenkel's (above n. 1) very sensible evaluation of Horace's 'sources' in mind: 'Horace probably remembered many Greek passages similar in matter and form and used them freely. Nor was he influenced by poetry alone. The discussion of the various types of *bioi* and their relative merits played a great part in the treatises of Hellenistic popular philosophy with which Horace was familiar' (231–2).

[17] See G. M. Kirkwood, *Early Greek Monody* (Ithaca 1974) 104–8; in contrast is Pindar's defense of communal values through the priamel form in *Nem.* 8. 37–8.

[18] Schönberger 397 n. 20.

[19] *N&H* appositely gloss *nobilis* as *arignōtos* ('renowned') – there is a clear tension between the epinician vocabulary and the poet's evaluation here.

[20] Ps. Acro pronounces *terrarum dominos* to be *amphibolicos dictum* ('ambiguous'). O. Skutsch, 'Rhyme in Horace,' *BICS* 11 (1964) 76, argues that it should be taken in apposition to *deos*, since rhyme normally expresses a syntactical relationship in the lesser Asclepiad. The same view is held by Schönberger 393 n. 14. *N&H* hold out for agreement with the charioteers. I do not believe that the Roman reader could definitely resolve the ambiguity, so both meanings should be left operative.

[21]*O.L.D.* s.v. *Maecenas* 2; the first recorded generic use of 'Maecenas' is *Laus Pisonis* 238.

[22]Porphyrio oddly takes this as a reference to the bronze (*cupreus*) nails used in building ships. Ps. Acro is puzzled: either *Cypria* is used synecdochally (*abusive*) for any wood or wood was stronger on Cyprus. The usual modern explanation is that Cyprus was famous for its woods and ship-building (Ammian. 14.8.14). But in a lyric context Cyprus would probably recall the worship of Venus Cypria (Tib. 3.3.34).

[23]Kiessling-Heinze, *Q. Horatius Flaccus, Oden U. Epoden* (Berlin 1930) *ad loc.* Ps. Acro, perhaps influenced by *Cypria*, offers an interesting alternative: *a Venere propter mirtum* ('with reference to Venus because myrtle is her tree'). Cody 51 suggests that Horace is painting a word-picture of a man surrounded by the waters:

Myrtoum pavidus nauta secet mare.

But we know too little about the audial/visual effect of Latin poetry to judge — the image could just as well be of a man cleaving through the sea.

[24]*dimoveo* can only mean 'split/cleave' — see *O.L.D.* Cf. Verg. *Georg.* 2.513: *agricola incurvo terram dimovit aratro* ('the farmer splits the earth with his curved plough').

[25]There is some irony in the Homeric language used here to describe the storm (cf. *Il.* 2.144-6).

[26]Cody 60 notes this ambiguity, the existence of which is strengthened by the efforts of Ps. Acro to unravel the syntax into an unambiguous word-order.

[27]For the onomatopoeia in more extreme form, cf. Ennius, *Ann.* 140 V.: *at tuba terribili sonitu taratantara dixit* ('But the trumpet with terrible tone roared taratantara').

[28]While we logically translate *catuli* as 'hounds' it can hardly mean other than 'cubs': cf. *Odes* 3.3.41, 3.20.2 ('cubs' of wild animals), and *Epist.* 1.2.5-7: *venaticus ex quo/tempore cervinam pellem latravit in aula/militat in silvis catulus* ('the hunting-dog's puppy serves in the woods after it barks at the deerhide in the courtyard').

[29]On this *Musenhain*, see I. Troxler-Keller, *Der Dichterlandschaft des Horaz* (Heidelberg 1964) 32-47.

[30]*N&H* note the link between lighter poetry and Bacchus, comparing Prop. 4.1.61-2.

[31]Ps. Acro: *materiam ipsam carminis pro laude posuit* ('he sets down the very matter of his poetry as an object of praise').

[32]Porphyrio: *per ea se egregiam gloriam dicit consequi, de quibus canit; fere enim lyrico carmini materia de nemoribus ac fontibus est et si qua sunt his similia aut proxima* ('he says he is gaining great glory from the things he sings about; for generally the subject matter for lyric poetry is comprised of groves and fountains and things similar or close to these').

[33]Presumably Horace wishes to be listed in the canon of Greek lyric poets (Porphyrio: '*Graecis' utique intellegendum. nam nondum erant Romani* — 'For certain, "Greek" lyric poets must be understood; for there were no Roman lyric poets yet').

[34]On *vates* see *N&H*; J. K. Newman, *Augustus and the New Poetry* (Brussels 1967); G. Lieberg, 'Horace et les Muses,' *Latomus* 36 (1977) 974-6.

[35]For *carmen* as poem/spell, see Cody 47 n. 11, 48 n. 12.

[36]For the Callimachean rejection of popular taste here, see *N&H*. Horace's readers may also have seen a rejection of the epic mode in the exaltation of the *vates*, since Ennius *Ann.* 214 V. had set up a polemical opposition between the learned epic poet and the rustic *fauni vatesque*. Cody sees a close connection between the *gelidum nemus* ('cool grove') and the Callimachean *genus tenue* ('slight style'). C. O. Brink reviewing Cody's book (*Gnomon* 51 [1979] 60–62), rightly denies that the two symbols can be so easily related. Still, even if Cody exaggerates the 'Callimachean' and especially the 'Socratic' element in 1.1, there are Alexandrian literary symbols interacting in the poem (e.g. the 'learned' poet and the rejection of the common crowd).

[37]See Shey 195 n. 14 for *doctus* as both the 'learned' poet and the man who has learnt the lessons of life. Such play on the literary and social codes is typically Horatian. Not only does the poet have the *sophia* of the Alexandrians (*N&H*), but also the thoroughly political wisdom of Rome, as illustrated by *Epodes* 16.36, where all Romans will leave for the Isles of the Blest — or at least the part of the populace better than the ignorant crowd will (*aut pars indocili melior grege*).

[38]Cody 52: 'all the descriptive details embellishing the would-be *vates*...and his poetic apotheosis create a unified, ethically positive portrait. Horace's own poetic values are favorably presented without dissenting ethical judgment...' Cody (64–6) sees bucolic repose (*autarkeia*) as Horace's ideal in his portraits of the poet and the man at the spring.

[39]The particular artistry of these lines has been well revealed by M. O. Lee, *Word, Sound, and Image in the Odes of Horace* (Ann Arbor 1969) 10, 14.

[40]*N&H* 3.

[41]Ghiselli (above n. 7) 119.

[42]Vretska 334.

[43]Schönberger 397; Syndikus 26.

[44]Musurillo 233.

[45]Cody 49, who also gives 'wine-drinker' (63).

[46]K. J. Reckford, *Horace* (New York 1969) 15.

[47]Shey 180.

[48]Reckford (above n. 44): 'Is this Horace? The concept of "breaking off" a piece of time to accompany your drink is Horatian; the well-placed adjectives too, emphasizing the freshness, even sacredness of relaxation.' This identification with the poet is also made by Musurillo (233, 235), comparing *Epodes* 2.23ff. Similarly Vretska (329): 'In Ganzen erhalten wir hier das Bild eines Menschen, dem zur Identifizierung mit den Dichter nur das Dichten fehlt.' Cody (71) the figure as 'the archetype of the *vir beatus*, [who] by reason of his acceptance of the gifts of the present forms the very incarnation of *otium*.

[49]Wine and Bacchic inspiration are linked in *Odes* 1.18, 1.32, etc.

[50]Cf. Theocr., 1.15ff.; Lucr. 2.29ff; Tac. *Dial.* 12.1. Troxler-Keller (above n. 29) sees Horace's poetic grove as an intermediate stage between Vergil's Arcadia, filled with shepherd-poets, and Propertius' solitary grove of Callimachus (Prop. 3.1.).

[51]The description begins at line 19 of a 36 line ode, i.e. halfway through.

[52]*N&H ad* 1.1.22.

[53]Page (above n. 5).

[54]*N&H ad loc.*

[55]Cf. *Odes* 2.5.13–15: *currit enim ferox/aetas et illi quos tibi dempserit/adponet annos* ('savage time runs on and will give to him the years it takes away from you').

[56]Cf. Cic. *Att.* 6.1.3: *usura nec ea solida contentus est* ('he is content with the interest alone — and not the entire amount of that').

[57]E.g. Reckford (above n. 46) 15: 'to subtract part of the day's store.'

[58]There is also syntactical ambiguity in *nunc viridis arbutus* (apparently meaning 'a presently green arbute'), since the meaning of the first *nunc* has to be resolved into a temporal marker for *stratus* (hence, 'now stretching his limbs') only after the second *nunc* is read.

[59]In the famous *Fons Bandusiae* ode (3.13), the eternal coolness of the fountain is purchased at the cost of the warm life-blood of the amorous kid. This connection between the *gelidum nemus* ('cool grove') and *gelida mors* ('icy death') has been well explored by P. Pucci, 'Horace's Banquet in *Odes* 1.17,' *TAPA* 105 (1975) 259–281. Some dissatisfaction with the scene of the poetic grove is already apparent in Shey (188), who sees Horace wanting to state that his pursuits too are conventional. Syndikus (32–3) compares the *Musenhain* with ideal landscapes in

contemporary art—Horace then becomes an ideal poet-figure fastened in that landscape.

[60]G. Lieberg (above n. 34) 966 suggests that the Muses play their instruments for Horace, rather than give them to him to play. If so, this would reinforce the impression that Horace is here simply the object of divine activity (Vretska 330: 'Objekt einer Handlung die unpersönliche Subjekte, Efeukranz und kühler Hain, lenken'), not an active participant in the production of poetry. In the priamel, the men listed at least control their own actions. True seclusion in the poetic grove would break the writer-recipient formula which is such a part of Horace's poetry and exclude the essential human evaluation of that poetry.

It may be that Horace is again emphasizing his type of poetry by the unusual phrase *tendere barbiton* ('to tune the lyre'). The contrast would be between the high-pitched and shrill (*vox tensa*) and the deeper, fuller sound of a relaxed tone (Quint. *Inst. Or.* 11.3.42: *nam vox ut nervi, quo remissior, hoc gravior et plenior, quo tensior, hoc tenuis et acuta magis est*—'the voice is like the strings of an instrument—the looser it is, the deeper and fuller the sound; the more taut, the finer and more high-pitched the sound').

[61]The thought of Horace's stature adds further incongruity—if by becoming a *vates* Horace acts as intermediary between god and man (Syndikus 36), by his growth in height, he turns this image into a physical conceit.

[62]On the cliché 'to touch (*psauein*) the stars with one's head,' see Vretska 331-4. It is as old as Sappho 52 LP. The substitution of *arassein* (*feriam*: 'to strike') for *psauein* adds a comic touch: cf. com. adesp. 531K. and Cic. *Att.* 2.1.7.

[63]Fraenkel (above n. 1) 230.

[64]Shey 190-1.

[65]See p. 43f. and Musurillo 232-3.

[66]Musurillo 232-3; Syndikus 25 n. 12. In particular, cf. *Epodes* 2.23-4: *libet iacere modo sub antiqua ilice,/modo in tenaci gramine* ('it's pleasant to lie sometimes under an old ilex, sometimes on the matted grass'). The immediacy of the repeated *modo* functions similarly to the repetition of *nunc* when describing the man at the spring. Cf. also the urgent *nunc...nunc* of *Odes* 1.9.18-24.

[67]Schönberger and Vretska, in particular, have well illustrated the peculiarly Horatian use of language in this ode (e.g. *Lesboum tendere barbiton*: 'to tune the Lesbian lyre'—which is unusual in both vocabulary and syntax), so I need not repeat their findings here. Syndikus (25) similarly describes *Odes* 1.1 is as 'typical' Horace, not an overture.

[68]An earlier version of this paper was delivered at the 1978 meeting of the American Philological Association. I wish to thank Professors Fred Ahl and Pietro Pucci and the referees of *Ramus* for advice and encouragement which has substantially improved this article.

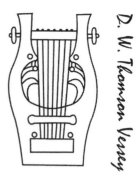

D. W. Thomson Vessey

PYRRHA'S GROTTO AND THE FAREWELL TO LOVE: A STUDY OF HORACE *ODES* 1.5

In Ode 1.5, we have the first chance to see Horace as a poet of love. He does something that is characteristic of his approach in other poems: he addresses a woman, Pyrrha, who is enjoying the ardent love of a young man, and he ignores his own connection with the situation until the last stanza, when he introduces his pronoun *me* (13). Vessey in this essay analyzes the ways the language chosen by the speaker exposes the lovers to penetrating realism. Pyrrha is a courtesan, and she has found her latest customer and victim in an unnamed slim, even scrawny "boy" (*puer* 1), with whom she is playing on a bed of roses to whet his passion. The boy, says the speaker, is overcome with desire and the delusion that this love affair will last forever, that Pyrrha will always be his. How credulous can a boy be! She has fixed her blonde hair (which is probably dyed) and dressed skillfully to enthrall the boy, but that only suggests the efforts she will take for any man. In contrast to the boy's romantic imagination of a serene and steady love, like perpetually smooth water, the speaker pictures for us and Pyrrha a future of stormy seas. How can he be so confident, we may ask? The answer lies in the last stanza, when he reveals that he himself has had some direct and traumatic experience of Pyrrha. He states that, after what we recognize as the "shipwreck" of his earlier affair, when he apparently anticipated the credulity of this boy, he has decisively ended his involvement, dedicating his "sailor's suit" to the deity who allowed him to escape. Vessey accepts this claim of wisdom from experience as true.

I am inclined to believe that the speaker talks too confidently about escaping Pyrrha, that his patronizing interest in Pyrrha's current affair betrays him. In the end, as often, Horace lets the speaker be ironized. (Ed.)

"*D*as Gedicht ist in seiner schlichten Einfachheit und klaren Gedankenführung überzeugend, dass es nicht viel Erklärung zu erfordern scheint. Aber gerade das scheinbar Einfache ist im Bereiche der Klassik ein Ergebnis höchster Kunst und raffinierter Überlegung" ["The poem convinces us by its smooth simplicity and clear development of ideas that it does not require much explanation. However, precisely the seeming simplicity, in the realm of Classics, is the achievement of the highest art and refined meditation."]—so Viktor Pöschl in his elegant interpretation of Horace *Odes* 1.5 (*Horazische Lyrik: Interpretationen* [Heidelberg 1970] 18–28, at p. 20). The poem has been so many times translated that it is tempting to suggest that one way of appreciating its artful simplicity is to fix the Latin firmly in the mind and then see how far one's understanding of it

This essay is reprinted from *American Journal of Philology* 108 (1984) 457–69, with permission of the Johns Hopkins University Press.

differs from that of its translators.[1] But that may not suffice: R. G. M. Nisbet and Margaret Hubbard (hereafter cited as N&H) in their commentary assert that the ode "is not sentimental, heart-felt, or particularly pretty" and that "it may be admired for rarer virtues, which have eluded the myriad translators, wit, urbanity and astringent charm."[2] This paper seeks primarily to reexamine the sense of the poem in an attempt to define what response it may have elicited in the minds of the Roman readers to whom it was addressed.

"The essential point to be made about this poem is that all the details in it were part of the normal daily scene in Horace's Rome," David West has written in his *Reading Horace* (Edinburgh 1967, p. 101). But our knowledge of what was or was not "daily" in Rome of that time can hardly be precise. No doubt it is true that there were women and young men, grottoes and roses (though making beds of them is no easy task or spontaneous gesture) and perhaps some people may have erected *tabulae votivae* for essentially frivolous reasons (though surely not often). Far more important than any supposed normality of the mise-en-scène, which must be regarded as doubtful and unprovable, is the indisputable fact that the motifs underlying and informing the poem have—like most motifs in Latin *Liebesgedichte* ["love poetry"], elegiac or lyric—Greek precedents immediately recognisable to an educated contemporary.[3] In any case, the idea that love is a perilous voyage and that, in theory, it is best avoided or renounced cannot be said to be, as metaphor or notion, startlingly original or (given that all poems, ancient and modern, are written by and for human beings) psychologically profound. It may be that, despite its prominence as a poetic theme, there is really not all that much that can be said about love itself, whether of pleasure or pain, but only about its attendant circumstances. These may be wholly factitious (as usually in ancient poetry) despite quasi-autobiographical accretions, or—more rarely, almost never demonstrably, and certainly never without transformation—based on some experience of the writer. Poets fall in love, to be sure; but the way they describe the experience is largely controlled by literary and cultural traditions. Motifs about love, and other universal emotions, after all become motifs because they reflect what is felt to be universally recognisable, even though the decor attached to them may, as time passes, become anachronistic, sedimented, and stylised. It would be quite fitting in principle to lend a Roman flavour to what is, at root, "an overworked topic of Greek erotic poetry" (N&H, p. 72), but it is hard to see that the flavour in *Odes* 1.5 is at all strong, far less "essential."

It is certainly Pyrrha who is best remembered by readers of this ode (perhaps by readers of Horace in general).[4] Her character is clearly and finely captured in lines 1–3: "Quis multa gracilis te puer in rosa / perfusus liquidis urget odoribus / grato, Pyrrha, sub antro?" *Quis* here implies two things: first, that a name is required or should be imagined as possible in reply, and second that Pyrrha might well be enjoying herself with any one of a number of *graciles pueri*.[5] The sense is: "Tell me just which of your slim boys...?" As has been often noted, the encirclement of *te* by the words *gracilis* and *puer* and the whole group by *multa...in rosa* cleverly suggests in itself close physical propinquity. The verb *urget* is specifically — and not especially genteelly — sexual; Orelli rightly saw it is as an equivalent to the Greek θλίβω ["press hard"], but it also has the sense of *urgere <ad coitum>* ["toward sexual intercourse"] by euphemistic suppression.[6] We are to infer that Pyrrha is playing hard to get, but that got she will certainly be. Foreplay of a heavy kind is in progress.[7]

We must turn for a time to the *puer*. He is *gracilis*: "the word refers objectively to the slight figure of an adolescent boy," according to N&H (p. 73). This attunes well with the modern Western notion, carried often to extremes, that slimness is a sexually desirable attribute. It is indeed an attribute of youth. The picture changes radically if we replace *gracilis puer* by *obesus senex*, its opposite; much of the significance of the "slim boy" depends on this occulted antithesis, which suggests the less pleasing aspects of aging such as putting on weight and waning sexual powers. But N&H, as they uneasily recognise (p. 74), may not be quite correct about *gracilis*, or at least their interpretation may not be the whole truth. West lists the epithet — doubtfully — among those words in the ode that are not "poetic" (op. cit. 101); *OLD* (IV.769, *s.v.* 1) provides examples of its use in a pejorative or scornful sense. N&H admittedly consider this facet of the word, but only to dismiss its relevance: yet the passage they cite (Ovid *Amores* 2.10.23) actually implies that a man who is *gracilis* might be expected to be *sine viribus* (but in this case was not). N&H add that "in girls *gracilitas* was much admired" (p. 74). It is quite reasonable to say, therefore, that a Roman reader might well have seen in the word *gracilis*, linked with the often condescending *puer*, not the connotations "slim and sexy" (the two not in their view being as inevitably linked as in ours, at least as far as men were concerned) but rather "skinny and girlish." This makes the proclivities of Pyrrha, whose age is not directly indicated, something quite other than charming, tender, or romantic. *Gracilis*, too, is placed next to *multa*; according to Storrs, the latter is to be seen as "enhancing (though not 'qualifying')" the former.[8] But neither "enhancement" nor "qualification' is at issue. If *gracilis* suggests a certain effeminate meagreness of physique, then *multa*, attached to the sexually symbolic *rosa*, evokes abundance and excess: and, as the rest of the poem leaves in no doubt, it must be Pyrrha's abundance and excess that is enveloping the boy as he plays the role of insistent lover for her gratification.

The boy is also "perfusus liquidis...odoribus." N&H remark (p. 74: "in ancient as in modern Italy young men in love paid inordinate attention to their hair": whether this (Anglo-Saxon) generalisation be true or not, it is hard to see why, despite the passages they cite,[9] the hair alone should be suggested by the phrase. It has been generally taken to mean that the *puer* has "thoroughly drenched himself in perfumes." This was, in the traditional Roman view, an unmanly habit; Jasper Griffin has asserted that by Augustus' time "men...used perfumes discreetly"[10] — but he sees this as part of a "life of luxury" that provides a realistic background to elegy and lyric of the period, an argument that is of doubtful value in that it freely uses evidence from the very poetry it seeks to explain in support of its premises and because it underestimates the continuity and coercive power of motifs inherited by the Romans from Greek poetry, to which "real life," even if it were in any way ascertainable, has little or no relevance.[11] But here we have not discretion but unrestraint. This might be taken as mockery of the extremism of youth in the pursuit of love, for Romans were not prone to sentimentality in such matters. Be that as it may, the whole phrase, with the intensive prefix *per-* and the plural *odores*, carries on the idea that is inherent in *gracilis*, that of a certain effeminacy about Pyrrha's *puer*. Pyrrha is a cradle-snatcher.

We must glance at the setting. "Multa...in rosa" is rightly taken by N&H (p. 74) to refer to a "bed of roses" (not to garlands as some have believed), adding that the motif "comes from Greek erotic writings" and that "to lie on roses was the height of hedonism." The roses heaped under Pyrrha and the boy are hardly to be included, as West (op. cit. 102) seems to believe, among the "familiar details from the daily life of ancient Rome"; they are clearly part of the decorative apparatus of love-scenes in literature (the rose was Venus' flower)[12] and divorced from reality. So too with the *antrum*, about which commentators have agitated themselves to no good purpose. N&H comment (p. 75): "caves are commoner in Italy than in England, yet the scene belongs to pastoral...or novelette rather than to real life." It is highly likely, need one add, that *antra*, whether natural or of human construction, were popular trysting places in Rome: but however strong the likelihood, Horace needed no such impetus to choose one as the venue for his imagined amatory encounter; the *antrum*, like the bed of roses, is a recognisable piece of literary decor.

Often overlooked, however, is the word *grato*. It is right to consider to whom and in what way the grotto is *gratum*. Certainly it is to Pyrrha who is no novice in love, and presumably to the boy on this occasion: but surely more to the former. With *grato* containing a suggestion of permanent pleasure[13] and conveying the notion "habitually welcome to her" or "her frequent resort for sexual enjoyment." Eyes blinded by a wish to see an idyll where nothing is in fact idyllic find it necessary to ignore the significance of *grato* and to devaluate it into little more than an *epitheton ornans*.[14]

The following sentence also demands close scrutiny: "cui flavam religas comam, simplex munditiis?" (4–5). As with *quis*, so *cui* should be taken to have the meaning "for whom (on this occasion)...?", as this is not, for Pyrrha, a new or unparalleled situation. The epithet *flavam* is, as N&H note (p. 75), "meant to suggest Pyrrha's own name," in that the Greek πυρρός was taken as equivalent to the Latin *rufus* or *flavus*, meaning "reddish-gold." But this *jeu de mots* is insufficient to explain why so careful a poet as Horace should have stressed the colour of Pyrrha's hair. The word can hardly be purely descriptive, and we must ask ourselves what this particular colour of hair would suggest to his readers about Pyrrha's hair. Obviously girls with reddish-gold hair existed, but in such a lyric this is not to the point. One relevant factor is contained in Fordyce's note on *flavo* in Catullus 64.63: "Fair hair conventionally belongs to the heroes and hero-ines of legend."[15] Pyrrha is a name taken from mythology (though used in Greek poetry to typify girls of a type certainly not dwelling in the age of legend);[16] so hair of a colour appropriate to a heroine is a pleasing touch — but not in any way chosen to suggest that this Pyrrha has the distant and alluring status of an Ariadne or a Dido (Virgil *Aeneid* 4.590). Far from it: because the colour was comparatively rare and much admired, "the defi-ciencies of nature were sometimes made good by art or even by purchase" (N&H, p. 75). The suspicion lingers to this day in countries where blonde hair is not the norm (including England) that those who have it have ob-tained it out of a bottle and are black at the roots. Ovid (*Amores* 1.14) has some fun with the dangers of dyeing the hair, an indication that allusions to the practice were a topos. Indeed, women's obsession with their hair was a stock theme in rhetorical and satirical ψόγος γυναικῶν ["attacks on women"].[17] It surely follows that Horace's emphasis on the *flavus* colour of Pyrrha's hair would lead to a presumption on the part of his readers that it is dyed hair — and that she is no better than she should be, lax in morals or pretending to be younger than she is (more probably the latter in view of her penchant for *graciles pueri*). It is worth adding that it was from the time of Pyrrha, wife of Deucalion, that moral corruption was conventionally held to have spread throughout mankind.[18] Her namesake proves it.

What of "simplex munditiis"? This "translator's despair"[19] has been unnecessarily obfuscated. *Simplex* is certainly intended to point a contrast with Pyrrha's true nature: "die *simplicitas* der Pyrrha…ist von Absicht nicht frei" ["the *simplicitas* of Pyrrha…is not without purpose"], remarks Pöschl, understating the case (op. cit. 21). Pyrrha's *simplicitas* is to be recognised as an aspect of her — to the *puer* — still latent complexity. *Munditiis* means not so much "neatness," far less "cleanliness," as "in the way it [the hair] is arranged"; and "uncomplicated" will serve to render *simplex*: the contrast is with the highly ornate hairstyles denounced by Propertius and Juvenal, for quite different reasons but both reworking the same topos.[20] The fun-damental point is that an elaborate coiffure is hardly conducive to pas-sionate lovemaking of the kind that is in progress *grato sub antro*; Pyrrha has dressed her hair not *ad ostentationem* but *ad lasciviam*, as suggested by the verb *urgere*. For this reason, West's tentative opinion (op. cit. 106–7), tempting at first sight, that the verb *religare* should here be taken as "un-bind" (a rare, if not unparalleled usage)[21] rather than "bind up" is not needed to explain Horace's train of thought.

It is remarkable that, in so few words, Horace should have fixed the nature of the encounter in the grotto, and of its participants, with a dispas-sionate precision. It is even more remarkable that the lines have been so often misunderstood and mistranslated: and, without understanding the opening lines, we are bound to take a distorted view also of the rest of the ode. This comprises a comment on the deceptiveness of love and on the wisdom of renouncing it. Both these themes may be said to go back to the beginnings of erotic poetry. The comparison between women and the sea may be traced back at least to Semonides of Amorgos[22] (and still lives on), and, as an image, it provides scope for subtle variation, while remaining identifiably within poetic tradition. So too the motif of the abandonment of love had ample precedent in poetry and philosophy;[23] and the renunciation symbolically objectified in the *tabula votiva* too has parallels in Greek poetry (N&H, p. 73). This literary background, of the fullness of which our knowledge remains imperfect, follows naturally on the largely motif-bound vignette with which the ode begins.

Venus was born from the sea. When the sea is calm, it is beautiful and alluring, but at other times fraught with peril. Like a woman (so male poets assumed), the sea is mutable and untrustworthy. The *gracilis puer* is envisaged by Horace as a voyager, who must inevitably come to grief and disillusion. Pyrrha is his sea,[24] on which he has rashly set sail; and we have already deduced from lines 1–5 what kind of woman she is and how inevitable is his doom. Once again, a closer examination of the words used by the economical Horace will aid us in following his development of the theme.

Lines 5–12 contain an extended sentence, which has been generally admired for interplay of nuance and for verbal patterning. In 5–6 we find the opening "heu quotiens fidem / mutatosque deos flebit." N&H (p. 76) quite properly mention the use of *fides* in "lover's language" (Catullus being the first poet known to us thoroughly to explore it in such a context) and opine that "it seems best to understand *mutatam* with the noun." This is surely true, and indeed *mutatam* may be said to be implicit in the masculine plural *mutatos*. It is, however, important to recognise how closely <*mutatam*> *fidem* and *mutatos deos* are related, for they form a single idea, almost a hendiadys. *OLD* (V.1150, *s.v.* 13, *b*) provides instances of *fidem mutare* in the sense of "to transfer allegiance" or "change sides," comparing the phrase *sacramentum mutare*. Such a "transference of allegiance" must be from one person or side to another, and covers more than a simple breach of faith. As it is here Pyrrha's *fides* (in the matter of love) that is in question, the sentence may be expanded as "how often he will bewail the fact that she has transferred her allegiance...from himself to another." As for *mutatos deos*, N&H (p. 76) compare Propertius 1.1.8: "cum tamen adversos cogor habere deos," but this is hardly an exact parallel: to have the gods against one is not the same as lamenting the fact that they are *mutati*. *Mutatos* must here be taken with a similar force to the *mutatam* which is understood with *fidem*, so that the whole sentence runs "how often he will bewail the fact that she has transferred her allegiance and the gods from himself to another." To transfer one's *fides* was in Roman eyes a serious matter, for the gods presided over *fides* and it had a cardinal importance in the moral order.[25] To play fast and loose with *fides* is to play fast and loose with the gods that are its guardians. What the *puer* will lament is the transference of an allegiance that he believed to have a divine sanction sacrilegiously away from himself; Pyrrha is foresworn and he will feel that the gods too, the guarantors of her oaths, have abandoned him along with her. It is not so much a belief that the gods have turned against him as that they have forsaken him altogether. Pyrrha, it seems, carries her own gods around with her.

The ideas of betrayal and mutability lead neatly into the marine imagery that follows and may, in a sense, be said to suggest it; the comparison of a woman to the sea was, as has been remarked, a well-established one in poetry, and behind it lies the still more familiar topos that the sea is in itself hazardous and to be avoided.[26] Admiration has been expressed for the skill with which Horace has deployed his adjectives in lines 6–12, with their various balances and antitheses:

> …et *aspera*
> *nigris* aequora ventis
> emirabitur *insolens,*

> qui nunc te fruitur *credulus aurea,*
> qui semper *vacuam,* semper *amabilem*
> sperat, *nescius* aurae
> *fallacis.*

The descriptive words applied to the *puer* (*insolens, credulus, nescius*) all relate to his naiveté and inexperience; those found in the comparison of Pyrrha to the sea stress her cruelty, darkness, and deceit (*aspera, nigris, fallacis*). In between them, in the two relative clauses, we find presented the false picture of Pyrrha, which the boy—while in the grotto or perhaps until her *fides* is transferred elsewhere—forms of her (*aurea, vacuam, amabilem*). Three words pertain to each category, for there may be said to be three characters in this part of the ode: the boy, the real Pyrrha, and the imaginary Pyrrha. The adjectives applied, metaphorically, to the real Pyrrha overwhelm and cancel both those applied to the boy and those that serve to mark out his naive vision of her: deceit in place of ignorance and credulity, harshness instead of availability and affection, blackness instead of gold. But there is more: whereas the boy and his imagined Pyrrha remain as human beings, with adjectives applied to them befitting their humanity, the real Pyrrha is presented only in terms of the violent, uncontrolled, and uncontrollable elements—it is they that sweep away and obliterate the human figures, one of which is indeed only the product of the other's fantasy.

The verb *emirabitur* "may well be a coinage of Horace's" (N&H, p. 76), one of the "long prosaic compounds" that "help to build the monumental masonry of a Horatian line." Bentley, seeing a logical conflict between *quotiens* and *insolens*, sought to eliminate it from the text.[27] That the sound of the pentasyllabic verb excellently evokes the state of long and stunned amazement which is in store for the *puer* is apparent, and N&H (p. 76) are probably right to suggest a parallel—or specific but unidentified echo— with a Greek compound verb such as ἐκθαυμάζω ["utterly astounded"]; the transformation of the sea from calm and fair to stormy and savage will take his breath away with shock and bewilderment. *Insolens* presents no real problem or inconsistency. N&H (p. 77) suggest that it "refers to the present time...and not to the future time of the boy's surprise," but this view is not wholly satisfactory. Horace surely implies that, when the boy is confronted by an angry and faithless Pyrrha, he will often, ingenuous as he is, be amazed; this is not an event that occurs once and then becomes familiar (or acceptable), but rather something that will continue to bewilder him until he has ceased to be *insolens* and has dedicated his own valedictory *tabula votiva*.

If there is any reference to "present time," by which is presumably meant the time envisaged in the first stanza, it is more likely to be contained in the secondary sense of *insolens*: "in his vanity" or "in his arrogant triumph."[28] The boy who now glories in his (supposed) conquest will later have to learn that he is quite unversed in the ways of women. This idea is clearly brought out in lines 9–11. These provide, as it were, a glimpse into the boy's thoughts while in the grotto, when he foolishly sees a Pyrrha who is *aurea* and always *vacua, amabilis*. West, while noting (op. cit. 104) that *amabilis* is an "unpoetic" word, asserts that these lines "call up a benign and empty sea at sunset before the impending storms and black winds..." (ibid. 104). This extrapolation misses the point. *Aurea* is a "lover's word" (N&H, p. 77, cf. *OLD* I.217, *s.v.* 5) and an inflation of *flavam* in 4 (Storrs, op. cit. 27); *vacua* ("available") and *amabilis* ("lovable," "gorgeous") are both words without high poetic force: indeed, all three are epithets that a boy might well, quite conversationally, use to himself or to friends about a girl. Lines 9–11, with their normal, slightly mundane vocabulary, give the reader an *aperçu* into the working of the boy's mind and are an index of his credulity. They contrast with the complex, *literarisch* imagery that surrounds them. The boy is naive, but Pyrrha is not; he responds to her in a simple and trusting manner—his "golden, willing and gorgeous girl"—without foreseeing at that point her tempestuous, destructive nature. Horace's choice of vocabulary enables him subtly to turn aside from the traditional metaphor and give his readers a short but unmistakable change of tone and mood; what a Roman would recognise as normal, if not everyday language, expressing authentically what the thoughts of such a boy might be in the depicted circumstances, disrupts the development of the traditional imagery, which is picked up again in 11–12 ("nescius aurae / fallacis"). The choice of *aura*, which at first glance seems a weaker word than *venti* in line 7 (cf. *OLD* I.216, *s.v.* 2), is made poignant by its responsion in sound to *aurea*, the "lover's word" in line 9. All of these nuances attune perfectly with the characterisation of Pyrrha and the boy so deftly established in the first stanza.

That the *puer* is only one among many on whom Pyrrha has preyed and will prey again is confirmed by the brief exclamatory interjection that follows: "miseri, quibus intemptata nites" (12–13). *Miser* is a quasi-technical word for those suffering through love.[29] Of the remark Pöschl writes: "Der Satz *miseri* etc. enthält die Quintessenz alles bisherigen. Er klingt

beinahe wie eine Sentenz" ["The sentence *miseri*…etc. contains the quin-
tessence of everything so far. It sounds almost like a general saying"](op.
cit. 23). Yet the words are not really gnomic, and the *miseri* comprise a
specific group: all the *pueri* who join Pyrrha in her *antrum* of passion. The
verb *nites* glances back, almost in mockery, to *aurea* (and so to *flavam*). As,
for example, in Catullus 2.5, *nitere* "suits a beautiful girl" (N&H, p. 77,
comparing *Odes* 1.19.5). It is less certain, however, that "it also suggests
the treacherous glitter of a shining sea" (ibid. pp. 77–78). No parallel is
adduced for this usage. *Nitere* is commonly used of gleaming and resplen-
dent surfaces (*OLD* V.1180, *s.v.* 2, 3), including metallic ones. It is more
likely to be intended to pick up the image contained in *aurea*, "golden," for
the exclamation refers to the shattering of the illusory dream-world of lines
9–11, of the hope the boys entertain about Pyrrha. *Intemptata* would then
mean "unassayed," "untried" in a metallurgical sense, not "unpenetrated
as a route" (cf. *OLD* IV.937, *s.v.* 1 *b*). Gold was normaliy tried by fire in
antiquity,[30] and this is entirely suitable to the context in view of the frequent comparison made in love-poetry between *ignis* and *amor*. All those
who "assay" Pyrrha in the fire of love find her base metal, despite the
superficial sheen that captivates them. The sentence forms a closure of the
ode as a comment on the relationship between Pyrrha and her *puer*, leading into the renunciation-topos with which it is formally ended.

    Me in line 13 is in emphatic contrast to *miseri* in 12. It is sometimes
rashly treated as if it referred to Horace himself; in fact it serves as a cover
for a definable category of men: former lovers of Pyrrha (and, by extension,
of her like), who have had enough of venturing on such faithless seas:[31]

> …me tabula sacer
> votiva paries indicat uvida
>   suspendisse potenti
>   vestimenta maris deo.

Walter Wili has perceptively commented on these lines: "Man sehe wie
diesseits und jenseits des tragenden Verbums indicat je zwei Wortpaare
gesperrt und zugleich unter sich verschränkt sind und so der ganze Satz
selbst gleichsam eine symmetrisch ausgewogene *tabula votiva* wird." ["One
can see that on either side of the main verb *indicat* two noun-adjective word-
pairs are poised and at the same time interlocked, so that the entire sentence itself becomes a symmetrically balanced votive tablet."][32] The juxtaposition of motifs is subtle and striking. Just as a craftsman might dedicate
the tools of his trade on retirement (cf. N&H, p. 73 on this as a literary
topos), so the nameless lover has hung up his dripping garments on escaping from the tempestuous waters of love. The traditional image of "woman
as sea" is suddenly given an almost mischievous specificity; because lovers are sailors only within poetry, so the votive tablet, commemorating the
renunciation of love symbolised by the *uvida vestimenta*, is itself a part of
the ode, is inscribed within it. The noun *vestimenta*, rightly classified as

"unpoetic," aptly evokes what is a down-to-earth and practical act, far from the world of grottoes, perfumes, and roses. A life on shore is safer.

The ode begins and ends with enclosed spaces. The *antrum* of Pyrrha is a suitable venue for erotic disportment; the temple of Neptune bears on its "holy wall" the imagined objectification of love renounced. Pyrrha herself, the golden Pyrrha, has the *gracilis puer* in her arms at the outset of a voyage that must prove disastrous to him, though not to her; neither she nor the sea ever changes or disappears. Only experience can teach her victims that all that glisters is not gold so that, soaked and buffeted by the waves of her perfidy, they at last retire from the life of love, moving, as it were, from grotto to temple. From a relatively small number of motifs and by a careful choice of word and image, Horace presented to his Roman readers — and to later ones — a fine statement on how the *ingénieux* should regard the *ingénu*. Love is not a bed of roses, when there is a Pyrrha to lie on it.[33]

Notes

[1]For a collection of translations, which could now be substantially increased, see *Ad Pyrrham: A Polyglot Collection of Translations of Horace's "Ode to Pyrrha" (Book I, Ode 5) Assembled with an Introduction* by Ronald Storrs (London 1959).

[2]R. G. M. Nisbet and Margaret Hubbard, *A Commentary on Horace: Odes, Book I* (Oxford 1970), 73. Cf. also R. G. M. Nisbet. "*Romanae fidicen lyrae:* The Odes of Horace," in *Critical Essays on Roman Literature: Elegy and Lyric* (ed. J. P. Sullivan, London 1962) 181–218 at p. 183: "The Pyrrha ode is remote from the lush effusions of modern translators, an anthology of whose futilities [i.e., Storrs] has recently been published."

[3]See the remarks of Giuseppe Giangrande, "Hellenistic Topoi in Ovid's *Amores, MPhL* 4 (1981) 25–51, esp. at p. 25.

[4]Nisbet (note 2 above) 181: "Everybody knows Pyrrha...."

[5]For *quis*, see *OLD* VII.1559, *s.v.* 1: most translations miss the point that a specific answer to the question is envisaged as possible.

[6]J. C. Orelli, 4th ed., rev. J. G. Baiter and W. Hirschfelder (Berlin 1886) ad loc., 41.

[7]It is to be noted that the verb *urget* contains within itself not only the boy's eagerness for copulation and the woman's (feigned) resistance to it, a normative situation, but equally the woman's pleasure in her lover's eagerness and in her own ability to defer his desire to increase her own, a notion usually suppressed in polite society.

[8]Storrs, op. cit. 27.

[9]Propertius, 2.4.5, Ovid, *Ars amatoria* 3.443, Aristaenetus 1.27.

[10]Jasper Griffin, "Augustan poetry and the life of luxury," *JRS* 76 (1976) 87–104 at p. 93.

[11]Indeed, the realism of "realistic" literature in modern times evaporates before close analysis: cf. Roland Barthes, *S/Z: Essai* (Paris 1970): the quest for verisimilitude is in itself a fantasy, as is well brought out by J. Culler, *The Pursuit of Signs: Semiotics, Literature, Deconstruction* (London 1981) 61–62.

[12]Of beds of roses, cf. Orelli (note 6 above).The association between the rose and love is perhaps the most persistent image in European love poetry.

[13]See *OLD* IV.774, *s.v.* 4, for this aspect of the meaning of *gratus*.

[14]Storrs' "straight" English rendition by A. D. Godley comes up with the notably inadequate "in the pleasant bower" (op.cit., p. xi), an adjective often repeated in other versions.

[15] C. J. Fordyce, *Catullus: A Commentary* (Oxford 1961) 287.

[16] N&H, p. 74: "It [the name Pyrrha] was probably favoured by hetaerae..."; as a literary instance they cite Marcus Argentarius, *AP* 9.161 (= A. S. F. Gow and D. L. Page, *The Greek Anthology: The Garland of Philip* [Cambridge 1968] I, p. 155, no. XV).

[17] On which, see E. Courtney, *A Commentary on the Satires of Juvenal* (London 1980) 253.

[18] See Propertius 2.32.49 ff., Juvenal 1.81 ff.

[19] Storrs, op. cit. 21.

[20] Propertius 1.2 (probably the poem that is parodied by Ovid *Amores* 1.14 as an exemplar of a stock amatory theme); Juvenal 6.-486 ff. (with Courtney's note and bibliographical reff., op. cit. 326).

[21] *OLD* VI.1606, *s.v.* 5, cites — doubtfully — only Catullus 63.84, where the meaning is inferred from *resolvens* in line 76.

[22] 7.37 ff.: N&H, p. 72. For the origins of this long-lived image, see R. B. Onians, *The Origins of European Thought* (Cambridge 1953) 230.

[23] N&H, p. 73. The remarks of Cephalus (citing the aged Sophocles) at Plato *Republic* 329 may be seen as a philosophical *point de depart* for a topos, which, handled by philosophers, poets, and rhetoricians alike, was to amuse Ovid in the *Remedia*.

[24] Cf. H. Musurillo, *Symbol and Myth in Ancient Poetry* (New York 1961) 144, with n. 24.

[25] Of the many treatments of *fides*, see now J. H. G. W. Liebeschuetz, *Continuity and Change in Roman Religion* (Oxford 1979) 12 ff. On *fides* in Catullus, D. W. T. Vessey, "Thoughts on two poems of Catullus: 13 and 30." *Latomus* 30 (1971) 15-55 at pp. 53-54

[26] For a collection of passages, see K. F. Smith, *The Elegies of Tibullus* (repr. Darmstatdt 1961) 216-17.

[27] N&H, pp. 76-77; see also Storrs, op. cit. 13-15 for an amusing eighteenth century reply to Bentley.

[28] *OLD* IV.926, *s.v.* 4: Horace *Odes* 1.16.21; 3.29.50.

[29] R. Pichon, *De sermone amatorio apud Latinos elegiarum scriptores* (diss. Paris 1903) 203 (*miser* specifically of love-sickness at Lucretius 4.1076).

[30] Cf. Cicero *Ad fam.* 9.16.2; Ovid *Tristia* 1.5.25; Pliny *N. H.* 33.126.

[31] N&H's advocacy (pp. 79-80) of Zielinski's emendation *deae* in the last line has — and rightly — not met with approval, though they have made what Jasper Griffin (*JRS* 70 [1980] 185) terms "a new and improbable attempt" to justify their view in *A Commentary on Horace: Odes Book II* (Oxford 1978) 91.

[32] Walter Wili, *Horaz und die augusteische Kultur* (Basel, Stuttgart 1965) 249.

[33] It is, all the same, the love of such as Pyrrha that has been renounced — a passing misfortune perhaps for *graciles pueri* — and not necessarily love as such.

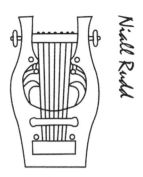

Niall Rudd

PATTERNS IN HORATIAN LYRIC

In this Ode, varying an opening scene in the Greek poet Alcaeus, Horace starts with an impressive picture of Mt. Soracte (visible from the highest hills of Rome) in the freezing temperatures of winter. It is, as Rudd in this essay nicely argues, a realistic but imaginary scene: Romans did not have picture windows through which they could enjoy outdoor scenery, for all Roman houses looked inward. So when the speaker urges young Thaliarchus to overcome the cold by heaping up wood on the hearthfire and generously pouring out wine from a Sabine jar, he is also describing in imagery how to change the "winter" of existence into the warmth of "spring." Amid the difficulties of our lives, we all have some possibility of affecting circumstances and our happiness. We have to concentrate on our immediate present. Leave to the gods, the speaker says, all other things (9 ff.): they don't let storms rage forever. Similarly, don't fuss about tomorrow or the distant future, which is out of our control (13 ff.). Make the most of the present, which, in the case of Thaliarchus, is the pleasures of a young man, especially those of love. Thus, Rudd marks another contrast in stanzas 3 and 4, between storms which image anxiety and the dismissal of anxiety for the delights of youth. And that system of contrast organizes the final two stanzas, where, against crabbed white-haired age, the ultimate threat of a man's future, we see assembled a variety of amatory details, which represent the available enjoyments of the "now" that is urged on Thaliarchus and us by repeated *nunc* in 18 and 21. (Ed.)

✧ ✧ ✧

What I should like to do is to give a brief outline of the poem and then go on to discuss some of its more controversial points.

Outside it is winter. Soracte is covered with snow. Trees droop under their burden, and rivers are frozen. From this frosty scene we move indoors to the warmth of a fire, wine, and good company. Forget your worries, says Horace, and make the most of life while you're young — *donec virenti canities abest morosa* (17). The contrast of white and green shows that Horace is again associating human life with the world of nature, and this at once suggests a more general contrast between the opening and the end of the poem. The winter scene remains as real as ever, but it has taken on symbolic overtones. The white snow, the trees' burden, and the frozen rivers contain similar implications to those of *bruma iners* in IV, 7; whereas the

This essay is reprinted from *American Journal of Philology* 81 (1960) 387–92, with permission of the Johns Hopkins University Press.

closing stanzas, with their references to outdoor activities, point rather to the spring or summer. This contrast is perhaps a little awkward, but it has brought Horace more censure than he deserves. People have complained that the ode is spoilt by having a winter opening and a spring conclusion, especially when the two scenes are made to appear contemporary by the reiterated *nunc* in 18 and 21. But this is unfair, because although the primary significance of stanza one is that of winter, the primary significance of the closing stanzas is not spring, but youth. The two *nunc*'s mean "now while you're young," not "now while it's spring." This is made perfectly clear by the *puer* of 16 and by the *donec* clause which follows it. The construction exactly resembles *dumque virent genua* in *Epod.* 13.

White/green, cold/warm, stillness/movement. These and a few other antitheses which do not really matter fit naturally into the larger patterns of winter/spring and youth/age. For L. P. Wilkinson these two sets of images are enough to interpret the poem, but I feel that he is not taking full account of the third stanza:

> Permitte divis cetera, qui simul
> stravere ventos aequore fervido
> deproeliantis nec cypressi
>   nec veteres agitantur orni.

These lines cannot form part of the Soracte scene. They are set on the sea coast and contain a picture of wild movement, whereas Soracte dominates a frozen landscape. Moreover, the Latin construction forbids us to assume either that the storm has immediately preceded the frosty scene[1] or that the two scenes are simultaneous.[2] The only possible view is that Horace is stating a general truth about the power of the gods.[3] This was perceived by Heinze and Wilkinson, but neither of them has explained the stanza's function quite satisfactorily. Heinze simply says that the power of the gods is most strikingly displayed in the quelling of storms, while Wilkinson maintains that the storm is the storm of life and the calm the calm of death. Now when Horace says *permitte divis cetera* he implies that things will eventually take a turn for the better and that the balance of nature will be restored.[4] We may compare II, 9, 1–8 (*non semper imbres…*), II, 10, 15–20 (*informis hiemes reducit Iuppiter, idem summovet…*), I, 7, 15–17 (*albus ut obscuro deterget nubila caelo saepe Notus …*), and a less confident version in *Epod.* 13, 7 (*cetera mitte loqui, deus haec fortasse benigna reducet in sedem vice*). Well then, are we to imagine Horace as saying "Don't worry, things will eventually take a turn for the better, you'll soon be dead"? Of course that won't do, but perhaps it is possible to guess at what led Wilkinson astray. Throughout his analysis of the Soracte ode Wilkinson was acutely conscious of its symbolic affinities with Housman's *On Wenlock Edge*. In fact he quotes the final verse in support of his argument:

> The gale it plies the saplings double,
> it blows so hard 'twill soon be gone,

to-day the Roman and his trouble
are ashes under Uricon.

As in Horace, the threads of humanity and nature are interwoven, but
Wilkinson may have overlooked the difference in mood between the two
poems. Horace never draws this kind of bleak comfort from the prospect
of death, and to introduce such a notion into the Soracte ode would surely
destroy its spirit, for it is above all else a happy composition.

Nevertheless Housman's poem does point the way to a more satisfactory solution of our problem. You remember the opening verse:

On Wenlock Edge the wood's in trouble,
his forest fleece the Wrekin heaves,
the wind it plies the saplings double,
and thick on Severn snow the leaves.

The wood's in trouble — *silvae laborantes*? Quite possibly. And does this not
lead us straight to the section we are discussing — *nec cupressi nec veteres
agitantur orni*? The winds struggle over the turbulent sea (*aequore fervido*),
and when they are laid low, the cypress and ash trees are no longer disturbed. *Fervidus* suggests violent emotion, and this appears to be the first
known instance of its application to the sea.[5] As for *agitantur*, the metaphorical sense can be illustrated from Horace, *Epist.*, I, 18, 98, where he is
speaking of tranquillity:

num te semper inops agitet vexetque cupido,
num pavor et rerum mediocriter utilium spes.

["Whether helpless passion will perpetually stir and harass you,
or fear and the hope for moderately useful possessions."]

So at its metaphorical level this verse would seem to deal with the change
from turbulent anxiety to calm cheerfulness.[6]

The seasons and the weather are beyond human control. Some greater
power, whether it be the gods or the rhythm of nature, will see to it that
winter does not last for ever. We should therefore ignore the snow and
make things as comfortable as possible within. A similar rhythm governs
our national and personal affairs. Dangers pass, troubles recede. Meanwhile we should turn away from all that is grim and depressing, and think
only of those things which make the moment happy. For to-day is a gift
which Fortune will not offer again.[7]

So it turns out that *Carm.*, I, 9 has four main pairs of antitheses:
winter/spring, age/youth, storm/calm, anxiety/cheerfulness.

Winter Spring Storm Calm Anxiety Cheerfulness

                                              Age   Youth

Putting the submerged or metaphorical themes in brackets we get a scheme like this:

1) Winter (age, anxiety).
2) Winter, cheerfulness (youth).
3) Storm, calm (anxiety, cheerfulness).
4) Anxiety, cheerfulness, youth.
5) Age, anxiety, youth, cheerfulness (winter, spring).
6) Youth, cheerfulness (spring).

The third stanza has always been something of a problem. Leaving aside the question of its interpretation, we may perhaps hazard a guess at its function in the Ode. In I, 7 Horace says "the wind does not always bring rain-storms, you too should relax from time to time"; in I, 26 the winds carry the poet's fear away while he remains calm; in *Epod.* 13 the storm outside will eventually cease, so Horace's friend should also forget his troubles. In I, 9, therefore, Horace may have felt that he needed a scene of confused motion in the world of nature to set against the inner calm which he was recommending. Such movement was not to be found in the frozen landscape of Soracte, so it had to be introduced in a verse of its own. Whether this whole business was deliberate or not it is impossible to say.

Two other points before leaving this ode. In the article already referred to M. C. Shields [*Phoenix*, IX (1995) and XII (1958).] compares the opening stanza with the introduction to a Christian parable like "consider the lilies." There would seem to be two main difficulties here. First I cannot see a parallel between "consider the lilies" and "consider Soracte." The lilies represent a model of tranquillity for neurotic and ulcerated mortals like ourselves, but Soracte and its environs do not reflect any such admirable quality. They stand rather for age and anxiety, as we have just seen. True, the scene has a certain icy beauty, but it is not a calm or a comfortable one. The woods are bowed beneath their burden, the rivers are caught in the sharp grip of frost, and one is glad to get indoors to the warmth of the fire. Secondly it was unusual for Soracte to be covered in snow, and it was this event which provided the occasion for the ode; the lilies, however, were part of the normal landscape, and were brought in to illustrate the religious message. Here is a slight but definite contrast in emphasis.

This leads on to the other point, namely the question of the poem's "reality." First of all does the opening stanza represent an actual experience? Orelli says no. After referring to the fragment of Alcaeus he concludes *qua ex imitatione ipsa equidem colligo totum argumentum esse ficticium ac liberae* φαντασίας *ludum.* In other words, since Alcaeus has spoken of a bad day it means that when Horace does the same he must be romancing. Apart altogether from the question of logical sequence, the great editor might have noticed that in Alcaeus there is no mountain and in Horace there is no rain. Yet there is something in what Orelli says. We must distinguish between the poem's dramatic setting and the place where it was written. While the scene in stanza two is authentic in the sense that its outlines are true to life, it is not being enacted at the moment of composition. We can scarcely visualise Horace sitting, tablet on knee, while the party goes on around him — not all lyric writers have the same detachment and facility as Mr. Cole Porter. Furthermore, since Roman houses faced inwards, Horace was not inviting Thaliarchus to look at Soracte through the window. The whole winter landscape — mountain, trees, and rivers — was to be seen by the eye of the imagination. The snow was there all right, but it was not visible from where Horace was writing or from where the party was supposed to be.

A few years ago a new question was opened in a stimulating article by Bagnani.[8] His point may be summarized as follows: if the living-room of a Roman house had no chimney, how are we to explain *ligna super foco*? You can burn charcoal without a chimney, but what about logs ? This is certainly a nice problem, and I am not so rash as to challenge Bagnani on a point of archaeology. However, a student of literature can always turn for aid to the *Thesaurus*. There he will find that Vollmer has listed twenty-five or thirty passages which show that in the humbler country houses at any rate wood was burnt on the hearth.[9] We will let the metaphysicians decide at what stage a log becomes a branch, but the pieces, whatever we call them, must have been reasonably small. They were certainly dry and well seasoned, and no doubt they were sometimes treated in the way recommended by Cato in his *De Agri Cultura*.[10] Nevertheless, smoke and soot could not be avoided, as several of the passages show.[11] The question, then, is whether wood was burned in the sort of house that Horace had in mind. If the archaeologists eventually prove that the burning of wood was confined to the peasants' dwelling-houses, then we shall have to suppose that *ligna super foco* is being used in a figurative sense. But this does not affect the points made in the previous paragraph. I would contend, therefore, that the opening stanza refers to an actual period of frost, that the poem was written during or shortly after the period described, and that the party scene is a piece of realistic drama.

This paper has tried, amongst other things, to illustrate how the investigation of a poem's imagery can give its meaning a new dimension. We cannot expect the method to yield equally fruitful results in the case of every poet. Yet it seems that even with a writer like Horace, whose work is of a relatively plain texture, the technique can be usefully combined with the more traditional means of interpretation.[12]

Notes

[1]This seems to be Pasquali's view, cf. *Orazio Lirico*, p. 82.

[2]Page, for instance, supplies *nunc* with *deproeliantis*.

[3]Examples of this construction are given in Gildersleeve's *Grammar*, § 567.

[4]Cf. Archilochus, 67a (Diehl) beginning θυμέ, θύμ' and ending γίγνωσκε δ' οἷος ῥυσμὸς ἀνθρώπους ἔχει (See Jaeger, *Paideia*, I, pp. 125 f.). Cf. also Uhland's *Frühlingsglaube*:

Nun, armes Herze, sei nicht bang!
Nun muss sich alles, alles wenden.
["Now, poor heart, do not be distressed!
Now everything, everything must change."]

[5]Isid., *Orig.*, XIII, 18, 2: *freta dicta ait Varro quasi fervida* ["Varro says that straits (*freta*) are called such as if boiling."] is slightly misleading; what Varro says is *dictum fretum ab similitudine ferventis aquae* ["a strait, derived from its similarity to boiling water."] (*L. L.*, VII, 22).

[6]As Pasquali says, " Spesso a Orazio, allorchè egli pensa a un' anima torbida e tempestosa, appare l'immagine del mare" ["Often the image of the sea occurs to Horace when he thinks of a troubled and temperamental soul."] (*op. cit.*, p. 82).

[7]Cf. *Carm.*, III, 8, 27; also *Epod.*, 13, 4, where the *dies* is, as it were, the vehicle of the *occasio*. As for *lucro appone*, we should avoid translating "Put down on the side of gain" (Page). The ancients did not have the bilateral system of bookkeeping. See B. R. Rees, *C.R.*, VIII (1958).

[8]*Phoenix*, VIII (1954).

[9]E.g. Varro, *R.R.*, I, 15; II, 10; Lucil., 966; Hor., *Epod.*, 2, 43; *Moretum*, 37; Ov., *Fast.*, IV, 510; *Medic.*, 16.

[10]*De Ag.*, 130. Cf. Forbes, *Stud. in Ancient Technology*, VI, p. 14.

[11]E.g. Verg., *Georg.*, I, 175; Ov., *Pont.*, I, 3, 34; Verg., *Ecl.*, 7, 49; Mart., II, 90, 7; Colum., XI, 3, 60.

[12]Professors G. Bagnani, D. F. S. Thomson, and L. E. Woodbury were kind enough to discuss certain questions which arose during the writing of this paper. They are not responsible for its defects.

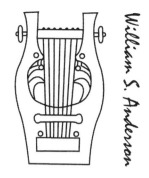

William S. Anderson

HORACE'S DIFFERENT RECOMMENDERS OF *CARPE DIEM* IN *C.* 1.4, 7, 9, 11

An ode of only eight lines, in an Asclepiadean meter of maximum length, this poem follows closely and aptly on 1.9. It introduces to world literature the phrase *carpe diem* and the type of poem where a man urges a maid to gather the rosebuds while she may, that is, to act on the brevity of youthful pleasure and satisfy his amatory passions. Although 1.11 was once appreciated in such terms, it has lost that meaning for most commentators, who tend to read it as merely one more poem of wise Horatian advice like 1.9. This essay argues that Horace, in fact, builds on the familiar formulae of 1.9 and two earlier odes, to show how, in the mouth of an interested speaker, they could be turned to ironically exploitative purposes. Whereas the speaker of 1.9 has encouraged Thaliarchus to go out to the Campus Martius and enjoy the love-games of one or another girl there, *puer* and *puella* in their natural inclinations, this speaker is arguing for himself, as the prominent placing of *mihi* in 1 implies, and for the sexual relationship which he plots to enjoy from Leuconoe. Thus, the arguments resemble those of 1.9, but they are put in a perfunctory, stylized manner that betrays the selfish motives of the speaker. After introducing the negative image of winter in 4–6, the eager adviser launches into three clauses of jussive subjunctives, the first of which is *sapias* 6. 1 suggest that we can catch his meaning with a translation like "Wise up, baby." If Leuconoe can only use the clear mind that her name suggests, she will resist this argument and definitely avoid the wine which is preliminary to the speaker's goal. (Ed.)

T he Horace who charms me is a poet of considerable versatility, not only in the genres which he mastered but also in the voices with which he puts forward views on the average crises of human existence. That versatility provides one of the special attractions of the *Odes*. Where so often the critics of a century ago were all too content, like Shorey, to epitomize with gleeful superciliousness the repetitive ideas and themes of Horatian lyric, we today can relish the subtle ways in which the poet differentiates his works by meter, by addressee, occasion, and by the relative involvement of the speaker. I should like to spend some time on four poems from Book I. About the first three, I shall have less to say, because, while each raises some critical problems, the matter of addressee, speaker and occasion is not seriously under dispute, and the common themes can be rapidly summarized. About 1.11, on the other hand, I shall take more time, especially because we need to see how skillfully Horace uses those same themes on a

This essay is reprinted from *Classical Journal* 88 (1984) 115–22, with permission of the publisher.

very different occasion, with a speaker whose peculiar self-interest qualifies his protreptic, in a meter that is new to the Book, to produce a final
lyric position that differs strikingly from those of 1.4, 7, and 9.

In his valuable new book, *Polyhymnia. The Rhetoric of Horatian Lyric
Discourse*, Gregson Davis has subtly elaborated the art with which Horace
manipulated the rhetorical materials of *carpe diem* argument (which he
abbreviates to *CD*).[1] In its basic form, the *CD* poem uses a description of
nature to elicit insight into the changes to which all human beings are subject, and then it proceeds to prescribe enjoyment of the moment, particularly in symposiastic pleasures.[2] Davis does touch on tone here and there,
but his primary concern to explicate the artful rhetoric of Horace tends to
emphasize the fundamental sameness of the rhetorical materials rather than
the different poems that result. For example, all four of the poems I have
selected do have a descriptive scene. *C.* 1.4 and 9 give that scene at the
start: the dissolution of winter's hold on nature in 1.4 and the static wintry
landscape around Mt. Soracte in 1.9. In their respective ways, then, 1.4 and
9 proceed to their human insights and prescription. In 1.7, the description
emerges only as the climactic part of a priamel (1–14), a device which Horace
employs to contrast and reject the places that other poets, even Homer,
have chosen to praise. Once he has established that Tibur is an idyllic spot
for both his poetic inspiration and for his addressee's pleasure, Horace
then can appeal to Plancus' insight and prescribe for him the convivial
ways of the usual *CD*.[3] In 1.11, however, Horace delays the description
until after the speaker has started his prescriptions. Davis notes the fact,
but, since the rhetorical function seems the same, he lets it pass without
further comment. I believe that the altered position of injunction and description points to a crucial distinction of meaning in the poem as a whole.

The addressees of the four poems are also significantly different. In
1.4, after his long opening description of springtime liberation, Horace
suddenly moves to his shocking mention of pale Death, which pounds at
the doors of poor and rich alike (13–14). And only then does he name an
addressee and start using the second person singular in his prescriptions.
The addressee, "fortunate" Sestius, happens to be the consul suffect of 23
B.C., the year of the publication of the *Odes*. Nisbet and Hubbard assert:
"the poem is in no way about Sestius;"[4] which is hardly accurate, though
we should not spend our time forcing the few facts we have about Sestius
into alignment with *carpe diem* themes. It is an editorial convention, after
all, to attach the vocative phrase *o beate Sesti* to the sentence in 15 rather
than to that which ends in 14. But in either case, Sestius the affluent consul
stands for all those who in middle age and relatively comfortable circumstances need to remember how close Death is. The addressee of 1.7, similarly postponed until the poet has reached the section on advice, is another
eminent Roman politician, L. Munatius Plancus. He is named and addressed

in the second person singular for a short stretch in the middle of the poem (15–21), after which Horace moves off into a story about Teucer (21–32). Because we happen to know more about Plancus' troubled life, there has been a fierce effort to fit the advice of CD tightly to this addressee. But Plancus, like Sestius, stands for wealthy, troubled middle age and its difficulties in relaxing.

When Horace returns to CD in 1.9 and 11, he chooses fictional addressees, both of whom are young and in more hopeful circumstances as far as death and politics are concerned. After sketching out the frozen wintry scene around Soracte in 1.9.1–4, the poet proceeds to his injunctions and then to the name of Thaliarchus (8). The Greek name, identifiable with no known figure of the day (and almost certainly not meant to be), invites us to generalize the situation and to look for meaning in the name rather than the historical person. As he carries out the injunction to "dissolve the cold," Thaliarchus is indeed the "master of pleasure" that his name implies. Thus, the advice consistently urges him to act out the meaning of his name or, in more symbolic terms, to use the limited mastery that all human beings have to affect the immediate quality of existence. In further protreptic, the speaker calls Thaliarchus *puer* (16) and urges him to take advantage of sweet love and dancing; and the poem ends on an alluring springtime scene, which has become "now" (18, 21) of playful youthful eroticism in the Campus Martius. The character and name that Horace assigns to Thaliarchus give a different flavor to the CD rhetoric. And what about Leuconoe in 1.11? This addressee is a girl, with a Greek name, too, but one not evidently in accord with the speaker's disapproval. If she is "clear- or white-minded," as the name implies, then the speaker is trying to change that mind radically and introduce another kind of "clarity." He names her in the second line, because he has started with his urgent injunctions, before describing the scene of nature that should inspire her. The advice, in fact, has proved so unclear for many readers, that we shall need to ask why this is so. Nevertheless, recent commentators agree somewhat tepidly that there is some talk of love. Not direct and forceful, as to Thaliarchus, but implicit. As Nisbet and Hubbard remark, "There are also hints of a love-interest which, though not conspicuous, may have been more prominent in Horace's models."[5] Equally restrained, Daniel Garrison writes: "Addressed to Leuconoe, *carpe diem* may carry a note of erotic suggestion."[6] So Horace chooses a problematic name, a young girl, for whom erotic advice is also problematic — or should I say devious? In any case, the addressee of 1.11 is several degrees beyond Thaliarchus away from the distinguished Romans Sestius and Plancus. And that makes for a different quality to the CD rhetoric.

Now what about the speaker of the four poems? In 1.4 and 7 the speaker has virtually no personality other than that of a familiar acquaintance of two notable Roman politicians; in that capacity, he has the status to offer them advice, free of criticism, to enjoy the ways of CD. He is presumably a man of their own age and general status, in other words someone substantially like the historical Horace, who was in his early 40's when *Carmina* 1–3

were published in 23 B.C. He seems to be a man of the same general circumstances in 1.9, addressing in avuncular fashion a young man (*puer*),
and in the disparity of their ages there emerges a tension in the advice and
concerns of the ode. The speaker has a double awareness, we might say, of
his own age and the closeness of life's "winter" and of the happy opportunities of youth, its delightful "springtime" of love and dance. Thus, snow-
bound Soracte serves more as the speaker's personal symbol, while love-
games in the warm Campus apply specifically to Thaliarchus, if he will
only act as master of pleasure while he enjoys the advantages of youth.

The first three *CD* poems of Book 1 all have in common a speaker who
offers disinterested advice: he stands to gain nothing. In 1.11, on the other
hand, the speaker is a very interested party in the outcome of his injunctions, for the call to enjoy the moment involves him as much as the addressee. His involvement in the situation qualifies—we must almost say,
disqualifies—his *CD* recommendations. Although most of his advice clearly
focuses on the second person, Leuconoe, and thus resembles the advice of
the normal *CD* rhetoric in content as well as in tone, his person does intrude from the beginning. In the opening line, he tries to dissuade the girl
from seeking to know the future, which is, after all, uncontrollable. That is
a standard injunction of the wise rhetoric of *CD*.[7] We can reduce Horace's
words to that and thus emphasize the common rhetoric of the *CD* poem.
However, the pronouns *mihi* and *tibi* stress the mutual involvement of
speaker and addressee as no other poem of this type has so far done.
Leuconoe is not merely foolishly inquiring into her own future, but into a
future that links her with the speaker. When, then, the speaker urges her to
forget the question of their future relationship, the advice may be more
self-serving than genuinely helpful to Leuconoe. After all, what is she asking of the astrology charts that seems so silly to our speaker? Isn't she
simply trying to find out how this erotic affair, so obscurely embedded in
this rhetoric, is going to turn out, for herself and the speaker? Thus, the
reversal of order of the standard *CD* has particular meaning for this poem:
the injunction does not spring from reflection on a scene of nature and
insight into the world; it arises from the impatience of the speaker over
Leuconoe's hesitation about his motives.

Later on in the advice, we encounter a *dum*-clause, which is another
standard element of the rhetoric, used to urge pursuit of the present pleasures while they are available.[8] However, instead of an impersonal phrase
like *dum licet*, this speaker betrays himself and his rhetoric with *dum
loquimur*. It seems plain that he has become restless with mere talk: he wants
the amatory action toward which his speech has been working.

Finally, we should consider the meters of these four *CD* poems. They
are all different: the first three form part of the virtuoso display of the so-
called Parade Odes, 1.1–9; and 1.11 introduces still one more new example
of Horace's metrical genius. The Fourth Archilochian of 1.4, an effective
combination of four dactyls and three trochees in a first line and an iambic
trimeter catalectic in a second, allows Horace to catch both the sense of

springtime release and the urgency that derives from the vicissitudes of human life, as implied in the break at the diaeresis of line 1. The three metrical units encourage the adviser to state his injunctions fully and emphatically. I find it significant that the temporal particles in 1–12 occur in the dactylic portions, as the speaker is mainly talking about the pleasures of springtime, but, as he becomes more urgent in 16–20 about the future's menace, they are moved into the iambic lines, with a very different rhythmic effect. Horace uses this meter only in 1.4. The Alcmanic meter of 1.7 occurs also in 1.28 and in the outspokenly obscene Epode 12. Its essentially dactylic base means that it can approach the solemnity of epic in the *Odes*, as in 1.7. Davis has brilliantly demonstrated how Horace exploits the meter to "assimilate" the manner of Homeric praise to his exaltation of Tibur and how he has transferred the heroic themes of Teucer's speech to his comrades in 21 ff. to the services of his lyric *CD* rhetoric.[9] Again, the dactylic flow contributes to the full and sonorous elaboration of the themes. In 1.9, the first of many Alcaic odes of the collection, Horace boldly starts off from a poem of Alcaeus in the same meter, on the same topic, pointedly adapting its literally wintry scene to his more obviously symbolic description. From there, he further adapts the injunctions of the 6th century Greek to the contemporary scene in Rome and to his young friend Thaliarchus, but always employing the energy of the Alcaic stanza in the service of energetic life-affirming recommendations, as Alcaeus tended to do. Although the lines of the Alcaic are shorter than those of the Archilochian and Alcmanic, the speaker develops his thoughts in ample units, whole stanzas or even more.

What strikes me as especially significant about the way Horace uses the Greater Asclepiadean meter in 1.11 is that his speaker there emerges as a person of clipped and perfunctory argument, who gets trapped, particularly by the choriambs, and exposed as a man of ready phrases and trite slogans. (Comparison with the two other odes where Horace employs this meter, 1.18 and 4.10, demonstrates that 1.11 exaggerates this potentiality of the Asclepiadean.) In the very first line, the speaker puts the formulaic *quaesieris* as well as the motto *scire nefas* into adjacent choriambs. In line 2, we encounter *di dederint* and the name of the girl, *Leuconoe*, in a pair of choriambs. The slogans continue in 3 with the successive *ut melius* and *quidquid erit*. Farther on, the injunctions *vina liques* (6), *carpe diem* (8), and the supporting units *dum loquimur* (7) and *quam minimum* (8) all become encapsulized in the choriambic rhythm. And even the protreptic wintry scene, on which normally the speaker and advisee solemnly meditate, is turned into a triple succession of lilting choriambs: *oppositis debilitat pumicibus* (5). This meter has long lines, but Horace has systematically used it to break up the speaker's thoughts, such as they are, and reduce them to what we are all familiar with: a "line" all right, not of elegant and solemn rhythm but of very obvious self-serving argumentation.[10] And the *CD* rhetoric, I would maintain, has also been reduced and essentially parodied, to work for the patent purposes of seduction.

Let me review, then, how I would read the poem to Leuconoe. Instead of starting dispassionately from a scene of nature and the wisdom that it can impart, as in the earlier *CD* poems, the speaker of 1.11 plunges directly into his advice. The initial pronoun *tu* and the perfect subjunctive with *ne* warn us that he is more insistently concerned with his addressee and this advice than are the earlier speakers. The choriambic unit *scire nefas* functions as a parenthesis, interrupting and strengthening the negative point which he now reveals. It was metrically optional for *tibi* to have come before *mihi*, but this "adviser's" urgency involves a large element of self-interest, and he puts himself first in this line and indeed in the entire argument. He does not like Leuconoe to inquire what end or result the gods have assigned for each of them. Why not? Is it because she is really in love with him, as Santirocco supposes, and wasting time and immediate pleasure, which he can count on anyway? I doubt it. Rather, as I said earlier, he is dealing with a reluctant woman, what Marvell called a "coy mistress," who distrusts him and the amatory pleasure he insistently advocates. It may be impossible to know the outcome of any love-relation in advance, but it can hardly be called a "sin" to know it, any more than coyness is a "crime" in the mouth of Marvell's lover. Those metaphors of "sin" and "crime" are part of the biased rhetoric of the man. But a practical woman does need some assurances that she has a reasonable chance of a durable mutual relationship: it is not to her interests, at least in the days of Horace and later of Marvell, to seize the moment carelessly. There are consequences that cannot be ignored, as every instance of sexual intercourse in New Comedy demonstrates. The "long hope" disparaged in 7 may indeed be foolish when it amounts to hope for a long life, as the phrase seems to imply in 1.4.15. But here Leuconoe has little interest in long life, only in a long friendship with this speaker; and that is something that she can try to plan.

The speaker exclaims how much better than making plans it is to "endure whatever comes to pass" (3). Again, that depends; the grasshopper might have said the same to the ant, and look what happened to those two. At this point, though, in a doublet, the speaker introduces the theme of time and life, which is *not* Leuconoe's concern; and his temporal term is "winter" (4), from which he mellifluously, in a single line of choriambic units (5) proceeds to sketch out a scene of winter storms on the coast. Having read three *CD* poems of Horace, we can sense how this reference to winter functions, especially by referring to 1.9.9 ff. We can hardly blame Leuconoe for failing to see how it should lead to the abrupt injunctions: *sapias, vina liques*, etc. And we should hardly fault her for rejecting this specious rhetoric. The speaker has no very convivial goal; he rather works from the tried and true macho philosophy of: "Candy is dandy, but liquor is quicker." And his libido says: now! But what advantage is there for Leuconoe in yielding to his amatory line? What does the "love," never promised, of this speaker offer to her now? Why not trust in the future, which, if it does not bring her much, may at least offer her another *man* who will prove more reliable? (Change *postero* of 7 to *altero*.)

The special quality of 1.11, I think, arises from the interested way with which the friend of Leuconoe perfunctorily exploits the serious rhetoric of *CD* that in three earlier poems has been developed elaborately, seriously, and convincingly by a disinterested and honorable speaker. Thereby, he transforms the wise advice into a plausible but dishonest line serving his goal of seduction. For me, as I stated at the beginning, this is one of the special appeals of Horace's *Odes*: the versatility of the speaker's voice. The different levels of interest in the ever-moralizing words of the poems give us new pleasure and a new awareness of their wisdom in the proper context. It seems that the Horatian lover, speaking in the first person, particularly represents the interested and flawed use of moral advice. He is regularly masking, aware or unaware, how poorly he has grasped and applied this wisdom which he utters. In the very first love poem of Book 1, C. 5 we meet this flawed moralist; and after 11, he reappears at 13, probably 14, 16, 17, 19, 22, 23, 25, again in Book 2 (e.g., 4), and right up to the final such poem of the collection, 3.26. Thus, that all too human and irrational amatory drive, as Horace ironically saw, helps to humanize the *CD* rhetoric as its speaker all too obviously tries to subordinate it to passion's purposes.

Notes

[1]Berkeley 1991, Chapter 3, 145 ff.

[2]Outlined by Davis, 145–47, then illustrated in a series of Horatian odes.

[3]Davis treats 1.7 in sections at several points, most fully on 16–18 and 191 ff.

[4]In their note on line 14, p. 68.

[5]In their introduction to 1.11, p. 135.

[6]*Horace. Epodes and Odes. A New Annotated Latin Edition* (Norman, OK 1991), note on line 8, p. 219. I cannot agree with the way that M. Santirocco puts it in his *Unity and Design in Horace's Odes* (Chapel Hill 1986), 44: "Despite these close similarities, there is one crucial difference between the two poems [1.9 and 11]. In C. 1.9 Horace advises his addressee to love. Such an injunction is missing from C. 1.11 since Leuconoe's inquiries reveal that she is in love—with the poet." In my opinion, Leuconoe's inquiries show that she is very cautious—and rightly so—about getting erotically involved with "Horace."

[7]Cf. 1.4.15 and 1.9.13, and Davis 155 ff.

[8]Cf. 2.3.15 and 2.11.16; also 1.9.17 (*donec* as synonym for *dum*).

[9]Davis 189 ff.

[10]Steele Commager, *The Odes of Horace* (New Haven 1962), 274, noted of 1.11: "The poem might almost be a more explicit redaction of the Soracte Ode." And he pointed out the phrases in 1.11 that parallel the more extended arguments of 1.9. But he did not apply those points to the characterization of the speaker in 1.11.

Charles Segal

FELICES TER ET AMPLIUS
HORACE, ODES, I. 13

In this ode, Horace once again, as in 1.5, represents a triangular amatory situation, with the speaker addressing the girl Lydia, who favors another male, Telephus. As Segal shows in his essay, Horace organizes the poem in three stages: (1) a long initial section of three stanzas, in which the speaker declares his jealous misery over the ardent passion of the two lovers, with obvious echoes of Catullus. (2) a stanza in which he affects some wisdom and advises Lydia not to expect the affair to last forever. (3) a concluding stanza that idealizes a love that unites lovers happily without friction until their death. What Segal does, is show that Horace, as in 1.11, reveals the interests of the speaker not only in calling attention at length to his jealousy, but also in those seemingly calmer words of the last two stanzas. His jealousy has turned into self-serving reasonability, as he implicitly offers himself as a valuable replacement for the supposedly unreliable and wild passion of Telephus. He would not bruise Lydia's lips as Telephus is doing (15), for he prizes her kisses far too highly. His romantic picture of love until death is a kind of wishful appeal to Lydia to consider him as a candidate for the ideal steady, reliable lover which, he suggests, is what she needs. Segal's appreciation of what he calls "a subtle drama of self-mockery" is refreshing.

*O*des, 1. 13 closes with one of Horace's most quotable *sententiae*:

> *felices ter et amplius*
> *quos irrupta tenet copula, nec malis*
> *diuulsus querimoniis*
> *suprema citius soluet amor die.*

Fortunately we no longer regard Horace merely as the conveyor of cameoed commonplaces. But this passage is so familiar and so obviously demanding of gnomic assent that the stock response of a solemn nod of agreement or the self-congratulation of shared moral uplift are easy temptations.

How seriously are we to understand this final stanza? Several critics have attacked this question and suggested the possibility of a deliberate uncertainty on Horace's part.[1] This uncertainty is probably an essential constituent of the tone of the poem. Not all interpreters have been equally resistant to the solemnity of the lines; but against total seriousness stand

This essay is reprinted from *Latomus* 32 (1973) 39–46, with permission of the publisher.

two *a priori* considerations: Horace lived a confirmed bachelor, and in the love-affairs of the *Odes irruptae copulae* are by far the exception rather than the rule. Horace generally looks on the elegists' idealization of a total, life-long union with the disenchanted eye of a wryly sceptical and somewhat cautious observer (*Odes*, I. 33 is the most obvious example).[2] The evidence of other poems is, of course, no sure proof of the tone of this ode. But a fresh look at the context of the passage will, I hope, confirm the view that the ending is not so serious as it might at first seem. Its very solemnity, in fact, may prove to be the key to a highly refined and subtle irony.

Horace has created an extreme polarity between the beginning and ending of the poem. What is one to think of the speaker who goes from such intense passion to almost sanctimonious calm? This is the central critical question of the ode. Differently put, how does Horace get from the emotion of the first three stanzas to the sententious objectivity of the last?

The ode has three main divisions. First come twelve lines in which Horace describes his raging jealousy of Telephus.[3] The juxtaposition of his rival's with his lady's name in line 1, the alliteration of *c-* at the beginning of the three main rhythmic cola in lines 1 and 2 (*cum, cervicem, cerea*),[4] the repetition *Telephi...Telephi* at the end of these same two lines, reinforcing the rhythmic and assonantal repetition within line 2 (*ceruicem roseam, // cerea Telephi*),[5] the list of the physical symptoms of love in the language of erotic violence drawing on and parodying the famous lines of Sappho and Catullus,[6] the quarrel and the mark of the lover's bite in lines 9–12 all prove a strong and deliberate foil to the peace of the stable union depicted in the last four lines.

The second section of the poem, lines 13–16, is transitional. From the impassioned vehemence of 1–12 the poet moves to the language of persuasion. Consequently the focus shifts from the speaker's own emotions to the sentiments and expectations of Lydia (13–16):

> *non, si me satis audias,*
> *speres perpetuum, dulcia barbare*
> *laedentem oscula, quae Venus*
> *quinta parte sui nectaris imbuit.*

The syntax also changes from the first person to the second: hence, despite the opening *tu* of line 1, *meum* in 3, *mihi* in 5, *macerer* in 8, *uror* in 9; but the second-person verbs, *audias* and *speres*, in lines 13 and 14.

Moving away from himself, the poet shifts his mood to greater calm and greater objectivity. He reasons and argues rather than shouts and gesticulates. The word *perpetuum* (14) introduces a broader temporal perspective which thus points ahead to the absolutes of *suprema die* and to the future tense of *soluet* in the poem's last line. In the first section of the poem, on the contrary, the poet would convince us that he is oblivious to all but the moment which rouses his passion. At the end of the second section the Olympian mythology and the more "literary" and artificial tone of the references to Venus and her nectar (15–16) continue and strengthen the atmosphere of removal and emotional control.

The last section (17–20) seems to be at first the natural consequence of this movement from passion to calm. The speaker has regained his poise and self-command. He holds out, implicitly, to Lydia the promise of the lasting, permanent love which the fiery passions of a Telephus cannot bestow. As part of this movement, the last four lines completely abandon the first- and second-person verbs of lines 1–16 for the impersonality of third-person gnomic generalization.

But is Horace so objective and impersonal? Do the lines do more than preach a moral about permanent union and fidelity? They have, I suggest, a dramatic function and contain a trace of subtle humor. The formula of *makarismos, felices ter et amplius,* suggests that the speaker in fact stands in a situation far from what he is praising.[7] It is in the midst of storm and suffering that the original behind these lines is spoken in the *Odyssey* (V. 306), and the case is the same with their famous imitation in the *Aeneid* (I. 94). Horace is desiderating an ideal which may in fact be quite remote from his own capacities or his own present condition (compare the similar irony in *Odes,* II. 4 or III. 26). What is more important, he uses the *gnome* about calm and tranquil union to support his own attempt to outmaneuver his rival.[8] This ostensibly disinterested advice to Lydia may thus reflect ironically on the still unassuaged passions of the lover who has spoken the preceding sixteen lines.

The transitional section, 13–16, is easily passed over, sandwiched as it is between the brilliant beginning and the weighty closure. But it is important for the irony of the last four lines. The references to Lydia's "sweet lips" and to the "fifth part" of Venus' nectar remind us that the speaker is still making love to the girl, not just instructing her in the proper values for her own edification and benefit. The phrase *barbare laedentem,* skilfully placed in hyperbaton between *dulcia* and *oscula,* keeps the speaker's jealousy of Telephus in the foreground. It also recalls the lovebites of the preceding section (11–12) and is an important link between the beginning and end of the ode. And commentators have perhaps not stressed sufficiently the conventionality of *perpetuus* in amatory poetry (cf. Catull., 109).

Despite the shift in tone, then, lines 13–16 still do not break completely with the preceding twelve lines. There is still a certain measure of continuity carried by the erotic language of 14–16.

That continuity has a further significance for the meaning of the ode. The physical beauty of Telephus, so strongly emphasized in the opening lines, intimates that Horace has very good reason to fear his rival. Outclassed (one presumes) in physique, he resorts to mind. The unobtrusive phrase in 13, *non, si me satis audias,* is the clearest indication of the speaker's purposes. He is trying to win by persuasion a contest which he must lose on the grounds of immediate physical appeal. The passionate jealousy of 1–12, as many interpreters have noted, is a self-consciously exaggerated handling of the conventional themes of the lover's ardor.[9] Is it possible that this very stylized and literary handling of love is an attempt to match in words the youthful *furor* which Telephus expresses in acts — as if the poet acknowledges, not without a twinge of regret, his distance from such *furor*?

The disproportion between the vivid description of passion in 1–12 and the calm of 17–20, however, does more than just create a black and white contrast between Horace and Telephus, the gnomic wisdom of maturer years and the impulses of youth. The last four lines also form an implicit criticism not only of Telephus, but also of the speaker himself. It is part of the dramatic situation and the irony that the speaker is supposed to be unaware of this criticism although it is apparent to the observing audience. He has not in fact attained the calm or the disinterested concern of which he would convince Lydia (and perhaps himself). He is still very much involved in the passions of rivalry which he had so vividly described in lines 1–12. The irony is not unlike that which reflects back on Alfius at the end of *Epode*, II. Here, of course, the effect is more subtle, for it is not indicated in an obvious closing παρὰ προσδοκίαν ["surprise"] (*Epode*, II, 67–70), but is conveyed only in the structure of the poem (the disproportion between twelve lines on passion and four on eternal fidelity) and in the parenthetical hint of line 13, *si me satis audias*.

The contrast between reflective objectivity and passionate involvement in the last four lines remains an open, dramatic force in the poem. The conclusion is not an inert, static piece of moralism or a temporary lapse into the world of the elegists, but an indication of unresolved tensions within the speaker between calm and passion. Hence the blessings of a happy union are defined (in part) as the *negation* of the passions of the ode's first section: note especially *irrupta copula* (18) and *nec malis / diuulsus querimoniis* (18–19). The violence of the beginning, therefore, is by no means forgotten in the serenity of the end.

Horace's emotions in the first twelve lines are not merely jealousy, but also envy. He envies Telephus his beauty (2–4) and his total abandon to and enjoyment of the tumultuous vicissitudes of love (10–12). The reversal of direction in *non, si me satis audias* (13) is significantly juxtaposed against the graphic vignette of Telephus' amorous *furor* (11–12). Even as he praises the calm union which remains until "the last day," Horace, as elsewhere, is not entirely convinced that the calm of age is superior to the heat of passion (cf. *Odes*, II. 4 or IV. 1). Indeed, the first twelve lines of this ode depict him as rather enjoying (and perhaps enjoying too much) the attitude of the impassioned lover.[10]

At the same time Horace is careful to provide the perspective which keeps us from taking this role of *amoroso* too seriously. The poet may burn within with the flames of love (8); yet it is Telephus, the *puer furens* (11), who actually makes love to the girl and marks her lips with ardent kisses (12). Horace begins the third stanza with a strong declaration of his passion: *uror* (9). But as he develops the image of that passion, it appears to have something of a vicarious character. He himself stands at a safe distance; the quarrels and love-bites belong to Telephus. His passion seems directed less toward the girl *per se* than to the thought of Telephus making love to the girl. For this reason too we hear less of Lydia herself than we do of Telephus (cf. 1–3, 9–12). Up to line 13, in fact, Horace is remarkably inattentive to Lydia. Instead he dwells lovingly on his own passions (3–9) and on Telephus' beauty and ardor (1–3, 9–12).

The penultimate stanza (13–16) reveals the irony inherent in the whole situation. The poet who has so jealously depicted his seething passions in 1–12 suddenly exhorts the object of those passions to calm reasonableness and a large view. The criterion of "eternity" (*non...speres perpetuum...*) undercuts the position not of Telephus, but of Horace himself, or at least of the "persona" of Horace developed in the first twelve lines. If Lydia does indeed "listen sufficiently" to Horace's advice, she should be as suspicious of him as of Telephus.

The irony of this and of the last stanza may also have a larger aim than delicate self-mockery. If lines 1–12 parody poems like Catullus 51, lines 13–20 extend that parody to the *perpetuus amor* of poems like Catullus 45 or 109 or Propertius II. 15. Horace achieves something of a *tour de force* by catching in the net of his irony both elegiac passion and elegiac bliss, both the frivolity and the seriousness of love-poetry. He plays off against one another two antithetical literary representations of love: on the one hand oblivion in the moment of all-encompassing passion; on the other the ideal of eternal devotion. It is one thing for a Catullus, wracked by the agonies of unhappy love, to hope for *amor perpetuus*. It is quite another to set that ideal in an exaggerated and artificial situation and to preface it by a low-keyed, colloquial, almost "chummy" phrase like *si me satis audias*. It is hard to think of a Tibullus or a Propertius—to say nothing of a Catullus— addressing his mistress in quite this tone.

If lines 13–16 are understood in this way, the last four lines of the ode cannot be entirely serious. Since they expand the notion of the *perpetuus amor* introduced in line 14, they too are affected by the contradiction contained in that advice. The solemn rhetoric and emotionality with which this last stanza clothes the ideal of *perpetuus amor* carry the parody of the elegiac stance as far as the subtlety of the Horatian ode will permit.

Yet it would be false to the delicacy of Horace's art and Horace's sensibility to deny all seriousness to the final stanza. But this seriousness is of a special kind. Horace is one of the few poets who can combine tenderness with a light touch of irony and leave the reader suspended—if humanly suspended—between them (compare the end of *Odes*, II. 6).

The last line of the poem juxtaposes death and love: *amor* and *suprema...die.*[11] The elegiac note and the reminder of death add a characteristic Horatian poignancy to the contrast between youth and age, passion and tranquillity, Telephus and Horace. This contrast is part of larger dialectic within Horace's work, a recurrent pull between the poet as troubled participant and the poet as wise, aloof spectator. Like all dialectic, it has no easy resolution, perhaps no resolution at all. Although Horace can often congratulate himself on escaping from the toils of love (cf. *Odes*, I. 5), he can also look back upon the *rixae* and *insani amores* (*Odes*, III. 21.3) with a touch of wistful regret beneath the wise, self-protective detachment (III. 14.25–28):[12]

> *lenit albescens animos capillus*
> *litium et rixae cupidos proteruae:*
> *non ego hoc ferrem calidus iuuenta*
> *consule Planco.*

["Graying hair calms spirits
that once passionately engaged in arguments and violent quarrel:
I would not stand this in my hot youth
when Plancus was consul."]

He is realist enough ("furchtbare Realität" was Goethe's phrase) to feel at times that wisdom cannot quite compensate for youthful vitality. The lovers' playful trysts (*Odes*, I. 9. 21–24) remain inviting despite the poet's mature knowledge of winter and grey hairs.

The closing cadence, *suprema...soluet...die*, therefore, is less final than it looks. Beneath the assured tone of reflective, removed wisdom lurks a hint of the involved lover who has so nakedly exposed his passions, and the foolishness of his passions, in 1–12. The result is a subtle drama of self-mockery, a playful trying on of different poses, and the urbane presentation of a conflict which is as eternal as it is human.

Notes

[1] See Gordon Williams, *Tradition and Originality in Roman Poetry* (Oxford, 1968), 575: "...The seriousness of the tone and sentiments tempts the reader into considering whether the whole poem is not intended seriously." Elsewhere Williams rightly emphasizes the irony of the first half of the poem, but is rather unsatisfactory on the ending (p. 564): "...i. 13 ends with a sweeping general statement that collects and caps the various themes of the poem." So too David West, *Reading Horace* (Edinburgh, 1967), 67, is keenly sensitive to the self-mockery and irony of the first part (see below, n. 6), but is untroubled by the discrepancy with the ending: "Now the serene and lasting love chimes beautifully with the rest of the poem..., an eloquent statement of what is sensible and true." Yet even West has to concede (in the next paragraph) that the ending is "astounding." The most successful analysis is probably that of Steele Commager, *The Odes of Horace* (New Haven, 1962). 152–56, who concludes (p. 155), "Probably Horace intended the poem's close to leave us in uncertainty. He refuses, as he does so frequently, to allow us the satisfaction of restricting him to a single attitude." Similarly, Williams, p. 564–5: "It is a difficult poem to pin down, and that is part of its charm, as of the best of Horace...." The ending of the ode is interpreted in a more serious vein by Walter Wili, *Horaz und die augusteische Kultur* (Basel, 1948), 183, who sees its sentiments arising "aus der stillen Sehnsucht und Erfahrung des Dichters" ["from the quiet passion and experience of the poet"]. Horace, he suggests, is deliberately going beyond the Sapphic descriptions of the physical symptoms of love to "die Kraft des beseelten Eros, der die Konvention persönlich adelt" ["the power of the animated Eros, which personally ennobles convention"]. Similarly the

recent commentary of R. G. M. Nisbet and Margaret A. Hubbard, *A Commentary on Horace: Odes, Book 1* (Oxford, 1970), 170: "...The serious ending makes a telling contrast with the frivolities that have gone before... Our poem should be regarded as a skit on the absurdities of Hellenistic epigram, set off against a more serious and Roman attitude." For an interesting, though I think also excessively serious, interpretation of the closing stanza somewhat along these lines see also Kenneth J. Reckford, *Horace* (New York, 1969), 101–2. Since I am not concerned with the (probably fruitless) question of whether the poem reflects Horace's "real" experiences or not (see West, p. 67), I use the terms "Horace," "the poet," and "the speaker" more or less interchangeably throughout this paper.

[2]One should mention *Odes*. II. 9 here also. For Horace's attitudes toward the elegists' "unattainable ideal" of one all-absorbing union see Kenneth J. Reckford, *Some Studies in Horace's Odes on Love* in *CJ*, 55 (1959/60), 25–26. Wili (above, n. 1), 183 and Kiessling-Heinze, *Horaz*, I[9] (Berlin, 1958), in their introductory note to the poem, remark how rare this expression of personal jealousy is in the *Odes*. On the political and other implications of Horace's attitudes toward the elegists see Brooks Otis, *Horace and the Elegists* in *TAPA*, 76 (1945), 177–90, with the further literature there cited: Kenneth Quinn, *Latin Explorations* (London, 1963), 154–62.

[3]For a more detailed subdivision of the first section (1–12) see N. E. Collinge, *The Structure of Horace's Odes* (London, 1961), 105.

[4]For a good analysis of the sound-patterns of this passage see Commager (above, n. 1), 154. See also M. O. Lee, *Words, Sounds, and Images in the Odes of Horace* (Ann Arbor, 1969), 32 ff., with the parallels cited at p. 111, note 6.

[5]Line 2 is, in fact, the only place in the poem where the two halves of the lesser Asclepiad line fall into such balanced symmetry: two trisyllabic words on each side of the caesura, one a noun, one an adjective, in chiasmic order, and each half beginning with the syllable, *cer-*. The controlled formal symmetry, in characteristic Horatian fashion, comes at the point of greatest passion.

[6]For the Catullan and Sapphic echoes and further parallels see Commager, p. 153; Wili, p. 183; Williams, p. 564; Nisbet and Hubbard, p. 169–70 (all in n. 1, above). For the exaggerations and metaphors in lines 4–8 see also West (above, n. 1), 66–71, who stresses the "amusing mock-poetic kitchen metaphor" (p. 67) of line 4.

[7]See the remark of Commager (above, n. 1), 155: "Does the epic echo in *felices ter et amplius* prolong the parody? Or does it signal a change to high seriousness?"

[8]L. P. Wilkinson, *Horace and His Lyric Poetry* (Cambridge, 1951), 50, rightly sees that in 13–16 Horace is trying "a subtler way of loosening a passionate young rival's hold on her."

[9]See the references cited above, n. 6.

[10]See Commager (above, n. 1), 153: "So extreme is Horace's despair as to suggest a parody of the habitual agonies of the elegiac poets." Williams (above. n. 1), 564 also observes the "amused irony in this self-exposure." See also West (above. n. 1), 67.

[11]On this emphatic use of *suprema*, with other parallels, see Karl Büchner, *Der Superlativ bei Horaz* in *Studien zur römischen Literatur*, III, *Horaz* (Wiesbaden, 1962), 30–31.

[12]On Horace's self-parody as "self-protection" see Commager (above, n. 1), 155. Commager goes on to observe (p. 156), "The initial parody in poems like that to the *filia pulchrior* (*C.*, 1, 16), that on the *triste lignum* (*C.*, 2.13), or that to Lydia (*C.*, 1.13) acts almost as a shield... Speaking as it were, through an elegiac mask of himself, he may indulge the extravagant sentimentality that he never permitted himself in any direct way."

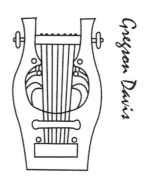

Gregson Davis

CARMINA/IAMBI: THE LITERARY-GENERIC DIMENSION OF HORACE'S INTEGER VITAE (C. 1, 22)

The first two stanzas of this ode became a popular student song in the nineteenth century, because of their apparently moralistic emphasis. But the poem as a whole records the speaker's reactions to a miraculous escape from a monstrous wolf. Why did he escape? Because he was in the act of singing about his beloved girlfriend Lalage. As Davis remarks at the beginning of this essay, the situation chosen by Horace is analogous to others where, because he describes himself as a poet, he experiences a charmed existence. Davis goes on from this to focus on other self-conscious aspects, and particularly the fearsome wolf, to read the poem as a statement of Horace's generic choices. If the speaker symbolizes the poet, and Lalage suggests the attractions of love poetry, then the wolf is associated by Greek and Romans with anger, biting, sudden attack, and then with the iambic verse that featured personal attack. It was the style of the lyric poetry which Horace had experimented with and published under the title *Epodes* in the years before he wrote these Odes. Therefore, while we can read 1.22 as the account of a miraculous incident, we can enrich our appreciation if we also realize that Horace is subtly making a "generic disavowal" of the iambic manner as he amazingly frightens away this wolf. (Ed.)

This paper proposes an interpretation of the flight of the wolf in C. I, 22 in terms of an antithesis between literary genres. Our working assumption is that the fugitive *lupus* is a symbolic figure whose general, if not precise, significance is indissociably related to that of the other major *personae* in the poem: "Lalage" and the singer. All three members of the configuration perform important roles in the interplay of literary kinds. Let us consider in turn the generic affiliations of each figure in the trio.

1. "Lalage"

It is generally agreed that the *amata* of Horace's *carmen* is transparently emblematic. To begin with, the Greek name "Lalage," which first appears in 10 and is reiterated in 22, is onomatopoeic. As is commonly observed, the word is cognate with the verbs λαλεῖν and λαλαγεῖν ["to prattle"]. Horace marks the etymological aspect of the *nomen fictum* by making a salient pun in the last line of the poem: *dulce loquentem* (where the participial phrase virtually transcribes the name's import). Furthermore, in one of the series of Hellenistic epigrams that have demonstrably

This essay is reprinted from *Quaderni Urbinati di Cultura Classica* 27,3 (1987) 67–78, with permission of the publisher.

contributed to certain of the poem's motifs, the instrument that the speaker employs to scare away the beast is dubbed a λαλάγημα.[1] Besides its acoustical referentiality (cp. *dum meam canto "Lalagen"*: "while I was singing my "Melodious talk"),[2] "Lalage" is also linked to the erotic theme, in particular, by another (generally overlooked) Hellenistic text: Moschus I, 8,[3] where Aphrodite characterizes Eros as ἁδὺ λάλημα. If "Lalage" represents erotic *melos* as performed by the singer of the ode, then the apotropaic effect of the song serves to validate the speaker's generic predilections.

2. *The Singer*

It has not escaped the notice of several critics that Horace's amusing encounter with the wolf is but another variant of the recurrent motif of the poet as magically protected from harm.[4] What needs to be additionally stressed, however, is that the topos of the sacrosanct poet who is *pius* (cp. *integer; purus*) often has a generic dimension in the *Odes*. To cite a conspicuous instance, the poet who escapes from the falling tree in *C.* 2, 13 specifically aligns himself with the Lesbian *lyrici* in the latter portion of the Ode, where his imagined after-life in the *sedes piorum* is spent in the company of Alcaeus and Sappho (21–32). In the case of the *Integer vitae*, it is precisely as a love-poet in the Lesbian tradition that the speaker is mysteriously rescued from death. The *dum* clause that constitutes part of the "proof" (cp. *namque* =καὶ γάρ) of the poet's "integrity" highlights the circumstance that the wolf's appearance (and disappearance) is contemporaneous with an ongoing lyric performance (a *carmen* in progress):

> namque me silva lupus in Sabina,
> *dum meam canto Lalagen...*

The debt to Lesbian lyric, in particular, is afforded prominence by a citation of the Catullan imitation of a celebrated Sapphic text: *dulce ridentem.*[5] The Sapphic tag (mediated through Catullus' diction), when compounded with the self-referential nomenclature ("Lalage"), provides a strong final cadence to the speaker's oath of allegiance to the genre of erotic Lesbian *melos*. The final asseveration of the poem with its "voluntative future,"[6] *Lalagen amabo*, reconfirms that allegiance as much by its content as by its placement — embedded, as it is, between the Sapphic imitation and the etymological *jeu de mots* ["wordplay"].

The focus on love-lyric and its zealous practitioner is rendered sharper by the conventional antinomy, which is implied by the speaker, between *amor*, on the one hand, and Martial pursuits, on the other.[7] The exaggerated catalogue of military and cynegetic implements (*Mauris iaculis; arcu; venenatis sagittis*) that are judged superfluous to the *integer* promotes this underlying antinomy; while the epithet *militaris*, applied to Daunias in 14, recapitulates the same topic. The exclusion of the "military" habitat of "wolves" complements the exclusion of military instruments in the hypothetical "marches" (cp. *iter facturus*: 5–6) that the love-poet may choose to undertake. In fine, the double exclusion of places and weaponry appropriate to the soldier is paradigmatic of the erotic life-style, which is distinguished by the conventional fiction of an "anti-bellicose" posture. Thus the definition of the *integer* as a non-combatant helps to characterize the developing *ethos* of the speaker as one who is faithful to erotic lyric.[8]

3. *Lupus*

If we grant that there is an overt metonymic bond between the singer and his sweetheart, *cantor* and *cantata*, it is a plausible hypothesis that Horace's potential adversary in C. I, 22, the spectral wolf, is also an integral part of a symbolic ensemble. As a preliminary defense of our hypothesis, let us observe that the speaker alerts us against understanding *lupus* in a literal (trivial) sense:

> *quale portentum* neque militaris
> Daunias latis alit aesculetis
> nec Iubae tellus generat, leonum
> arida nutrix.

The word *portentum* ("sign," "token")[9] points to the emblematic aspect of the beast in question. The content of the disjunctive clauses suggests that the wolf-portent is not merely abnormal but extra-natural, i.e. extraneous to any "real" habitat, such as Apulia and Numidia, both of which are put forward as typical (and natural) haunts of wolves. The contrast between an extra-mundane phenomenon, on the one side, and its mundane biological counterparts, on the other (cp. *alit; generat; nutrix*) precludes any ordinary species of wolf from the poetic agenda. To insist on a purely literal reading of *lupus*, therefore, would be to downplay the rhetorical caveat inscribed in the text.

With this caveat in mind, however, we are in a better position to reformulate the question of the symbolic identity of the wolf in more precise terms: in what variety of poetry is it appropriate to state that the wolfish *persona* gives its character to the whole genre? In what follows, I shall argue that the pertinent genre is invective (*iambi*), and that Horace achieves the double aim of repudiating the Archilochian manner of the Epodes and reaffirming his current attraction for the *Lesboum barbiton*.

Following the pioneering observations of K. J. Dover,[10] several scholars of Horace's Greek iambic models[11] have built a formidable case for onomastic symbolism with reference to the main figures who are the target of those poets' invective. "Lycambes," the butt of Archilochus' attacks, is the most notorious case in point. His tell-tale name bears not only a "wolf" component (*lyc-*), but possibly a generic component as well, for the ending -*ambes* appears to have a curious linguistic affinity with the genre itself.[12] As M. L. West, in particular, has emphasized, the very name of

Archilochus' stock adversary appears to reflect iambic invective not only in terms of meter, but also in terms of the "wolfish" disposition of the *personae*, since there exists a well-documented tradition that associates the aggressive nature of the wolf with the truculence of both the iambographer and his opponent.[13] Horace, who professed quite openly his qualified debt to the iambic poetry of Archilochus and composed his own *iambi* (as he labelled his *Epodes*) before graduating to the radically disparate genre of *carmina*, was by no means unaware of the conventional link between the mask of the *lupus* and *iambos*.

Epode 6 provides an instructive example of the iambist's bestial incarnations. The speaker there assumes the metaphorical role of a sheepdog[14] (*amica vis pastoribus*) in contradistinction to the addressee, a *canis ignavus* (presumably a poetic rival in *iambos*):

> Quid immerentis hospites vexas canis,
>   ignavus adversum lupos?
> quin huc inanis, si potes, vertis minas
>   et me remorsurum petis?
> nam qualis aut Molossus aut fulvus Lacon,
>   amica vis pastoribus,
> agam per altas aure sublata nives,
>   quaecumque praecedet fera.

> ["Why do you bother innocent passersby, you dog, a coward in the face of wolves? Why don't you transfer your empty threats, if you can, in my direction and attack me who will bite you back? Because like a Molossian or a tawny Spartan hound, the powerful ally of shepherds, I shall drive through the deep snow, with my ears pricked, any beast in front of me."]

The appropriate targets of attack for the canine iambists (whether brave or cowardly) are *lupi* — an undomesticated species whose biological affiliations with dogs are, of course, axiomatic.[15] Towards the end of his vituperation (13–14) the Roman epodist goes on to compare his own ferocity to that of Archilochus and Hipponax in a simile that alludes to these poets' generic antagonists, "Lycambes" and "Bupalos," respectively (13–14). In a less elaborate, but no less mordant fashion, the initial simile of *Epode* 4 (1–2) compares the staged verbal combat between abusive iambist and victim to that between wolves and lambs:

> lupis et agnis quanta sortito obtigit,
>   tecum mihi discordia est...

> ["As great as the natural hostility of wolves and lambs
> is my enmity toward you."]

In view of the traditional connections between "wolfish" aggression and iambic *personae* (both assailant and victim)—connections that, as we have seen, Horace blatantly exploits in his own youthful imitations of Archilochus and Hipponax—it is conceivable that the fugitive *lupus* of the *Integer vitae* is a kind of literary "ghost from the past," a trope for the sort of defamatory poetry that the lyric speaker is now claiming to have transcended.[16] According to this scenario, the unarmed love-poet who sings the praises of "Lalage" easily wins out against the former detractor (emblematized by the wolf).

Within such an inter-generic perspective, the confident opening declaration of the *integer* to the effect that he has no need for martial implements in his projected journeys may be a token of his renunciation of a militant iambic posture:

> Integer vitae scelerisque purus
> non eget Mauris iaculis neque arcu
> nec venenatis gravida sagittis,
>   Fusce, pharetra.

To disavow the need for weapons is to signal their inappropriateness for the disparate enterprise at hand, in which lyric decorum will take the place of belligerent utterance. The exclusion of warlike figures from the gentle environment of *melos* is a motif that recurs in C. I, 17, where the singer seeks to seduce an *amata* named Tyndaris (who, incidentally, is portrayed as a poet in her own right) by assuring her, *inter alia*, that the young animals will be secure from *Martialis...lupos* (9). Lyric compositions in the manner of the congenial Anacreon (cp. *fide Teia*, 18) will offer prophylaxis against the intrusions of the predatory *lupi*.

In regard to wolves as exemplars of the martial spirit, it is pertinent to recall that the metaphorical association goes back to the Homeric poems, in which the rampaging super-warrior displays, on occasion, "wolfish rage" (*lyssa*).[17] The related Greek verb λυσσάω commonly applied to wolves (see Theocr. 4, 11). Moreover, a late epigrammatist uses the lexeme to characterize *iambi* (λυσσῶντας ἰάμβους ["raging iambics"]).[18] If wolves conventionally signified the spirit of martial invective, then the speaker's initial disavowal of weaponry in C. I, 22 is all of a piece with his subsequent alienation from the lupine "portent."

The economy of the *Integer vitae* appears even more rigorous when we examine the dominant mythological affiliations of the two geographical regions mentioned in 13–16: *Daunias* (Apulia) and *Iubae tellus* (Numidia). At first inspection, these toponyms may seem merely ornamental—the first refers to the poet's familiar native haunts, the second, with equal banality, to a territory traditionally fertile in wild animals. A closer scrutiny, however, reveals a much more organic development of Horace's argument than is suggested by a cut and dried geography. The lands of the mythical Daunus and the historical Juba are predominantly marked in local legends by the presence of wolfish personalities associated with warlike kingdoms. Some of this ancillary popular lore is worth at least a brief digression from our central exegesis. Daunus, to begin with, is, according to one strand of the tradition, a son of none other than Lycaon — the very archetype in Greek myth of the temperamentally "wolfish" human being.[19] According to S. Italian legends (which, it need hardly be stressed, were familiar to Horace and his circle), Daunus, whether autochthonous or an emigré, was the eponymous ancestor of a region of N. Apulia. The legends of N. Africa and S. Italy are, in turn, closely interlinked through the intermediary figure of the Greek Diomedes who, in his later career as an exile, settles temporarily in Libya before coming to Italy and receiving refuge and support from Daunus. In both geographical locations the hero is compassed by men of wolfish disposition: negatively, in Libya, by a ruler named "Lykos" who tries to sacrifice him to his father, Ares; positively, in Apulia, where Daunus awards him a part of his kingdom in compensation for his military assistance against the Messapians.[20] N. African elaborations of the Diomedes legend might be supposed to have been obscure or recherché were it not for the fact that some of them (in particular, the "Lykos" episode) appear to have originated in the *Libyka* of Juba II himself — a ruler-author contemporary with Horace and favored by Augustus.[21]

Since *Jubae tellus* is mentioned in the *Ode* in connection with lions rather than wolves (*leonum / arida nutrix*, 14–15), a clarification of the generic interrelationship between the two beasts is in order at this juncture. That "lions" are strictly complementary to "wolves" in their contribution to the literary subtext — the disavowal of iambic invective — emerges most clearly in an ode that is related to the *Integer vitae*, viz. the so-called "palinode" (*C.* 1, 16):[22]

O matre pulchra filia pulchrior,
quem criminosis cumque voles modum
    pones iambis, sive flamma
      sive mari libet Hadriano.

non Dindymene, non adytis quatit
mentem sacerdotum incola Pythius,
    non Liber aeque, non acuta
      sic geminant Corybantes aera,

tristes ut irae, quas neque Noricus
deterret ensis nec mare naufragum
    nec saevus ignis nec tremendo
      Iuppiter ipse ruens tumultu.

fertur Prometheus addere principi
limo coactus particulam undique
    desectam et insani leonis
      vim stomacho apposuisse nostro.

irae Thyesten exitio gravi
stravere et altis urbibus ultimae
 stetere causae cur perirent
  funditus imprimeretque muris

hostile aratrum exercitus insolens.
compesce mentem: me quoque pectoris
 temptavit in dulci iuventa
  fervor et in celeres iambos

misit furentem: nunc ego mitibus
mutare quaero tristia, dum mihi
 fias recantatis amica
  opprobriis animumque reddas.

["Daughter, more lovely than your lovely mother, put an end to your libelous iambics, any end you choose, whether you prefer the fire or the Adriatic Sea.

Neither the goddess Cybele nor Pythian Apollo shakes the mind of the priestesses from the inmost shrines, nor Bacchus, and the Corybantes do not clash the piercing bronze cymbals

like bitter anger, which is not deterred by the Noric sword nor by the shipwrecking sea nor the savage lightning nor even by Jupiter hurtling down in a fearful crash.

There is a story that Prometheus, when forced to add to our primal mud a particle cut from every source, applied to our irritability the violence of a wild lion.

Anger laid Thyestes low with tragic doom and is the ultimate reason why tall cities utterly perished, why the haughty enemy army pressed

the hostile plow through their walls. Control your wrath: I, too, was possessed by a hot spirit when I was young and launched myself wildly

into swift iambics; but now I seek to transform bitterness by gentleness, if only you will give up your insults and become my friend and restore your good will."]

There are several motifs in this playful recantation of *iambi* that shed light on the symbolic meaning of C. I, 22. In a lyric poem that formally disavows the genre of invective (cp. *criminosis iambis*, 3; *celeres iambos*, 24),

the speaker presupposes an intrinsic bond between excessive *ira* and defamatory verse.[23] The epithet *tristis*, which is attached to the genre in 25–26
(*nunc ego mitibus / mutare quaero tristia*), is also used, in the third strophe, to
refer to the emotion of anger (*tristes ut irae*, 9). What is of immediate perti-
nence to our hypothesis, however, is the speaker's humorous derivation of
man's potential for immoderate anger from the "leonine" component in
the human make-up (13–16). This bit of lore (perhaps derived from Plato's
Protagoras) serves to establish an affinity between the mad anger of the
lion (*insani...leonis*) and the raging effusions of the iambographer (*in celeres
iambos / misit furentem*, 24–25). Such a posited affinity makes sense of the
juxtaposition of wolves and lions[24] in C. I, 22. Far from being otiose, let
alone contradictory, the mention of lions there reinforces and amplifies the
significance of the *lupus*-figure as a bestial incarnation of the iambic animus. The emblematic role of the wolf as a foil to lyric affirmation is struc-
turally analogous to the role of the "leonine" iambist of *O matre pulchra*.

The notion that anger is endemic to the genre of *iambos* is nicely articulated in a passage of the *Ars poetica* in which the context is generic decorum :

Archilochum *proprio* rabies armavit *iambo* (v. 79).

["Rage armed Archilochus with its natural iamb."]

If we accept the cogent interpretation of *proprio* (endorsed by Brink *ad loc.*)[25]
that *proprio* refers ownership of iamb to *rabies* rather than to Archilochus,
as it is commonly construed, then we may plausibly infer that the "mad"
persona armed with the "weapons" of *iambi* (cp. *armavit*) was a literary-
genetic cliché — a cliché that is also implied in the popular derivation of
ἴαμβος from ἰάπτειν ("shoot"). The symbolic nexus here attested between
anger (*rabies*), martial weaponry and invective poetry provides a crucial
basis for comparison with the persona of C. I, 22, who begins with a cer-
emonial renunciation of "weapons."

Horace's "recantation" unequivocally associates the renounced genre
of *iambi* with a reckless youthful phase of poetic endeavor:

> me quoque pectoris
> temptavit in dulci iuventa
> fervor et in celeres iambos
>
> misit furentem: nunc ego mitibus
> mutare quaero tristia...

In this formulation, the mature lyricist presents himself as drawn to
"mellow" compositions (*mitibus*), such as love-poems. The generic antithesis
between *melos* and *iambos* is also the topic of a priamel in the *Epistle to
Florus* (2, 2, 59–60):

denique non omnes eadem mirantur amantque:
carmine tu gaudes, hic delectatur *iambis*...

["Finally, not everybody admires or loves the same verse:
you like lyric, but another delights in iambics."]

If we accept Daube's brilliant interpretation of the verb *recantare* ("remove by song"),[26] there is an additional nuance in the poet's generic conversion in *O matre pulchra*, since the celebrated phrase *recantatis opprobris* may foreground the magical *carmen* that has the power, in performance, to cancel out the offending verses. The exorcising of the iambic *animus* is perhaps foreshadowed in the very first line of the *Ode* where the expression *O matre pulchra filia pulchrior* seems to emblazon a *topos* that appears in the *Cologne Epode*—a poem which flatters a Lycambid in order to seduce her[27] (cp. Horace's *dum mihi /fias...amica*).

Our brief analysis of the Horatian "palinode" is consistent with the hypothesis that the deeper structure of the *Integer vitae* depends upon a latent antinomy between *carmina* and *iambi*. The "armed," martial iambist, whether lupine or leonine in his bestial *persona*, disappears before the image of the peace-loving melic poet who is forthright in singing the praises of his beloved.[28] Lyric "integrity," then, is the pivotal concept that the poem sets out to adumbrate and it is this new *poetic* engagement that is threatened by the bestial apparition. The idea of the potentially baneful consequence to the singer (qua *singer*) of a chance encounter with "wolves" receives trenchant formulation by the young Vergil in the context of pastoral song (*Ecl.* 9, 53–4):

nunc oblita mihi tot carmina, vox quoque Moerim
iam fugit ipsa: *lupi Moerim videre priores.*

["Now I have forgotten all my poetry, and my very voice
has deserted me: wolves have seen Moeris first."]

Moeris' lament, which seems to reflect a popular superstition akin to the notion of the "evil eye," implies a magical negation of the poetic function by the wolfish apparition.[29] If Horace's *portentum* poses an analogous threat (as the bucolic setting of the poem in the Sabine *silva* suggests), we may infer that loss of his lyric "voice" is what is principally at stake in the confrontation. The success of the *cantor* vis-à-vis the wolf is therefore celebrated, appropriately enough, by the vociferous *reaffirmation* of the final stanza, which proves in effect that the poet, far from losing his voice, is unswerving in his devotion to *carmina*:

pone sub curru nimium propinqui
solis in terra domibus negata:

dulce ridentem Lalagen amabo
      dulce loquentem.

To conclude our interpretation of *C. I.* 22: the secure love-lyricist strenuously proclaims and reiterates his present adherence to *carmina* (emblematized in the vocable "Lalage") by dramatizing his successful banishment[30]
of the "wolf" of invective poetry (the genre of the past) from the creative
locus of lyric, the Sabine *silva*. The narrative sign of his generic conversion
is the pseudo-biographical anecdote of the wolf that is represented as fleeing at the mere perception (sound and/or sight) of the singer.[31] From this
perspective, the *Integer vitae*, charming *bagatelle* though it remains, is to be
understood as yet another example of the subtle art of generic disavowal —
an art that Horace developed to an exquisite degree in his *Carmina*.

Notes

[1] *Anth. Pal.* 6, 220, 15 (Dioscorides). On the subgroup of epigrams (*Anth. Pal.* 6.
217–221) that feature the commonplace of the isolated wanderer in the woods who
charms or scares away a beast by the sound of his musical instrument, see Gow-
Page apropos of *Anth. Pal.* 6, 218 (Alcaeus); Nisbet-Hubbard (hereafter N.-H.) *ad C.*
I, 22 (with references therein cited); H. W. Prescott, 'Horace's *Integer Vitae*,' *Class.
Philol.* 20, 1925, 276–277

[2] The duplicated syllabic "la-la" is an onomatopoeic signifier for "melody."
Cp. Ernout-Meillet on the analogously formed verb, *lallo:* "dire la, la." Theocritus
20, 29 is an instructive example of singer and instrument conjoined in the single
phrase, αὐλῷ λαλέω.

[3] For further evidence of Horace's acquaintance with Moschus, cp. G. Pasquali,
Orazio lirico, Florence 1920 (repr. 1964), 495–497.

[4] E.g. Pasquali (*supra* n. 3), 470–475, and S. Commager, *The Odes of Horace*, New
Haven 1962, 130–136, both of whom illustrate the *topos* with primary reference to
Latin love-elegy (Tibullus; Propertius). The occurrence of the *topos* in elegy does
not *per se* warrant the inference that Horace is here posing as an elegiac *amator*. On
the contrary, the lyric speaker of the *Carmina* is commonly critical of the elegiac
amatory posture. In my view, it is *qua* love-poet, not simply *amator*, that the singer
is magically protected. On the idea of the bard's sacrosanctity (implied in *sacrilega
manu*, 2), cp. especially *C.* 3, 4, 9–28; 2, 17, 12–13.

[5] Sappho 31, 3–5 L.-P.; Catullus 51, 5. Consult N.-H. *ad* 23.

[6] See W. Slater, 'Futures in Pindar,' *Class. Quart.* n.s. 19, 1969, 86–94. For another Horatian instance, see G. Davis, 'Silence and Decorum: Encomiastic Convention and the Epilogue of Horace *C.* 3.2,' *Class. Ant.* 2/1, 1983, 24.

[7] Horace and the other Augustans also exploit the conventional opposition by
"contaminating" (figuratively) the two domains, as in *C.* 3, 26, 1–8; 4, 1, 1–2. Cp.
Prop. 1, 6, 29–30; 2, 1, 14; Ovid, *Am.* 1, 9; 1, 2, 19–52.

[8] Strictly speaking, the fact that the "fidelity" claim has a multiple reference to
eros and *melos* as well as *ethos* does not fully emerge until the end of the poem, as
N.-H. point out.

[9] As with the synonym *monstrum*, "sign" or "omen," is, of course, the primary
denotation of *portentun* (see Ernout-Meillet s.v. 'portendo'), though the *connotation*
"monster" may in certain contexts be included (e.g. *Epistles* 2, 1, 11). For the standard meaning see Vergil, *Aen.* 7, 52 and 81 (*portenta* form the class of which *monstrum*

is the individual instance); *idem* 8, 533 and 534 (a particular example of the listed *portenta* is designated *signum*). On the wolf as an omen, see the article by W. Richter, *R.E.* Suppl. XV (1978) coll. 968–987, s.v. 'Wolf.'

Citations of Horace's text are from *Q. Horati Flacci Opera*, ed. E. C. Wickham, 2nd ed. rev. H. W. Garrod, Oxford 1901.

[10]K. J. Dover, 'The Poetry of Archilochus,' in *Archiloque. Entr. Hardt* X, Vandoeuvres-Genève 1964; 181–212.

[11]M. L. West, *Studies in Greek Elegy and Iambus*. Berlin 1974, 25–27; G. Nagy, *The Best of the Achaeans*, Baltimore-London 1979, 243–252.

[12]West (*supra* n. 11), 26, and 'Archilochus *ludens*: Epilogue of the other Editor,' *Zeitschr. f. Pap. u. Epigr.* 14, 1974, 219; Nagy (*supra* n. 11), 248. The putative name of Archilochus' mother, "Enipo," is also diagnosed by West as genre-related (the poet is "child of abuse").

[13]See also J. Pòrtulas, 'The Iambic Poet as a Wolf,' in C. Miralles and J. Pòrtulas, *Archilochus and the* (sic) *Iambic Poetry*, Roma 1983.

[14]L. Watson has argued cogently that sheep-dog, rather than hunting-dog, is the role envisaged in lines 1–10; see 'The Iambist as Sheep-dog: Horace. *Epode* VI, 7–8,' *Mnemosyne* 36, 1983, 156–159.

[15]Besides the canine *persona*, the *Epode* includes an apparently anomalous theriomorphic shift to a bull: *cave, cave: namque in malos asperrimus / parata tollo cornua...*, 11–12. Perhaps this is to be explained in reference to the first syllable of the stock antagonist's name in Hipponax, *Bu*-palos (parallel to *lyc*-ambes). Cp. *S.* 2, 1, 52.

[16]There is an obvious point of convergence between *satura* and *iambi* as forms of invective. It is possibile, therefore, that the *lupus* emblem encompasses both genres of invective in which Horace indulged *in dulci iuventa*. For "wolfish" manifestations of the satyric animus, see *S.* 2, 1, 68 (where an adversary of the satirist Lucilius bears the tell-tale name "Lupus"). Cp. Persius, *S.* 1, 114–115.

[17]See B. Lincoln, 'Homeric λύσσα: "Wolfish Rage."' *Indogerm. Forsch.* 80, 1975, 98–105.

[18]*Anth. Pal.* 7, 674, 1 (Adrianos). Cp. Catullus 36, 5 *truces vibrare iambos* (in a context of renunciation of invective).

[19]On the wolfish nature of the mythical Lycaon, consult W. Burkert, *Homo Necans*, Berlin 1972, tr. P. Bing, Berkeley 1983, 84–93. The Lycaonian parentage of Daunus is attributed to Nicander *apud* Ant. Lib. 31. According to F. Altheim, *A History of Roman Religion*, tr. H. Mattingly, New York 1937, 209–211, the name Daunos itself may betray a wolfish origin in its IE root (<*dhauno*: "throttler" = "wolf"). Bömer *ad* Ovid, *Fasti* 2, 267 argues, *inter alia*, for an autochthonous Daunus-figure.

[20]The major source for the Libyan episode of Diomedes' travels is Juba *apud* Ps. Plutarch, *Parall. min.* 23 (*FGrHist* 275 F 5); for the more familiar S. Italian legends surrounding the hero, see, *inter alia*, Ant. Lib. 37; Ovid, *Met.* 14, 417ff; Pliny, *Nat. hist.* 3, 103. Mythological variants are amply assembled in *R.E.* s.v. 'Diomedes.' Consult further J. Bérard, *La colonisation grecque*, Paris 1957, 368–376.

[21]The prosopography of Juba II is adequately discussed by N.-H. *ad* 15 (*Jubae*).

[22]On the Genre of the Palinode, see F. Cairns. 'The Genre Palinode and three Horatian Examples: *Epode*, 17; *Odes*, 1, 16; *Odes* 1, 34,' *Antiquité class.* 47, 1978, 546–552.

[23]L. A. McKay has succinctly argued that the *iambi* in question are to be understood as authored by the *puella* rather than the speaker ('*Odes*, 1, 16 and 17: *O matre pulchra...,Velox amoenum...*,' *Am. Journ. Philol.* 83, 1962, 298–300). In any event, Horace is now careful to distance himself from the production of vitriolic lampoons whatever their source (*me quoque...*).

[24]Not surprisingly, wolves and lions are commonly conjoined as bestial paradigms of the ferocious spirit (cp. *Epodes* 12, 25–26). In *Epodes* 7, 11–12 (a context

decrying the Civil Wars) Horace compares the paired species to fratricidal humans —
to the moral detriment of the latter: *neque hic lupis mos nec fuit leonibus / umquam nisi
in dispar feris.* Cp. Aeschylus, *Agam.* 1256–1259; Martial, *Epigrams* 2, 75.

[25]C. O. Brink. *Horace on Poetry: the Ars Poetica,* Cambridge 1971, 168
[Archilochum]. Brink ascribes the interpretation to Steidle.

[26]See D. Daube. 'Withdrawal: Five Verbs,' *Calif. Stud. Class. Ant.* 7, 1974, 93–112.

[27]*Pap. Colon.* Inv. 7511, 7–8.

[28]Pindar names Archilochus, the paradigmatic poet of detraction, as foil for
the forthright *laudator* in *P.* 2, 55. Observe that the encomiast later paradoxically
professes his willingness to adopt the devious lupine methods of a carping adversary when the occasion demands: ποτὶ δ᾽ ἐχθρὸν ἅτ᾽ ἐχθρὸς ἐὼν λύκοιο δίκαν
ὑποθεύσομαι ἄλλ᾽ ἄλλοτε πατέων ὁδοῖς σκολιαῖς (ll. 84–81). Horace's lyric *laudator*
is no less committed to forthright eulogy of "Lalage."

[29]The folklore belief is documented in the commentary of R. Coleman, *Vergil:
Eclogues,* Cambridge 1977, *ad loc.*

[30]My use of the word "banishment" is not fortuitous: Horace, I suspect, may
be playing on a latent connotation of *fugere* (= φεύγειν: "go into exile") as he does at
C. 1, 7, 22 and 2, 16, 20 (see I. M. Du Quesnay, *Vergil's First Eclogue* [Liverpool Lat.
Seminar 3], Liverpool 1981, 67 and n. 171 [with references cited therein]). If so, the
nuance harmonizes well with the view of the poet as wishing to distance himself
from a former literary identity.

[31]For the magical idea of apotropaic *sound* (as opposed to *sight* as in the Bucolic example) see the epigmmatic sources cited *supra* n. 1. Dioscorides (*supra* n. 1),
l. 15, for example, makes the λαλάγημα the cause of the flight: καὶ λαλάγημα /
τοῦτο τὸ θηρὶ φυγῆς αἴτιον ἀντιθέμαι. Cp. K. N. Macfarlane, 'Integer Vitae. A Wolf
by the Ears,' *Class. Journ.* 77, 1981, 23–25; Gow-Page *ad* l. 15.

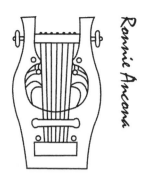

Ronnie Ancona

THE SUBTERFUGE OF REASON: HORACE, ODES 1.23 AND THE CONSTRUCTION OF MALE DESIRE

In this elegantly composed ode, Horace writes three stanzas, each one a complete sentence. His speaker begins by proposing a simile, to describe the behavior of Chloe, the girl he is trying to seduce. Like a nervous fawn, she does her best to avoid him, seeking refuge with her mother doe. But according to this speaker, the fawn's nervousness is based on groundless fear of insubstantial breezes or the rustling of the bushes. He elaborates this aspect of the fawn's terror in stanza 2. Of course, what frightens the creature is the possibility that the noise in the woods signifies the approach of a beast of prey. Working from that implicit comparison, the smooth seducer smilingly denies that he resembles a tiger or a lion: he is simply a man. And Chloe should, he argues, act like a woman, for after all she has reached the age when she should be pleasing men. Ancona's useful essay explores the gendered manner in which the speaker operates. Ostensibly appealing with calm good humor to the reason of Chloe and reassuring her absolutely of his dispassionate good will, he in fact refuses "to specify precisely what his desires are," but conveys them by the language of denial in the third stanza. He does want to "break" her (10). In showing the way this man masks his desires and works through "emotional suggestiveness," Horace demonstrates, as in earlier odes we have read, that he recognizes and aims to analyze the complex of emotionality and reason in the self-presentation by males of their desire. His love poetry is anything but insignificant. (Ed.)

✧ ✧ ✧

Fraenkel, one of the most influential Horatian scholars of this century, devotes little attention to the poems of Horace that deal with love, despite the fact that more than a quarter of the odes involve erotic themes and another quarter or so contain additional uses of erotic language, that is, language associated with love, sexuality, or desire.[1] Fraenkel's relative neglect of this aspect of Horace's work, namely the erotic, is not overly surprising, for it is representative of a widespread assumption among Horatian critics that love — at least in the case of a Horace — is a less important subject for poetry (and consequently for literary criticism as well) than are politics, poetics, patronage, and the state.[2]

One approach that acknowledges the erotic interest in Horace, but only to disparage it, is perhaps best exemplified in the statement of R. G. M. Nisbet, coauthor of the current standard English commentary on the first two books of *Odes*: "None of Horace's love-poems (if that is the right name

Reprinted with permission from the publisher and the author. From *Helios* 16:1 (1989), by Ronnie Ancona, Texas Tech University Press, copyright 1989.

for them) reaches the first rank."[3] Implicit in this remark is a judgment about Horace's love poetry that is based on an unstated assumption of what a love poem should be; yet Nisbet offers no clear and consistent notion of what would constitute a love poem, or more specifically, a good love poem. Nevertheless, the faults that he attributes to Horace as a love poet (lack of seriousness and involvement, artificiality, and unbelievability), and the poets with whom he compares Horace unfavorably (Catullus and Propertius), would suggest that the model that Horace fails to live up to is that of the romantic love poet. What Nisbet finds disturbing about Horace's love poetry is its remoteness from a romanticism that exhibits desire with the kind of directness and immediacy of, for example, a Propertius whose poems (according to Nisbet) "are written with an earnestness and intensity that seem to be derived at least partly from real life."[4] Thus, because Horace deals with desire in less overt ways than do the romantic poets, he is unable to meet Nisbet's standards for good love poetry.

A possible alternative to Nisbet's reliance on standards of judgment external to Horace's assumptions about love would be to use the poems themselves as a basis for determining the nature of Horace's love poetry, and further, for deciding whether the love poems are sufficiently powerful to warrant our attention. Unfortunately, such a reliance on explication of the text has produced not infrequently a denial that issues of love and desire are particularly significant to what is central in Horace's poetry. Thus R. O. A. M. Lyne, author of *The Latin Love Poets: From Catullus to Horace*, who is obviously interested in Horace *qua* love poet, endorses a view that subordinates Horace as love poet to Horace as primarily a "committed public poet."[5] Although this may be an adequate view of how Horace viewed the position of his love poetry in the *Odes*, what is problematic in this approach is Lyne's uncritical acceptance of this description as authoritative. As Jonathan Culler has written recently,

> In general, self-referentiality does not create a self-enclosed organic unity where a work accounts for itself or becomes the thing that it describes but rather produces paradoxical relations between inside and outside and brings out the impossibility for a discourse to account for itself. A work's self-descriptions do not produce closure or self-possession but an impossible and therefore open-ended process of self-framing.[6]

The question that Lyne's analysis cannot address is whether love in the *Odes* stays as self-contained as Lyne's acceptance of Horace's version of his love poetry would have us believe, or whether there are factors at work in the poems that undermine this description.[7]

While there are several other critics who have attempted to interpret Horace's love poetry without privileging a romantic version of love (as does Nisbet) and without relying excessively on the poet as guide to his own love poems (as does Lyne),[8] their work has not been entirely successful because they remain trapped, perhaps by necessity, in male assumptions about desire that they are unable to question. Thus, while these scholars have succeeded in advancing our understanding of particular odes and in forcing us to recognize the validity of studying Horace as a love poet, their work falls short of the kind of exploration of love and desire that the love poems demand. What they have failed to see is that the aspects of the love poems to which they pay attention have been shaped by unacknowledged assumptions about desire — assumptions that in turn determine the aspects of Horace's poetry to which we pay attention.[9]

In turning our attention to how assumptions about desire have shaped our sense of Horace as a love poet, I want to focus on a single poem, *Odes* 1.23, which serves as a microcosm of more general problems in Horatian criticism. Although one critic dismisses *Odes* 1.23 as "hardly...much more than a pretty little artefact,"[10] many others have given it considerable attention, focusing on various issues of a literary-historical, philological, or structural nature.[11] The characterization of Nisbet and Hubbard of the poem as "tender, humorous, and discreetly sensuous" is not atypical."[12] Nielsen, who questions the supposed ingenuousness of the poet's denial of predatory intent, goes furthest perhaps in recognizing and exploring the sexual tensions in the poem.[13]

However, what critics have thus far largely ignored (and their gender probably in part accounts for this) is the specific nature of desire in the poem. All of the above approaches to the poem reflect, to a greater or lesser extent, an identification with the perspective and values of the poet (or the speaker of the poem), which precludes an analysis of those values. Or, to put it another way, they reflect what Judith Fetterley in *The Resisting Reader* has called "the pretense that literature speaks universal truths through forms from which all the merely personal, the purely subjective, has been burned away or at least transformed through the medium of art into the representative."[14] In Fraenkel's day it was considered not only possible but laudable to "remove from the poems of Horace some of the crusts with which the industry of many centuries has overlaid them and to enable a sympathetic reader to listen as often as possible to the voice of the poet and as seldom as possible to the voices of his learned patrons."[15] More recent literary theory, however, has made us aware that poetry (or the text) is not completely isolable from the reader,[16] and that all criticism involves a political stance (acknowledged or unacknowledged) toward the text.[17] Consequently, the universality of the "sympathetic reader," that is, the assumption that the "good" reader will share the values of the text, can no longer be taken for granted.

In examining the nature of desire in *Odes* 1.23, I will take into account what I think has largely been ignored in previous analyses of the poem, namely, the gender specificity of desire.[18] What I hope to show is that the basis of the poem (and what has as yet remained largely uncharted) is a version of male desire that expresses itself in a language whose rational argumentation is completely undercut by its emotional or affective power.

That is to say, the language of the poem expresses a tension between reason and emotion in the poet/lover which forms the basis for the poem's
expression of male desire. By exploring how desire is constituted in the
poem, we will be able to discuss the consequences of this particular version of male desire.

Recent work in feminist psychoanalytic theory provides a framework
for interpreting the Chloe ode's tension between emotive language and
rational argumentation. Jessica Benjamin, in her provocative essay "The
Bonds of Love: Rational Violence and Erotic Domination,"[19] shows how
rationality functions in our culture (and I would argue in Horace's as well)
as a sort of erotic subterfuge. Benjamin begins with Hegel's idea that au-
tonomous selfhood develops through being able to affect others by one's
acts, that is, that to exist for oneself one must exist for an "other."[20] She
then turns to Bataille's claim that eroticism centers around transgressing
the boundaries of another (or having one's own boundaries transgressed)[21]
and argues that here the Hegelian notion of autonomy turns into a fantasy
of erotic domination. According to Benjamin, this fantasy reflects a failure
in "differentiation," a failure in "[the childhood] process of acquiring a
self" of "developing the ability to see ourselves and others as independent
and distinct beings."[22] She argues further that the fantasy of erotic domination exhibits a need both for autonomy and for recognition by the "other,"
and that the expression of these paradoxical needs, that is, the need for
autonomy and the need for recognition, in the fantasy of erotic domination entails finally its own ineffectiveness because an extreme assertion of
self denies agency to the other, who needs agency in order to have the
power to recognize. While Benjamin acknowledges that this general structure of erotic development is applicable to both women and men, she argues that the denial of recognition to the "other" stems from the "male
experience of differentiation and the repudiation of maternal nurturance,"[23]
and that "this repudiation gives rise to a form of individuality and rationality that permeates our culture and intensifies the conflict between our
needs for self-assertion and transcendence."[24]

My focus here is not, however, on the origins in childhood of this version of male desire, but rather on its expression in a particular construction
of adult male desire. I am not suggesting an actual scenario for either the
poet's or the poet/lover's childhood; instead, I want to explore how this
phenomenon, analyzed by Benjamin, underlies a specific text that inscribes
male desire. What Benjamin's interpretation of the fantasy of erotic domination allows us to see in the dynamics of desire in the Chloe ode is that a
seemingly rational assertion of power or knowledge conceals a refusal to
recognize or acknowledge emotional need. The poet's insistence that his
own desires pose no threat (indeed, his refusal to specify precisely what
his desires are), far from indicating innocence or selflessness, is in fact a
subterfuge designed to preserve both the autonomy and dominance of a
self incapable of recognizing the object of its desire as an agent. The dichotomy between the rational discourse of the poem (the arguments that

the poet makes) and its emotive power (primarily the figurative language in which those arguments are expressed) thus reveals, in Benjamin's terms, a version of male desire that seeks an autonomy secured by rational detachment, while exhibiting a dominance over the other that is the necessary consequence of an extreme assertion of self.

This dichotomy between the rational discourse of the poem and the affective power of its language can be made explicit through an examination of the rational arguments of the poem and the specific ways in which they are undercut. To begin with, the word order of the poem's first line mirrors the conflicting interests of the poet/lover and Chloe, the addressee. While the rational meaning of the simile in the poem's first line, "You are avoiding me like a fawn, Chloe," is reflected in the separation of verb (*vitas*), direct object (*me*), and vocative (*Chloe*), it is undercut by word order as well, for the poet surrounds himself (*me*) with "Chloe words" (*inuleo...similis*). Furthermore, the apparently rational characterization of Chloe's fears as empty or groundless (*vano*) in the fawn simile is undermined by the emotionally disconcerting tone produced by the presence of the fawn's fearful mother (*pavidam...matrem*) and the pathless mountains (*montibus aviis*) through which the fawn flees. Then, in the guise of expanding upon the fawn's empty fears (note the explanatory *nam*), the poet/lover begins to image both arousal in Chloe and the fulfillment of his own desire. Chloe's name (Greek for "green bud" or "shoot"), introduced earlier in the poem, has prepared the reader to associate Chloe with spring, which, as Commager argues, functions as the controlling metaphor of the poem.[25] Thus, we associate the poet's description of the bristling forth of foliage at spring's arrival (*mobilibus veris inhorruit / adventus foliis*) with Chloe. And through the words *mobilis* ("pliant," "flexible") and *inhorrēo* ("shudder" or "become erect") the poet images symptoms of (Chloe's) physical arousal. Still further, the erotic potential awakened in this description of spring is realized in the vivid picture of sexual intercourse imaged by the lizards parting the brambles (*virides rubum / dimovere lacertae*). The description, following directly, of the fawn's or Chloe's trembling knees and pounding heart is equally evocative of both fear and desire, thus mingling symptoms that describe the effect the poet / lover presumably desires (namely, Chloe's desire) with the effect he describes himself as having on Chloe (namely, fear). As we can see, then, the rational argument that Chloe is avoiding him because of unnecessary fears is undermined radically through word order and suggestive sexual imagery. The figurative power of the language evokes designs the poet has on Chloe which do not surface in his rational argumentation.

What follows in the poem on the rational level (expressed once again through simile) is the poet/lover's attempt to reassure Chloe that he has no plans to attack her: *atqui non ego te tigris ut aspera/ Gaetulusve leo frangere persequor*; yet through word order that embodies pursuit (*non ego te*), and similes of predatory animals, each made more empathetic with a modifier (*tigris...aspera* and *Gaetulus leo*), the poet/lover undercuts his reassurances.

The postponement of *frangere persequor* until the end of its phrase, its lengthy separation from the negative *atqui non,* and its demarcation through its appearance after the metrical pause in the line all serve to undercut still further the denial of predatory intent. Moreover, it is "pursuit" (*persequor*) with which the phrase concludes.

Frangere, finally, demolishes the poet/lover's seeming reassurances. The "rational negation" of *atqui non* is boldly effaced by the figurative power of *frangere.* Indeed, *frangere* functions as the climax of the poem, for it captures the poet/lover's unacknowledged need to overpower Chloe completely. The choice of *frangere* to embody this climax is particularly effective because of the word's range of meanings, which extends from the rational to the emotional spheres. The word encapsulates the poet/lover's multiple goals of *influencing* Chloe through rational argumentation, *taming* her the way one tames an animal,[26] and *breaking down* her resistance. Indeed, *frangere* (which can be used of breaking down doors or barriers)[27] may even hint at the breaking of the hymen, which would make real, and more specific to Chloe's youthful state, the sexual intercourse imaged earlier by the lizards parting the brambles.[28] Perhaps now we can understand *frangere* as a powerfully evocative expression of the destructive component of a desire that requires a subordination of the other.[29] To be sure, the poet backs off a bit from the explosiveness of the word *frangere* in the poem's final lines. Yet here, too, the seemingly objective language of *tandem* and *tempestiva* is undercut by the realization that Chloe's "readiness for a man" has been defined all along solely in relation to the interests of her would-be lover. In the guise of a rational polemic on the necessity for Chloe to adapt to the "natural order of things" the poet/lover conceals his own impatience and desire.[30]

We can see now that the tension between the rational discourse of the poem and its affective power can be explained by the dynamics that Benjamin describes of a self torn between its desire for autonomy and its need for the other. The particular form of desire that emerges from the Chloe ode — a paradoxical desire for both control of the other and recognition by her — is expressed through a combination of rational detachment and emotional suggestiveness. "Reason" allows the poet/lover the appearance of speaking from a dispassionate and uninvolved position, while it, in fact, functions as a kind of erotic subterfuge that masks an overpowering desire in the cloak of objectivity.

In the Chloe ode the ultimate futility of the poet/lover's strategy is evidenced by the fact that what is absent from the poem is any clear sense of Chloe's will or of Chloe as the subject or agent of desire. We are left with only the surface of Chloe, with a Chloe whose trembling reaction to the poet/lover suggests both her fear and (to the poet/lover) her potential for erotic response. As a consequence, the lines between seduction, domination, and invasion begin to blur. By denying Chloe agency, the poet/lover precludes the kind of response he presumably wants from Chloe, namely, desire.

Not recognizing the intimidating aspect of the poet's persona entails mistaking the poem for a "sweet" portrait of a girl leaving childhood behind. If, however, we replace such a simplistic reading with the sort of reductiveness that sees nothing more in the poem than an uncomplicated expression of male dominance, we make it impossible to understand the poet/lover's desire for Chloe. By interpreting the split between the rational discourse of the poem and its affective power as analogous to the conflicting needs and desires found in the fantasy of erotic domination, we have a way of dealing with the poet/lover's simultaneous distancing of himself from Chloe and his expression of desire, an expression that verges on the obliteration of the object of his desire.

In the preceding discussion I hope to have made explicit the dynamics of desire in *Odes* 1.23. Using Benjamin's theory of the fantasy of erotic domination, I have tried to explain the ways in which these dynamics take shape in the language of the Chloe ode. Specifically, I have outlined a version of male desire that expresses itself indirectly (often through figurative language) as well as through a rational discourse that seeks autonomy at the risk of denying desire. This analysis of the dynamics of desire in *Odes* 1.23 shows that the traditional image of Horace as the rational, detached (love) poet has made it too easy for critics both to ignore the emotive power of the poem and to fail to recognize the way in which the poet's rational detachment is itself constitutive of desire. The lack of attention to these aspects of the poem is explainable in part by the (predominantly male) critics' blindness to the gender specificity of desire in the poem and, more particularly, by an unacknowledged identification with the male poet's desire. This produces an avoidance of analysis of the poem's *subject* of desire (which would entail self-reflection) and a more comfortable focusing on the "other," namely, Chloe, the *object* of desire. And yet, finally, the poem is only "about Chloe" to the extent that Chloe embodies the construction of what the poet's male desire desires.

In conclusion, it must be acknowledged that Horace's detached, ironic stance, so common in the love poems, does not signify a lesser interest in love, but is instead a particular way of expressing (male) desire, for the distancing created by the use of reason functions as a vehicle through which the poet/lover attempts simultaneously to seduce, that is, to elicit desire, and to maintain his autonomy, thus masking his own desire. If we question the nature and function of Horace's detachment as a love poet—a task which I hope to have begun here, but which has yet to be undertaken comprehensively—what I think we will discover is a far more complicated, and perhaps more disturbing, version of love and desire than critics have yet considered.

Notes

An earlier version of this paper was presented at the Fall 1986 meeting of the Classical Association of the Atlantic States at Columbia University, and at the 1986 annual meeting of the American Philological Association in San Antonio.

I would like to thank the guest editor of this issue [of *Helios*], Adele Scafuro, and the two anonymous referees for their helpful comments; thanks are owed as well to Charles Babcock for having first shared my exploration of the Chloe ode, to David Konstan for his responses to an earlier draft of the paper, and to Steven Cole for encouragement and criticism throughout this project.

My research was supported by Grant #667020 from PSC-CUNY Research Award Program of the City University of New York.

[1]Eduard Fraenkel, *Horace* (Oxford: Clarendon Press, 1957).

[2]Even a work as valuable as Matthew Santirocco's *Unity and Design in Horace's Odes* (Chapel Hill and London: University of North Carolina Press, 1986) suggests that what Horace has to say about love is fairly obvious: "In all of his love odes...whether he is the observer or the participant, Horace's stance is basically the same as in the first ode [1.5]: never obsessive like Catullus and the elegists, he is mildly bemused, even detached, and appreciative of the ironies inherent in the situation" (33). As I show below, the ironic detachment of Horace in the love poems (with which Santirocco expresses no discomfort) is, in fact, quite sinister.

[3]"Romanae Fidicen Lyrae: The Odes of Horace," in *Critical Essays on Roman Literature: Elegy and Lyric*, ed. J. P. Sullivan (Cambridge, MA: Harvard University Press, 1962), p. 184.

[4]*Ibid.*, p. 194.

[5]*The Latin Love Poets: From Catullus to Horace* (Oxford: Clarendon Press, 1980), p. 203 and *passim*.

[6]"Changes in the Study of Lyric," in *Lyric Poetry: Beyond New Criticism*, ed. Chaviva Hošek and Patricia Parker (Ithaca and London: Cornell University Press, 1985), p. 52.

[7]For an examination of the disquieting elements in one of Horace's love poems, see Pietro Pucci, "Horace's Banquet in *Odes* 1.17," *TAPA* 105 (1975), 259–81. I would like to thank John Van Sickle for calling my attention to this article which, in many ways, anticipates and corroborates the disturbing qualities of desire that I explore in this paper.

[8]Useful studies of this kind that either focus on or include discussion of Horace as a love poet include A. J. Boyle, "The Edict of Venus: An Interpretive Essay on Horace's Amatory Odes," *Ramus* 2 (1973), 163–88; Steele Commager, *The Odes of Horace: A Critical Study* (New Haven and London: Yale University Press, 1962); Richard Minadeo, *The Golden Plectrum: Sexual Symbolism in Horace's Odes* (Amsterdam: Rodopi, 1982); Michael Putnam, *Essays on Latin Lyric, Elegy, and Epic* (Princeton: Princeton University Press, 1982); Kenneth Quinn, "Horace as a Love Poet: A Reading of *Odes* 1.5," *Arion* 2.3 (1963), 59–77; Kenneth Reckford, *Horace* (New York: Twayne Publishers, 1969).

[9]What is virtually absent from these interpretations (above, note 8) is a critique of the status of the poet lover's desire that a feminist perspective allows. (I should add, however, that several of these same interpretations have played an essential role in the development of my own thinking about Horace as a love poet.)

[10]Fraenkel (above, note 1), p. 184.

[11]See, for example, R. G. M. Nisbet and Margaret Hubbard, *A Commentary on Horace: Odes Book I* (Oxford: Clarendon Press, 1970), pp. 273ff., for discussion of the poem's Anacreontic models and problems with and suggested emendations for *veris inhorruit adventus*. I agree with Commager (and others) that "Bentley's attempt to amend *veris...adventus* (5–6) to *vepris...ad ventum* ignores the ode's controlling metaphor, which is a seasonal one" (Commager [above, note 8], p. 238). On the poet's use of simile and metaphor, see M. Owen Lee, "Horace *Carm.* 1.23: Simile and Metaphor," *CP* 60 (1965), 185–86; on simile and logical structure, see Victor Estevez, "Chloe and the Fawn: The Structure of *Odes* 1.23," *Helios* 7.1 (1979–80), 35–44.

[12]Nisbet and Hubbard (above, note 11), p. 274. See also Lyne (above, note 5) who comments on the poem's "charm and discretion" (p. 215) and calls the "message [of the poem] essentially complimentary — but [one that] needs sensitive handling" (p. 216).

[13]Rosamary Nielsen, "Horace *Odes* 1.23: Innocence," *Arion* 9 (1970), 373–78. Although I do not agree with all of Nielsen's conclusions, her exploration of the nature of Chloe's fears and her recognition of the poet/lover as a possible threat show an interest in and a sensitivity to Chloe's perspective not common in the scholarship on this poem.

[14]*The Resisting Reader: A Feminist Approach to American Fiction* (Bloomington and London: Indiana University Press, 1978), p. xi.

[15]Fraenkel (above, note 1), p. vii.

[16]On the relationship between reader and text in the field of Classics, see "Audience-Oriented Criticism and the Classics," *Arethusa* 19.2 (Fall 1986).

[17]On literary criticism as political, see, for example, Fetterley (above, note 14), *passim*, and "Conclusion: Political Criticism" in Terry Eagleton, *Literary Theory: An Introduction* (Minneapolis: University of Minneapolis Press, 1983), pp. 194–217.

[18]On gender and the interpretation of literature, see, for example, *Writing and Sexual Difference*, ed. Elizabeth Abel (Chicago: University of Chicago Press, 1982); and on the intersections of writing, gender, and desire, see, for example, Hélène Cixous, "The Laugh of the Medusa," in *New French Criticisms*, ed. Elaine Marks and Isabelle de Courtivron (New York: Schocken Books, 1981), pp. 245–64.

[19]"The Bonds of Love: Rational Violence and Erotic Domination," in *The Future of Difference*, ed. Hester Eisenstein and Alice Jardine (New Brunswick, NJ: Rutgers University Press, 1985), pp. 41–70. This article appears with minor changes under the same title in *Feminist Studies* 6.1 (Spring 1980), 144–74. An abbreviated (and somewhat different) version is found as "Master and Slave: The Fantasy of Erotic Domination," in *Powers of Desire: The Politics of Sexuality*, ed. Ann Snitow, Christine Stansell, and Sharon Thompson (New York: Monthly Review Press. 1983), pp. 280–99. 1 became interested in Benjamin's work while participating in Carol Gilligan's seminar "On the Psychology of Love" at Douglass College in 1986. Benjamin was a Fellow at the Laurie New Jersey Chair in Women's Studies (then held by Gilligan), sponsor of the seminar.

[20]G. W. F. Hegel, "The Independence and Dependence of Self-Consciousness: Master and Slave," ch. IV.A, *The Phenomenology of Spirit (Phänomenologie des Geistes)* (Hamburg: Felix Meiner, 1952), pp. 141–50, as cited by Benjamin (above, note 19) in *Future of Difference*, p. 68.

[21]Georges Bataille, *Death and Sensuality* (New York: Walker and Company, 1962), as cited by Benjamin, *ibid.*

[22]Benjamin (above, note 19), *Powers of Desire*, p. 281.

[23]Benjamin (above, note 19), *ibid.*, p. 282; on the role of gender in the experience of differentiation, see Nancy Chodorow, *The Reproduction of Mothering: Psychoanalysis and the Sociology of Gender* (Berkeley: University of California Press, 1978).

[24]Benjamin (above, note 19), *Powers of Desire*, p. 282.

[25]Commager (above, note 8), p. 238 (cited above, note 11).

[26]For the purpose of my argument H. J. Rose's interpretation of *frangere* as requiring "mule-colt" not "fawn" for the animal to which Chloe is compared ("Some Passages of Latin Poets," *HSCP* 47 [1936], 1–15) is not of consequence, for it makes little difference whether the poet/lover in the tiger lion simile is (as Rose argues makes sense with Chloe as "mule-colt," but not as "fawn") "an actual or potential owner, not eater, running after a creature which he wants to use for his business or pleasure (p. 3)." The dominating attitude of the lover is equally apparent even if Chloe is merely "owned," not "eaten"!

[27]Cf. *quis nostras sic frangit fores?* (Plautus, *As.* 384) and *ianua frangatur* (Horace, *Sat.*1.2.128).

[28]Of course, the desire to break down a barrier to gain access to a beloved takes conventional literary form in the *paraklausithyron/exclusus amator* motif. The need to overcome or violate another's boundaries imaged in this motif is central to the fantasy of erotic domination under discussion. For references to this motif in the *Odes*, see W. J. Henderson, "The Paraklausithyron Motif in Horace's Odes," *AC* 16 (1973), 51–67.

[29]On *frangere* as "epexegetic inf. after *persequor* implying *desire* [emphasis mine]," see T. E. Page, *Q. Horati Flacci: Opera* (London: Macmillan, 1896), p. 225.

[30]It is interesting to note that the poet/lover's desire for Chloe urges a rupture in Chloe's relationship with her mother. If the dominating quality of the poet/lover's desire can be understood, in Benjamin's terms, as reflecting the male's repudiation of the mother in the childhood process of developing a self, how appropriate that the male poet/lover should see this "bond with the mother" as impeding Chloe's development.

H. Akbar Khan

HORACE'S ODE TO VIRGIL
ON THE DEATH OF QUINTILIUS: 1.24

Some time in 24 B.C., Quintilius Varus, a poet-friend of both Vergil and Horace, died prematurely. In this ode, Horace adopts as the occasion an attempt to console Vergil for his deep feelings of loss. Readers have regularly viewed it in terms of the conventions of the formal consolation known to Romans. As such, it devotes precisely half its lines (1–10) to Vergil's feelings of loss for the dead man. Then, it turns to the second part of the form in 11–20, namely, to the need of the living to return to reality and put an end to their sorrow. In addressing Vergil on this sad occasion, Horace may well be using him, as many think, to represent the grief of all Varus' friends. However, in this essay Khan goes farther and suggests that Vergil's way of grieving is the actual origin of these verses. There is good reason, he argues, to think that, when Varus died, Vergil launched into a threnody, that is, an elegiac lament over his friend. If so, it went too far in its sentimentality for Horace's stomach, and therefore Horace was impelled to write this poem to express his disagreement and to give Vergil a "lesson on how to strike a balance between the expression of sorrow and the maintenance of decorum." Although one might be reluctant to admit that Vergil had ever erred in his published poetry, nevertheless, the argument is well worth consideration. (Ed.)

The following observations were called forth primarily as a result of R. G. M. Nisbet's remarks on this ode in his essay on Horace in *Critical Essays on Roman Literature*, vol. 1, Routledge & Kegan Paul, 1962, p. 194 f. With Nisbet's remarks I will deal later in detail. For the present it suffices to say that he perpetuates the tradition which regards this ode as chiefly an effort by Horace to mourn the passing of a mutual friend of his and Virgil's, generally agreed to be Quintilius Varus, and to enshrine his memory for posterity. Most critics start with the assumption that Horace's main purpose was to compose an elegy, and in their evaluation of the poem they use this preconception as the yardstick with which to measure Horace's success.

There are in the poem, however, elements which parry the emotional thrust with which most critics would have an elegy endowed, and in recognition of such elements, some have resorted to drastic measures, while others, themselves more restrained, have cast an appreciative eye on the moderation they detect in this poem. So T. E. Page[1] thought, with others, that if the first stanza were excised, we would have a more forceful and satisfying beginning. A. Y. Campbell[2] considered the poem basically an

This essay is reprinted from *Latomus* 26 (1967) 107–17, with permission of the publisher.

elegy, and said: "In XXIV we see that even an elegy has become in Horace's hands an admonitory address against over-indulgence in grief." L. P. Wilkinson[3] admired Horace's controlled manner here as a manifestation of emotion in the truly classical fashion. He too thinks of the piece as first and foremost an elegy, in which the poet uses the cloak of advice given to Virgil to palliate his own strong feelings.

The prejudices which modern sympathies erect can form truly damaging barriers to level-headed literary criticism. The fact that elegy-motifs occur in this poem, and are a more attractive theme and capable of greater poetical possibilities than an admonition to a friend whose grief has led him to throw up all sense of decency, would tend to make many see in the poem nothing else but this aspect which fastens on our sensibility: make a critic in fact appreciate the poem more in terms of his preconceptions about what an elegy ought to be, than in terms of what Horace wrote. The critics so far referred to considered this poem basically an elegy, but they also took note of the element of restraint and dealt with this aspect in a way consistent with their ideas of what elegies should be like. H. D. Sedgwick,[4] on the other hand, makes no reference to this restraint in the poem, and he is indeed himself all emotion in his appraisal of the poem as an elegy. He calls the ode, significantly, "the requiem on the death of Quintilius, Horace and Virgil's friend." He comments, "What more can mortal say when death knocks at the heart of a friend? What can consolation do but praise the dead, share another friend's grief, and bid him summon up his courage to bear with patience what must be borne? And how harmonious and tender some lines are: *nulli flebilior quam tibi, Vergili,* etc."

The question I would ask strikes at the very roots of these criticisms. Was Horace's primary intention, judging from the treatment of the theme, to write an elegy whose sole purpose was to praise Quintilius? Was it sympathy with Virgil, quite simply, and a desire to console him, that prompted him to include the remarks addressed to the epic poet ? If we assume that Horace was not single-minded in his composition of this ode, but that the writing of a threnody and the admonition to Virgil went hand in hand, we might be on the way to a fairer assessment of the piece. I am not for a moment doubting that there are elements in the poem which can make it qualify for inclusion in the category of elegies. The formal elements are beyond dispute.[5] There is, however, an unmistakable tone of irony aimed at the emotionally unrestrained Virgil, and the form in which this dose of gentle reproach is administered is an example—the ode itself—of how a balanced threnody ought to be composed. We have here a lesson to Vergil in the composition of an elegy. The poem is therefore in emphasis at least equally apportioned between Quintilius and Virgil—if indeed it is not Virgil whom we should put in the foreground as the person responsible for the composition of the poem in this form. The admonitory strain is not merely stuff thrown in to prevent Horace from becoming too involved in his own grief at Quintilius' death. It is an important and integral part of the poem. The lesson given to Virgil lies in the controlled manner in which Horace can mourn the death of a person whom he would have considered no less dear to himself than he was to Virgil. Logically, then, the lesson, the controlled threnody, the elegy included in the admonitory poem, *follows* the admonition. We have, for Virgil's benefit, an appreciation of the common friend Quintilius, *in terms of an elegy*. This is, I believe, a very helpful way of seeing the poem, and one which I think must have been before the eyes of the ancient scholiast who wrote of the poem: *Haec ode ΘΡΗΝΟΝ continet in Quintilium, sodalem Vergili morte exemptum* ["This ode contains a lament for Quintilius, a friend of Virgil who had died"], etc. That Quintilius was the mutual friend of both Horace and Virgil places in a position of even greater prominence the difference in their attitude to his death. By virtue of conscious ambiguities and the treatment in general, I hope to show the extent of Horace's disagreement with Virgil, in this poem which contains (*continet*) a specially composed lament for a common friend.

The poem begins with what seems to be a rhetorical question, the idea being that there can be no sense of proportion, no limits to be set when one is mourning such a heavy loss as the passing of Quintilius. But even here, at the very start, there is ambivalence which becomes more explicit, or rather more likely to be sensed by a sensitive reader, by virtue of the other instances of ambiguity which are revealed as the poem progresses. The first sentence reads: *quis desiderio sit pudor aut modus / tam cari capitis*? The construction seems to be a rhetorical question with the implications mentioned above, if we understand *sit* as a potential subjunctive, and we translate "What...can there be?" But there is nothing, from a grammatical point of view, to prevent us from understanding *sit* as a subjunctive used in an indirect question of the kind I shall explain immediately. If *A* asks *B* a question, the question may be repeated with the verb put into the subjunctive by *B*, since some such word as *rogas* is understood, and surprise may be registered by *B* that *A* has in fact thought the question worthy of being asked.[6] I rather believe that this way of taking the first sentence was conscious to the mind of Horace, and that he meant Virgil to be conscious of the note of ambivalence on which the poem began, and to trace the thread through the rest of the poem. The more ambiguities piled up in the rest of the poem, the more their accumulated weight would become an effective retroactive force upon the first sentence with its ambiguity, and the idea that Horace was surprised that Virgil would ask the question would gain prominence over the other notion — that there could be no limits to the grief for Quintilius.

It could well be that in an elegy written for Quintilius, Virgil had showed no restraint whatever, and had asked the question "what moderation or end can there be to mourning such a dear friend as Quintilius?"[7] The beginning of Horace's ode takes this question as its cue, and says "Do you actually ask?" Then Horace goes on to write the elegy with the restraint he thinks should be employed. The edge is taken away from the admonition by Horace's appeal to the Muse. It is she who teaches the way to compose elegies, rather than Horace himself. Horace, would, according to this interpretation, go on to say what limits there were to mourning. This is indeed how the scholiast understood the words: he says on *praecipe* — *dic praecepta carminis, id est scientiam, O Musa, ut ostendam quis modus desiderii esse debeat carissimi amici* ["Speak the precepts of poetry, that is, wisdom, o Muse, that I may show what limit there should be to the longing for one's dearest friend"].

If Virgil did indeed write an elegy which, in Horace's eyes, went beyond the bounds of *pudor*, then there would be more point in his giving Virgil this lesson on how to strike a balance between the expression of sorrow and the maintenance of decorum. In the following stanza, we are told that everlasting sleep weighs down Quintilius, and then we are given a list of his worthy attributes. The first mentioned of these qualities is *pudor*. It emerges from the poem that Virgil in his asking the gods who have claimed Quintilius, to return him, and in his 'outweeping' others to whom the death of Quintilius brought grief, transgressed the limits of *pudor* — that sense of restraint and of moderation which controls man's relations with his fellow men and with the gods. Horace might well be hinting that Virgil does not possess to a sufficient degree a quality so obvious in the man whose death he mourns! I think Horace is saying, hinting — and not very darkly at that, some such comment as this: "You are inconsolable in your sorrow for this friend of ours who had such admirable qualities, the foremost of which was indeed *pudor*, but, alas, *pudor* is what you yourself are lacking in." When a person as cultured as Virgil shows himself deficient in *pudor*, one might well doubt whether anybody at all could equal that of Quintilius : ... *quando ullum inveniet parem?*

Perpetuus sopor urget (5-6) is, on one level, a consolation to Virgil, since Horace uses a euphemism: Quintilius is only in an unconscious state, though it lasts forever. But by the very use of euphemism, by making the calamity lighter than it is in fact, Horace can enhance Virgil's neurotic behavior. After all, it is not even a case where Quintilius is weighed down by the heavy earth; and it is a common prayer that when one dies, the earth would rest lightly upon the deceased person. It is merely sleep which 'weighs down' Quintilius![8]

Nisbet (*op. cit.* p. 195) says of the second stanza, "The abstractions tell us nothing about Quintilius... Horace goes on to say that Quintilius is mourned by all good men, and especially by Virgil, but we are not told why these people liked him." Nisbet is evidently an adherent to the tradition of the critics cited above who consider Horace's primary aim to have been the composition of an elegy on Quintilius' death. But the ode is logically first and foremost a warning to Virgil, and of this the elegy-motif forms a part. Both Horace and Virgil knew Quintilius. It is possible that there were aspects of Quintilius' character, which the general reader would have found interesting, had Horace wished to tell us of them. In an ode of this kind where two friends are involved in a situation touching a mutual friend, many things can be left unsaid, for they would themselves be in a position to fill in the gaps. When, however, Horace decided to publish the poem, he must have known that what he had written was sufficient for the general reader to know in order to appreciate the piece. It is, I feel, more likely that Horace had good reasons for handling his theme in this fashion, than that he was aesthetically faltering by his omission to mention why other people besides Virgil loved Quintilius.

It seems that Nisbet assumes that Horace's main purpose is to write a lamentation, and therefore when he comes across elements which check a stream of emotion, he considers these aspects as militating against the poem's success. This sort of thinking seems responsible for his remark, (*op. cit.* p. 195), that "The opening sentence is admirable for its gravity and restraint, but Melpomene fails to satisfy; the allusion goes on too long, and does not help to convince us that Horace is in earnest. The second stanza again begins well, but the rest is vague and exaggerated." But it may well be that the fact that the Muse does not satisfy, and the lengthy allusion, aid Horace's purpose rather than detract from the efficacy of his art. The allusion *cui liquidam pater / vocem cum cithara dedit*, is not at all otiose. It is precisely because Melpomene has these attributes that Horace can depend on her to begin the *lugubres cantus*. He is saying in effect "Teach me funeral strains, for you can." The *cui*-clause functions here as the *namque potes* of prayers. For Horace, this formal element is a necessity, even when he is writing about a dead friend for whom he cared and was presumably under some emotional strain.[9] Grief is not allowed to overthrow his sense of propriety. There is also a sort of formal correspondence between the first and second stanzas, with their questions and *cui*-clauses. It is not that Horace is insensible to grief, rather he knows how to practice the rule "Nothing too much." Horace can feel and yet suppress his feelings. His attitude is the same as that expressed by Seneca writing from his place of exile to his mother (*ad Helviam* 16.1): *...nam et infinito dolore, cum aliquem ex carissimis amiseris, adfici stulta indulgentia est, et nullo inhumana duritia. Optimum inter pietatem et rationem temperamentum est et sentire desiderium et opprimere* ["It is stupid self-indulgence to be afflicted with limitless grief when you have lost one of your dearest friends, but it is inhuman hardness to have no feeling. The best thing is a compromise between deep feeling and rationality: both to feel longing and to control it"]. Horace's classical restraint reminds one of that scene in the *Iliad*, 3.243–4, in which Helen looks out upon the plain of Troy to see if she can set eyes upon her brothers, Castor and Pollux. But they are already dead, and Homer says that the life-giving earth had them within it:

Ὣς φάτο τοὺς δ᾽ ἤδη κάτεχεν φυσίζοος αἶα
ἐν Λακεδαίμονι αὖθι φίλῃ ἐν πατρίδι γαίῃ

["Thus she spoke, but already the life-giving earth possessed them, in Lacedaemon in their beloved native land."]

He does not become weepy and sentimental over the affair. Despite the fact that it is touching to depict the picture of the sister scouring with her gaze the open field for her brothers, who, unknown to her, are now dead, the earth, for all that, does not become any whit less life-giving.

If we examine the form of

> *multis ille bonis flebilis occidit,*
> *nulli flebilior quam tibi, Vergili...*

we cannot help seeing a hint of impatience in the repeated *flebilis...flebilior.* Also, there is the straightforward notion of Virgil's excessive grief, but there is also the subsidiary idea—played as it were in a minor key, but no less perceptible—of an argument from proportion. Good men wept for Quintilius, but Virgil wept more bitterly than they all. I do not think that we can escape the hint which such a statement of the matter, in conjunction with the other elements of irony, suggests: that Virgil must have been trying to show that his loyalty to Quintilius outstripped that of all the others, since it was he who could weep the most copiously. This extra overtone enhances the effect of the poetry, not passing, but provoking a comment on the fact that Virgil outwept the other mourners. Horace is with subtlety upbraiding Virgil.

On lines 11–12,

> *tu frustra pius heu non ita creditum*
> *poscis Quintilium deos,*

critics are divided in their interpretation. Following the lead of the scholiast's comment: *frustra reposcis, inquit, Quintilianum non sub hac spe illis commendatum,* some take this to mean that Virgil entrusted Quintilius to the gods in prayer for safe keeping, taking *non ita creditum* to mean 'not on condition that the gods should claim him forever,' as they have done. This interpretation will also satisfy those who wish to give the same subject to *credere* and *poscere,* following the principle that *is poscit qui credidit.*[10] Others think especially of the analogy from usury, used to accentuate the transient nature of human life and our enjoyment of the goods of this world, which are but *lent* to us, to be claimed by the gods whensoever they see fit. This sentiment is found elsewhere and in Seneca, (*ad Marciam,* 1.1-4), and especially *Itaque non es! quod nos suspiciamus tamquam inter nostra positi; mutua accepimus. Usus fructusque noster est, cuius tempus ille muneris sui temperat; nos oportet in promptu habere quae in incertum diem data sunt et appellatos sine querella reddere: pessimi debitoris est creditori facere convicium* ["So you are dead! Let us treat the situation as though placed among our possessions: we have received them as a loan. The use and enjoyment of them is ours as long as the giver determines. We should have ready what are given for an unspecified time and when called restore them without complaint. It is the act of the worst kind of debtor to hurl insults at his creditor"]. Some critics, conscious of the thought here expressed by Seneca, consider that the subject of the action in *creditum* must be the gods, who have lent Quintilius to his friends on earth, and now Virgil claims him back *non ita creditum* — although the gods did not lend him on such terms — that Virgil or any of Quintilius' friends should feel justified in recalling him when once the gods had withdrawn him from their company.

In solving our problem of interpretation here, there are several points which we have to take into account. The strongest of our arguments and the most definitive will be the grammatical. Grammatical necessity dictates that we should have as the subject of *credere* the same person who is the subject of *poscis*. It is a commonplace in Latin syntax that where modern European languages would use two or more verbs with a personal subject and connected by 'and,' in order to describe a series of consecutive actions, Latin substitutes for all these verbs, except one, participles. Paul Veyne recently[11] applied this inescapable argument from grammar to Horace's ode I.31, *Quid dedicatum poscit Apollinem / vates*? and he showed that the subject of the action expressed in *dedicatum* must be the same as the subject of *poscis*, thus demolishing the myth that the poet composed this poem after the dedication of a temple to Apollo on the Palatine on the ninth of October, 28 B.C. by Octavian. So here too, in ode I.24, it would be Virgil who is demanding from the gods his friend whom he entrusted to them for safe keeping.

The second point which I believe that we cannot leave unsaid is that commentators seem to have been confusing two concepts. A person may entrust a friend for safe keeping to a god or an equivalent — as for instance Virgil was entrusted to the ship of the ode I.3. In this ode, the analogy with usury is forcefully upheld. The ship has been entrusted with Virgil, and therefore owes him, and must restore him safe and sound, (I.3.5–7). I think, however, that the fact that we are here dealing with a ship is of no small consequence. As we have seen from the passage of Seneca quoted above, a common way of looking at the relationship between men and gods was in such terms that the gods loaned us our blessings which they were at liberty to withdraw whensoever they chose. It is the gods who are the creditors, mortals the debtors. It is the gods, then, who *credunt, poscunt*. It would be natural therefore for a sensitive reader to get a jolt when confronted with a conceptual framework in which the roles of men and gods are suddenly reversed — in which it is a man who *credit, poscit*. A reader of Horace would be hard put to find in his poems, outside our I.24, an instance of indignation at the will of the gods so untempered and brazen as to arrogate to man the special privileges of the gods. Horace might well conceive of entrusting a friend to a ship and then asking it for his restitution; it is, I think, highly doubtful that he should treat the gods in a like manner.

I submit, therefore, that Horace is here either setting his own interpretation upon what he considers a brazen act of Virgil's, the fact that the latter brought himself to demand from the gods the restoration of Quintilius, or he is drawing, in an adapted form, on the sentiments expressed by Virgil in an elegy written on Quintilius' death, in which Virgil used the analogy from usury and argued that he had entrusted Quintilius to the gods, but not on condition that they should keep him forever. The exclamation *heu* in line 11 would, as it normally does,[12] take its meaning from the context, and according to this interpretation, would hold in solution an admixture of both sympathy on the part of Horace as well as irritation at the lack of control which Virgil exhibited. Horace would doubtless have seen that Virgil used *credere* to mean 'entrust in prayer,' but by the use of *poscere* as well, anyone would be put in mind of the gods, who vis-à-vis human possessions, *credunt, poscunt*. The transference of such terms in Virgil to the mortal sphere was terribly risky. Here was a sort of cleverness at the expense of *pudor*. A sane and sober Menandrean figure would have remarked to Virgil:

Ἄνθρωπον ὄντα δεῖ φρονεῖν τἀνθρώπινα.

["Being a man one should think mortal thoughts."]

Of the fourth stanza Nisbet says that (*op. cit.* p. 196) "the story about Orpheus and the trees is too fanciful and too trivial for the context." The point is that as far as the passionate attachment of Virgil for Quintilius goes, he in this respect resembles Orpheus and his great passion for Eurydice. It seems to me very likely that in Virgil's elegy for the lost Quintilius, he had sighed in passionate disillusionment at his own inability to rival the melodious strains of Orpheus,[13] and now Horace picks up the reference and says, "What if you did indeed prove a match for Orpheus? Do you think that by that sort of art you could revive the dead?" Here, as in the ode to Valgius, where the tone of admonition is similar though stronger and less disguised, Horace tries to draw the addressee away from the world of myth and fairy tale to the world of reality and hard fact. Such desires as recalling the dead from Hades should, Horace would have thought, be kept securely in that pretty region of fables, and not allowed to intrude into our daily lives. The juxtaposition *sanguis imagini* (15) brings out sharply the extraordinary nature of Virgil's wish. We get the impression not only of life-blood returning to the ghost, but also of the bust of the deceased person, his *imago*, blushing to life once more.

The parallelism between the case of Orpheus, who exerts influence on trees, and Virgil who tries to influence Hades is put over with great subtlety by Horace. The pivotal link that binds the two cases together is the point of contact between *arboribus* (14) and *virga* (16). Orpheus could sway trees, whole trees; Virgil, by contrast, has no control even over a part of a tree — *virga*, that special switch, the rod of Mercury, the marshaller of souls. Horace stresses the wish of Virgil to be like Orpheus by referring to them both in similar terms, and this places in still greater relief the difference between the two characters. The fact that *arboribus* and *virga* are in the same stanza, and that *Mercurius*, the subject, is kept back until the end of the sentence helps to enhance the important role played by the symbols 'tree' and 'switch.' The link between *arboribus* and *virga*, with their notions of the trees which obeyed Orpheus, and on the other hand Mercury and the gates of the Underworld, which would not listen to the requests of Virgil, this idea is reflected by the common notion, in *auditam* (14) and *precibus* (17), of listening. Trees listened to Orpheus, whereas Hades will not listen to the entreaties of Virgil. This special aspect of trees listening is chosen to correspond to the idea of prayers to which deaf ears are turned. When it is the power of the music which Orpheus makes that Horace wishes to stress, he observes that music makes things act contrary to their natural mode of behaviour. So, for instance, in the ode I.12.7-12, we are told that things normally stationary are made to move, while those normally in motion are brought to a standstill. Both Orpheus and Mercury are shepherds, but whereas we could imagine Orpheus letting his sheep out of their pens, *claustra recludens*, Mercury would not open the gates of death *fata recludere* (17), once he had admitted a soul to his flock, the *niger grex* (18).

It was not only in *pudor* that Virgil was lacking, but also in *patientia*. This quality Cicero defines thus (*Inv.* 2.54.163): *patientia est honestatis aut utilitatis causa rerum arduarum ac difficilium voluntaria ac diuturna perpessio* ["Patience is voluntary and lasting endurance of troubling and difficult circumstances for the sake of what is honorable and useful"]. Both *honestas* and *utilitas* would have been served had Virgil manifested adequate endurance against the shafts of adverse fortune. He would have been practical enough to know that it was futile to recall Quintilius from Hades, to dissolve in tears to no purpose; he would have been respectful enough to the gods not to make such ridiculous and even blasphemous demands of them. Also, there is a balance between *urget* (6) and *durum* (19) both of which come first in their verse and are followed by a long pause. *Levius* (19) acts in responsion to them both. Horace ends the ode with the weighty word *nefas*. It means 'impossible.' But it would surely be a misguided opinion that prompts us to focus all our attention upon this bald meaning to the detriment of the atmosphere that has been set for it by the nineteen preceding verses.[14] In the ode I.3.26: *gens humana ruit per vetitum nefas*, Horace wished to underscore the audacity of mankind in overleaping those boundaries which nature herself had set to his enterprises. Man was unable to take the hint from the fact that the sea was a barrier to overseas adventure. So here too, in I.24, *nefas* carries with it the notion of transgression of set limits. Nor was Horace in this ode giving advice to a Virgil who did not care for *patientia*. For Fabricius reports that among the writings of Donatus is the saying of Virgil himself, that there is no virtue that is more useful to a man than is the power of spiritual endurance, and there is no stroke of fortune so harsh that a stout-hearted man cannot overcome its effect if he has sense enough to bear up under the strain.[15]

In conclusion, this ode to Virgil takes its inspirational cue from a definite situation in the relationship of Virgil and Horace. Virgil wrote an elegy on Quintilius' death, caring nothing for mortal propriety. Here, in I.24, we have a rejoinder by Horace, which is at once a cautionary poem, with a lesson (by example) on how a sensitive threnody ought to be composed — one which can pay an elegant tribute to a dead friend without flying in the face of Heaven. We should have no misgivings about this type of composition, derived from a personal relationship, which would lie outside the common knowledge of all modern readers and outside of the experience of a great number of the contemporaries of the two poets. Had Horace thought that the general reader required anything for the comprehension and the enjoyment of the poem over and above that which we can derive from the poem itself, he would have had second thoughts about including it in his collection. Also, here, as in the case of the ode II.9, to Valgius, Horace's poem is quite sufficient for us to understand the background to it. We do not need to read the weepy poem of Valgius first, nor indeed the elegy of Virgil on Quintilius' death. We have seen in the course of this analysis that Horace, stanza by stanza, uses various devices, which we may class as instances of ambiguity, in the widest sense of the word, and in so doing creates a dichotomy of purpose that pervades the entire poem. We must not push into insignificance, or find fault aesthetically with, the admonitory aspect of the ode, concentrating solely upon the elegy-motif. Rather we have to take the ode as Horace gave it to us, not as we would prefer to have it. It is above all, an ode with a message to Virgil: that even in the case of an inestimable friend's death, *pudor* and *modus* are guiding principles of which a man should never lose sight.

Notes

[1]In his edition of the Odes and the Epodes, London 1959, p. 188.

[2]In his *Horace, a New Interpretation*, Methuen, 1924, p. 223.

[3]In his *Horace and His Lyric Poetry*, Cambridge, 1951, p. 93. On p. 105, Wilkinson implies that in I.24, we have the motif of advice to Virgil acting as "a mere disguise for self-expression." One of the chief points I make is that logically, the advice comes first, before the threnody for Quintilius, and that Horace is as much, if not more, concerned with Virgil's conduct, as he is with singing the praises of the lost Quintilius.

[4]In his *Horace, a Biography*, Harvard 1947, p. 100.

[5]For a section by section analysis of the ode see José Esteve-Forriol, *Die Trauer- und Trostgedichte in der römische Literatur*, Munich 1962, p. 27f.

[6]See S. A. Handford, *The Latin Subjunctive*, Methuen, 1947, p. 173-74.

[7]In the ode II.9, Horace tells Valgius: *tu semper urges flebilibus modis Mysten ademptum* etc. (9–10), and *flebilis, flebilior* occur at 9–10 in our ode. It is quite easy to take the basic notion of *flere* out of the adjectives in I.24 and to interpret the idea in Virgil's *flere Quintilium* to mean that he wrote a maudlin dirge on Q.'s death. For II.9 see K. Quinn, *Latin Explorations*, Routledge & Kegan Paul, 1963, p. 158f.

[8]We find that *sit tibi terra levis* is a recurring formula in sepulchral inscriptions; see J. B. Pighi, *Lyra Romana*, Como, 1946, for examples. Cf. also Ovid, *Amores* I.8.107–8, Propertius, II.20.15–17, Euripides, *Alc.* 463-4.

[9]The opinion that restraint in a man's poetry allows the reader to say that he did not feel strongly is naive and misleading. There is a great difference in the frame of mind of the man who feels the jab of anguish and the poet who has afterwards summoned up enough composure to put pen to paper in order to record that emotion. See the late Prof. C. S. Lewis' remarks in *The Personal Heresy*, Oxford

Paperback Ed. 1965, p. 9: "It is, in fact, quite impossible that the character represented in the poem should be identically the same with that of the poet. The character presented is that of a man in the grip of this or that emotion: the real poet is a man who has already escaped from that emotion sufficiently to see it objectively — I had almost said to see it dramatically — and to make poetry of it."

[10]Cf. J. Esteve-Forriol, *op. cit.*, p. 29, who puts the case thus: "Wenn man hier nicht eine äusserst dunkle Ausdrucksweise annehmen will, muss man den einleuchtenden Gegensatz anerkennen: *is poscit qui credit*, und nicht das Motiv des menschlichen Lebens als ein Darlehen der Götter" ["If we don't assume an extremely obscure expression here, we must recognize the illuminating opposition: he demands who entrusts, and not the trope of human life as a loan of the gods"].

[11]In his article "Quid dedicatum poscit Apollinem?" in *Latomus*, 24, 1965, p. 932f.

[12]Cf. the note of W. A. Camps in his *Propertius, Elegies Book III*, on poem 15.5–6: *Illa rudis animos per noctes conscia primas / imbuit, heu nullis capta Lycinna datis!* Camps says there (p. 126): "*heu* conveys emotion, not necessarily (though often) grief; it takes its tone from the context. In this context the emotive thought is of the innocent spontaneity of Lycinna (evidently a maidservant), compared with the calculating acquisitiveness of other women the speaker has known."

[13]It seems to me that Virgil means that, had he in fact the musical ability of Orpheus, he would have been able to rescue the dead Quintilius from the halls of Hades. The fact that Virgil made, in his treatment of the story, Orpheus lose Eurydice since he looked back at her before she had really left Hades, and that in spite of his music, has tended, it would seem, to make critics forget or neglect the version of the story in which Orpheus *did* rescue her. The allusion would therefore be not as otiose as Nesbit supposes. Virgil would not be wishing to be an Orpheus who, though capable of softening the hearts of the Underworld dwellers, was of no avail in rescuing the person he loved, but rather he would be implying the ability to rescue Quintilius, granted the ability of Orpheus. Virgil wanted Quintilius back. His attitude would have been similar to that of Admetus in Eurip.'s *Alcestis*, 357f. Here we have the earliest mention of Orpheus' journey to the Underworld. In a very illuminating article, by Peter Dronke, "The Return of Euridyce," *Classica et Mediaevalia*, 23, 1962, p. 201–2, the argument is put forward, with regard to the passage of Euripides: "Although Admetus does not say in so many words that Orpheus succeeded, the logical point of his speech makes this clear. He is saying 'If I could *succeed* as Orpheus did, I too would go down to fetch you back.' It would have been absurd to reinforce a wish for success by reference to a well-known failure." The same arguments can be used to support my case for Virgil's attitude. It would seem, then, that in this ode, Virgil is represented as having, in his lamentation for Quintilius, used, implicitly or explicitly, the version of the Orpheus/Eurydice tale in which the husband actually rescues his wife.

[14]The simple meaning "impossible" for *nefas* here is implied by Douglas F. S. Thompson in his review of C. J. Fordyce's edition of Catullus in *Phoenix* 15, 1961, p. 245–8. But it damages the poem to underscore the purely logical meaning at the expense of the implications the word has for Horace's philosophy of temperance. Wilkinson, *op. cit.*, p. 92, says: "…the whole burden of the philosophies he (Horace) pondered, those of the Hellenistic Age, was that passion should be damped." It was the failure to appreciate Horace's upstanding and controlled attitude before grief that led Bentley in his third edition, published at Amsterdam in 1728, to misunderstand Horace's purposeful ambivalence in the first lines of the ode and disagree with the scholiast's interpretation on *praecipe*, which ran: *praecipe cantus, quis sive quibus desiderio pudor sit et modus*, a meaning which, as I have argued, is not at all to be overlooked. Bentley says "*intempestiva sane haec videntur et cum sequentibus pugnant. Nam continuo luctum orditur noster, praecepti istius nimis immemor, Ergo*

Quintilium perpetuus sopor/urget? Quid, quod odiosum est luctui modum ponere" ["These ideas seem badly timed and in conflict with what follows. For immediately the poet marshalls his grief, all too forgetful of his very precept: *ergo Quintilium perpetuus sopor/urget?* What about the fact that it is hateful to set a limit to grief?"], and then goes on to quote from Statius. Bentley, with a simplicity that baffles, assumes here that *pudor* and *modus* in the poem as understood by the scholiast mean for the latter that a sense of shame and a respect for limits would prevent the poet from mourning Quintilius altogether. The scholiast's comment he finds inconsistent with what follows because he construes *modus* as meaning that an end or limit has been put to mourning, not that one may mourn but within limits. As for the statement that *odiosum est luctui modum ponere*, this would run counter to all Horace believed. At *Epistles* I.14.36, Horace says *nec lusisse pudet, sed non incidere ludum;* he would have said here that he found nothing wrong with mourning the loss of a dear friend, but one had to know what limits to respect.

Against those who would suggest that it is in some way perverse composition if we have to read the rest of the poem and then in retrospect reinterpret the first two lines, I would maintain that a poem takes shape in the mind of the poet as a composite entity, but since he must set out in speech or in writing, in space and time, and as it were, in linear form the *Gestalt* which we may imagine to exist in his mind in a *circular* form, we cannot escape seeing one part of the poem before another. The claim for the colouring of an earlier passage by the influence of a later one is therefore quite as justifiable as the impact of an earlier on a later one.

[15]*Donatus scribit Vergilium solitum dicere: nullam virtutem commodiorem homini esse patientia ac nullam fortunam adeo esse asperam, quam prudenter patiendo uir fortis non uincat. Propria igitur sententia ipsum nunc consolatur Horatius* ["Donatus writes that Virgil used to say regularly: no good quality was more suitable for a man than patience, and no situation was so cruel that a strong man could not defeat it by prudent patience. Horace, then, now consoles him with his own saying"].

THE SECRET OF LYDIA'S AGING: HORACE, ODE 1.25

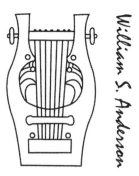

William S. Anderson

The older commentaries on this poem tended to be embarrassed by its bad form in jeering at an old woman who is a failed prostitute. Newer commentaries do not seem to like it any better, but now they patronize it as an obvious pastiche of conventions. We have quite a number of Greco-Roman poems in which a man ridicules an older prostitute and exults in her misery. Nobody should deny the fact that Horace was steeped in the poetry of his predecessors. However, a long tradition has never kept a good poet from composing effective poetry and often it has in fact inspired him to significant modifications and adaptations of the conventions. In this essay, I attempt to show that the prevailing interpretation has misread the conventional verse it cites and therefore failed to see how ingeniously Horace manipulates the dramatic situation he has chosen as his starting point. Lydia is not an old crone, in spite of the speaker's impatience with her: she is quite as attractive to lovers as she was in 1.13 to Telephus, and Horace's speaker, in his jealousy and frustration, is resorting to another attempt at persuasion, which is likely to be as unavailing as the line was in 1.13. He masks his desire behind his intemperate predictions of the future, but what he really wants is for her to open her door and welcome his erotic longings. If you were Lydia, how would you respond? (Ed.)

Readers for two thousand years have tended to accept as fact the statements of the speaker in *Ode* 1.25 and agree that Lydia is already nearly past the age when she can hope to attract men to her bed; that indeed she is very close to the disgusting old age which emerges in lurid detail in the final three stanzas. The scholiast Porphyrio in his commentary of the third century introduces the poem as follows: "This Ode was composed against a greedy prostitute, but one who was already somewhat old and therefore destined to suffer deservedly from lovers the indignities which she once had inflicted."[1] Even though Horace has only recently been entertaining us in *Ode* 1.13 with the unhappy triangular situation of a speaker who miserably views the passionate embraces of Lydia and Telephus and clearly depicts that Lydia as a most desirable companion not only for young (*puer*) Telephus but also for himself, we are apparently to forget that previous poem and its sufficiently youthful and lovely Lydia and to concentrate with complete trust on this speaker's words and his image of this new (that is, elderly) Lydia.

This article appears for the first time in this volume.

What he says is relatively easy to summarize: in the first two stanzas he declares what the present condition of Lydia is, basically an aging and failing prostitute, all her business declining, as the emphatically initial comparative adverb *parcius* (1) and the repeated *minus et minus iam* (6) emphasize; the last three stanzas then proceed to elaborate the pathetic and offensive old age that lies in store for Lydia, with an animosity that hardly befits a gentleman. Accepting the present state as factual and the predicted misery as likely, readers have tended to feel uncomfortable with this poem. Even the modern commentary of Nisbet and Hubbard laments the "inhumanity" of the work.[2] And the commentaries I grew up with were deliberately laconic and embarrassed about the situation and intention of the speaker; indeed I never had a teacher who dared to assign 1.25 to any class I took. We are in a happier new era today.

The other liability that Nisbet and Hubbard attribute to this ode is "conventionalism." By this, they mean the way in which Horace combines a number of Greco-Roman or Hellenistic conventional themes of male lovers when speaking to the women they are pursuing. We can find a short list of Latin passages in the introduction to the poem by Kiessling-Heinze: namely, Ovid, *Ars Amat.* 3.69 ff. and Propertius 3.25.11 ff. Both poems are later than Horace's, so they illustrate the common use of motifs in the confident prediction (Ovid) that old age will reduce the humbled prostitute to misery; or the fervent wish in subjunctive (Propertius) that the cruel woman may become a wrinkled old hag and suffer contempt in her turn. It was Giorgio Pasquali, however, who first fully explored this conventional material in Greek as well as Latin, using the rich resources of Books 5 and 11 of the Palatine Anthology.[3] In Book 5, the editor Planudes combined collections of Meleager (1st century B.C.), Rufinus (uncertain date, but much later), and Agathias (6th century C.E.) about erotic liaisons. Although the earlier poems of Meleager's collections don't provide significant parallels for 1.25, the later ones of Rufinus and Agathias richly document the conventions which Horace has exploited in his ode. In Book 11, Pasquali noted a cycle of epigrams (66–74) which ridicule the ugliness and debased condition of aged prostitutes.

According, then, to Nisbet and Hubbard, "this ode is an elaboration of a traditional motif: the rejected lover tells his beloved that her beauty will fade, and then she will be sorry."[4] Later, having added to the poems cited by Pasquali and listed nine from Book 5 of the Anthology, they comment: "Horace combines these various themes in his usual manner, though without achieving complete consistency....Horace does not even persuade us, as do Catullus and Propertius, that his conventional formulas reflect real feelings. He is simply exhibiting his usual virtuosity in weaving together diverse poetical strands."[5] I do not want to spend time on arguing against their requirement that Horace convey "real feelings" with his conventional material: it will soon be obvious that this ode does not expect us to identify sympathetically with the speaker, and it follows that his feelings indeed are not worth much. But the implication that this ode consists of mere virtuosity in combination demands our attention.

Of the nine poems cited by Nisbet and Hubbard, I shall choose but two to illustrate the range of conventionality. Here is Rufinus in *A.P.* 5.103:

> For how long, Prodice, shall I weep at your door? How long shall I beg on my knees, harsh woman, without being heard? Already white hairs are attacking your head, and soon you will give yourself to me, as Hecuba did to Priam.

And here is Julianus, Prefect of Egypt, in *A.P.* 5.298:

> Charming Maria makes too much of herself. Lady Justice, please go after that boastful arrogance; but not by killing her. On the contrary, let old age come to her hair and let her hard face come to wrinkles. May gray hairs avenge these tears of mine; may her beauty pay the penalty for her soul's error, since it is responsible for that error.[6]

In 5.103, Rufinus sets the stage: his speaker is shut outside the door of Prodice and begging vainly to be let in. After that first couplet of frustration, the man tries his ploys in the second: Prodice, he claims, already has graying hair, and, in a sudden jump to a distant and hyperbolic future, he predicts that "soon" she will be his, but it will be like aged Hecuba with Priam. There is no question of the speaker's situation and motivations: the two couplets go from the lover's rejection directly to his warnings of Prodice's present aging and predictions of drastic decline into the state of the legendary old Hecuba. In *A.P.* 5.298 Julianus' speaker simply declares that Maria acts too big, in three Greek words implying that she spurns him. The remainder of his three couplets is devoted to a curse, which he spells out as gray hairs and wrinkles, old age to undermine her sinful beauty. But he does slide into the last couplet that this will avenge his own tears. So it is not hard to imagine that this speaker is rejected perhaps in the same way as Rufinus': by weeping vainly at Maria's closed door and reacting against her arrogance. Rufinus depicts a man who uses some rhetorical art against his rejection, in the hope of persuading Prodice to avoid that predicted future as long as possible with him; whereas Julianus' speaker immediately resorts to curses that might terrify Maria into compliance. Rejection is the clear beginning of each epigram. Reaction to rejection varies in manner but has the same final goal: to force the girl to submit because of anxiety over the future (predicted or invoked). These and other epigrams exhibit the use of those conventions which Nisbet and Hubbard, following Pasquali, identify.

Now consider the alleged "conventionalism" of Horace's poem. He begins with a speaker whose situation and motivation are not initially declared, in sharp contrast with the clarity of the two epigrams I have cited.

This speaker simply starts suggesting that, comparatively speaking (hence, *parcius* and *minus*), his addressee (identified only in line 8) is suffering a decline in popularity with her former lovers. He seems to be stating facts with his present indicative forms, but why he does so is not apparent. Kiessling and Heinze built up a vividly imaginary situation on the basis of these first two stanzas: "The occasion and situation of this poem become entirely clear only on the presupposition that Lydia once...rejected the poet and now he avenges himself with this insulting song which he sings before her door, the opposite of a paraclausithyron. Only in that way does the citation in 7–8 work with full effectiveness."[7] Their presupposition, however, while no doubt possible, is certainly not our only one, and certainly not the right one for Horace. Nisbet and Hubbard are far more cautious and evasive about the occasion and situation. That the speaker reacts to rejection is assumed. But how these first two stanzas operate is never declared; they only deny that "one is meant to suppose that Horace is lying at the door as he utters the poem."[8] It seem as though they assign the conventional reaction to rejection to the vivid final three stanzas, where the predictions of old age are vigorously deployed.

But the key to the art of Horace, I think, lies in determining how to read the first sentence and then the first two stanzas. Why does Horace make this speaker start off with apparent objectivity about pebbles tossed against another's windows, using this comparative adverb *parcius*, instead of declaring openly and subjectively his personal situation and emotions? Kiessling-Heinze, following the old interpretation of Porphyrio, argued that the speaker was gloatingly comparing the failed present with the once-successful past of Lydia (when she had spurned him). Nothing in Nisbet and Hubbard corrects that view of the temporal situation. But if they had grasped the argument of the very poem *A.P.* 5.103, which they and I have cited, they might have suspected that Horace's speaker is in the responsive mood from the start, like Prodice's victim, who tries to remind her that "already" (= Horace's *iam* 6) she has begun to have her hair turn white, in his ingenious desperation at the very time she is keeping her door closed to him. The speed with which Rufinus lets his frustrated lover talk about the white hair of the woman he tries to seduce, then rush on to the decrepit old age of Hecuba, shows up his argument in a comic fashion. He is simply lying (or vastly exaggerating) about Prodice's present decline. And the same is the case for the Horatian speaker. What he claims to be "now" is a part of his self-serving argument of persuasion: the comparatives are invalid; the real and true present is the cruel fact that Lydia has the power now to reject him, and that most definitely implies that she is entertaining someone else quite lovingly and profitably at the very moment this speaker so cleverly (but vainly) plays fast and loose with the actuality of what he asserts.

If Horace's speaker is, as I suggest, reacting to rejection as of his first reported words and therefore resorting to some of the stereotyped response patterns, we need to locate the moment when he reveals that he has been or is being spurned. The first sentence, which continues into line 6, makes observations about the house where the as yet unnamed woman addressed resides: we hear about its shuttered windows and its door and the lusty young men who do or do not hang around the place. Where does this familiarity with this house come from? The second sentence (6–8) introduces a speech which supposedly Lydia hears less and less often these nights: "Are you sleeping while I, your devoted lover, am dying outside here in the cold [and the damp—if we add rain to the scenario]?" But this is a brilliant instance of the rhetorical device of *praeteritio*: what she rarely hears, Lydia—and we in the audience with her—is made to hear by this speaker, who rehearses the standard complaints of the excluded lover at the closed doors of his beloved. The pathos (or bathos) of this speech, the naming of Lydia, and the lover's plea that he belongs to Lydia (*me tuo*) imply the speaker's personal identification with its words. He is, I believe, reciting his own appeal and documenting his own rejection. That she hears such words less often now, is comic nonsense. That he complains of her sleeping just after claiming that she is getting more sleep (3) than she wants; that he laments being shut outside the closed doors just after claiming that her "door loves its lintel" (3–4), shows up his inconsistency. Thus, in these first two stanzas, Horace has projected his speaker into a conventional situation, but he has done so with an inversion of the normal dramatic order that invites the audience to discover and re-adjust the order and to determine its attitude towards this speaker.

The present indicatives, shaded by the comparative adjectives or the facile comparisons with an earlier time (imperfect *movebat* 5), are exposed as argumentative claims. They speak slyly of a time that will no doubt be coming, using the presents to make it more threatening and useful to the speaker. But the true present situation is inevitably betrayed by his predicament as an excluded lover: he is excluded because Lydia has another lover in her bed at this very minute. She intends her door to be shut, "loving" its lintel as she loves her companion, her shutters remain "joined" as she and her lover are joined in passionate embrace; and the rivalry between the successful lover and this unsuccessful speaker provides solid evidence that this courtesan is doing quite well, thank you, with no gray hairs or wrinkles, not likely to be deterred by the self-interested spiel of the excluded speaker. She is definitely not the aged courtesan that Porphyrio and subsequent commentators into the twentieth century have imagined. In short, she is essentially the same Lydia that Horace presented in 1.13; and the speaker is in much the same disadvantage of a triangular situation, trying to argue his way into an advantage that, as far as we in the audience can see, he is not likely to achieve.

If Horace has used the first two stanzas to clarify the true situation of this speaker as an excluded lover, who tries to sound reasonable and factual as a rhetorical cover for his deceptive self-serving, what is the purpose of the longer ending of the ode, stanzas three to five? It begins with the important words *in vicem* (9), which establish a close link to the cited speech of 7–8.[9] In return, in punishment for excluding our speaker, he now launches into one long sentence of grim, confident prediction that consists of stanza 3, a future clause (*flebis*) supported by an ablative absolute clause also implicitly in the future; stanza 4, a *cum*-temporal clause in the future with its own relative clause; and stanza 5, two *quod*-causal clauses in the present subjunctive, which makes them part of her predicted complaint (*questu* 16). We can of course say with Pasquali and Nisbet-Hubbard, but *a fortiori* after our analysis of the first two stanzas, that the rejected lover goes over very familiar and conventional ground in foretelling the inevitable old age of the courtesan. He has moved from one fairly useful argument to the council of desperation, to prophesy the change of a currently attractive and desirable courtesan into a hag (*anus* 9) in an unspecified future. No doubt, he is telling Lydia that she will be sorry, and the details of his prediction are so vivid and inhumane that the audience has a hard time with them and with the character of the speaker who could voice them with such apparent gusto.

Notice, however, the pattern of the details that the speaker marshalls for his prediction. Not a single physical item about this future old hag, none of the conventional elements of gray or white hair, wrinkles, and studying one's loss of beauty helplessly in the mirror. What occurs to this prophetic speaker is that indeed there will be a reversal (*invicem*): the status of the excluded lover, which I have argued reveals the humiliated position of the speaker as he is in the act of trying to persuade Lydia to relent and let him inside her house, will some day, he confidently asserts, become hers as punishment for her present arrogant cruelty. Although he is not so sure of himself to foresee that Lydia will come crawling to *his* home and *he* will reject her, he does imagine that she will vainly hang around alleys at night and solicit young men and be contemptuously spurned by them. The howling wind, which often forms part of the scenario of the excluded lover (as in Horace's Ode 3.10.5–8) and so might be assumed for this situation, will be suffered by Lydia. That accounts for the detail of stanza three.

The next portion of the prediction, which forms stanza four, attributes to Lydia, in that wretched future old age, burning lust in lurid terms. The speaker doubles his nouns *amor et libido*, then compares the notorious violence of mares in heat, and imagines that all this multiplied passion will rage in her ulcerated liver. Where did we last encounter a burning liver? Why, back in 1.13.4, when the unhappy speaker was describing his own symptoms of jealousy at Lydia's preference for Telephus. So again in this stanza the detail is simply transferred, but angrily magnified, from the speaker's experience of frustration. Mares may indeed be proverbially lusty when in heat, but stallions are even more proverbial for sexual desire, and at all times. Again, then, the reference to the mare suggests the current status of the speaker as an over-excited stallion. He is wishing for Lydia the same suffering that he is now enduring.

Stanza four ends with the introduction of the "complaint" (*questu* 16) which, in indirect form, will form the contents of stanza five. It is a curious lament, all detail turned into symbols about the separate associations of youth and old age. Youth is happy and takes pleasure in green ivy; old age is the dark myrtle and dried leaves, destined to be blown about by the winter wind. I think it odd that this contrast between youth and age is genderless and accordingly general enough to apply to the speaker as well as Lydia whom he addresses. It is as if he knows personally the humiliation of being rejected as too old and, in his prediction of her complaint, voices his own. The Horatian lover that we have met in 1.5 and more recently 1.13 regularly finds himself frustrated by the girl's preference for a lover whom he labels as *puer*. Thus, in the final stanza, this speaker summarizes the plight of the aging lover with a poetic sympathy that both alludes to his own unhappiness and closes the poem with what I would call, in contrast to Nisbet and Hubbard, a poignant humanity. We can all respond to that.[10]

With this interpretation, then, the puzzling problem of how Lydia grew so old and desperate in the space of a few lines between *Odes* 13 and 25 is solved. She did not grow old at all. The speaker has merely been reduced to a different series of ploys, equally unsuccessful, to gain her sympathetic attention. Though he admits none of her attractions, we can infer them from his desperation. He neither gains her sympathy nor ours, for the exploitative male perspective that Horace represents cannot work with her and is not meant to work with us in the audience. The lies that men tell to win domination over females, when exposed in all their ugliness, as Horace (and later Ovid) tend to do, alienate.

Notes

[1]"Haec ode in meretricem rapacem, sed iam vetulam, et merito ab amatoribus passuram, quae fecerat, scripta est."

[2]N.-H. p. 292.

[3]G. Pasquali, *Orazio lirico: Studi*, (Florence, 1920), pp. 441 ff.

[4]N.-H. p. 289.

[5]N.-H. p. 291.

[6]I have modernized the Loeb translations.

[7]Anlass und Situation unseres Gedichtes wird völlig klar erst unter der Voraussetzung, das Lydia einst...den Dichter verschmäht hat und er sich nun durch dies vor ihrer Tür gesungene Hohnlied, das Gegenstück eines *paraklausithyron*, rächt: erst so wirkt auch das Zitat v. 7fg. mit voller Lebendigkeit." Introduction to 1.25.

[8]K.-H. p. 291. They go on to stress "the unreality of the situation."

[9]Kiessling-Heinze realized this, but drew the wrong conclusion about the situation.

[10]Ronnie Ancona, in her fine chapter on this poem, "The Temporal Adverb," *Time and the Erotic in Horace's Odes* (Duke University Press, 1994), argues that the speaker's male gender does slant this ending, and so he insists that, for a woman, temporality and eroticism cannot be joined. On which she astutely comments: "There is no reason that we must share such privileging." (p. 30)

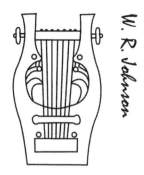

W. R. Johnson

A QUEAN, A GREAT QUEEN? CLEOPATRA
AND THE POLITICS OF MISREPRESENTATION

The Battle of Actium in September, 31 B.C. was a turning point in Roman history: it brought defeat to the efforts of Antony to use the forces of the East and win mastery of the Roman world from Octavian (soon to be Augustus). He withdrew to Egypt with his beloved Cleopatra and waited for the inevitable arrival in force of the Roman navy and army. It came the following Spring, and the demand for unconditional surrender seems to have driven both lovers to suicide, possibly with the complete co-operation of Octavian, who might have found them awkward alive. Horace's poem adopts the occasion of the arrival of the news in Rome, which is greeted first by frenzied nationalistic celebrations and wild patriotic insults for the defeated and dead Queen of Egypt. Then, there is a sudden shift in tone, in the course of the simile of 17–21, and thereafter Cleopatra becomes a heroine who, some believe, becomes worthy of her Roman conqueror and, others believe, actually triumphs in the grandeur of her chosen end.

In his essay, Johnson explores the world of propaganda, with which we have much experience today, and he suggests that Horace did the same. Few people were actually certain of how or why Cleopatra died; Horace may well not have known for sure. But in Johnson's view, his primary interest lay in exposing the clash of two prevailing strands of Octavian's propaganda that had been developed for Roman consumption. In the first, Cleopatra was a besotted barbarian enemy, a major threat to the survival of Rome. (Note how he avoids the slightest allusion to Antony.) Then, in defeat, the time of which the poet carefully foreshortens, making his swift transition in that simile, he picks up that other strand of propaganda, which developed after the mysterious circumstances of her death (murder? forced suicide? nobly chosen suicide?) and recites in all seriousness the incredible, unexplained conversion of the hated barbarian into virtually a heroic Roman matron like Lucretia, who kills herself to preserve her integrity. That story served the purposes of the future Augustus, suggests Johnson, more than it did the memory of Cleopatra. But it is the clash between those two public versions of Cleopatra that Horace emphasizes, that and the pernicious ways of propaganda in distorting the truth. (Ed.)

> The true history of Antony and Cleopatra will probably never be known; it is buried too deep beneath the version of the victor.
>
> Tarn

> Voici Tarse, où l'attend le guerrier désarmé;
> Et la brune Lagide ouvre dans l'air charmé
> ses bras d'ambre où la pourpre a mis des reflets roses;

This essay first appeared in *Arion* 6 (1967) 388–402 and is reprinted here with permission of the author.

Et ses yeux n'ont pas vu, présage de son sort,
Auprès d'elle, effeuillant sur l'eau sombre des roses,
Les deux enfants divins, le Désir et la Mort.

["Here is Tarsus, where the disarmed warrior waits;
and brown Cleopatra opens into the charmed air
her amber arms that reflect in rose her royal purple;
her eyes have not seen, omen of her fate,
near her, brushing over the dark water of the roses,
those two divine children, Desire and Death."]

*L*ovely as they are in their Vergilian echo and in their Vergilian cadences, these verses of Heredia's are thoroughly grounded in *topoi* which Augustus devised and which Horace gilded with great poetry. *Le Désir et la Mort,* the alcoholic slut turned Stoic saint? Was there no more to Cleopatra than that? We cannot, of course, produce a real Cleopatra, for Augustan propaganda, the ravage of time, and the limitations of history have done their work well, but we can, with the aid of Tarn and Volkmann,[1] catch brief yet vivid glimpses of the great Macedonian princess, a politician shrewd at her worst and brilliant at her best, witty, intellectual, disciplined, very imaginative and rather realistic, worthy of the Ptolemaic line, more an Elizabeth I than a Marie Antoinette or even a Mary Queen of Scots. Such a woman could hardly find a place in Augustus' own version of Octavian's "res gestae," and so, not surprisingly, found no place in Augustan history, and in Augustan poetry found only a subtle, shifting reflection: in Vergil alone is Cleopatra possessed of anything like her real vigor and intensity, for the verses which form the climax of *Aeneid* 8 rightly center on a clash of cultures and religions in which Alexandria, that peculiar blend of erratic, hard-pressed but vigorous political acumen and of fine spirituality, lights up the triumph of Octavian and his Rome.

Since the essential power and brilliance of Alexandria and its queen have no more place in Horace's ode than they have in Propertius' strange pasquinade on Augustus, and since I therefore cannot concur with Commager's belief in Horace's "genius for weaving history into a poem's essential structure" or his "alchemy of history,"[2] I suggest that we can only account for the absence of the real Cleopatra from 1.37 either by supposing that Horace was the dupe of Augustus' propaganda or its willing or hesitant minister or by discovering even in this ode the ironic detachment and the profound striving for oxymoron which are of the essence for Horace's lyric genius and which Commager himself has brilliantly defined.[3]

We need not much bother with the opening cliché (6–15); Cleopatra's drunkenness, like her equally notorious fondness for sexual amusement, is merely perhaps a matter of fact and perhaps not, and we have no way of knowing which it is. The great, even the great whose real *idée fixe* is power and its manipulation, can afford to indulge their thirst and lechery as they choose; on the other hand, anyone who remembers Cicero's speeches will know that charges of habitual intoxication and unbridled lubricity are standard formulas for the ancient propagandist. We had best suppose that Cleopatra was *une femme moyenne sensuelle* ["an average sensual female"], and read the first cliché as jingoistic hyperbole-synecdoche, i.e., another of Octavian's lies. In any case, at 16 the crapulent wanton flees, and her flight provokes a stanza which, for metaphysical wit, has few equals in Donne or even in Herbert:

> ...remis adurgens, accipiter velut
> mollis columbas aut leporem citus
>   venator in campis nivalis
>   Haemoniae, daret ut catenis....

> ...he hastened after her with flailing oars, he was like a hawk that falls on delicate doves or like a huntsman who sprints after a hare through the snowy wastes of Thessaly, determined to load the awesome fiend with chains....

Horace dismisses what must have been to his contemporaries the most decisive battle since Salamis and Zama in a line ("vix una sospes navis ab ignibus" — hardly a ship got away from the battle seaworthy), then converts victor to hawk and hunter, victim to dove and hare. The similes function in three ways: they define Octavian's determination and Cleopatra's cowardice, treachery and despair; they prepare (after a fashion) for the transformation from wine-sodden ogre to royal masochist by distracting us with emblems of pathos from the matter at hand; finally, "remis adurgens" (oar-wing-hawk) by its fine velocity cheats even those of us who know better into thinking that Octavian chased Cleopatra straight from Actium to Alexandria, that nearly a year did *not* elapse between Actium and the asp. The foam that churns beneath the desperate oars of pursuer and pursued becomes Thessalian snow, hawk becomes hunter and dove becomes hare till a single standard epinician motif ("daret ut catenis") propagates beautiful and utterly false oxymora: Caesar-hawk-hunter-hero; Cleopatra-"regina demens"-dove-hare-wicked dragon—"quae generosius"![4] *Stimmungsbruch* ["break in tone"], Cromwell and Charles I, a double epinician, then, in which nobody loses? It is all very tidy, it is all very noble, satisfying and uplifting; unfortunately it seems not to be true, and I doubt very much that Horace thought it was true.[5]

The barbaric whore has disappeared into the fine legerdemain of hawk and dove, sea, sky and snowy expanse and has reappeared chastened, sober and virtuous. What in fact was she doing while our gaze was fastened on those strange, enchanting likenesses? Tarn, I think, can tell us better than anyone else:[6]

> Though Antony was broken by the catastrophe of Actium, Cleopatra was not. She sailed into the harbour of Alexandria with

head erect and ships garlanded for victory; it gave her the few hours she needed, and she seized and executed all who might have raised a revolution against her....[She] began to make plans; they might set sail to Spain, seize the silver mines and play Sertorius; they might find a new realm in the Indian seas, beyond the reach of Rome. This was feasible enough, and she drew some ships over the isthmus to Heroônopolis; but Malchus joyfully attacked and burned them....Cleopatra had to decide whether she would defend Egypt by herself; she faced the situation with her usual courage. After her two bids for supreme power she was again what she had been at the start, a client-queen of Rome. That she must lose her throne, if not her life, she knew. But if she fought, her children would fall with her, for the result was certain; if however she acted as client-kings did in such circumstances...and put her crown in Octavian's hands, there was a chance that he might follow the Roman custom and give it to one of her sons.

For Wurzel[7] the undaunted activity that Tarn here describes, the plots and counterplots, the profound, single-minded striving to secure the house of Lagus, the embassies to Octavian,[8] are nothing more than "gehässige und herabwürdigende Gerüchte" ["hateful and demeaning rumors"]. Why we should be asked to assume that behavior which is both natural to and worthy of a great queen had no existence but in malicious gossip, I fail to understand. As a matter of fact, Cleopatra's resourcefulness and spirit during the year after Actium were not part of the tradition which was hostile to her, and the hostile tradition, so far as we can tell, suppressed the tale of her real courage and ingenuity.[9] Velleius, having dealt with Actium in 2.85, devotes 86 to a discussion of Octavian's clemency and begins 87 in this way:

> Proximo deinde anno persecutus reginam Antoniumque Alexandriam, ultimam bellis civilibus imposuit manum.

> Then in the next year he followed the queen and Antony to Alexandria and put the finishing touches to his work of ending the civil war that had raged for decades.

Though the fact that the *periocha* for Livy 133 bears no trace of his having discussed Cleopatra's activities after Actium does not mean that Livy did not treat of them, it should be remarked that Florus ignores them. Our chief sources of information on this subject, Plutarch and Dio, seem to use traditions that were favorable to Cleopatra as well as traditions that were hostile to her, and it seems likely that, whereas Augustus would be anxious to minimize not only his own Machiavellism against Cleopatra after Actium but her vigorous if hopeless parrying as well, her partisans would be anxious to celebrate her pertinacity, her ingenuity and her devotion to her line and her country.

For what emerges from the romantic filigrees of both Plutarch and Dio is a story that, for the most part, does more credit to Cleopatra than to Octavian. Cleopatra's only concerns in the last year of her life were to thwart Octavian as long as she possibly could and to secure Egypt's throne for her children, to assure that the house of Lagus should continue. Whatever we may make of the Cleopatra prophecy and of Tarn's notion that Cleopatra, of all her line, most nearly resembled Alexander in temperament, talent and ambition,[10] it is fairly clear that Cleopatra sought to restore and at times came rather close to restoring the fortunes of the Ptolemies, that her plans to use Rome to free Egypt from Rome, with Caesar, then with Antony, to divide, conquer and rule the Mediterranean world, were at once daring and (despite the outcome) by no means impracticable, that her will and courage were proof against brutal reversals. Yet if she refused to surrender her grand design after Caesar was murdered, if she was patient while Antony doomed his hopes (and hers, but she could not know that) in paltering and temporizing, if she waited his return to Alexandria to seize her last and greatest opportunity, if even Actium could not subdue her spirit and her cunning, her finest hour came when all but the last of her cards were played, when she could only bluff, and so bluffed magnificently.

She could not rule the world, but she was determined that her children should rule Egypt. Octavian desperately needed money, and Cleopatra was prepared to purchase the crown of Egypt for her line with "the last great accumulation of wealth in the ancient world."[11] For his part Octavian was terrified that Cleopatra would remove the treasure of the Ptolemies beyond his grasp, and, when he had succeeded in destroying the fleet that was to have escaped with the treasure, he was unnerved to learn that she had gathered her wealth into the Mausoleum and purposed to burn it if and when he should take Alexandria. The year after Actium, then, shows deft games of cat-and-mouse and treasure-hunt, embassies to and fro, cryptic offers and cryptic counter-offers, Cleopatra's skilled but desperate bargaining and Octavian's familiar poker face.[12]

This part of the story ended only when Proculeius succeeded in taking possession of the Mausoleum, when Cleopatra attempted to stab herself (*"nec expavit ensem"* — she did not pale at the thought of a dagger) — and when Octavian, the wealth of the Ptolemies intact, sighed with relief. He does not cut a particularly handsome figure, this victorious imperator dangling on the string of a clever, frightened woman: it is the stuff neither of high poetry nor official versions. "Nec latentis / classe cita reparavit oras?" — Nor did she sail swiftly away, seeking refuge in some distant, impenetrable country. No, but she tried to, and we may wonder why the story of her attempt and her failure and of Octavian's considerable discomfiture is buried away beneath an explicit denial of the truth. "Her expression untroubled and calm," *vultu sereno*? There seems to have been no real failure of nerve until Proculeius broke into the Mausoleum, but at no time during the year after Actium was Cleopatra possessed of the chilling, regal resolve to die *à la mode sidonienne* ["in the Sidonian manner"], "et nunc magna mei sub terras ibit imago" — and now I shall take with me to Hell's darkness this radiant phantom of greatness — which the closing stanza of Horace's ode has unalterably fastened in our memories. There was no such resolve because, even had she been a Cato in petticoats, there could be none until Cleopatra admitted to total defeat, and her spirit and her intelligence were such that she did not make that admission (if she ever made it) until she had been irretrievably forced into a corner. Until the moment that Octavian had got control of Alexandria, the treasure and herself, her maneuvering, however nervous, however anxious, was supple, tough and inventive: *sereno* is hardly the word.[13] It is this resilience and imagination as well as this tenacity of the year after Actium, not the jeweled despair and the haughty, grandiose tableau with which we are familiar from Horace, Plutarch and Shakespeare, that bespeak the great queen. The traditional gouache, all shimmering fin-de-siècle silk, ivory and emerald, smacks rather of Firbank at work on the last chapter of a book on Oscar Wilde.

Volkmann on this point ignores Tarn and approves the poetic image wholly, "all passion spent":[14]

> The contributions of human beings to history, and our final verdict on them, are certainly not dependent on the success of their efforts. Rather, their value is determined by the way in which they grasp and endure their fortune. Cleopatra's opponents were already passing judgment on her according to this standard. After her death Octavian himself acknowledged her noble bearing with admiration; and the poet Horace found the appropriate words for her greatness: "non humilis mulier," "a woman of mighty spirit."

Well, it was indeed a shrewd stratagem to focus on the manner of her death (rather than on the quality of her life), to fabricate and do homage to a splendid failure: such fabrication and such homage distract us from her real greatness, her real problems, and, of course, from the problems Octavian did not care to see clarified. Let us recall how she "grasped and endured" her fortune.

This is precisely what we cannot do, because, as Plutarch candidly admits in discussing the circumstances of her death, nobody knows what really happened.[15] The notion that Octavian simply had Cleopatra murdered has been emphatically rejected,[16] but it has at least the merit of drawing our attention to the dilemma that confronted Octavian when he finally had Cleopatra in his power. Stähelin, Groag and Tarn[17] all argue persuasively that a live Cleopatra represented a very real and very hopeless problem for Octavian. The populace might be ferocious in its desire to enjoy the spectacle of its most savage enemy (since Hannibal) being led in triumph, but Octavian was not one to confuse symbols with realities, and though he knew how to stage a spectacle it is clear that he was never (unless, perhaps, towards the end) a victim of the illusions he engineered. Could he

send her to be slaughtered when the procession had ended and the costumes and props were being packed away, she, the mistress of his "father"? Would her presence, even as a captive in the ritual of triumph, revive and magnify unwelcome memories of the days when Julius and
Cleopatra were lovers, allies and rulers of mankind? Could she be safely
committed to exile and obscurity? Did she not know too much, perhaps
more than anyone else, of secrets of statecraft which Octavian hoped to
scatter to oblivion? "His problem was to induce her to kill herself in such a
way that he could not be blamed."[18] Or, more precisely, in such a way that
he could not be blamed for having driven her to death and could not be
blamed for having failed to provide his people with the sight they most
wanted to see. We know no more of the first and only interview between
victor and vanquished (if there was one) than we know of the asp or poisoned hairpin or dagger that rescued Cleopatra from utter despair and
Octavian from embarrassment. However she died, whatever motive or
threat or wan hope impelled her to suicide (if it was, strictly speaking,
suicide), the asp, whether introduced in a basket of memorably beautiful
figs or sequestered in a water jar, rapidly and conveniently became part of
the official version, and it was not by accident that the statue of Cleopatra
which was carried in the procession was, apparently, decorated with an
asp or two.[19]

But the myth of the asp and of Octavian's haste in summoning the
Psylli to suck out the asp's venom before it was clear that asps were at all
in question[20] is hardly less curious than Octavian's response to Cleopatra's
death. We have grown accustomed to supposing that *non humilis mulier*
represents Horace's unique, deeply personal, possibly even courageous
protest against the slander of a great and noble lady. But it is at least possible that *non humilis mulier* is no less a part of Octavian's propaganda than
the wine-bibber and her asp. Both Plutarch and Dio record Octavian's gal-
lantry with hushed tones: "Although he was deeply annoyed at Cleopatra's
suicide, Caesar marveled at her good breeding, and accordingly he or-
dered that she be buried alongside Antony with royal splendor and pomp"
(Plutarch, *Ant.* 86.4); "For all his efforts Caesar was unable to effect her
resurrection, but he marveled at her and pitied her too, deeply pained
though he was at having been thus deprived of his triumph's crowning
glory" (Dio, 51.14.6). Though the *non humilis mulier* cliché and Octavian's
response to it are juxtaposed only by Plutarch and Dio, traces of such an
intricate pattern may perhaps be seen in Livy (Pseudoacronius):

> Augusto invidens, ne captivitas sua illi speciosiorem faceret
> triumphum. nam et Livius refert Cleopatram, cum de industria
> ab Augusto capta indulgentius tracteretur, dicere solitam: Non
> triumphabor.

> Begrudging Augustus the full glory of his triumph (for she rightly
> guessed that her absence from it would impair its magnificence).

Livy reports that Cleopatra, although Augustus had treated her with the greatest possible consideration, kept repeating, "I will not march in his triumph!"

In the *periocha* for Livy 133:

After Alexandria had been taken and Cleopatra had killed herself ("voluntaria morte defuncta") rather than live or die as her conqueror might choose ("ne in arbitrium victoris veniret"), Caesar returned to Rome and celebrated a triple triumph.

"Non triumphabor, invidens" and "ne in arbitrium victoris veniret" represent the *non humilis mulier* cliché as does Velleius' pronouncement at 2.87.1:

At Cleopatra frustratis custodibus inlata aspide in morsu et sanie eius expers muliebris metus spiritum reddidit.

But Cleopatra cheated the vigilance of her guards, procured herself an asp and by its venomous bite (for she scorned the squeamishness of her sex) contrived to die.

Though "de industria...indulgentius tracteretur" is perhaps no more than a way of excusing Octavian's carelessness in allowing Cleopatra to commit suicide (he had, after all, to keep her in good spirits to get her to Rome, but, ingrate that she was, she took advantage of his kindness), "voluntaria morte" may perhaps be thought to have strange overtones: Velleius emphasizes the fact that both Antony and Cleopatra did away with themselves voluntarily and fervently praises Octavian's *clementia* in this matter. Keeping Velleius' admiration on this point in mind and remembering Suetonius' remarks on Antony's suicide ("Antony tried to sue for peace at the last minute, but Caesar saw to it that he killed himself [or died], 'ad mortem adegit,' and viewed the corpse, 'viditque mortuum'," 17.7), we may wonder if there were not vicious rumors that needed smothering. In any case, even Suetonius relates the story of Octavian's great gesture of magnanimity (her magnanimity — his wonder at her magnanimity — his greater magnanimity in response to his wonder at her great magnanimity): "He accorded them the tribute of double interment [ambobus communem sepulturae honorem tribuit] and, since they had not had time to do it themselves, saw to it that the Mausoleum was completed [tumulum ab ipsis incohatum perfici iussit]": a handsome gesture, this finishing touch.

We might suppose that Horace's ode is the source of this part of the myth, that Horace's own admiration for the *non humilis mulier* was transferred to Augustus by his historians (or lifted by Augustus himself), that this admiration engendered the story of "communis sepulturae honor." But it is unlikely that the magnificent tomb (and the tribute of which it is emblematic) was created out of thin air, and I think it probable that

Octavian's magnanimous gesture in providing his victims with the tomb and its honor was real and is to be connected with his bogus awe at the fabulous resolve and fortitude of a woman who was in fact by the time she died (however she died) trapped in a despair that rendered resolve, fortitude and magnanimity less than shadows. If she killed herself, she did so not out of pride, Olympian scorn and courage, but out of bitter and irretrievable despair. It is not improbable, then, that the wonder and pity of it all may have found some place in Augustus' autobiography, that the victor's clemency, fair-mindedness and sheer good manners may have been decorously celebrated by the victor himself.

Public opinion wanted Cleopatra in the triumph, convention and *Realpolitik* demanded that she be in the triumph, and, accordingly, the victor was publicly grieved when the finest plume in his war-bonnet was snatched from him. But how to mollify and gratify a public opinion no less grieved? — Take a desperate woman with her back to the wall, invent a melodramatic suicide for her, a bold lady, splendid even (or especially) in ruin, worthy to have marched, certainly, in the most magnificent of triumphal processions, whose vehement refusal to participate in that procession magnifies it, of course, as her presence in it (even if it were otherwise acceptable) probably would not. Publicize our own wonder at this incredibly great woman so as to magnify her response to our own greater incredible greatness. A suitably dramatic plastic representation of her can be found for the procession — perhaps one of those cult statues which depict her as the new goddess with her snakes. So, as usual, all the difficulties are crushed, evaded or turned to our advantage, and all that is really necessary is scrupulously secured.

What then of Horace's ode? If this view of Cleopatra's death were correct, what should we say of Horace as "alchemist of history"? That he was a dupe or party-hack? Or that he was, here as elsewhere, a deceptively genial critic of the idols of the market place no less than of the idols of the cave, the tribe and the theater? Vergil eschewed both *le désir et la mort*[21] to concentrate on the new Isis and her ferocious challenge to Rome: the central panel of that elaborate, ironic, fateful shield consists of brilliant emblems of Cleopatra's genius and the greatness of Alexander's own city. Ignoring *la mort*, at least insofar as *la mort* is informed by the *non humilis mulier* cliché, Propertius also pays handsome if oblique homage to Cleopatra by making her the definitive exemplum in a small erotic joke which ends as flippant panegyric on Augustus.[22] Horace defines both clichés with the utmost elegance and verve, then sets them both in motion to watch them collide and shatter. A mindless harlot might well end as a paragon of all that is best in a solid, stolid Roman matron, but we want perhaps, if we are to be persuaded by such a metamorphosis, something more in the way of transition: the trembling dove and the frightened rabbit are not for this purpose entirely adequate. The Macedonian princess, the protégée and the instructress of Julius, the vivacious bluestocking, the arrogant, ambitious and extremely competent queen who snubbed Cicero because he tried to treat a reigning monarch and a goddess as his peer, Tarn's creature—any of these ladies would have sufficed to explain how one cliché might cancel out the other. But none of these ladies is in evidence, for this poem is not Cleopatra's.

Instead we have two antithetical oversimplifications in deft and casual juxtaposition, two melodramatic caricatures, and *Stimmungsbruch*; we have skepticism, oxymoron, a suave and ruthless mockery. Since it is uncertain which moods Horace meant or did not mean, Commager's suggestions about the ode's "double moral commitment"[23] seem to me rather uncertain. Need we believe, can we clearly know, that the ode is about what Horace felt about Actium and Cleopatra's death? Is it not also possible that the ode describes what Horace felt about other people's feeling on these matters? We need not believe this alternative, we certainly cannot know that it is clearly correct, but it seems, in many ways, as valid as its alternate. Suppose both moods are not expressions of Horace's own moods but caricatures of moods he happens to distrust? This would not necessarily mean that he despised the moods and opinions of other people; it might mean that he had, as poets often have, an unusual insight into the velleities, inaccuracy and terrible power of human moods and human opinions.

Allowing for various intentional fallacies, we may allow that Horace sometimes does not mean what he says or say what he means, that when *Stimmungsbruch* and oxymoron are in evidence we must be prepared for anything from complex poignance to sheer drollery, we must be prepared for a shredding of pathos and a scrambling of high seriousness and low fun:

cur heu, Ligurine, cur
manat rara meas lacrima per genas?

Why, dear boy, o why do occasional tears glisten down my cheek?

Here if anywhere is *Stimmungsbruch*, and oxymoron ("dure, volubilis") knots it firmly. Commager snatches up the wit of the penultimate stanza only to let it loose in the ultimate: "The overwhelming sensuousness of the final image irretrievably banishes not only Horace's earlier excuses but the atmosphere of stylized complaint as well."[24] But "irretrievably banishes" does not allow for the possibility that for some readers of *Carmina* 4.1 the mockery of "cur heu, Ligurine, cur" endures, strengthens and is strengthened by this clear-eyed, clear-voiced final sensuousness. *Volubilis*? Horace does not, for the swiftness of the quarry and the wildness of the course, catch what he chases (nor, apparently, does he, will he ever, desist from the chase): the ode, in some sense, has no stop. In the limitless expanse of reality and our consciousness of it, in the endless shifting of minds and hearts, there are neither finalities nor simple questions and answers—there are desires, regrets, oxymora and skepticism. When our dearest clichés have been broken, and, as the fragments of our *idée reçues* flutter off, we come smack against *rerum concordia discors,* our imaginations are set free, we breathe clean air: the function of Horatian lyric is disenchantment.

It seems to me rather unlikely that poets whose minds and hearts were nourished in large measure on the greatness of Alexandria would easily have lent credence to the notion that Alexandria's queen was a barbarian, that a woman who had schemed so brilliantly was, or was nothing more than, a wine-swiller. Nor, however little they may have known of state secrets, however uncertain they may have been in the swirl of rumors after Actium, would these poets necessarily have been persuaded by the pious tableau which was staged to account both for Cleopatra's death and Octavian's complex but most honorable response to that death.

Second-raters may dabble with jingoism, but poets of the first rank tend to approach the clichés of their time with deep skepticism, nor is it peculiar that men whose chief business it is to handle and arrange images, likenesses and correspondences should be especially sensitive to half-truth, innuendo and shameless falsehood, nor is it peculiar that they should revere truth. The great Augustan poets were to a man sensitive to the ambiguities and vices of their age, and if they did not rebel against them or try to over-turn them (only Ovid did that), they nevertheless admonished them sternly; like good poets of any age, they wrote to exalt *to kalon* ["true virtue"] and to suggest that much or most of what their age demanded was irrelevant or boring or vicious. I suggest, then, this possibility: when Horace came to view the images of Cleopatra which had been designed to pass for the truth about her, he responded by writing an indictment of propaganda; he neither believed nor condoned nor constructed the lies he treated of; he ridiculed and dismissed them.[25]

Notes

[1]W. W. Tarn, *CAH* 10, ch. 3,106ff; H. Volkmann, *Cleopatra: A Study in Politics and Propaganda,* tr. T. J. Cadoux (London 1958).

[2]S. Commager, *The Odes of Horace* (New Haven, 1962) 88, 94.

[3]*Ibid.,* 116.

[4]"Quae generosius perire quaerens" has at least two meanings: (1) "seeking to die nobly rather than to die (or live) ignobly;" (2) "seeking to die more nobly than she had lived." I prefer the second because it seems to be related to Octavian's public expressions of awe ("thauma," "monstrum") — I should never have thought she had it in her to behave like a real aristocrat; the second also provides some sort of bridge between mere drunkard and regenerate drunkard.

[5]Commager, 93, rejects too lightly Wickham's notions that Cleopatra's glory is designed to reflect on and magnify Augustus' glory. What Wickham (and Augustus) had in mind may be seen in Quintilian's discussion of *amplificatio* at 8.4.9 and 8.4.20.

[6]Tarn, 106–07.

[7]F. Wurzel, *Der Krieg gegen Antonius und Kleopatra in der Darstellung der augusteischen Dichter,* Diss. (Borna-Leipzig 1941) 20.

[8]Tarn, 107; Volkmann, 195. Plutarch, *Ant.* 72–73; Dio, 51.6.4, 8.1, 8.2 (three embassies to Plutarch's one: for the discrepancy see T. Rice Holmes, *The Architect of the Roman Empire* I [Oxford 1928] 166).

[9]See Volkmann, 220ff, for a discussion of the ancient sources.

[10]Tarn, 82–83. It may be objected that it was naive of Cleopatra to suppose that Octavian would allow Ptolemies to continue to sit on Egypt's throne, but Octavian seems to have hinted that he was entertaining her suggestions (see n.12 below). In any case, she had nothing left to hope for, and as long as Octavian was not in possession of her wealth she had, or thought she had, something to bargain with. See Volkmann, 193–94.

[11]Tarn, 107–08; Volkmnnn, 189–90, 195–96, 210. This tradition is emphatic in Plutarch, 74.2, 78.3, and in Dio, 11.3, 13.1.

[12]For Volkmann, 195, Octavian turned the embassies into "a clever game designed to wear down the morale of his opponents." Plutarch, 74.2: "As he approached Alexandria with his army, he kept sending her warm messages of good will;" in Dio *philanthropous* is embroidered at 8.7 with romantic panache where Augustus sends her word that he has fallen in love with her, and she is taken in! For the pretty fiction about Octavian's intrepid chastity when Cleopatra attempts to seduce him (Dio, 12.3–7, Florus, 2.21.9) see Volkmann, 203–04, who suggests that Augustus may have had something of the sort in his autobiography. For fine shredding of the nonsense about her treacheries see Tarn, "The Battle of Actium," *JRS* 21 (1931) 196ff, and C. W. Richardson, "Actium," *JRS* 27 (1937) 163.

[13]Cf. Stähelin, *RE*, 11:1, 773, for whom "ein Übermass von Plänen" signals only "Planlosigkeit."

[14]Volkmann, 219.

[15]Plutarch, 86.2; Dio, 14.1.

[16]Holmes, 166, who cites Groag.

[17]Tarn, 109–10; Stähelin, 778–79; E. Groag, "Beiträge zur Geschichte des zweiten Triumvirats," *Klio* 14 (1914) 65–66. Cf. Holmes, 165–66, who opposes such views but allows that Octavian may have had serious misgivings about her return to Rome. Holmes' evidence that Octavian "tried to prevent her from committing suicide" is rather uncertain. If Octavian was merely pretending that he wanted to keep her alive, such stories were useful. Groag, 65–66, neatly condemns the laxity and incompetence of the guards set over her, nor is Plutarch's suggestion at 83.5 ("thinking he'd hoodwinked her, but the rather hoodwinked he") altogether convincing: that too may have been in the autobiography.

[18]See Tarn, 109, for Dolabella's role in hastening the suicide.

[19]In this regard Tarn himself prefers romanticism and rejects out of hand the notion of E. Hermann ("Kleopatras angeblicher Schlangentod," *PW* [5 Sept. 1931] 1100–02) that a cult statue of Cleopatra as the new Isis (Plutarch, 54), complete with asp, confirmed unwarranted assumptions that she died by asp bite. Tarn prefers to think that Cleopatra chose an asp because "the creature deified whom it struck," 110–11. But as reigning Ptolemy and new Isis she may possibly have thought of herself as deified already; see *CAH* 7, 18ff and 114ff and G. Lafaye, *Histoire des cultes des divinités d'Alexandrie* (Paris) 15ff. For the connection between Isis and the asp (perhaps she *was* the asp who threatened and preserved Re's identity) see E. A. Wallis Budge, *From Fetish to God in Ancient Egypt* (Oxford 1934) 94, 459–63, and A. Erman, *A Handbook of Egyptian Religion* (London 1907) 226. One wonders how the Roman devotees of the goddess would have felt had the new Isis been led in chains before them; see Lafaye, 44ff.

[20]Suetonius, *Div. Aug.* 17.8; Dio, 14.45. Tarn, 110, doubts that the story is true, but its truth is not the point. If no one but his guards knew anything at all, Octavian was free to invent any story he chose—asps, poisoned hairpins, water jugs, fig baskets, Psylli, rage, concern, grief, wonder, pity and magnanimity (the vaguer, perhaps, the better).

[21]I mean *la mort* as informed by the "no lowly female she" cliché which is utterly denied by "illam inter caedes pallentem morte futura"—fleeing amid the

carnage, she blanched, for she guessed that soon she too must die. If anyone mourned Cleopatra, it was the great poet of universal human suffering: the tortured woman disappears into the splendid pathos of the grieving Nile and his shelter. It is another fiction, but a noble and beautiful one.

[22]Nor should we take Propertius very seriously at 4.6.63–66; the verses are unkind, but I am not certain that the unkindness is directed against Cleopatra: "quantus mulier foret una triumphus" denigrates Octavian's victory at Actium in a peculiar way, as, indeed does the entire pastiche. "Sum deus; est nostri sanguinis ista fides" — I'm a real god after all; the wonderful actions of that boy today are proof positive that the ichor in my veins runs blue and true — is hardly less funny than Ovid's "O et de Latia, o et de gente Sabina" (*Met.*14.832), nor is it impossible that at least some of the inspiration for Ovid's ferocious frivolity came from Propertius.

[23]*Ibid.*, 91.

[24]291ff. Cf. T. Oesterlen, *Komik und Humor bei Horaz* II (Stuttgart 1886) 54–56.

[25]The ode "dates itself" (E. Fraenkel, *Horace* [Oxford 1957] 158f) only if we assume that it was written in the white heat of the news of Cleopatra's death because it expresses Horace's passionate, complex and immediate response to this news; if we assume that it expresses Horace's disgust or irritation or cool irony in respect of Augustan propaganda and the Augustan settlement, there is no reason why the poem cannot have been written even as late as 23: such a date might even throw some light on the ode's penultimate position in the opening book (it would, for instance, balance 1.2 rather nicely). In any case, the peculiar rhythm of v.14 ("mentemque lymphatam Mareotico," — her brain oozing with cheap muscatel), together with its general crabbedness, may be used to argue a master's ease rather than a tyro's faltering: the verse both mimics and, at a crucial place, emphasizes drunken confusion.

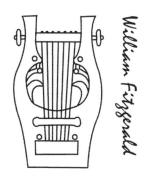

William Fitzgerald

HORACE, PLEASURE AND THE TEXT

The final poem of Book I, along with 1.30, consists of two brief Sapphic stanzas. In his essay, Fitzgerald reads it as a significant example of Horace's tendency not only to compose "poems that give pleasure," but also to raise "the question of pleasure as he defined his own situation as a poet." It has been conventional to see the ode, especially because of its terminal position in its book, as programmatic: emphasizing, as Horace does elsewhere, that he is a poet of simple pleasures. However, as Fitzgerald notes, Horace does not address his audience or openly declare his poetic program of simplicity: on the contrary, he speaks to a nameless young slave *(puer)* and tells him pointedly not to do anything for him, not to fuss with elaborate Oriental preparations, not to fashion for him a crown, not to hunt for the last rose of summer, not to do anything special with the myrtle. To Fitzgerald, then, this suggests that Horace does not want pleasure to be "created" for him by the labors of another, especially a slave. As son of an ex-slave, the poet had a definite sense of how the work of a slave could distort one's own achievement and one's pleasure in it. He will be responsible for his own pleasures, which will indeed be simple. And our last picture of him is of a man by himself, his slave dismissed or at least stilled, quietly drinking his wine in the shade of an arbor. Fitzgerald continues his discussion with 3.13. (Ed.)

There is no doubt that reading Horace can be one of the greatest pleasures that classical literature has to offer, but there is also no doubt that at some point most of us suspect that it is a guilty pleasure. Of course, there are not one but many pleasures to be had from reading Horace. There is, first of all, the vicarious pleasure to be had from what Horace himself so manifestly enjoys. Here is Thomas Otway in an epistle to Richard Duke:

> But when to give our minds a Feast indeed,
> *Horace*, best known and lov'd by thee, we read,
> Who can our Transports or our Longing tell,
> To taste of Pleasures, prais'd by him so well?
> With thoughts of Love, and Wine, by him, we're fir'd,
> Two things in sweet Retirement much desir'd.
> A generous Bottle and a Lovesome She,
> Are th' only Joys in Nature, next to Thee.[1]

This essay is reprinted from *Arethusa* 22 (1989) 81–93, with permission of the Johns Hopkins University Press.

Clearly Leishman, who quotes these lines in his book *Translating Horace*, regards these as guilty pleasures since he spends several pages defending Horace from the advocacy of "Restoration Wits." We are more sophisticated readers now, and are happy to relinquish these all-too-substantial pleasures to the vulgar. A more subtle pleasure, frequently cited by classicists, is the pleasure of subtlety itself: the pleasure of savoring and describing those infinite shades of tone, obliquities of statement, and that civilized balance of attitude, all of which are closely related to the patrician pleasures of good conversation.[2] If we feel a bit squeamish about this, we will probably take refuge in what is the most neutral pleasure of all, that of reading the "mosaic of words" so definitively described by Nietzsche: the pleasure of reading Horace is the pleasure of experiencing Latin exercised to the limits of its potential. Nietzsche is an eminently respectable authority in modern literary studies and is quoted profusely by Barthes in *The Pleasure of the Text*, which is a powerful attempt to make pleasure respectable. Barthes does not quote Nietzsche's description of the strongest "artistic delight *(Entzücken)*" he ever had, and that is hardly surprising, since this is what he has to say about it:

> To this time I have not had the same artistic delight from any poet that an ode of Horace gave me from the beginning. In some languages what is here achieved cannot even be *hoped for*. This mosaic of words, where every word as sound, as position, as concept radiates its power to the right, to the left and over the whole, this minimum in the extent and number of the signs, this maximum in the energy of the sign achieved thereby — all that is Roman and, believe, me, *elegant (vornehm)* par excellence. All the rest of poetry by contrast seems somewhat too popular, the mere garrulousness of feeling *(Gefühls-Geschwätzigkeit)* ....[3]

Here we have the canonical description of the pleasure of reading Horace, but even this is permeated by the language of class. Commager seems to have been disturbed by this aspect of the passage, since when he quotes it he leaves out the last sentence, which distinguishes elegant aristocratic conversation from plebeian chatter.[4] Nietzsche does not say why this mosaic of words is so Roman, but we might speculate that the few words so strategically placed that they spread their influence in all directions represent the legions and colonies of Rome exerting their influence over the vast empire. There would appear to be no innocent pleasures to be had from Horace, but then pleasure is seldom innocent. Barthes laments the fact that the concept of pleasure has become so suspicious and complains that there is a whole "mythology" that would consign pleasure to the (political) right: "On the right ... everything abstract, boring, political, is shoved over to the left and pleasure is kept for oneself; welcome to our side, you who are finally coming to the pleasure of literature! And on the left, because of morality (forgetting Marx's and Brecht's cigars), one suspects and disdains any 'residue of hedonism.'"[5] Certainly, it is with some justice that people who speak of the pleasures of art are suspected of wanting to protect it from becoming the object of engagement, but Barthes is surely right when he goes on to argue that pleasure is not something simple, an *element* of the text, and that the complexity of its mechanism should rescue it from the crude alternatives of disdain or championship. However, his book suffers from a confusion of goals that is never really confronted; in fact, I would say that it is deliberately equivocal about what it is doing because in the end Barthes wants to use the concept of pleasure to produce exactly the kind of exclusive club that the "mythology" sees in the rightist use of the word. Barthes's first project, and the one that I find most promising and useful, is to analyze the mechanism of pleasure in its general sense, to reveal the structure of this mechanism and so to break open the apparently irreducible simplicity of an essence; this allows us to see the exercise of and claim to pleasure as an action that can be performed in various contexts and relationships. His second project is to distinguish a classical, bourgeois pleasure from what he calls *jouissance,* and when Barthes uses that versatile word the meaning "orgasm" is primary. In this context, vulgar, classical pleasure is reduced to a litany: "Classics. Culture (the more culture, the greater, more diverse, the pleasure will be). Intelligence. Irony. Delicacy. Euphoria. Mastery. Security: art of living. The pleasure of the text can be defined by *praxis* (without any danger of repression): the time and place of reading: house, countryside, near mealtime, the lamp, family where it should be, i.e., close but not too close (Proust in the lavatory that smelled of orrisroot), etc. Extraordinary ego-reinforcement (by fantasy), the unconscious muffled. This pleasure can be *spoken*: whence criticism."[6] By contrast, the text of *jouissance* produces a *loss* of ego-stability and ruptures the plenitude of the classical text of pleasure. Perhaps the most useful description of this kind of text (usually modern) is in Barthes's *The Zero Degree of Literature,* a description that allows us to see the difference between this kind of text and Nietzsche's Horace: "These word-objects, without connection, adorned with all the violence of their explosion, whose purely mechanical vibration touches strangely the next word but extinguishes itself immediately, these poetic words exclude humanity."[7] The bourgeois pleasure withdraws, conserves and gathers, the aristocratic *jouissance spends*."[8] *Jouissance* defies criticism—either one is up to it or one is not and, to borrow the words of the "mythology" that would consign pleasure to the right, "Welcome to our side, you who are finally coming to the *jouissance* of literature." Thus Barthes, prophet of *jouissance*.

Fortunately, *The Pleasure of the Text* provides a more subtle analysis of the classical pleasure than the litany that allows it to be opposed to *jouissance.* Certainly much of that litany might be applied to the pleasures of Horace, and has been, though the returns are rapidly diminishing. I would like now to consider two poems of Horace in the light of some observations of Barthes connected with what I have called his first project, and I call it that only because it interests me more than the other. Barthes would certainly have given precedence to the latter: on the jacket of the French edition it is stated that the intention of the book is to affirm the pleasure of the text against the indifferences of science and the puritanism of ideological analysis (hence its unsystematic procedure), and to affirm the *jouissance* of the text against the leveling of literature to mere charm.[9] My own approach is closer to ideological analysis, but if it is puritanical that is because it would also resist the leveling of literature to mere charm. My readings will not display the critical tact that is sometimes demanded of those who would display a sensitivity to the charms of Horace, a sensitivity that consists in echoing his delicate tone and balance. In other words, I do not intend to *reproduce* what is conventionally taken to be the pleasure of Horace's charm. The poems I shall deal with are not only pleasurable poems, but poems that produce pleasure in the context of particular relationships and connect it with particular purposes. Horace was not simply a poet who wrote poems that give pleasure, he was also a poet who raised the question of pleasure as he defined his own situation as a poet; several of the poems addressed to his patrons, for instance, situate him in relation to those patrons in terms of the opposition politics-pleasure, and in many other poems Horace presents himself as the spokesman of what one might call an ethics of pleasure.[10] These aspects of Horace were highly influential, and it is important to understand the function of the mechanism of pleasure in Horace if we are to understand the tradition of the writing and reading of lyric in which he played such an important role.

The poem that stands at the end of book one of Horace's odes is one of the shortest and slightest of the whole corpus.

The immediate pleasure of this poem, and here the pleasure that it gives and the pleasure that it claims are intimately connected, is derived from its emphatic, even aggressive shortness, especially as it comes after the grandiose Cleopatra ode and at the end of the long first book.[11] Barthes has pointed out that the text about pleasure is necessarily short, provoking the question "Is that all?" This in turn produces the answer, "Yes, I have a *right* to pleasure," for pleasure can only be spoken through the indirection of a *claiming* (*revendication*). The text about pleasure is therefore always implicated in a short dialectic with two moments: "the moment of *doxa*, of opinion, and that of *paradoxa*, of contestation."[12] The shortness of a literary work is not simply a matter of size—witness the "tedious brief scene of young Pyramus" in *Midsummer-Night's Dream*—and what makes this ode of Horace short (and slight) is best understood with the help of Barthes's dialectic. First, we wait to hear from what standpoint the speaker rejects the various luxuries paratactically accumulated in the first six lines; this puts into play what Barthes calls *doxa*, which is here the moral rejection of superfluous pleasure, or perhaps of pleasure itself, insofar as it is always superfluous. But we are pulled up short when the statement that grounds these accumulated rejections turns out to be, putting it bluntly, "I'm having a nice drink."[13] "Is that all?" we ask, to which the implicit answer is "I have a *right* to pleasure." In the end, Horace simply reveals himself, in the accusative of the present participle, drinking beneath the shady vine: this is the *paradoxa*, the contestation of the *doxa* that one must give an account of one's relation to pleasure; Horace appeals to the self-evidence of pleasure itself, adducing no other context for the decorum implied by *neque dedecet*. In this contestation of *doxa* pleasure is claimed.

Let us now consider another strand of the immediate level of the poem, which also reveals the mechanism of Barthes's dialectic. Like most ancient poems, this one is addressed to someone—a slave. In the context of this situation the utterance of the poem is strange, since the slave is given no order.[14] Like the reader, the slave stands ready, waiting to hear what he *should* do if not what his master so compendiously dislikes, but he is merely told that the unelaborated myrtle is not unbecoming for either him or his master. It might be objected that this constitutes an implicit order, and, as we shall see, the lines about the myrtle are very complex, but for the moment I would like to isolate the formal aspects of the utterance as they relate to the address of the master to the slave. Against the expression of the master's dislikes, conveying the authority of the one who must be pleased, there is no balancing expression of preference, for the slave is not told what the master likes/wants instead, merely that the myrtle is not unsuitable for either of them; both agents are now in the accusative. The fact that this final statement is cast in a double negative (*neque...dedecet*) contributes to the draining of authority from the voice of the master, and we can now see that there is a single diminuendo of emphasis and will from *odi, displicent* and *mitte sectari*, through *nihil...curo* to *neque...dedecet*, and that this diminuendo comes to take the place of the two-part form that we would expect of the master's address to a slave ("Don't do this, do that!" or "I don't like this, I like that.") Again, we have a dialectic of opinion and its contestation. This time, though, pleasure is claimed by contesting its implication not in a moral discourse, but in a discourse of authority, an implication that was considerable in a slave-owning society. In the context of the poem as address to a slave, we again find ourselves asking "Is that all?" and the answer is "*I* (rather than the master) have a right to pleasure."

Horace's poem exemplifies an important aspect of Barthes's analysis of pleasure: pleasure is not so much represented as claimed, and it is claimed by the short dialectic that we have seen functioning in Horace's poem through the short-circuiting of two forms of discourse that would absorb pleasure; insofar as pleasure can be spoken, it can only be spoken through the indirection of a claim which realizes it against those discourses. On the surface, though, the poem seems to imply that pleasure is something simple that is there independently of the fuss and paraphernalia that simply has to be removed in order for it to be revealed. It has been pointed out that, in spite of this stance, the poem is a highly wrought artefact whose lingering over the things that are rejected suggests that it is at least half in love with them. This is certainly true, and there is more to it than the "tension of attitudes" that Commager describes when commenting on this contradiction.[15] I propose now to examine this and similar contradictions in relation to the poem's problematic of pleasure, simplicity and work in the context of the master-slave relationship.

Let us begin with the first two and a half lines of the second stanza, which seems to be the turning-point of the poem. I say "seems" because although it introduces the first positive (*simplici myrto*), and a change in the authoritative tone (*nihil...curo*), it can be read in a quite different way that would align it with the first stanza. If we follow the word-grouping suggested by the line-break, we get: "I diligently see to it that you make no special effort with/add nothing to the unadulterated myrtle."[16] *Sedulus curo* recalls the committed voice of the first stanza, but the contrast between *nihil allabores* and *sedulus curo* suggests that it is Horace who is now the worker, as well as the voice of authority. Both readings are needed here, for the poem stages the conflict between the idea of pleasure as a simple given that can be indicated by removing the luxuries that smother it, and as something that can only be claimed through a more complex operation in which the poem diverts, transforms and appropriates the work of the slave rather than simply ordering it away. The poem subverts its own claim that pleasure can be simply uncovered and revealed by a rejection of the superfluous; instead, it shows pleasure to be the result of operations performed on the unpleasure from which it must be claimed.

In the light of the above we can return to the first stanza. After the opening line, which sandwiches the two agents as puny disyllables between the burdensome luxuries that would drown them, the next three lines take a more complex attitude to what is being rejected. Crowns woven with bast may displease the speaker, but the act of rejection produces a vivid sense of their tactility that belies what is being said. The word *displicent* contains the element -*plic*-, the compounded form of *placeo*, which in this context brings to mind the word *plico* (fold); the appearance of *simplici* in the metrically equivalent position of the fifth line reinforces our tendency to register *displicent* as an unfolding as well as a displeasure. The line *displicent nexae philyra coronae*, with its interlocking of the juxtaposition of weaving and unweaving (*displicent nexae*) with the interwoven structure of *nexae philyra coronae* creates an intense effect of textuality (the ancients also used this metaphor for writing), and thereby undermines the rejection of this intricacy that is carried by the semantic level of the sentence. Horace is substituting his own labor for that of the slave, reclaiming pleasure from its alienation in the division of labor between master and slave, a division that robs the master of the crown's wovenness, since all he can do in this context is receive it as *product*. Explicitly, the poem claims that the pleasure of the master is independent of the work of the slave, and furthermore that only the sensibility of the master is capable of understanding pleasure, since the slave needs to be prevented from his officious and mistaken servility. In fact, though, the expression of the pleasure of the master depends on the work of the slave, since it must be claimed as something that has been alienated by the slave's work, and claimed through a parody of the slave's work: *nihil allabores/sedulus curo*. Pleasure is not there independently of the contexts from which it must be claimed.

In the final two lines of the first stanza, the master tells the slave not to go looking for the late rose, implying that for him true pleasure has nothing to do with the luxury of knowing that one's leisure has cost others a great deal of work. Here again, the object that would come to the master through the work of the slave is not so much rejected as reclaimed from the work of the slave through the work of the poet. Horace has himself installed the rose in, or as, the exquisite lingering of the stanza, but it is not the same rose as the slave would have fetched, rather it is the rose that has been carefully preserved from that officious fetching.[17] Once we place Horace's textual work in its proper relation to the aborted work of the slave, we see that Commager's suspicion that Horace may desire the rose that he apparently rejects is not quite correct, for the rose that is the object of his desire is realized only through the action that preserves it from the slave's search and that stands in a competitive relation to that search. Similarly, it is not true that the master's pleasure is independent of the slave's work, for it can only be represented through the dialectic of the two types of work. In the light of this poem we may ask whether pleasure is really an originally available experience for the master, the purposes of which the slave merely serves, and is all too apt to smother, or whether it in fact emerges from this relationship as an ideal, whose formulation is prompted by a feeling of alienation arising from that relationship. If the latter is the case, pleasure can only be reclaimed (though not recovered) through the meta-work of textuality, which is here a diversion or appropriation of the work of the slave.

The time has now come to answer an important objection. There are those who will have become increasingly irritated by my analysis of the master-slave relationship in this poem; all this talk of alienation, they will say, is simply importing modern ideas into the thought of a society that was perfectly at ease with the presence of slaves and their role in the production of pleasure. This may be so, but Horace's relation to the slave is colored by the fact that he was not just a Roman, but a Roman poet, and as such fitted uneasily into the network of Roman social relations. The earliest poets at Rome were slaves, freedmen and foreigners without Roman citizenship and Horace himself, who had risen to a position of considerable prestige through the patronage[18] of Maecenas and Augustus, was the son of a freedman. His constant insistence on his independence, and particularly his use of the very Sabine farm that was the most concrete result of that patronage, as a symbol of independence,[19] proves the need for Horace to situate himself socially against the appearance of subordination and illiberality, although he does not have any recognized or established status to which to refer. This lack of a clear social position, even for poets who did not need any financial support (which means most of the major poets from

Catullus on), led to a fascinating process of self-definition by poets against certain Roman norms that their very pursuit of poetry as a serious calling challenged.[20] Whether the appropriation of the language of Roman social, political, religious, military and conjugal life by these liminal agents is to be read as a reversal of the Roman hierarchy of values or as a parasitical attempt to hold on to a Roman identity that was, after all, the only one they had, or, more probably, a tense combination of both, is a question that would be worth pursuing. In the case of Horace's relation to the slave, we see two things happening: first, Horace as slave-owner attempts to disconnect his own pleasure from the illiberal mentality of the slave who provides it, and then Horace the hard-working purveyor of pleasure to the occupied Roman replaces the slave and so defines his own work against that of the slave. The second aspect of Horace's position is not explicitly brought up in this poem, except insofar as the very position of the poem leads us to read it as some kind of statement about Horace as poet (which is what we get at the end of the second, third and fourth books), but we have only to compare the relation of Horace to Maecenas in poems like 3.29 to the relation of the slave to Horace in this poem to see its relevance. In 3.29 Horace calls Maecenas away from his business in noisy Rome to the place (Sabine farm?) where "I (Horace) have had for a long time ready a cask not yet broached, along with flowers of roses, Maecenas, and balsam pressed for your hair" (1–5). In *Satires* 2.7.81–2, where Horace's slave Davus tells him that, though he is Davus' master, he himself serves others who manipulate him like a puppet, we should not let the humor drown out the anxiety, and similarly in Epistles 2.1–25, where Horace excuses his lack of literary production to Iulius Florus with the help of an extended parable about buying a slave.

Perhaps the most famous ancient description of the pleasure of the Horatian text is Petronius' *curiosa felicitas*.[21] It is a phrase particularly apposite to this poem, paradoxically combining a spontaneous luck or happiness (*felicitas*) of expression with careful and painstaking work. What it describes is that bifurcated sensation of reading Horace in which we feel both the knotty composition and the almost epiphanic rightness of the larger unit, a sensation that accords with Barthes's description of pleasure as the exercise of a "different physiology." In 1.38 Horace has situated this paradox, as the dialectic between *nihil...curo* and *sedulus...curo*, in the dynamics of the relation between master and slave, so that this text on pleasure is firmly rooted in the particular context in which it is an issue for Roman society and for the Roman poet. The complexity of the poem as a text on pleasure reflects Horace's anomalous position as both man of leisure and purveyor of pleasure to the unleisured, and it is this that produces the situating of pleasure in the dialectic between the work of the slave and that of the poet.

✧ ✧ ✧

Notes

[1]Quoted by Leishman 1956.30–31.

[2]A representative example of this approach to Horace would be the following words of Gordon Williams 1970.174: "Stylistic tact and appropriateness are Horace's outstanding qualities, but for this to be appreciated the reader's ear needs to be constantly attuned to the tone of the poet's voice, for it is in such small-scale works as the Odes that significant tonal effects, often dependent on but a single word, are possible."

[3]Nietzsche 1967–77, Vol. 6.154–55.

[4]Commager 1962.50.

[5]Barthes 1975.22–23.

[6]Barthes 1975.51.

[7]Barthes 1953.39.

[8]"To spend" is the Victorian expression for having an orgasm. In the preface to Richard Miller's translation of *Le plaisir du texte*, Richard Howard comments: "The Bible they translated calls it 'knowing' while the Stuarts called it 'dying,' the Victorians called it 'spending,' and we call it 'coming;' a hard look at the horizon of our literary culture suggests that it will not be long before we come to a new word for orgasm proper — we shall call it 'being.'" (vi).

[9]Barthes 1973.

[10]For the opposition politics-pleasure, see C.1.6; 1.20; 2.12; 2.17; 3.4.37–40 and the remarks of Anderson 1974.45–46. The "ethics of pleasure" is developed in those poems in which the *carpe diem* theme links enjoyment with a proper recognition of our mortal status, for instance, C.1.4; 1.9; 2.3 and 3.19.

[11]On the question of what significance to attach to the poem's position, see Nisbet and Hubbard 1970.422–23. Nisbet and Hubbard cite some of the symbolic readings of the poem that have intended to give it more weight and to make a more impressive end to the book. I will argue that the poem is, by implication, concerned with Horace's status as a poet, though I do not think that it is an apology for a particular kind of style (Fraenkel) or subject matter (Pasquale). Certainly the rejection of "Persian" luxuries is relevant to its position next to the Cleopatra ode, see Nussbaum 1971.91–97.

[12]Barthes 1973.31. Translation mine.

[13]Syndikus 1972.341–42 points out that the opening prepares us for a tirade from a Stoic *"Sittenprediger"* ["moral preacher"] but the luxuries that are in fact cited turn out to be rather tame, and are not subjected to a moral perspective. One might compare C.2.18 for a more conventional, morally motivated rejection of luxury.

[14]Contrast the epigram by Philodemus quoted by Nisbet and Hubbard 1970.422.

[15]Commager 1962.117–18.

[16]Most commentators take *nihil...curo* together and *sedulus* with *allabores,* but Quinn 1980.195 takes *sedulus curo* together and translates "I am particularly anxious that you should not go out of your way to add anything..." My translation, "I diligently see to it that ..." reflects the almost invariable association of *sedulus* with action (see examples in *OLD*) better than Quinn's "I am particularly anxious."

[17]In her answer to the *Arion* (1970.128–29) questionnaire on Horace, Brigid Brophy tells how, as a struggling Latin student, she was betrayed by Horace in this passage. Having read *mitte sectari* as "send to seek ..." she fell in love with this passage on the rose: "The dying, artistically-aristocratic command to pursue last beauties became a talisman to me." When she was informed that the passage meant just the opposite, she was disillusioned by a Horace who, having created such a splendid image, could "negative it with a puritanical, but not a passionately puritanical,

prohibition." My reading of the passage would preserve Horace's honor, for the negation of the command, as I see it, is the condition for the preservation of the rose as an artistic, aesthetic object.

[18]This word needs to be used with some caution in connection with Roman poets, as White 1979 has shown. In the late Republic and early Empire, poets were not supported or commissioned in the way that they have been by modern patrons. White has shown that the relation between poets and their "patrons" at Rome was simply another manifestation of the general and informal relationship of *amicitia* that pervaded Roman social life; he argues that, though poets did often receive gifts (but not regular stipends), the motive for attaching oneself to a powerful *amicus* was more probably the opportunity for publicity that this offered. He also makes the important point that between senatorial politics and demeaning work for hire there was not much in the way of professions for the educated man and, of course, writing poetry was not recognized as a profession in the same way that oratory was. This meant that "Poets attached themselves to the houses of the great in the first place because there was nowhere else for them to go" (85). The question of patronage at Rome is examined in the important collection of essays edited by Gold 1982. In his contribution to that collection, James Zetzel argues that Horace, like most poets of the late Republic and early Empire, was not financially dependent on patronage and that "the existence of artistic patronage must be understood as the social reality against which the major poets were working, the conventions that they transformed in their verse." (Gold 1982.89). While his implication that patronage cannot simply be treated as a determining factor for these poets is surely correct, his argument that these self-sufficient poets were employing "as a literary convention what was, for less fortunate contemporaries, as for earlier generations, a reality" (90) is misleading, as is his opposition between art and life ("In the *Satires*, as in most poetry of the Augustan age, art not life is both the subject and object of poetic creation" 95). For all of these poets there was a real anxiety about their status in Roman society, and it is against this anxiety that we must see the reversals of normal hierarchy and "poeticizing" of Roman social realities; Zetzel states that when Horace presents himself as conqueror and *princeps* he has "transcended the need for Maecenas and even Augustus" (96), but this elides all the complexities of this gesture in a leap to the modern conception of the autonomy of art. Perhaps he is assuming that Horace must be either entirely dependent or entirely independent in relation to his patrons, and this may be due to his focus on the financial aspect of the relationship.

As far as the concrete rewards of the protection of Maecenas go, it may be true that Horace's *paupertas impulit audax/ ut versus facerem* (*Epistles* 2.5.53–4) does not square with the facts, as Zetzel points out (89–90), but there is no reason to doubt that after Philippi Horace found himself deprived of his father's estate (*Epistles* 2.2.50–1) and that this loss was made up by Maecenas' gift to him of the Sabine farm.

[19]See Commager 1962.312.

[20]See Ross 1975.9–15 on Catullus' application of the terminology of *amicitia* to his affair with Lesbia. There are many other examples of this kind of strategy in the Roman poets of which the most striking is the *militia amoris* of the love poets.

[21]*Satyricon*, 118.5.

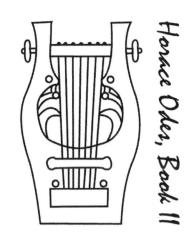

Horace Odes, Book II

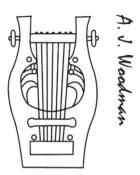

A. J. Woodman

HORACE, ODES, II, 3

In his second book of Odes, Horace addresses some of the great men who survived the Civil Wars and settled down in various ways to the orderly rule of Augustus. Quintus Dellius, named in line 4, was a successful politician, a man of dubious morality who had survived by deserting one sinking cause after another until he finally made the decisive jump to Octavian before Actium and thus achieved survival and prosperity. Augustus had no important role for him to play, so he wrote his memoirs and had to content himself with his wealth. It might seem odd that Horace should write a poem for such an opportunist, odd, too, that he would encourage so strenuously a man of such affluence to practice Epicurean moderation with his vast estate and wealth. This is the target of Woodman's trenchant essay: that Horace has let his clichés run away with him and and fallen into patent illogicality in urging on Dellius the trite theme of *carpe diem*. According to Woodman, "Horace has made it plain in lines 2–4 not that Dellius is having fits of depression..., but that he in fact enjoys himself too much" (p. 171). If, then, he is constantly living it up, it is entirely illogical for Horace to encourage him to seize the day and snatch its fleeting pleasures before his inevitable death, in a series of felicitous but fundamentally trite recommendations. I am not so sure that it is clear that Dellius over-enjoys himself, either in Horace's opening address or in actual history. It has never necessarily followed that, because one is rich and survives to retirement, one is guaranteed happiness. Many politicians and millionaire businessmen don't know how to use their wealth to enjoy life: that was the theme of *Citizen Kane* and of more than one novel. It then may be ironic that rich Dellius needs to be advised to take advantage of his wealth, but it need not be illogical. The commonplaces of *carpe diem* are apt for rich as well as poor, old as well as young and potential lover. But ponder Woodman's well-made points. (Ed.)

In the words of Horace, it is said, there are found the "mature, ironical, sensual, and irreligious opinions of a middle-aged Roman, one whose chief counsel to youth was to drink and make love to the best of its ability, as these were activities unsuitable to a middle age given over to worldly-wise meditation and good talk. Afterwards there remained only an equal oblivion for the virtuous and the wicked in the unconsulted tomb."[1] *Aequam memento* seem to epitomise this Horatian outlook on life, and the poem's blend of euphonic maxims and rural vignettes (together with traditionally improving thoughts on death) has made it one of the more popular odes.[2] Such odes, however, are normally taken for granted and rarely

This essay is reprinted from *American Journal of Philology* 91 (1970) 165–80, with permission of the Johns Hopkins University Press.

subjected to analysis or examination. *Aequam memento* is no exception,[3] yet even the poem's sequence of thought, a fundamental aspect, is difficult to comprehend.

The ode, as it stands, divides into two unequal parts of 16 and 12 lines respectively: lines 1–10 deal with ἀταραξία and *carpe diem*, lines 17–28 with death (the transition coming with the repeated *cedes* at 17 ff., just as the transition at *Carm.*, II, 14 comes at 13 ff., also with the repeated *frustra*).[4] However, the theme of death has been initiated in line 4 with *moriture*, and, though abandoned immediately, is resumed exactly half-way through the poem at line 15 (*dum res et aetas...*, which is thus ideally connected to the second part of the ode, though syntactically, of course, to the first part). Such duality of structure is a typically Horatian technique. The first part of the ode is remarkable for its slowness of progress:[5] for just as 15 f. *dum res et aetas* recall 4 *moriture*, so also 5 *maestus omni tempore* recalls 1 *rebus in arduis*; 6 *te per dies festos bearis* recalls 2–4 *in bonis*[6] and *laetitia*; 13 f. *vina, unguenta* and *flores rosae* recall 9 ff. *pinus, populus* and *lympha*. Horace continually repeats ideas or themes,[7] and by means of such retrospection very little actual progress of thought is made in the first part of the ode. This is a quite common feature in the odes of Horace.[8]

In the second part of the poem (17–28), however, Horace repeats words and thus obtains an effect of speed or urgency: *cedes...cedes*,[9] *divitiis...dives, omnes...omnium*. Even *serius ocius*, though more a homoeoteleuton than a strict word-repetition, helps this effect, which is also maintained by energetic phraseology such as *coemptis saltibus* and *exstructis in altum*. The metre is used here by Horace along these lines, to imply the inevitability of death:[10]

> sors exitur(a) et nos in aetern(um)
>   exsili(um) impositura cumbae.

But the long *o, er*; and *ur* sounds could perhaps indicate a slowing down in the pace of the ode at its conclusion, while the short *i* sounds recall the lots jumping in the *urna*.[11] Horace here seems to achieve a duality of both speed and tone.

Much of the first part of the ode owes its thought to popular Epicureanism,[12] and the first stanza itself is ultimately derived from the Epicurean tenet of ἀταραξία,[13] a favourite of Horace.[14] The doctrine would be especially applicable to Dellius, for he was a person notoriously given to extremes.[15] It is, however, clear that in the first stanza Horace is hardly concerned with *res arduae*, much rather with *res bonae*; and indeed *insolens laetitia* seems more to be his theme.[16] This much is obvious from the relative amount of detail given by Horace to the depiction of *bona* and *mala*: *arduis* itself is a "euphemistischer Gegensatz zu ["euphemistic antithesis to"] *bonis*,"[17] and Horace is careful to omit all detail in the first clause but to insert *ab insolenti temperatam laetitia* in the second; his only reason for so doing is because it is *insolens laetitia* that is applicable to Dellius. The stanza concludes with the words *moriture Delli*, which are doubly ironical: first, because they imply inevitability — Dellius is in no way *aequus*, but the one thing he can be relied upon to do is to die; secondly, Dellius had become notorious during the Civil Wars for his extravagant attempts at saving his skin[18] — and the one epithet which Horace in the whole ode addresses to him is *moriture*. This vocative participle has perhaps a further extension of meaning. Towards the end of the fourth Georgic Virgil tells the tale of Orpheus and Eurydice (457 ff.):

> illa quidem, dum te fugeret per flumina praeceps,
> immanem ante pedes hydrum *moritura puella*
> servantem ripas alta non vidit in herba.

> ["She indeed, while she was fleeing headlong from you along the river, a girl doomed to die, did not see in front of her feet, lurking in the deep grass, the huge snake."]

moritura puella is Virgil's own personal and ominous observation on what is about to happen,[19] and this use of the participle is common in Virgil, though not always constituting his own subjective comment.[20] It is not improbable that Horace had implications similar to those in Virgil's phrase, and others like it, in mind when he wrote *moriture Delli*; at least, the existence of this device may be said to add a new and sinister dimension to Horace's words.

It is upon *moriture*, as the commentators remark, that the *seu...seu* clauses of the second stanza depend; but the tenses of the verbs (*vixeris, te...bearis*) indicate that the force of the whole sentence falls upon *moriture* and not the *seu...seu* clauses themselves.[22] Nevertheless, in this stanza also it is implied how Dellius is expected to spend his life:[23] *maestus* is a weak abstract expression[24] in comparison with the detail (e.g. *reclinatum*, a physical description indicating the notion of ease) of the vivid rural scene which follows, and the generalised *omni tempore*[25] is purposely dull alongside the more specific temporal element of the succeeding clause, *per dies festos*. The second stanza too shows that it is not *res arduae* that is Dellius' trouble.

It was one of the counsels of Epicurus that the wise man will love the country,[26] and in the third and fourth stanzas Horace proceeds to issue, at first indirectly by the questions *quo?* and *quid?* (9–12), and then almost imperatively by *ferre iube* (13–16), an invitation to come out into the countryside and enjoy life. It is not too fanciful to see in the phrase *in remoto gramine* a reference to the Epicurean belief of λάθε βιώσας ["Live a hidden life."],[27] elsewhere a favourite of Horace;[28] but this is not to say that Horace was not a true lover of the Italian country[29] and did not regard it as a most desirable retreat.[30] That such an invitation to come into the country and enjoy life is being given may be confirmed by the *dum*-clause (15 f.), reminiscent of the *dum licet* at *Carm.*, II, 11, 16; IV, 12, 26. This *dum*-clause reintroduces the theme of death, with which the final three stanzas are wholly concerned.

There are, then, in this poem three themes: ἀταραξία in *insolens laetitia*, *carpe diem*, and death. All commonplaces of Horace. But a moment's consideration will reveal that the invitation to *carpe diem*, which forms the kernel of the ode (9–16), is extremely paradoxical: for Horace has made it plain in lines 2–4 *not* that Dellius' trouble is having fits of depression (in which case Horace's invitation would be most timely), but that he in fact enjoys himself too much. Horace appears to be recommending to Dellius a way of life quite inconsistent with his present needs.

Also in the second book of Odes there are two poems which together deal with these three themes. They are the consecutive poems 10 *Rectius vives, Licini* and 11 *Quid bellicosus Cantaber*, and it will be instructive to digress and observe the sequence of their thought. In the former ode the thought proceeds as follows:[31] 1–4 two themes are stated, the golden mean is best, bad times are transitory; 5–12 the advantages of *aurea mediocritas* (with the emphasis on prominence and excess); 13–20 *non, si male nunc, et olim sic erit*; 21–4 restatement of both themes. Murena has been going through troubled times (2 f. *dum procellas cautus horrescis*), and has been adopting extreme behaviour (1 ff. *neque altum semper urgendo neque...nimium premendo litus iniquum*):[32] Horace therefore, quite logically, states that the *res malae* will soon pass away, but meanwhile it is much better to observe an *aurea mediocritas*. In the latter ode Horace says: 1–12 cease worrying, for life is short; 13–24 why not come out into the country and enjoy life? Hirpinus has been worrying about the current political situation abroad (11 f. *quid aeternis minorem consiliis animum fatigas?*), but Horace reminds him that life is short (9 f. *non semper idem floribus est honor vernis*):[33] the advice proposed by the poet is again relevant (17 f. *dissipat Euius curas edaces*). In both odes the addressee is suffering from some kind of depression, and in the one case Horace recommends *aurea mediocritas*,[34] in the other *carpe diem*. It would be difficult enough for Horace to recommend both remedies for the trouble in the same poem, but it would by no means be illogical. When it is a case of someone suffering, not from *res malae*, but from *insolens laetitia*, then the advice of *aureas mediocritas* is still apposite; the admonition to *carpe diem*, however, is wholly illogical, and the combination of *aurea mediocritas* and *carpe diem* is in this context unwarrantable. Yet this is what happens in the ode to Dellius: the lines advocating *carpe diem* (9–16) are completely paradoxical with what has gone before.

There would appear to be at least three not necessarily exclusive explanations for this inconsequence in *Aequam memento*.[35] The first is that Horace has let the poem run away with him and at the expense of his famous *curiosa felicitas* has inserted two irrelevant stanzas into the middle of the ode to the detriment of the rest of its meaning.[36] Horace may not have felt able to omit what is one of his favourite themes, and indeed the rest of the poem too seems simply to be a collection of Horatian clichés.[37] If this is so, the conclusion cannot be avoided that the ode is unsuccessful. The second explanation depends upon the presence of *insolenti* in line 3. It is just possible that Horace is telling Dellius to keep equable in his *insolens laetitia* but that since he is to die (*moriture*), he must still enjoy life, though in moderation. But this requires a great deal of emphasis to be placed upon *insolenti*, which must be retained in the memory as far as line 16; it also requires the supplement of "in moderation" throughout lines 9–16, for *temperatum* in line 3 seems to restrict its influence to the first stanza alone. This explanation too implies that Horace has not been successful in the presentation of his sequence of thought.

The third explanation is that Horace is intentionally employing a bitter paradox. Such paradox may be exemplified by one point of detail. The normal type of Horace's invitation, as observed above, proceeds roughly as follows: stop worrying about present difficulties, life is short, come and enjoy yourself in the carefree countryside. It may, however, be gathered from lines 17 ff. of this ode (*coemptis saltibus, domo villaque*,[38] *exstructis in altum divitiis*) that Dellius is so rich that he has no need to work or worry,[39] no need to *laborare*.[40] Indeed, he seems to be enjoying himself too much. But when he arrives in the supposedly trouble-free countryside, as Horace recommends, there he will find that even the stream *laborat* (11f.).[41]

There is certainly an element of bitterness underlying the first stanza of the poem, and such paradox or irony is perhaps the clue to the first part of the ode. For it would appear that the opening γνώμη is derived from a poem of Archilochus,[42] a poet whom Horace in the Epodes was the first Roman to imitate,[43] and who had a reputation for his biting θυμός.[44] In writing his lyric poetry Horace was mainly concerned with following Alcaeus, Sappho, and Anacreon,[45] but on a very few occasions he seems to imitate Archilochus.[46] For example, Horace addresses Lyce,[47] *fis anus, et tamen vis formosa videri*; the language is sharp, and apparently modelled on a line of Archilochus,[48] οὐκ ἂν μύροισι γρῆϋς ἐοῦσ᾽ ἠλείφευ ["Old as you are you should not anoint yourself with myrrh"]. It might not be untrue to say that in certain contexts in the Odes when Horace imitates Archilochus, he wants his readers to be aware of the Archilochian spirit pervading the *carmen*.[49] It is naturally most important to take into account the contexts of the two poems in question (Horace's ode and its Archilochian model), and the lines of Archilochus here imitated by Horace[50] might seem to be plain moralising. But is not at all impossible that Horace wanted a certain pungency to be evident in *Aequam memento*, because these verses of Archilochus had already been adopted by Lucilius, Horace's model for the *Sermones*, and thus made common to the Roman audience by means of the genre *satura*.[51] It should he stressed that it is generally the context of a poem of Archilochus or Lucilius, and not the actual name of the poet, which provides any imitation with a specific tone. But even though the contexts of these two models for *Aequam memento* are missing, the recurrence of the theme in Archilochus and Lucilius could be a significant coincidence, and a Roman reader may well have known in which spirit to take Horace's moralising.[52]

The above discussion, therefore, postulates that Horace has been unsuccessful in the organisation or presentation of his thought in this ode. At best he may have been too subtle. But there are many who have had no difficulty with this aspect of the poem, and these have had their attention diverted by its individual traits. For it has been seen how much of the ode consists of familiar Horatian clichés, which appear all the more welcome in *Aequam memento* because Horace has felicitously been able to endow many of them with a new vitality. Thus the normal Latin manner before Horace for expressing ἀταραξία is *aequo animo*, frequent in comedy and perhaps therefore colloquial.[53] Horace, however, produces what up to his time was the rarer variant *aequa mens*, and in the accusative after *servare*, as if in ironic indication[54] that Dellius' mind is already *aequa* and that all he must do is keep it so (*servare*). Horace preferred *mentem* to *animum* not only because the change itself provided emphasis,[55] but also because he desired the aphoristic rhyme of -*ment*- in the same place in the Alcaic line:[56]

> Aequam me*mento* rebus in arduis
> servare *mentem*.

Even the trite *aequa* assumes life and colour from the context into which Horace has placed it: Dellius' mind must be *aequa* as opposed to the θυμὸς κυκώμενος of Archilochus, *aequa* (level) in contrast with *res arduae* (steep),[57] *aequa* in the sense of 'right, fitting, *iusta, recta*,' *aequa* in the sense of 'equal to,'[58] — to say nothing of its fundamental meaning here, 'even.'

Commentators have objected that the epithet *flavus* for *Tiberis* in line 18 is weak because it is the usual word for describing the River Tiber.[59] But they failed to see that this was exactly what Horace wanted. Whenever Dellius was at his villa he saw the Tiber as *flavus* as it rolled past; and whenever he imagined the river it would always be *flavus*. In making the picture as familiar as possible, Horace by contrast emphasises the pathos of Dellius' eventual loss. Commentators are also to blame for taking line 10, where Horace with appropriate elisions is entwining branches, simply at its face value with never a thought for the notion of love-making:[60]

> umbr(am) hospitalem consociar(e) amant.

But "the use of the words *consociare amant* is meant to give a hint that Horace seldom omits when his theme is the brevity of life, that love-making as well as drinking should not be neglected."[61] The line itself presents a tranquil image, whereas often "dans le detail de paysage, il s'arrête surtout sur l'instable."[62] Sure enough there appears the *lympha fugax* in the following lines and it is hard not to agree that "the laboring stream, trembling along in its devious course, suggests the transience of all human efforts."[63] In describing the course of the stream (*obliquo...rivo*), Horace separates adjective and noun as far as possible from each other, thus emphasising his description, since *pinus, populus*, and *umbram* are all juxtaposed to their respective epithets.[64] This does not prevent Horace from employing another familiar technique: for in the phrase *pinus ingens albaque populus* "the double contrast between the slender poplar white in the wind and the gloom of the heavier pine is indicated, after Horace's manner, by one epithet with each of the pair of substantives."[65] Similarly in the previous stanza Horace echoes *remoto* with *interiore*: both mean, in effect, "the farthest away possible," but *remoto* indicates a place far into the open countryside, *interiore* the deepest and darkest recess of a wine-cellar.

Such care over word-order is highly characteristic of Horace and evident elsewhere in the ode. Thus in the penultimate stanza he says that it matters not to death whether you are rich or poor; and the words which express impartiality (*nil interest*) are neatly inserted, as if in actual neutrality, between the phrase denoting riches (*divesne prisco...*)[66] and that denoting poverty (*an pauper...*). Horace concludes the stanza by referring to man as *victima nil miserantis Orci*, which recalls his Homeric description at *Carm.*, II, 14, 10 *quicumque terrae munere vescimur.*[67] The mention of *victima* has led commentators to think that *cogimur* in the final stanza is used metaphorically, as if man were a flock of sheep;[68] but since the subsequent mention of *urna* and *sors* represents an image "durch den im öffentlichen Leben Roms vielfach geübten Brauch der Losung nahe gelegt" ["closely allied to the frequent practice of drawing lots in the public life of Rome"],[69] then *cogimur*, a verb often used in the context of public life,[70] perhaps belongs rather to this picture. At any rate the motif of the *urna*, used elsewhere at *Carm.* III, 1, 16, appealed to Horace and perhaps corroborates a hint of Homeric colouring at the conclusion of *Aequam memento.*[71]

Such individual traits as have been noted here, evidence in themselves of Horace's famous *callida iunctura* and *curiosa felicitas*, ought nevertheless not to blind the critic to a proper examination of the thought of Horace's Odes. It has been suggested in this paper that Odes, II, 3, at least, can be faulted in this respect,[72] and if a similar method of analysis were to be applied to other of the more popular odes it might again reveal Horace's clichés running away with him.[73]

Notes

[1]Cyril Connolly, Preface to *The Rock Pool* (1935).

[2]E.g. for A. W. Verrall, *Studies in Horace* (London, 1884), p. 137, "One of those seething commonplaces whose triteness Horace forces us to forget by sheer beauty of style."

[3]Such remarks as "Il serait difficile d'être plus heureux dans l'expression, plus claire dans la pensée, plus riche en suggestions, plus impeccable dans l'harmonie du rhythme" ["It would be difficult to be more felicitous in expression, clearer in thought, richer in suggestion, more faultless in the harmony of the rhythm"] are not even "appréciation générale" let alone proper criticism (P. Colmant, S. J., "Horace, *Odes* II, 3," *L.E.C.*, XXIV [1956], p. 378). But there is worse to follow: "cette poésie, si belle soit-elle, a quelque chose qui l'assombrit; c'est l'incurable egoïsme du pauvre païen Horace." ["This poetry, beautiful as it may be, has a troubling feature: it is the incurable egotism of the poor pagan Horace"].

[4]*Aequam memento* thus "falls into the major Horatian category of odes wherein meaning and feeling undergo an abrupt change" (N. E. Collinge, "Form and Content

in Horatian Lyric," *C.P.*, L [1955], p. 164). It may be more exact to see a threefold structure: lines 1–8 ἀταραξία, 9–16 *carpe diem*, 17–28 death. The structural ambiguity is characteristically Horatian. Cf. also W. Wili on the fourth stanza, "Vorher feiern drei Strophen den goldenen Weg der Mitte, nachher weisen drei Strophen auf alles Vergängliches und den Tod. Wahrhaft vom goldenen Mass und Tod umgeben ist hier das festliche Trinken" ["First, three stanzas celebrate the Golden Mean, then three stanzas point to all that is transitory and to death. Indeed, in this poem festive drinking is framed by the Golden Mean and Death"] (*Horaz* [Basel, 1949], p. 223).

[5]The following few remarks derive from N. E. Collinge, *The Structure of Horace's Odes* (O.U.P., 1961 [hereafter Collinge]) , p. 85.

[6]But for the text note Bentley's *ac bonis* and Housman's *ut bonis* (*C.R.*, IV [1890], p. 341).

[7]Contrast the manner in which each of the first three lines ends with an adjective (*in arduis, in bonis, temperatam*), so that a minor image, complementary to the message of the stanza as a whole, is conjured up. Compare *Carm.*, I, 22, 5–8 "sive per Syrtes iter *aestuosas* / sive facturus per *inhospitalem* / Caucasum vel quae loca *fabulosus* / lambit Hydaspes" (cf. J. Marouzeau, *Emerita*, IV [1936], p. 4).

[8]Collinge, p. 85, n. 2.

[9]Contrast how the succession of three nouns in the previous stanza (*huc vina et unguenta et nimium brevis flores*) almost shows Horace ticking these items off on a list before the country symposium starts. Not without considerable irony he balances these three by a further three (*res et aetas et sororum fila trium*), all incalculable elements. [As the commentators remark, *res* here could mean either 'fortune = wealth' (so Wickham, whose only support is perhaps the following *coemptis saltibus*) or 'circumstances' (so Orelli Kiessling-Heinze, Plessis, Page, who justly remarks, "the suggestion that he may become poor some day is wholly out of place here").]

[10]Hypermetre occurs only once elsewhere in Horace's Alcaics, at *Carm.*, III, 29, 35, also for special effect.

[11]Cf. L. P. Wilkinson, *Horace and his Lyric Poetry*[2] (Cambridge, 1951 [Hereafter Wilkinson]), p. 37, "The lots are shaken in the urn, and the round monosyllable *sors* is held in suspense, to fall out at the beginning of the next line."

[12]Too much must not be made of the paradox that Horace spends the second part of the ode (cf. also line 4) in discussing death in sinister tones which all true Epicureans would scorn (e.g. P. Merlan, *J.H.I.*, X [1949], p. 448, "As death does not concern us at all, the certitude of our impending death can have no significance on our way of life—not to the slightest extent. This is just the opposite of Horace's point of view"), for Horace should properly be described as eclectic (cf. O. Immisch, "Horazens Epistel über die Dichtkunst," *Philol.*, Suppl. XXIV, 3 [1932], pp. 26 ff.; W. S. Maguinness, *Hermathena*, LII [1938], pp. 27–46). Nor does it seem possible to agree with K. Quinn, *Latin Explorations* (London, 1963), p. 108, n. 1, when he says that what is perhaps truly Epicurean about this ode is less its philosophy than the way in which it allows Horace "to play the serene spectator of life." Horace appears not as spectator but preceptor.

[13]Lambinus and Orelli quote Lucr., V, 1117 ff., *quod si quis vera vitam ratione gubernet, / divitiae grandes homini sunt vivere parce / aequo animo*; K(iessling)-H(einze) quote Epic., fr. 488 Us. The doctrine of the mean was also a feature of Peripatetic philosophy.

[14]E.g. *Carm.*, III, 29, 32 f. "quod adest *memento* / componere *aequus*," *Epist.*, I, 18, 112 "*aequum* mi *animum* ipse parabo."

[15]Cf. Sen., *Suas.*, 1, 7 *desultorem bellorum civilium...quia ab Dolabella ad Cassium...a Cassio deinde transit ad Antonium, novissime ab Antonio transfugit ad Caesarem.* ["the rider who leaps from one horse to another, in the Civil Wars...because he shifted

from Dolabella to Cassius…then from Cassius to Antony, and finally he fled from Antony to Caesar"]. Collinge, pp. 138 f., has some apposite observations on the character of Dellius, and cf. V. Cucheval, *Hist. de l'éloquence romaine* (Paris, 1893), I, p. 177. This ode is not a failure in so far as it may be regarded as a *Gelegenheitsgedicht* (often perhaps a dubious term with reference to Horace, although cf. L. E. Lord, *C.J.*, XXXI [1935], p. 152, "Horace as an occasional poet is almost supreme"; E. Fraenkel, *Horace* [Oxford, 1957], pp. 313 f. [here after Fraenkel]), with Horace supposedly supplying insufficient information on Dellius within the poem itself. For the Odes of Horace, usually having an addressee, were written exclusively for a literary coterie of great refinement whose members were aware of any necessary background.

[16]Collinge, p. 72, n. 1, comes to the same conclusion, "In the opening of ii.3, two extremes are mentioned, but only *insolens laetitia* is really in point." Both Peerlkamp and Doering in their editions, however, take the opposite view. They are followed by H. Düntzer who, in his edition of 1849, provides the following interpretation: "vide, quam scite tristitiam, qua Dellius laborat, vix attingat (v. 5), sed disertius versetur in laeto vitae usu (v. 6–12)." ["Note how discreetly [Horace] touches the sadness with which Dellius is afflicted, but how he waxes more eloquent over his happy experiences."] Düntzer's may be the only possible explanation for the opinion of Peerlkamp and Doering, but its subtlety would seem to be too extreme for the ode as a whole.

[17]K-H. The word is also ironical; for if Dellius' trouble is exclusively *insolens laetitia*, Horace appropriately tones down the opposite of *res bonae* to make it slightly less inapplicable.

[18]Cf. Sen., *Suas.*, 1, 7, *salutem sibi pactus est.*

[19]On this phrase A. S. Pease (at *Aen.*, IV, 415) comments, "*moritura* reveals the reflection of the poet rather than the consciousness of Eurydice herself."

[20]E.g. *Aen.*, II, 408, 511; IV, 308, 519, 604; XII 55, 602.

[21]Horace has the comparable *animo…morituro* at *Carm.*, I, 28, 6, but with less effect since the person in question is already dead. Cf. also *interitura aestas*, also less effective, because the example is non-personal. Nor is either instance in the vocative, which really sets off *moriture Delli.*

[22]If the verbs had been future tense Horace would have been saying this: "You will die whether you live sadly now or happily (implying, therefore, you may as well live happily)." But the verbs are future perfect, and Horace means this: "Whether you have lived sadly or joyfully, you will die." It is death, one of his other themes, that he wants to stress.

[23]Velleius Paterculus shrewdly observes that Dellius was consistent in his inconsistency II, 84, 2): *exempli sui tenax.*

[24]Purely psychological indications or abstract nouns are rare in the Odes (cf., e.g., *Carm.*, I, 7, 18 *tristitiam vitaeque labores*), but "cette parsimonie n'a rien qui étonne: le monde d'Horace est celui des images" (H. Bardon, "Carpe diem," *R.E.A.*, XLVI [1944], p. 348). It is true that *ab insolenti laetitia* is also an abstract phrase and hence to a certain degree balances *maestus*; but it is in itself forceful and contrasts with the bareness of lines 1–2. It gains its life from its context, whereas *maestus* does not.

[25]The ablative of the duration of time is unusual, though there are examples in Varro, Caesar, Cicero, Livy, Velleius, and Tacitus (cf. Kühner-Stegmann, II, 1, 360, Anm. 12; E. Löfstedt, *Philologische Kommentar zur Peregrinatio Aetheriae*, pp. 51ff.): Cat., 109, 5 is the earliest example in verse. E. C. Woodcock, *A New Latin Syntax*, p. 38, observes that generally the verb "is in a tense of completed action, so that the ablative may denote the limits within which the action was completed." This would support the view proposed above, note 22. It is to be noted, however, that W. Medley, *Interpretations of Horace*, p. 58, translates the phrase as "Life in all its crises."

[26]It is of course also a Stoic text that one should live in harmony with nature, as at *Epist.*, I, 10, 12 ff. *vivere naturae si convenienter oportet / ponendaeque domo quaerenda est area primum, / novistine locum potiorem rure beato?* Such ideas form a general theme for diatribe, cf. A. O. Lovejoy and G. Boas, *Primitivism and Related Ideas in Antiquity* (Baltimore, 1935), pp. 120 f., 261.

[27]"Fern vom Lärm der Welt und dem Gedräng der Menschen" ["Far from the noise of the world and the crowd of mankind."] (K-H, quoting *Serm.*, II, 6, 16 *ubi me in montes...ex urbe removi*; 1, 71 *ubi se a volgo...in, secreta remorant*).

[28]E.g. at *Epist.*, I, 18, 103 *secretum iter et fallentis semita vitae.*

[29]*Epist.*, I, 14, 7 ff. *tamen istuc mens animusque / fert et avet spatiis obstantia rumpere claustra. / rure ego viventem, tu dicis in urbe beatum.*

[30]*Ibid.*, I, 16, 15f. *hae latebrae dulces etiam, si credis, amoenae / incolumen tibi me praestant Septembribus horis.*

[31]See Collinge, pp. 70 ff.

[32]Murena was noted for his intemperate character (Dio, LIV, 3, 4).

[33]This hints at the perpetual Horatian theme of death; and the actual invitation *carpe diem* includes the inevitable *dum licet*. Dellius' ode has the comparable *dum res et aetas...*, and the final three stanzas, thus introduced, present no problem.

[34]On which cf. W. Kroll, *Wien. Stud.*, XXXVII (1915), p. 225.

[35]It would seem impossible that the offending stanzas are interpolations; Peerlkamp, who might otherwise have been the likeliest to suggest this approach, found no fault with the poem, because he misinterpreted the first stanza (see above, note 16). Nor can the stanzas be transposed to improve the sense of the whole.

[36]Stanza 3 at least would be less inapposite if Caldenbach's *qua* for *quo* is read at line 9, and Haupt's *ramisque et* for *ramis? quid* at line 11, with a comma instead of a question mark at line 12 (*Opuscula*, I, p. 92, following Bentley's *ramosque et*).

[37]A selection of parallel words, phrases and ideas will suffice: 1–2 *aequam mentem*, cf., e.g., *Serm.*, I, 5, 8; II, 3, 16 *animo aequo*; *Epist.*, I, 11, 30 *animus si te non deficit aequus*; 6–7 *in remote gramine reclinatum*, cf. *Epod.*, 2, 23 f. *libet iacere modo sub antiqua ilice, modo in tenaci gramine* [these two later imitated by Martial, IX, 90, 1]; *Carm.*, II, 11, 4 *iacentes sic temere*; 9 *pinus ingens*, cf. *Carm.*, II, 10, 9 f. *ingens pinus*; 11, 13 f. (*sub alta*)*...vel hac pinu; albaque populus*, cf. *Epod.*, 2, 10 *altas... populos*; 10 *umbram*, cf. *Carm.*, I, 17, 22 *sub umbra*; 12 *lympha fugax trepidare*, cf. *Epod.*, 2, 27 *fontesque lymphis obstrepunt manantibus*; 16, 48 *levis crepante lympha desilit pede*; *Carm.*, II, 11, 20 *praetereunte lympha* (11, 4 *nec trepides in usum*); *Epist.*, I, 10, 21 *quae (aqua) per pronum trepidat cum murmure rivum*; 13–14 *breves flores*, cf. *Carm.*, I, 36, 16 *breve lilium*; 14 *flores rosae*, cf. *Carm.*, III, 15, *flos purpureus rosae*; 29, 3 *cum flore...rosarum*; IV, 10, 4 *flore...rosae*; 15–16 *dum res et aetas...*, cf. *Carm.* II, 11, 16; IV, 12, 26 *dum licet*; *Epod.*, 13, 3 ff. *rapiamus, amici, occasionem de die, dumque virent genua et decet*; *Carm.* I, 9, 17 f. *donec virenti canities abest morosa*; 18 *flavus Tiberis*, cf. *Carm.*, I, 2, 13; 8, 8 *flavum Tiberim*; 26 *urna*, cf. *Carm.*, III, 1, 16 *omne capax movet urna nomen.* The comparative frequency in this list of *Epod.*, 2 (whose theme is, albeit ironically, the delights of country life) and *Carm.*, II, 10 and 11 (whose themes are, it has been seen, similar to II, 3) perhaps indicates the platitudinous nature of this poem. The two stanzas themselves much recall Lucr., II, 29–33 (= V, 1392–6) but this may only reinforce their triteness, the *vita rustica* being a stock theme with limitations as to how it may be treated (cf. A. Oltramare, *Les origines de la diatribe romaine* [Lausanne, 1926], p. 141). Other commonplaces occur, such as *vina* (line 13, cf. *Carm.*, II, 7, 21 f.; 11, 17 f.), *unguenta* (13, cf. II, 7, 22f.; III, 14, 17), *rosae* (14, cf. I, 36 15; III, 19, 22), the motif of the *heres* (19 f., cf. II, 14, 25 ff.; III, 24, 61 f; IV, 7, 19 f.), the contrast of rich and poor (21 ff., cf. I, 4, 13 f.; II, 18, 32 f.). It must, however, be noted that some of these clichés are remarkably successful (e.g. *aequam mentem*, *flavus Tiberis*, *urna*, discussed below): a moderate example is 6 f. *te per dies festos bearis*, where the temporal phrase is hackneyed and

almost technical (e.g. *Serm.*, II, 2, 83 [the origin of *Carm.*, III, 8, 9]; II, 3, 143; *Carm.*, III, 14, 13; 28, 1; *Epist.*, I, 5, 9 f.), but given interest by the verb *bearis*, "archaïque ou familier" (Plessis, cf. Fr. Ruckdeschel, *Archaismen und Vulgarismen in der Sprache des Horaz* (diss. München, 1910], p. 56).

[38]"Villae autem propter Tiberim sitae ob commeatus facilitatem magni aestimabantur" (Orelli).

[39]Cf. Collinge, p. 139, "Taking all he could from the war, he (Dellius) then flourished materially in the peace; we need not doubt that *coemptis saltibus et domo villaque flavus quam Tiberis lavit* refers directly to his possessions."

[40]Wealth can, of course, imply *cura* (cf. *Carm.*, II, 16, 11 f. *curas laqueata circum / tecta volantes*; III, 16, 17 *crescentem sequitur cura pecuniam*; *Epist.*, I, 10, 47) and it was a common text that the *avarus* is unhappy (cf. Dio Chr., 4, 96; Oltramare, *op. cit.*, pp. 63, 142). Some might therefore say that this is the clue to the ode. But this is difficult in so far as it is Horace, the poet/teacher, who ought to be pointing out to Dellius the misery which results from his wealth; on the contrary, however, Horace has already isolated Dellius' trouble in vivid language, and it is *insolens laetitia*. To make this explanation work, Horace would have to be counselling on two different levels about two superficially opposed problems. An unlikely hypothesis in the context of the poem as a whole.

[41]Wilkinson, p. 129, well describes *laborat* and *trepidare* as "words that recall the feverish toil of worldly affairs" (cf. the use of the verb at *Carm.*, II, 11, 4 f. *nec trepides in usum / poscentis aevi pauca*; III, 29, 31 f. *si mortalis ultra / fas trepidat*).

[42]As pointed out by Orelli and Ussani. The poem is Arch., 68a D(iehl, *Anth. Lyr. Gr.*[3] [1964]) = 118 L(asserre)-B(onnard) (*Arch. Fragments* [Paris, 1958]), and commences as follows:

θυμέ θύμ' ἀμηχάνοισι κήδεσιν κυκώμενε,
†ἀνάδυ†, δυσμενέων δ' ἀλέξευ προσβαλὼν ἐναντίον
στέρνον, †ἐν δοκοῖσιν ἐχθρῶν† πλησίον καταστηθεὶς
ἀσφαλέως.

["Soul, soul overwhelmed by impossible cares, rise up, defend yourself from your enemies, setting your face firmly against them...and standing close to them in security."]

[43]Cf. Hor., *Epod.*, 6, 13 ff.; *Epist.* I, 19, 23 ff.; Fraenkel, pp. 60, 342.

[44]E.g. Pind., *Pyth.* 2, 99; Diog. Laer., II, 95; Hor., *A.P.*, 79; Ov., *Ib.*, 53. It must, of course, be admitted that Archilochus had other aspects to his talent (cf. Philod., *de Poem.*, II, 29 [p. 252 Hausrauth, p. 138 Treu; καὶ Σαπφώ τινα ἰαμβικῶς ποιεῖ, καὶ Ἀρχίλοχος οὐκ ἰαμβικῶς) ["Sappho does some things in the iambic manner, and Archilochus does some not in the iambic manner."], but it was his θυμός for which he was really remembered.

[45]Cf. *Carm.*, I, 1, 34; 32, 3–5; III, 30, 13; *Epist.*, I, 19, 32 f.; Fraenkel, pp. 154 ff.

[46]D. West, *Reading Horace* (Edinburgh, 1967), p. 114, n. 68, parallels Hor., *Carm.*, I, 2, 6–12 with Arch., 74 D = 82 L-B, lines 6 ff. (but μετακόσμησις in general is quite common, e.g. Theocr., I, 134; Herod., V, 92 *init.*; Her., *Epod.*, 16, 33 f.; Virg., *E.*, 1, 60; 8, 53 ff.; Ov., *Tr.*, I, 8, 1 ff.); I, 35, 1–4 with Arch., 58 D = 123 L-B (but note also Pind., *Ol.*, 12). For Horace's Odes and Archilochus see R. P. Schulze, *Berl. Phil. Woch.*, XXXVI (1916), pp. 348–9; V. Pöschl, *L'influence grecque sur la poésie latine de Catulle à Ovide* (Fond. Hardt, Entretiens, II, 1953), pp. 96–8.

[47]*Carm.*, IV, 13, 2 f.

[48]27 D = 237 L-B. The theme recalls that of *Carm.*, I, 25, one of Horace's most bitter odes.

⁴⁹The relationship of the Odes to the Epodes is close (cf. Fraenkel, p. 65) and might assist this notion. E. Wistrand, however, *Archilochus and Horace* (Fond. Hardt, Entretiens, X, 1963), p. 279, goes much too far in saying "Archilochus opened the source of the rich and varied flow of Horace's lyric poetry." R. Bardon, on the other hand, *op. cit.*, p. 354, warns against imputing too much importance generally to Greek models: "chez Horace, tout nous ramène à Horace." ["In Horace, everything takes us back to Horace."]

⁵⁰Arch. 68a D = 118 L-B, lines 4–7:

καὶ μήτε νικέων ἀμφάδην ἀγάλλεο,
μηδὲ νικηθεὶς ἐν οἴκωι καταπεσὼν ὀδύρεο,
ἀλλὰ χαρτοῖσίν τε χαῖρε, καὶ κακοῖσιν ἀσχάλα
μὴ λίην· γίγνωσκε δ᾽ οἷος ῥυσμὸς ἀνθρώπους ἔχει.

["Do not exult openly when victorious, and do not, when defeated, collapse wailing in your house; but rejoice in happy situations and grieve in troubles, but not excessively. Keep in mind what rhythm controls the lives of mortals."]

Keller and Holder in their edition quote also Eur., fr. 963 N, *Iph. Aul.*, 920 ff. (where Wecklein remarks, "Der Gedanke ist eine Erinnerung an Archilochus"). The last line of Arch., 68a D is reminiscent of Anacreon, 65 D.

⁵¹Lucil., 699 ff. M:

re in secunda tollere animos, in mala dimittere,
ceterum quid sit, quid non sit, ferre *aequo animo* ac fortiter
cum sciam nihil esse in vita proprium mortali datum.

["In favorable times to raise my spirits and in bad to let them go, but, whatever may happen or not happen, to endure it serenely and bravely, since I know that nothing in life is given to a mortal as his possession."]

On the relations of Lucilius here to Archilochus see M. P. Piwonka, *Lucilius und Kallimachos* (Frankfurt, 1940), pp. 49 f. G. C. Fiske, *Lucilius and Horace* (1920), p. 385, is followed, e.g., by N. Terzaghi, *Lucilio* (Torino, 1934), p. 158, in observing that Horace recalls this theme also at *Serm.*, II, 2, 135 f.

⁵²*satura* at Rome originally consisted of just such simple moralisings, but it was Lucilius who directed the genre towards censure and polemic. On the origins of *satura* see, e.g., U. Knoche, *Die römische Satire*² (1957), pp. 2 ff.; E. Burck, *Nachwort und bibliographische Nachträge* to K-H's ed. of the *Satiren*⁸ (1961), pp. 367 ff.; C. A. van Rooy, *Studies in Classical Satire and Related Literary Theory* (Leiden, 1965).

⁵³Cf. *T.L.L.* I, 1035, 70 ff., Marx on Lucil., 700.

⁵⁴For the whole stanza, of course, shows that Dellius' trouble is that he has no *aequa mens.*

⁵⁵There could also be a change of meaning: Horace might be referring to a balanced view of life as opposed to keeping (physically) calm or unruffled.

⁵⁶Insufficient attention is paid to Horace's employment of words with relation to his metre, but it must be remembered that a happy combination can produce "une occasion...de jeux et d'effets" (J. Marouzeau, "Horace assembleur de mots," *Emerita*, IV [1936], p. 1). For some exemplary remarks on internal rhyme in Horace see Wilkinson, pp. 137 ff., and cf. also J. Marouzeau, "Horace artiste de sons," *Mnem.*, IV (1936), pp. 85 ff.; O. Skutsch, *B.I.C.S.*, XI (1964), pp. 73–8.

⁵⁷This excellent point was made by Wickham.

⁵⁸Cf. *Epist.* I, 17, 24 *temptantem maiora fere praesentibus aequum.*

[59]Cf. above, note 37. Wickham, however, provided the right interpretation.

[60]Macleane (ed. 1853) makes the classic observation, "How little that notion suits the epithet *hospitalem* must be obvious to anyone!" Critics of Latin poetry seem apt to forget that the assumption *plus significas quam loqueris* was apparently as familiar then as it is now (cf. Quint., VIII, 2, 11).

[61]Wilkinson, p. 129, rightly, following Orelli. There is a similar undertone at *Carm.*, I, 25, 3 f. *amatque / ianua limen*. It is perhaps unlikely, in fact, that Dellius needed any encouragement along these lines: quite apart from his other activities in the Civil Wars he was known to have sent *epistulae lascivae* to Cleopatra (Sen., *Suas.*, I, 7, but suspected as an interpolation by Kiessling).

[62]H. Bardon, *op. cit.*, p. 347.

[63]S. Commager, *The Odes of Horace* (Yale Univ. Press, 1962), p. 284. Cf. especially *Carm.*, II, 4, 23 *trepidavit aetas*. It is not, however, possible to agree with Commager that lines 17–20 may be an extension of the idea of building into the sea, to which Horace supposedly returned "persistently, with a mixture of fascination and outrage" (cf. Commager, p. 82; Hor., *Carm.*, III, 1, 33 f.; Sall., *C.*, 13, 1; Vell., II, 33, 4; and W. Kroll, *Wien. Stud.*, XXXVII [1915], p. 228). All may depend on whether Dellius had a "sea-house" or not; but without further information it requires too much to be read into *in altum*.

[64]So C. Witke, *C.P.*, LXI (1966), p. 251. He has other more fanciful ideas about the trees, but for a more balanced view see Collinge, p. 5.

[65]Wickham, *ad loc.*

[66]The asyndeton of line 21 balances ill with *pauper et infima...* of line 22. Peerlkamp favoured *prisco <et> natus ab Inacho*, which may well be right.

[67]In the previous line *sub divo moreris* "hints at the custom of letting *victimae* out into the fields for a while when they were due for sacrifice" (Wilkinson, p. 37, n. 1).

[68]E.g. Plessis, Wickham, Page. Cf. *Carm.*, III, 9, 18.

[69]Kiessling-Heinze.

[70]Cf. *T.L.L.*, III, 1519, 79 ff. This is not to say that the common and more general idea of the confines of death is not present (cf. *Carm.*, I, 4, 16; II, 14, 9; IV, 7, 25 ff.)

[71]Lambinus and Ussani quote Hom., *Il.*, III, 316, VII, 175. For ideas or language related to the last stanza in general see the parallels quoted by A. Zingerle, *Ovidius und sein Verhältniss zu den Vorgängern und gleichzeitigen röm. Dichtern*, I (Innsbruck, 1869), p. 456; K. P. Schulze, *op. cit.*, p. 350.

[72]This paper was accepted for publication before the appearance of Gordon Williams' *Tradition and Originality in Roman Poetry* (Oxford, 1968), who on pp. 112 f. has some brief but relevant remarks on the ode.

[73]Prof. C. O. Brink, Mr. R. G. G. Coleman, and Mr. J. C. Bramble kindly read and commented on an earlier draft of this paper.

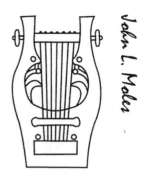

John L. Moles

POLITICS, PHILOSOPHY, AND FRIENDSHIP IN HORACE: ODES 2,7*

Horace welcomes home in Ode 2.7 a friend, otherwise unknown, by the name of Pompeius. He organizes the seven Alcaic stanzas around favorite Alcaean themes: active war service and the pleasures of wine and companionship in the interludes of battle. The three first stanzas recapitulate shared experiences in the past, when Horace and Pompeius enlisted under Brutus, killer of Caesar, and followed him and the Republican cause to defeat at Philippi in 42 B.C. Their companionship is epitomized by *mecum* (1), *cum quo* (6), and *tecum* (9). In the fourth, central stanza, Horace records their separation after the defeat: Mercury miraculously lifted him from the battlefield to safety, whereas the tide of war swept Pompeius back into further warfare.

In other words, Horace gave up resistance to Octavian, returned to Rome, and launched into the career of poet, which has given him such satisfaction. The escape from Philippi, like the one from the wolf in 1.22, was divine intervention on behalf of the destined poet. Now, however, after fifteen or more years, Pompeius has come back to Rome under Augustus' amnesty, and, in the final three stanzas, Horace tries to get him to forget about the bitter past — or at least put it into a useful perspective — and to seize the moment in renewed friendship and drinking with him. Moles' essay cogently argues that Horace puts forward a perspective on the campaigns of Brutus and the Republicans that should help Pompeius abandon his bitter hostility to Octavian (Augustus). In his view, the terms in which Horace reviews the generalship of Brutus, the defeat at Philippi, and the general behavior of the Republicans are damningly accurate and also reflect the propaganda of the victorious regime. Brutus was incompetent; Pompeius and Horace suffered ignominious defeat and had to flee or plead for their lives. Thus, the sooner Pompeius can celebrate the present and their reunion under optimistic conditions, the sooner he can fit into the new environment of the Augustan world. For Horace has asked a question at the start — who has restored Pompeius? — which gains its answer in the course of the poem. Augustus has brought the two old friends back together, genuinely achieving for them what the flawed leadership of Brutus failed to do. (Ed.)

In Horace's welcome poem to his friend Pompeius, Nisbet and Hubbard detect hints of criticism of Brutus and the Republican cause. Similarly, Quinn writes: "Pompeius' return provides an opportunity for Horace to say in effect (on behalf of others as well as Pompeius and himself) 'it's no use pretending we weren't on the wrong side in the Civil Wars.'" New interpretations of well-loved texts inevitably encounter resistance.[1] Here I

This essay is reprinted from *Quaderni Urbinati di Cultura Classica* 25,1 (1987) 59–72, with permission of the publisher.

shall reaffirm the case that Horace is indeed critical of Brutus and the Republican past and I shall further argue that this criticism is an important part of the poem's meaning.

> O saepe mecum tempus in ultimum
> deducte Bruto militiae duce,
>   quis te redonavit Quiritem
>   dis patriis Italoque caelo,
>
> Pompei, meorum prime sodalium
> cum quo morantem saepe diem mero
>   fregi coronatus nitentis
>   malobathro Syrio capillos?

Nisbet and Hubbard comment on v. 2: "the *figura etymologica* with *deducte* seems to imply reproach; the participle, which need mean no more than a colourless 'brought,' now begins to suggest incompetent manoeuvres." But to most scholars *deducte* is a standard, neutral, military term, used, like *mecum*, *tempus in ultimum*, and the ablative absolute, to give Horace's reminiscences an appropriately military flavour.

Deduco in the latter sense is indeed very common, but Nisbet and Hubbard reasonably cite *bell. Alex.* 7.1 *ut ad extremum periculi omnes deducti viderentur* for the implication "lead incompetently." We might also recall that *deduco* can mean "lead astray" metaphorically.[2] But the question cannot be decided by appeal to parallels, on one side or the other, for *deducte* in isolation. *Deducte... duce* is certainly a *figura etymologica*, hence Nisbet and Hubbard's interpretation immediately comes into consideration, since in compounds the prefix *de* can function analogously to the Greek alpha-privative, implying reversal, negation, or defectiveness.[3] It would not be inappropriate, in a poem so heavily influenced by Greek models, if Horace were employing a *figura etymologica* designed to recall Greek oxymorons based on negative compounds, such as γάμος ἄγαμος, ὕπνος ἄϋπνος ["marriage that is not marriage, sleep that is no sleep"], etc. Graecisms of this kind are infrequent in Latin, but we find *funera... nec funera* (Catullus 64.83), *insepulta sepultura* (Cicero, *Phil.* 1.5 and *innuptis nuptiis* (a tragic quotation in Cicero, *de orat.* 3.219). Most strikingly of all, Cicero, in clear imitation of the Greek idiom, describes Pompey as a *dux...*ἀστρατήγητος ["a general who is not general"] (*epist. ad Att.* 7.13.1, cf. 8.16.1).

As a form of words, then, *deducte... duce* "could" mean "*mis*led under the *leadership* of Brutus." Is this appropriate to the context?

Several considerations indicate that it is:

1. Brutus was indeed an incompetent general and was widely so regarded by his contemporaries and later tradition. Modern scholars agree.[4] The Republican decision to fight the first battle of Philippi was a bad strategic error, but it had been urged by Brutus (Plutarch, *Brut.* 39.8); in that battle his troops (his discipline being poor) charged αὐτοκέλευστοι ["on

their own decision"] (Plutarch, *Brut.* 41.4; Appian 4.110). Brutus' decision
to fight the second battle of Philippi was equally mistaken (Plutarch, *Brut.*
56.2; Appian 4.124). When Mark Antony had heard of the death of Cassius
after the first battle, he had known at once that final victory would be his
(*de vir. ill.* 83.7). Appian 4.123 and Frontinus 4.2.1 contrast Brutus' poor
discipline with Cassius' strict discipline and provide convincing documentation for their views. Velleius, a military man, comments illuminatingly
on the differences between Brutus and Cassius (2.71.1–2): *fuit... dux Cassius
melior, quanto vir Brutus: e quibus Brutum amicum habere malles, inimicum
magis timeres Cassium; in altero maior vis, in altero virtus.* ["Cassius was as
much a better general as Brutus a better man: of the two you'd rather have
Brutus your friend, but you'd fear Cassius more as an enemy; in the one
there was greater violence, in the other greater virtue"] The implication is
clear: Brutus was a very good man, Cassius a rather bad one; Cassius was
a very good general, Brutus a rather bad one. Horace, a military tribune
under Brutus, present at the debacle of Philippi, cannot have been unaware
of Brutus' shortcomings in battle.

2. The statement in v. 1 that Brutus led his men *saepe... tempus in ultimum*
is extremely challenging, for that, surely, is the very last thing a good general should do.[5]

3. *Deduco* literally means "lead *down*" and "down" in Latin, as in other
languages, often has negative connotations (for example, of failure or defeat). A significant pattern can be detected in the prefixes of some key verbs
in the ode. Brutus led his men *down* (de*ducte*, cf. v. 12 *solum tetigere*, in
contrast to the anonymous *quis* of v. 3 ff.[6] who brought Pompeius *back* to
safety in his native land (re*donavit*, cf. v. 27 *recepto*, and to Mercury, who
lifted Horace *up* from the mêlée at Philippi (v. 14 sus*tulit*). The three external figures in the poem transport their charges in significantly different
directions.

V. 2, then, does indeed hint at Brutus' well known military incompetence, Cicero's description of Pompey's faulty generalship being a close
parallel, close both verbally (*deducte... duce* and *dux... ἀστρατήγητος* are
Graecizing oxymorons) and thematically (Pompey's and Brutus'
generalship was deficient in very similar ways).[7]

I pass over discussion of the second stanza for the moment, for it is
part of my argument that its full meaning only becomes clear when the
reader comes to the third stanza:

Tecum Philippos et celerem fugam
sensi relicta non bene parmula,
    cum fracta virtus et minaces
        turpe solum tetigere mento;

Before we analyse vv. 11–12, which are (I believe) the crucial lines of
the poem, we must again note that here, as in the first stanza, Horace is,
quite simply, critical of the Republicans: good soldiers do not indulge in

celeris fuga, or throw away their shields. The ῥιψασπία is of course peculiar to Horace himself and is (no doubt) just a fictitious literary reworking of similar incidents recorded by Archilochus (5 W. = 8 Tarditi), | Alcaeus (401B Voigt) and Anacreon (381[b] P. = 85 Gentili), but it still exemplifies the general Republican military collapse, and good armies do not collapse in this way.[8]

Cum fracta virtus. This cannot just mean "when brave men were crushed" (the usual interpretation), for two reasons: (1) *fracta* picks up *fregi* (v. 7): the tables are turned and those who "broke" were "broken." It follows that Horace must somehow be included in the general category *fracta virtus*, but Horace, who threw away his shield *non bene*, was *not* a "brave man;" (2) *celerem fugam, non bene*, and, as we shall see, *minaces/turpe solum tetigere mento* are all critical observations about the Republicans: *fracta virtus* cannot be a single positive element.

A good many scholars, following the lead of Porphyrio (who commented *ad loc.: quia virtute se Cassius et Brutus praecipue iactabant*), have detected here an allusion to the "virtue" of Brutus. Nisbet and Hubbard see an even more specific point: "there is a paradox in Horace's words: one does not expect *virtus* to break. He is clearly alluding to Brutus' unbending Stoicism."[9]

Let us consider first the case for a general allusion to Brutus' "virtue," aside from his alleged Stoicism.

Brutus was indeed renowned for his virtue even in his own lifetime (cf. e.g. Cicero, *epist. ad fam.* 9.14.5, *orat.* 10.33), and prided himself on it (cf. *epist. ad Brut.* 1.16.8; Plutarch, *Brut.* 52.5). Further, the relationship between Brutus' much-vaunted *virtus* and his political and military failure *was* discussed after the Republican defeat at Philippi. In the rout after the second battle Brutus' faithful friend Lucilius told Antony that Βροῦτον...οὐδεὶς ᾕρηκεν οὐδ᾽ ἂν ἕλοι πολέμιος· μὴ τοσοῦτον ἡ τύχη κρατήσειε τῆς ἀρετῆς ["No enemy overpowered Brutus nor would one: never would chance exert such power over virtue"] (Plutarch, *Brut.* 50.1–9, cf. the closely similar account of Appian 4.129, 542–545). The ultimate source for this incident is almost certainly Asinius Pollio, the great contemporary historian and friend of Horace.[10] Like Lucilius, Brutus himself defiantly claimed that his *virtus* was wholly unaffected by wordly failure (Plutarch, *Brut.* 52.5). The source for this is P. Volumnius, "philosopher" and friend of Brutus.[11] On the other side, there is the tradition that the dying Brutus quoted the tragic couplet ὦ τλῆμον ἀρετή, λόγος ἄρ᾽ ἦσθ᾽, ἐγὼ δέ σε ὡς ἔργον ῎ησκουν· σὺ δ᾽ ἄρ᾽ ἐδούλευες τύχη ["O miserable virtue, you were only a word and I cultivated you as a fact; but you were a slave of fortune."] (Cassius Dio 47.49.1–2, cf. Florus 2.17.11). This presumably reflects Augustan propaganda, designed to discredit Brutus.[12] Brutus' resort to suicide, instead of attempting to carry on the struggle, seems also to have aroused contemporary criticism.[13] Finally, the relationship between Brutus' "virtue" and his downfall is discussed in the historians Velleius and Valerius Maximus, both of whom, of course, reflect an Augustan perspective, and seems already to have been discussed by Asinius Pollio.[14]

In sum, Horace's emphatic reference to the defeat of *virtus* at Philippi would surely remind a contemporary reader of Brutus' *virtus* and prompt the question: which side does Horace take in the contemporary debate about the role of that *virtus* in Brutus' failure?

What, then, of Nisbet and Hubbard's further suggestion? Their argument seems to be this: Brutus was a Stoic, renowned for his *virtus*; it is a notorious Stoic paradox that virtue is immune to physical assault of all kinds (cf. *SVF* III, fr. 567 ff.), including "breaking" (cf. e.g. Plutarch, *Stoic. absurd. poet. dic.* 1057D); thus Horace's wording gains additional point from being itself the paradoxical contradiction of a celebrated Stoic paradox, with direct allusion to Brutus' Stoic *virtus*. In describing Brutus as "Stoic" Nisbet and Hubbard are of course technically in error,[15] but this does not count seriously against their suggestion, since Brutus was a follower of Antiochus of Ascalon, whose "Academic" philosophy was very heavily influenced by Stoicism and was indeed popularly regarded as indistinguishable from it.[16] Moreover, among his own philosophical works, Brutus' *de virtute* was strongly Stoic in tone,[17] and several pieces of evidence show that even by his contemporaries he could be seen as a sort of Stoic sage figure (his close association — on a family, personal, and political level — with Cato the Younger will of course have contributed to this process):

1. Cicero, *epist. ad Brut.* 1.15.5 *cedebas... Brute, cedebas, quoniam Stoici nostri negant fugere sapientis* ["You yielded, Brutus, you yielded, since our Stoics deny that wise men flee"]; Cicero's jibe assumes Brutus' status as a Stoic exemplar.

2. Plutarch, *Brut.* 50.1–9 (cf. Appian 4.129, 542–545), quoted above, p. 139. The equation here of Brutus with Virtue is distinctively Stoic, since (a) the absolute immunity of virtue to physical assault is a Stoic conception (above) and (b) the idea of the sage as Virtue incarnate is also Stoic.[18]

3. Cassius Dio 47.49.1–2 (cf. Florus 2.17.11), quoted above, p. 139. This tradition also makes Brutus a Stoic, since in the tragedy the couplet was spoken by Heracles, who was a Stoic hero and whose suicide, like Brutus' (above), aroused moral controversy; the tradition, in other words, represents Brutus as a debased Stoic, whose "virtue" did not stand up in practice.[19]

4. Velleius Paterculus 2.72.1: *incorrupto animo eius* (sc. Bruti) *in diem quae illi omnes virtutes unius temeritate facti abstulit* ["His soul was free of corruption until the day that stripped him of all his virtues in the rashness of a single act"] (cf. Valerius Maximus 6.45.5 *uno enim facto et illas* [sc. *virtutes*] *in profundum praecipitavit*) also makes Brutus a corrupted Stoic, the language recalling the Stoic doctrine that there are no gradations of vice.[20]

In the light of all this, Nisbet and Hubbard's suggestion that Horace's *fracta virtus* sharply contradicts the famous Stoic paradox seems highly attractive. If so, the allusion must be pejorative. The point is that Brutus' *virtus* did not come up to expectations — was not in fact true *virtus* at all (true *virtus* cannot "be broken"). *Virtus*, then, does not here refer to what was in fact *virtus*, but rather to what was *claimed* (as it turned out, *wrongly*) to be *virtus*. Now, as we have seen, the word *fracta* picks up *fregi* in v. 7,

hence Horace and Pompeius are somehow included within the description
fracta virtus. But Horace also was not in fact a "brave man" (he threw away
his shield in the general *celeris fuga*), so that once again we have confirmation
that *virtus* refers to a *false claim*, not an objective reality. The word *virtus*
thus does duty for both (1) military *virtus* and (2) the philosophical *virtus*
of Brutus, conceived as a Stoic quality. And both, Horace implies, were
defective.

But there is still more to the words *fracta virtus*. *Virtus* basically means
"manliness" and this basic meaning is rarely forgotten in Latin, whatever
the context. Soldiers (like Horace and Pompeius) claim "manliness" and
so do Stoic philosophers, as Brutus is here conceived to be (Stoic *virtus* is a
"manly" thing, and the words ἀνήρ and *vir* are almost technical terms in
Stoic, or Stoic-influenced, philosophical texts).[21] But the "manliness" of both
groups was *fracta*. *Fractus* is a very common Latin term for "unmanly."[22] To
Roman ears, therefore, *fracta virtus* would be a striking oxymoron: "manliness was unmanned." Horace, Pompeius and the rest of the Republicans,
who had thought themselves to be "manly," were in the event revealed as
"unmanly," when they fled ignobly in the second battle of Philippi. The
idea of "unmanning" also suits the allusion to the "breaking" of Brutus'
virtus, since in Stoicism, Stoic *virtus* being "manly," failure to achieve, or
maintain, virtue can be characterised as "unmanliness."[23] "Unmanning" is
also quite a common notion in political contexts,[24] so that *fracta virtus* may
also refer to the political "emasculation" of Republicanism at the decisive
defeat at Philippi. The idea that Philippi marked the end for Republicanism
is easily paralleled: even after the first battle Brutus had hailed Cassius as
"the last of the Romans" (Plutarch, *Brut.* 44.2; Appian 4.114.476 f.), implying
that Rome was "dead,"[25] and Lucan was later to describe Philippi as *Romani
bustum populi* (7.862). Indeed, throughout the *Odes*, Horace himself shows
clear awareness of the fact that, whatever the constitutional veneer, in reality
Rome was now under the rule of one man.[26]

Interpretation of the sentence *et minaces/turpe solum tetigere mento* is
equally vital for our understanding of Horace's attitude to the Republican
past, yet once again, whatever we make of the detail, we should note immediately that the word *minaces* has a critical flavour.

Some scholars here see a reworking of the Homeric motif of warriors
"biting the dust," others a reference to *proskynesis* ["prostration before and
worship"] of the victors by the vanquished, and still others a fusion of
both ideas.[27] In my opinion, a *proskynesis* reference makes much the best
sense. Caesar, *bellum civ.* 3.98.2 (*re* Pharsalus) *passisque palmis proiecti ad
terram flentes ab eo salutem petiverunt* ["With arms spread, lying prone on
the ground, they tearfully begged safety of him"] proves that *proskynesis*
descriptions (whether literal, metaphorical, or rhetorically exaggerated)
are available in contemporary literature. We know also from Appian 4.135
that "proud" Roman aristocrats did "submit" to Antony and Octavian after
Philippi. *Tetigere* is not a natural word to use of the Homeric motif but is
the *vox propria* for *proskynesis*; similarly in the Homeric motif contact is not

made with the ground by the chin, but this is precisely the part of the body used in formal *proskynesis* (on both points cf. especially Curtius 8.5.22 *unum ex iis mento contingentem humum*). Finally, and most important, *turpe* clearly implies moral degradation: just as *minaces* contrasts with *mento* and *solum* (the "high" and "proud" are "made low"), so *turpe* contrasts with *virtus*. The idea of moral degradation is alien to the Homeric motif, which stresses rather the pathos of the dying warrior's fall, but highly appropriate to an allusion to *proskynesis*.[28] The associations of *proskynesis*, an Eastern custom, also go well with the earlier notion of "manliness unmanned": the *fracti viri* are like orientals, "unmanned," who prostrate themselves before their master. Degrading social or political customs are often described in Latin in terms of "unmanliness." So, for example Seneca, (*ep. mor.* 47.13) attacks those who kiss the hands of the great as *delicati*, whose behaviour is *humilis* and *turpis*. In our passage, therefore, not only is Horace critical of the arrogance of the Republican *principes* but he also sees a certain poetic justice in the fact that arrogant men sued for their lives in so degrading a manner. Again, it is instructive to compare Horace's attitude with that of Cicero, who inveighed against not only the incompetence of the Pompeians (*epist. ad Att.* 7.13.1; 8.16.1; *epist. ad fam.* 7.3.2), but also their arrogance, rapacity, and cruelty (*epist. ad Att.* 11.6.2; *epist. ad fam.* 7.3.2).

One last point of the *proskynesis* allusion: like *fracta virtus*, it unobtrusively conveys the thought that the Republican past is finished; for *proskynesis* is paid to an autocrat.

In the light of our interpretation of *fracta virtus*, let us now return to the second stanza. On the face of it, it simply recalls the drinking sessions Pompeius and Horace enjoyed together in their youth. But it seems to me that it also suggests that Horace and Pompeius were "soft," thus linking with the notion of "unmanliness" in v. 11.

The two friends drank heavily (*mero* of unmixed wine) and began carousing early in the day. The Romans disapproved of such behaviour, associating it with moral degeneracy,[29] yet that is how Horace and Pompeius behaved during the Philippi campaign, when their "valour" was revealed as empty (*fracta virtus*): small wonder!

Horace and Pompeius also "broke" the "lingering" day. This use of *frango* with *diem* cannot be paralleled exactly: the use of such words as *divido, diffindo, sumo*, etc. (cf. Nisbet and Hubbard on 2.7.6 and 1.1.20) is not quite the same. Consequently, some scholars have supposed that the expression *fregi... diem* evokes soldiers' boastful talk of "breaking" the enemy line;[30] the detail *morantem* coheres with this picture (the enemy line "holds" until "broken"), the description of Horace's garland might also suggest an implicit contrast with the decoration of the soldier, and the paradoxical juxtaposition of *mero/fregi* ("breaking" with a *liquid*) might allude to Hannibal's celebrated feat of splitting the rock with wine (these last two suggestions come from Nisbet and Hubbard *ad loc.*). How far this interpretation should be pressed may be disputed, yet it is (I think) clear that Horace is suggesting that he and Pompeius were only playing at being soldiers (which again links with the idea *fracta virtus* — the *virtus* the Republicans claimed was in fact illusory). *Frango* is a word that can be used in military contexts and this association is brought out in v. 11 *fracta virtus*. Indeed, the verbal contrast between *fregi* and *fracta* forms part of a more general contrast between the symposium scene of vv. 5–8, where Pompeius and Horace are *active* (*fregi*), and the battle scene of vv. 9–16, where the situation is reversed, and they are *passive* participants in events which they cannot control; cf. *sensi relicta... parmula, fracta, tetigere, me... sustulit, te tulit*, just as they were throughout the Philippi campaign (vv. 1–2 *saepe... tempus in ultimum/deducte*).[31] This general implication goes well with *fracta virtus*: the friends thought that they were *viri* (active), but in fact their role was purely passive. Their only real *activity* was... heavy drinking! The latent idea of boasting also looks forward to vv. 11–12 *minaces/turpe solum tetigere mento*: the Republican *principes* who had been *minaces* had to perform *proskynesis* — again, the tables were completely turned. Finally, we should note that, as a matter of historical fact, Brutus' army had been over-confident and "boastful" about the outcome of the second battle of Philippi (Appian 4.125: φρόνημα ...μέγα καὶ θρασύτης ...ἐθρασύνοντο ["high hopes and over-confidence...they boasted"]). As participants in that battle, Horace and Pompeius must have known of this thoroughly misguided state of mind on their own side.

Other details in the symposium description maintain the implication that, despite their claims, the Republicans were "soft." The implied contrast between drinking and proper soldiering is further brought out by the verbal parallelism between *saepe mecum* (v. 1) and *cum quo... saepe* (v. 6). Although symposiasts naturally wear garlands and sleek their hair with unguent, the idea of "crowning" can be related to the imagery *minaces/turpe solum tetigere mento* (*proskynesis* is performed to autocrats and *kings* — Horace is again utilising a reversal motif), the emphasis on "sleekness," besides connoting youthfulness, seems to suggest the "softness" of Horace and his companions,[32] and there is also an implication of oriental luxury (*malobathro Syrio*), which again looks forward to the *proskynesis* description. And we know from Plutarch, *Brut.* 38.5–7 and Pliny, *nat. hist.* 33.12.39 (quoting a letter of Brutus) that the officers of the Republican army were in fact devoted to *luxus*.

> Ergo obligatam redde Iovi dapem
> longaque fessum militia latus
>   depone sub lauru mea nec
>   parce cadis tibi destinatis;
>
> oblivioso levia Massico
> ciboria exple, funde capacibus
>   unguenta de conchis; quis udo
>   deproperare apio coronas
>
> curatve myrto? quem Venus arbitrum
> dicet bibendi? non ego sanius

> bacchabor Edonis: recepto
> dulce mihi furere est amico.

Horace now invites Pompeius to repose his weary frame and a symposium begins in his honour. As in the description of the carousing which he and Pompeius did together in their youth during the Philippi campaign (vv. 6–8), several phrases draw a contrast between the activities of drinking and soldiering: *depone, sub lauru mea, nec parce,* perhaps also *bacchabor, furere,* and the whole phrase *non ego sanius/bacchabor Edonis*.[33] But whereas the effect of the contrasts in the second stanza was to suggest the gulf between Horace's and Pompeius' claims and the reality of Republican military incompetence, here it is to underline the fact that for Pompeius, as for Horace himself, the days of soldiering are finally over. Not only that, it is better so: "now the wine is of reassuring Italian vintage... in the East the *malobathrum* was worthier of an adjective" (Nisbet and Hubbard). Similarly, the *coronae* of v. 24 are now simply the normal accoutrements of symposiasts, not, as in v. 6, decoration suggestive of misguided pride, and there is a further contrast between the simplicity of the garlands[34] and the *luxus* of the earlier symposia. The implicit rejection of the soldiering life is neatly pointed by Horace's injunction to Pompeius in vv. 18–19: *longaque fessum militia latus/ depone sub lauru mea.* Horace's laurel is the laurel of poetry, in implicit contrast with the laurel of military victory: there is a formal contrast with v. 18 *militia.* It is as if Horace is saying jokingly: "I am your general now — I am the one you must obey." The two friends are to drink and "forget" (*oblivioso*) their Republican past. How should we interpret this?

For one scholar: "the hidden pain of the Ode is momentarily bared in the final two stanzas, when the poet proposes to get himself and the friend of his lost youth royally drunk... : this is to be no celebratory toast, but a hard drinking revel whose primary purpose is to blot out the pain of the past."[35]

This reading cannot command assent. Certainly, Pompeius is adjured to "forget" the past, but that past has been described in terms which imply Horace's repudiation of it: Brutus, the Republican general, was "no general," the "manly" Republicans turned out to be "unmanly," arrogant "minaces" were humbled and there was a certain justice in their comeuppance. The stress at the end of the poem falls, rather, on the *joyousness* of the occasion: *recepto/dulce mihi furere amico. Amicus* is a warmer, more intimate, word than *sodalis.*

But there is, I believe, still more to the meaning of the last three stanzas and the poem as a whole.

The Stoic implications of the phrase *fracta virtus* are very important. In this ode Horace, I suggest, is drawing a generic contrast between the Stoic and Epicurean attitudes to political participation. The bogus *virtus* of the Republicans and the "Stoic" Brutus, the inadequacy of which was revealed at Philippi, involved participation in political and military life. Stoics characteristically advocated such participation. The second half of the poem urges Pompeius to forget his misguided past—his soldiering is over and he should instead celebrate with Horace, his friend. It is *dulce* to do so. Here surely we have a contrast between Stoic *virtus* and Epicurean ἡδονή, that ἡδονή which necessarily involves disengagement from public life. In philosophical texts the contrast between Stoic "virtue" and Epicurean "pleasure" is commonplace.[36] The second half of the poem also celebrates friendship for its own sake: the *sodalis*—the military or symposiastic ἑταῖρος ["companion"]—becomes the *amicus*. No philosophical school attached a higher value to friendship than Epicureanism or interpreted the concept in a warmer way.[37] Several touches in the last three stanzas combine to give Horace's prescriptions a lightly Epicurean note. The two friends are to drink in a garden (*sub lauru mea*) and this garden has a certain symbolic quality, since it is contrasted with the *militia* which Pompeius has finally put behind him. Of course symposia may take place in gardens, but Horace is also deftly alluding to the Epicurean *hortus* which symbolises retreat from the world of politics and war. Pompeius' *militia* is described in sea imagery—conventional enough, yet we may also detect an Epicurean contrast between Epicurean "pleasure" and the "sea of troubles" which engulfs the non-Epicurean (as in Lucretius 2.1 ff.). The two friends will drink *oblivioso Massico*. Wine traditionally brings λήθη ["forgetfulness"], but here Pompeius is forcefully urged to "forget." The word can also have philosophical implications. In *sat.* 2.6.60 ff. Horace laments: *quando... licebit/... ducere sollicitae iucunda oblivia vitae!* There, as here, it is the Epicurean life which affords *oblivium* from cares.

To sum up. This poem is not simply an outpouring of emotion, studded with appropriate reminiscences, on the return of a long absent friend, genuine though its emotion is. Rather, Horace is concerned to give his friend some sound practical advice on the political attitude he should now take. Pompeius should not idealise the past: it was in fact much less glorious than it appeared at the time to the friends in their youth—their general was incompetent (he was), his *virtus* not what it was claimed to be (debatable, but certainly a tenable position and one propagated by the Augustan regime), their leaders were arrogant (they were), the Republicans were soft (true) and brought about their own downfall (also true—over-confidence lay behind the Republican *principes'* insistence on joining battle), and it is now gone for ever—power now resides with Octavian, the sole ruler to whom the Republican survivors prostrated themselves on the field of Philippi (a correct political analysis). Better to forget, and to find true repose in private life, in the company of an old friend, with whom he had shared both happiness and suffering long ago, and with whom he is now joyously reunited.

As I have tried to show by my bracketed comments, there is nothing remotely implausible about such an interpretation of Horace's views on the Republican past: in every single respect it corresponds to historical realities of which Horace must have been aware. But of course Horace expresses these views obliquely and with tact: he can hardly tell Pompeius

outright that the last 15 years or so of his life have been completely mis-
spent. Hence the punning *deducte... duce*, prompting the question: "what
sort of *dux* was Brutus?," and the inevitable answer: "a rather poor one," and
the challenging oxymoron *fracta virtus*, suggesting, to anyone with a feeling
for language and contrast (*fregi/fracta*), that the much-vaunted Republican
virtus was a sham. Thought-provoking also are the matter-of-fact allusions
to the *celeris fuga* (surely not what a man committed to the Republican past
would mention? He would rather recall the splendid deeds of heroism of
Lucius Cassius, Cato's son, and Antistius Labeo)[38] and not the arrogant
temper of the Republican *principes* (*minaces*). Horace is indeed critical of
Brutus and the Republican past and this criticism is an important element
in his address to Pompeius.

Notes

*I am grateful to Professors R. G. M. Nisbet and F. Cairns for helpful com-
ments on an earlier draft of this paper.
[1]R. G. M. Nisbet and M. Hubbard, *A Commentary on Horace Odes II*, Oxford
1978, pp. 106–121; K. Quinn, *Horace: the Odes*, London 1980, p. 210; Nisbet and
Hubbard's views are sharply criticised by (e.g.) J. Griffin, *Journ. Rom. Stud.* 70, 1980,
p. 183; E. A. McDermott, *Am. Journ. Philol.* 102, 1981, pp. 234–235. The neglected
study of L. Edelstein, *Am. Journ. Philol.* 62, 1941, pp. 441–5, contains several antici-
pations of the views of Nisbet and Hubbard. Quinn and myself, though I disagree
with the substance of Edelstein's argument.
[2]*Thes. Ling. Lat.* 5.1, col. 276.80 ff.
[3]On the range of possible meanings of the prefix "de-" see *Oxford Lat. Dict.*
and Lewis and Short s.v.
[4]For critical modern estimates of Brutus' generalship see e.g. R. Syme, *The
Roman Revolution*, Oxford 1939, p. 205; M. L. Clarke, *The Noblest Roman*, London
1981, p. 67.
[5]Attempts to discern "irony" or "parody" in this statement (so Nisbet and
Hubbard, Quinn) are surely misguided; the contrast between the first two lines
(dreadful dangers) and the third and fourth lines (safe return to Rome) must be
real, otherwise the emotional effect is completely lost.
[6]The form of the question, which expresses surprise rather than a desire for
knowledge, should discourage us from seeking to identify the *quis*. Therefore it is
inappropriate to see an allusion to Octavian, as urged by (e.g.) L. P. Wilkinson,
Horace and his Lyric Poetry, Cambridge 1951², p. 33 f; Nisbet and Hubbard *ad loc.*; G.
Nussbaum, *Aufstieg u. Niedergang* 31.3, 1981, pp. 2122–2123.
[7]Cf Appian 4.124 (an explicit comparison between Pompey's mishandling of
the Pharsalus campaign and Brutus' mishandling of the Philippi campaign). It is
interesting to note that Appian makes Brutus say, when forced to join battle by his
officers, that he is οὐ στρατηγοῦντες ἔτι μᾶλλον ἢ στρατηγούμενοι. Since Appian's
account of this incident derives from Asinius Pollio (as I show in a forthcoming
article in *Latomus*), it is tempting to suppose that Pollio's narrative contained some
kind of derogatory pun on Brutus as *dux*. And Horace, of course, had read Pollio
(*Odes* 2.1).
[8]Indeed, Horace may even be exaggerating the speed of the Republicans' collapse: Plutarch, *Brut.* 49.4–10, Appian 4.128,, and Cassius Dio 47.48.4–5 make it
much more of a flight. On the other hand, all three of these accounts contain con-

ventional literary "big battle" elements and are sympathetic to the Republican side. If Horace is indeed exaggerating, his intention is not to be flippant (*celerem fugam/ sensi* is grimly serious) but rather to intensify his criticism of the Republicans.

[9]E.g. S. Commager, *The Odes of Horace*, New Haven 1962, p. 172 (and scholars there cited); Nisbet and Hubbard, p. 114.

[10]For Plutarch's and Appian's use of Pollio cf. recently C. B. R. Pelling, *Journ. Hell. Stud.* 99, 1979, pp. 84–85; J. L. Moles, *Class. World* 76, 1983, pp. 287–288 (and n. 7 above); for more detailed argument that Pollio is the source of the Lucilius story see my unpublished doctoral dissertation, *A Commentary on Plutarch's Brutus*, Oxford 1979, pp. x–lvii, 467–468.

[11]Volumnius is explicitly mentioned in Plutarch, *Brut.* 52.2–3.

[12]I discuss this tradition in detail in my *Latomus* article.

[13]Cf. the ὦ τλῆμον ἀρετή tradition (with discussion below, p. 140) and Plutarch, *Brut.* 56.2–3 ὁ δὲ Βροῦτος τὸν ἔσχατον ἀγῶνα ὑπὲρ τῶν ὅλων οὐθ' ὑποστῆναι δοκεῖ φρονίμως, οὔτε σφαλεὶς ἐπανόρθωσιν εὑρεῖν, ἀλλ' ἀπεῖπε καὶ προεῖτο τὰς ἐλπίδας, οὐδ' ὅσον Πομπήϊος ἐπιτολμήσας τῇ τύχῃ ["Brutus does not seem to have stood up rationally under the final battle that determined everything nor, after defeat, to have found encouragement, but he disowned and abandoned his hopes, daring to resist fortune not even as much as Pompey had"]. The Brutus-Pompey σύγκρισις in this passage may derive from a motif in Pollio—cf. n. 7 above.

[14]Velleius 2.72.1 ff.; Valerius Maximus 6.4.5; Pollio; cf. the Lucilius story and the long discussion of the relationship between Brutus and Cassius' "virtue" and their downfall in Appian 4.132–134, which presumably reflects a similar discussion in Pollio.

[15]Cf. Griffin (above. n. 1), p. 183.

[16]Cf. Cicero, *acad. prior.* 2.132.

[17]Cf. G. L. Hendrickson, *Am. Journ. Philol.* 60, 1939, p. 401 ff.

[18]For this kind of Stoic equation cf. e.g. Velleius 2.35.2 *homo virtuti simillimus* (of Cato the Younger); Tacitus. *ann.* 16.21.1 *Nero virtutem ipsam excindere concupivit* (of Thrasea Paetus and Barea Soranus).

[19]Cf. my *Latomus* article.

[20]Cf. J. Hellegouarc'h, *Velleius Paterculus* II, Paris 1982, p. 218.

[21]Cf. e.g. Diogenes Laertius 6.14 = Antisthenes fr. 135A Caizzi; Theon, *progymn.* 33 = Antisthenes fr. 195 Caizzi; Diogenes Laertius 6.59; Seneca, *de tranq. anim.* 5.4, *de vit. beat.* 13.6–7.

[22]For extensive documentation see *Thes. ling. Lat.* 6.1, col. 1252.26 ff.; R. G. Austin, *Quintilian Book 12*, Oxford 1948, p. 158; J. Bramble, *Persius and the Programmatic Satire*, Cambridge 1974, pp. 44, n. 1, 76. For specific *fractus – vir* contrasts cf. e.g. Quintilian 5.9.14, 12.10.12; Seneca, *ep. mor.* 115.2, *de vit. beat.* 13.4.

[23]Cf. e.g. Cicero, *Tusc. disp.* 4.30.64; Dio Chrysostom 4.35 ff.; Plutarch, *Stoic. absurd. poet. dic.* 1058C.

[24]Cf. e.g. Cicero, *de orat.* 3.41.16; Polybius 30.30.8; Plutarch, *Brut.* 7.7; the idea is of course also implicit in accusations of ἀνανδρία μαλακία, *mollitia* etc.

[25]"Death" and "infertility" are related ideas in this motif: cf. Plutarch, *Philop.* 1.4.

[26]Cf. F. Millar, *Journ. Rom. Stud.* 63, 1973, p. 66, with references.

[27]"Biting the dust;" cf. especially Nisbet and Hubbard, p. 115; *proskynesis*: ps.-Acro, Heinze, Syndikus, Quinn; fusion of both: e.g. N. E. Collinge, *The Structure of Horace's Odes*, London, 1961, p. 130 n. 2.

[28]For incisive discussion of the problem cf. especially Heinze in A. Kiessling and R. Heinze, *Horaz: Oden und Epoden*, Berlin, 1955, pp. 188–189.

[29]Cf. Nisbet and Hubbard, p. 112 (with references).

[30]So (e.g.) Nisbet and Hubbard. pp. 111–112; Quinn, p. 210.

[31]Cf. Nussbaum (n. 6 above), p. 2123.

[32]Cf., for this possible implication, Cicero, *Cat.* 2.22 *quos pexo capillo,* nitidos *aut imberbis aut bene barbatos videtis, manicatis et talaribus tunicis, velis amictos, non togis;* Seneca, *ep. mor.* 115.2 *nosti comptulos iuvenes, barba et coma* nitidos, *de capsula totos: nihil ab illis speraveris forte, nihil solidum;* Horace, *epist.* 1.4.15–16 *me pinguem et* nitidum *bene curata cute vises, / cum ridere voles, Epicuri de grege porcum* (for Epicurean *mollitia* cf. e.g. Seneca, *epist. mor.* 33.1–3).

[33]*Bacchari* and *furere* can be used in military contexts, and the allusion to the Edoni may evoke not only hard drinking and Bacchic rites but also Thracians' traditional bloodthirstiness in war (perhaps the Edoni contributed auxiliary troops to Brutus' army).

[34]Cf. Nisbet and Hubbard, p. 120.

[35]McDermott (n. 1 above), p. 235.

[36]Cf. e.g. Cicero, *epist. ad fam.* 15.16.3 (with Tyrrell and Purser *ad loc.*); *de fin.* 1.12.42–13. 42; 1.18.61; 2.13.44 (all *virtus–voluptas* contrasts). *Virtus* in isolation, with, as it were, a capital *v*, often denotes *Stoic* virtue in particular: cf. p. 140 and n. 18 above.

[37]For the role of friendship in Epicureanism cf. recently J. M. Rist, *Class. Philol.* 75, 1980, p. 121 ff.

[38]Plutarch, *Brut.* 49.9–10 and Appian 4.135 show what could be done by those who wished to paint a heroic picture of the Republican defeat at the second battle of Philippi.

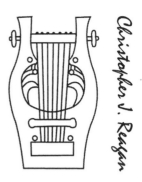

HORACE, CARMEN 2.10: THE USE
OF OXYMORON AS A THEMATIC STATEMENT

The year 23 B.C., in which Horace completed and published his Odes, was a troubled one for the regime of Augustus. The troubles included a conspiracy against Augustus' life by his fellow consul (detected and quickly punished by execution); the replacement of the dead consul by Piso and the appointment of Sestius (of Ode 1.4) to be suffect consul; serious illness of Augustus himself that was feared fatal; a new distribution of power that led to the pre-eminence of Agrippa (of Ode 1.6) and the steady decline of Maecenas (of Ode 1.1); and the death of Marcellus, nephew, son-in-law, and destined successor of Augustus. The most obscure of these events, perhaps even at the time, was the consul's conspiracy. He appears to have had the public name of Aulus Terentius Varro Murena, but the four names indicate that he had been born as Licinius Murena, then been adopted into the family of Terentius Varro and kept only the cognomen. Horace addresses that man as Licinius in this poem. We would love to know when he composed the poem and how the publication of the Odes relates in time to the conspiracy. Did Horace anticipate the instability of Licinius that would lead, in spite of advice, to rash action as consul; did he deliberately leave the poem in the collection after the plot's discovery and Licinius' death, partly to prove his own loyalty and political acumen, partly to exploit the inevitable dramatic irony that readers would enjoy? Or did the publication precede the conspiracy; for he would never have allowed his familiarity with Licinius to have been immortalized after the scandal? Scholars disagree on the sequence of events. Nevertheless, whether intended by Horace or not, the dramatic irony of advice to a man who died when he failed to heed wise words, constitutes an important element in our reading. Reagan's essay concentrates on the wise words and their poetic expression, and he chooses the rhetorical term oxymoron (the juxtaposition of contradictory words) as a way of summarizing Horace's art. As he shows, Horace has composed a complicated system of alternations and variations on the theme of moderation or what, ever since he coined the phrase in line 5, has been called the Golden Mean. In the first stanza, the poet urges Licinius to steer his course carefully between the deep ocean and the dangerous shore, not to strain outwards nor to repress too much. There is security (6) in the Golden Mean, from either abject poverty or wealth that provokes envy. Reagan notes how Horace alternates his advice with scenes of turmoil, how he weaves action and inaction into the fabric. Licinius is encouraged to understand that the universe itself experiences patterns of change and that he has only limited powers to control events. If he had listened to this advice, then he would have been able to survive the crisis which led to his impatient decision to conspire. The oxymoron of 21, *angustis animosus*, would have been his wise manner: "full of life in tight times," he would have waited out the troubles. Unfortunately, he appreciated neither the oxymoron nor the Golden Mean. (Ed.)

This essay is reprinted from *Rivista di Studi Classici* 18 (1970) 177–185.

Horace's Carmen 2.10, addressed to Licinius Murena, who was apparently badly in need of the advice,[1] is a presentation of the idea of the golden mean *(aurea mediocritas)*. This central idea of the ode was not original with Horace, but is a poetic statement of the Aristotelean, and generally Greek popular, view that virtue (ἀρετή) consists in the mean (μεσότης).[2] We must agree with Professor Silk, when he remarks:

> It was Horace's nature to discover poetry in the familiar and his incomparable art to make a limited repertory of traditional moral truths the starting point of a body of poetry of seemingly infinite diversity.[3]

The ode is one of Horace's most polished poems, yet it has received only passing notice or none at all from commentators. The poem presents two interconnected themes: the golden mean in behavior and the unavoidable but ephemeral nature of hardships through which only the virtuous man can pass safely and with equanimity. Hardship in life is man's testing ground; the tension within man, his dissatisfaction and his insatiable desire to achieve, are at once his claim to glory and potentially the means of his ruin. But it is more than this; in its fundamental metaphor, the voyage at sea in the ship of life, in its use of imagery and its structure, in its tone and texture, in its use of and play on words the ode is a comment on the cycle of life and death in which virtue plays an integral role and is the one insurance of reasonable happiness. I suggest also that Horace through the use of oxymoron, states these themes and ideas in a radical form first in the words *'celsae graviore,'* (9), then in *'angustis animosus'* (21).

The lesson is set forth in the metaphor of the voyage on the moody sea, the time-honored symbol of man's journey through life, of man's courage and fearlessness.[4] This vignette frames the poem (1–4; 22–24), producing a ring structure, a common feature of ancient poetry.

Two recent discussions of the structure of the poem are worth examining here. Professor Toll suggests that the poem is an elaborate interweaving of ideas, dividing the ode into two parts of two and four strophes each (ll. 1–8; 9–24). The first two strophes of the poem are an extension on the level of the ideas presented of the golden line with chiastic order. The ode begins with a warning *(rectius vives) neque...urgendo* (a), and *neque...iniquum* (b). The mention of the golden mean (c) separates the first warning from a second in which the metaphor has changed in reverse order: *obsoleti tecti sordibus* (b) and *invidenda...aula* (a). The poem continues with another warning (a) (ll. 9–12), followed by a note of hope (b) (13–20). The final strophe of the ode closes with admonitions in reverse order:

> rebus angustis animosus atque
> fortis appare; (b)

and return to the metaphor of the voyage at sea: *sapienter...vela* (a).[5]

Professor Collinge sees the structure of the poem as one in which there is a responsion between the two themes of the ode. The first strophe (1–4) presents both themes and this is followed by eight verses (5–12) which give a series of images and applications of the first theme. The second idea is treated in the following two strophes (13–20), followed by the last stanza which returns to the nautical imagery.[6]

There are elements in both of these structural analyses which are tempting. Miss Toll's analysis of the first two strophes is inviting, and certainly an attempt to create a golden line on the level of the ideas that are presented while putting forth the concept of the golden mean would not be beyond the conscious art of Horace. But unhappily she wishes to disjoin the third strophe from the first two when that strophe quite clearly presents us with *exempla* designed to illustrate by means of natural phenomena and man-made objects what happens in the case of extreme pride.

Professor Collinge's analysis of the poem's structure is neater. He sees the poem as a presentation of two ideas dividing the poem at line 12.

Whatever one may take to be the general structure of the ode, the thought pattern seems to me to be more complex. The structure of the ode is clearly based on the principle of the *harmonia discors*. Dynamic passages, usually *exempla*, depicting great activity are juxtaposed with static apophthegms where there is complete inaction. Looking at the poem in this way the scheme would appear as follows:

ll. 1–4   the storm at sea: *exemplum*: action
ll. 5–8   the prudent man avoiding extremes: apophthegm: inaction
ll. 9–12   nature itself destroying hybris: *exempla*: action (*celsae graviore* (9) sums up the thought of this section.)
ll. 13–14 ...*pectus:* apophthegm: inaction
ll. 15–17 ...*summovet.* Jupiter governing the cycles of the seasons and of life: *exemplum*: action
ll. 17–18 ...*erit:* apophthegm: inaction
ll. 18–20 Apollo as musician and archer: *exemplum*: action
ll. 21–22 ...*appare:* apophthegm: inaction (*angustis animosus* (21) sums up the meaning of this section.)
ll. 22–24 back to the sea: *exemplum*: action

The notions of life (activity) and death (lack of activity) are woven into the very texture of the poem itself and the radical statement of these ideas occurs on the connotative level in the oxymoron *angustis animosus* (21). Horace, as always, is here shown to be the master artisan with words and at the same time very much the philosophical eclectic. For this reason attempts to translate the ode and to interpret it solely as a discussion of Aristotelean ethical concepts fall short.

The diction of the first strophe, and indeed of the poem as a whole, is particularly striking and complex. The description of the stormy sea and the perils of the ship and its insolent and unwary navigator are vividly presented through the use of onomatopoeia. The alliterative effect of the 'p,' 't,' 'c,' 'v,' 'r,' 's,' 'm,' 'n,' and the assonant 'u' and 'o' found throughout the first three strophes suggest all the sound and fury of the marine and celestial turbulence, the wind, the thunder, the wave, the creaking and groaning of the hull and the mast, the tearing of the sails and later the crashing of tree and tower.

The words used throughout the poem are laden with meaning. Through the ambiguity of many words, Horace brings out meaning on a far deeper level than might appear at first. Descriptive linguists have for some time been aware that the words of any utterance carry both a lexical and grammatical meaning. Neo-critics have written extensively on the levels of meaning, of connotation and denotation in poetic expression. These critical and linguistic concepts are far too familiar to discuss here. When a critical reading of Greek or Latin poetry is attempted, these two points of view must be to some degree fused, else the real meaning of a poem may be lost. Ancient writers on the theory of rhetoric and poetics were keenly aware of the use and power of words, of the force and beauty of the euphonic placement and pattern of expression, and of the effect of the juxtaposition of words, phrases and clauses to one another. This awareness led to the naming of a whole host of figures of speech and figures of words, many of which we are not able to employ. The modern world has in a very real sense only rediscovered what was common knowledge to every schoolboy of the ancient Greek and Roman world.

Of particular interest are the metrical implications of the poem. On the one hand, the use of the Sapphic strophe for this ode is appropriate to the moralizing tone and content of the poem.[7] On the other, the metrics of the first three verses of the strophic pattern with their many long syllables lend a slow sonorous quality and particularly in this case the quality of the many 'o,' 'u,' long 'a' sounds as well as the diphthongs render an added somber effect.

A detailed analysis of diction will bring out more clearly the patterns of thought of this ode and will support the concept that its structure is based on the idea of the *harmonia discors*. It will also show that through the use of the discordant figure oxymoron, Horace has succinctly enunciated the themes and ideas he has presented.

Rectius (1) may carry the meaning 'virtuous' or 'just' but it was also used as a synonym for *honestus* and, as a noun, *rectum* was employed to translate the Stoic concept, κατόρθωμα, 'a morally right act performed with a knowledge that it is so.'[8] *Rectius* may then connote both the concept of justice as well as that of κατόρθωμα. The phrase *altum urgendo* (2–3) in context means 'to press out to sea.' But *altus* refers to height as well as depth;[9] and *urgere* is equally ambiguous, meaning either 'to push,' 'drive,' 'urge' or 'to weigh down or burden.'[10] The elliptical *altum*, then, may very well connote *insolens*, ὕβρις.[11]

Urgendo, the gerund with its fateful ring, is intended to stand antithetically to *premendo* (3). N. D. Levin is quite right to suggest that the

immediate intent here is to illustrate through the imagery of nautical ma-
neuvers the Aristotelean excess (ὑπερβολή) and deficiency (ἔλλειψις).[12]
Premere means 'to press,' 'to bear down'; in context: 'to hug the shore.' But
the two gerunds each have a deeper connotation. *Premendo*, a confining
action, connotes for Horace the act of dying. As Professor Commager says:
'Movement of life into death struck him (Horace) as an almost physical
contraction.'[13] If *premendo* suggests death for Horace, then *urgendo*, clearly
its opposite, connotes expansiveness and life. The voyage at sea, the quest
for the mean (virtue) is a life and death struggle, taking a man now nearer
one extreme, now nearer the other, and it is expressed uniquely through
kinesthetic imagery.

Iniquum (4), which in its context clearly means 'uneven' or 'rugged,'
also conveys the notions of 'unjust' and 'hostile.'[14] The former meaning
recalls *rectius* (1); the latter focuses upon the hostile or unfriendly situation
of the voyage itself.

Cautus (3), 'cautious,' 'wary' at first glance may appear to indicate the
mariner is prudently fearful, but the proximity of *nimium* to this adjective
which here is used adverbially may render a pejorative meaning: 'over-
cautious' i.e. 'lacking in courage.'[15] Thus the *cautus* becomes the antithesis
of *altum* on the connotative level and brings out the more basic meaning of
horrescis (3) 'to tremble with fear.'

The phrase *neque...semper* (1–2, repeated 19) not only admonishes
against inflexibility[16] but conveys the idea of the impermanence of things
as well. It also looks ahead to the apophthegm of lines 17–18 '*non, si male
nunc, et olim/sic erit*': and to the meaning of the mythological *exempla* which
surround it (15–17, 18–20). The adverbial *nimium* (3, repeated 23) calls to
mind the Delphic admonition μηδὲν ἄγαν.[17]

The statement of the first and major theme of the ode 'the golden mean'
is presented in the second strophe. Again there are *exempla* to illustrate
the extremes of deficiency and excess, the house that is in ruins (*obsoleti
sordibus tecti*) and the palatial establishment (*aula*). The order of presentation
is exactly the opposite of the *exempla* of the first strophe. Unlike the first
strophe where we see the insolent and over-cautious mariners, we observe
the extremes from the point of view of the man who is protected (*tutus*) by
his virtue, in particular by his prudence (*sobrius*). The verbs of the strophe
are deliberately weak: *diligit* (6) *caret* (6,7); the whole weight of meaning
and of emphasis is placed on the adjectives and nouns of the passage, especially *auream* (5), *tutus*, *obsoleti* (6), *sordibus*, *tecti*, *invidenda* (7), *sobrius*
and *aula* (8).

The 'golden mean,' *aurea mediocritas*, has become a veritable by-word
but at the same time has elicited little worthwhile comment.

Through generations of school editions of the *Odes*, and as recently as
Page, we are invited to look at 1. 5. 9. '*qui nunc te fruitur credulus aurea*' for
a parallel use of the word *aureus*.[18] But in the context of the ode 1. 5 *aurea*
cannot have the same connotation that it does in 2. 10. 5. It is quite clear
from the context that the last thing that Lydia's ensnared young lover is

interested in is her virtue. Rather the use in 1. 5 must without a doubt derive ultimately from such a phrase as χρυσέη 'Αφροδίτη. In context the young man thinks everything is golden, that is to say 'wonderful,' that 'golden Aphrodite favors him in his amatory enterprise.'

We are also treated to such literary insight as may be offered by the statement: 'the gold of the middle course, not the gold of a miser's dream.'[19]

No commentator seems to have noticed or bothered to point out that the phrase is unique. Only Horace uses the term *aureus* in speaking of the mean. Granted that Latin admits of such phrases as *aurei mores*[20] (where *aureus*, means 'splendid' or 'excellent'), all other Greek and Latin authors, so far as I know, use such adjectives as ἄριστος, βέλτιστος, *optimus* with respect to the mean.[21] *Auream*, emphatically placed at the beginning of the strophe, modifies *mediocritatem* (5) directly but offers an effective contrast to *obsoleti* (6) and *sordibus* (7) on the denotative level. The force of this adjective carries over to *aula* (8) as well as adding to the opulence already suggested by this Greek loan word.

The anaphoric use of *caret* (6, 7) occurring at the caesura and at the beginning of two *membra* of the tricolonic period emphasizes that word. It becomes the fulcrum or pivot around which balance the filth of a house grown old and decayed and the palace that is bound to be envied. *Tecti* (7) has the metaphorical meaning 'home' but on a literal level means 'roof' and in conjunction with the adjective *obsoleti* (6) brings out what Horace has in mind, namely that it is a home that is barely a roof to cover a man's head. *Sordibus* (7) means 'filth' but may also mean 'lowness or meanness of rank' and in its plural form may also mean 'mourning garments.'[22] The suggestion of death has, therefore, been restated.

Aula (8), a word borrowed from the Greek αὐλή and clearly antithetical to *tecti* (7), suggests all the sumptuousness of an eastern court. *Invidenda* (7), the gerundive, has a fateful, an inevitable, ring to it.

The third strophe sets forth by way of example the meaning of the previous two. The key words here are *saepius, ingens* (9), *celsae, graviore* (10) and *summos* (11). Again the structure of the strophe is tricolonic and the initial *saepius* (9) is meant to be taken with all three *membra*. The images are designed to show the punishment of nature itself for hybris. The emphatic position of the three key adjectives *ingens* (9), *summos* (11) at the end of their verses and *celsae* (10) before the *caesura* makes clear the intent of the strophe. All three words carry us back to the first stanza and the word *altum* (1); all suggest immoderation and pride. The onomatopoeic force of the verbs also heightens the imagery. In *agitatur* (9) we hear the shaking and rattling of the branches of trees; in *decidunt* (11) we hear the final rumbling thud of a falling tower; *feriunt* (11) suggests the flash of the thunderbolts.

But the most important of all, the juxtaposition of *celsae and graviore* (10) sums up the theme of the first three strophes by means of the figure oxymoron on the connotative level, recalling all the extremes against which Horace warns. *Celsae* 'high' or 'haughty' and *graviore* 'heavy,' 'burdensome,' 'oppressive' with its noun *casu*, which may mean not only a 'falling down' but a 'moral fall' as well,[23] suggest the same imagery on the connotative level that *urgendo* (2) and *premendo* (3) do in the first strophe. *Celsae* implies the expansiveness of life; *graviore* the confining oppression of death. At the same time on a denotative level perhaps no more succinct way has ever been found to express the idea "How are the mighty fallen" (II Sam. 27).

The fourth and fifth strophes should be taken together, for only at this point in the poem is there enjambment of strophes. *Sperat* (13), the initial word of the strophe, sets the keynote for this and the last three strophes. The two strophes form a tight interweaving of apophthegm and *exemplum* in carefully balanced periods where antithesis is the major figure employed. The parisosis and paromoeosis in line 13 is most striking. *Metuit* (13) does not suggest in this context the cowardly fear of the navigator in the first strophe, but a just and reasonable fear that begets temperance and prudence. Horace here warns against foolish overconfidence in favorable times and unreasonable despondency in the midst of misfortune.

But the two adjectives *infestis* and *secundis* (13) call to mind once again the sea imagery. *Infestus* has the literal meaning 'unsafe' as the vessel in the first strophe clearly is, but has the transferred meaning of 'troublesome.'[24] *Secundus*, with the literal meaning 'following,' derives a transferred connotation of 'favorable' from the nautical metaphor indicating that the winds are most favorable for sailing when the winds come from behind the ship.[25]

The only man who can maintain this balance between tensions has the heart or mind, *pectus*, (15) that is *bene praeparatum* (14) 'well disposed.' Horace has in mind here either the Aristotelean ἕξις or the Stoic διάθεσις.

The preposited adjective *informes* (15) occupies an emphatic position meaning 'shapeless,' then 'ugly.'[26] *Hiemes* (15), 'the winter' may connote old age.[27] *Reducere*, 'bring round' is used frequently of the movement of heavenly bodies and the seasons.[28] Hence, this verb together with *summovet* (17) introduces a cyclical notion of the cosmos and of life into the poem which serves to reinforce the meaning of the maxim (13–15), as well as that which succeeds (17–18). In this *exemplum* Jupiter, as Apollo in the next, is an ambivalent figure, for Horace suggests that he is the bringer of death as well as life.

The ephemeral, fleeting nature of all things is made the more poignant by the brief aphorism of 11. 17–18 *non, si male nunc, et olim / sic erit.* The key words here are the adverbs *nunc* and *olim*, ' here and now ' and ' by and by,' with *non* at the beginning of the statement negating the whole.

The following *exemplum* (18–20) brings out even more unequivocally the meaning of the preceding apophthegm. Apollo is the god of the cithara as well as of the bow. The cithara, the instrument of music and the symbol of the joy of living, and the bow, the instrument of death, are both constructed on the same principle of tension. Horace has here in a highly suggestive and imaginative way set forth the notion of the *harmonia discors*.

One recalls at once the comparison of the bow of Odysseus to the lyre
when Odysseus strings his famous bow in Book 21 of the *Odyssey:*

ὣς ἄρ᾽ ἔφαν μνηστῆρες· ἀτὰρ πολύμητις Ὀδυσσεύς
αὐτίκ᾽ ἐπεὶ μέγα τόξον ἐβάστασε καὶ ἴδε πάντη,
ὡς ὅτ᾽ ἀνὴρ φόρμιγγος ἐπιστάμενος καὶ ἀοιδῆς
ῥηϊδίως ἐτάνυσσε νέῳ περὶ κόλλοπι χορδήν,
ἅψας ἀμφοτέρωθεν ἐϋστρεφὲς ἔντερον οἰός,
ὣς ἄρ᾽ ἄτερ σπουδῆς τάνυσεν μέγα τόξον Ὀδυσσεύς.
δεξιτερῇ δ᾽ ἄρα χειρὶ λαβὼν πειρήσατο νευρῆς·
ἡ δ᾽ ὑπὸ καλὸν ἄεισε, χελιδόνι εἰκέλη αὐδήν.

(21. 404–411)

["So spoke the Suitors. But clever Odysseus, when he had picked
up the great bow and looked it all over, as when an expert in the
lyre and song easily stretches the string over the new peg, holding from both sides the well twisted sheep gut, so without haste
Odysseus strung the great bow. Then, holding it in his right hand,
he tested the bowstring; it sang back a lovely note, like the song of
a swallow."]

Or Heraclitus when he says:

οὐ ξυνιᾶσιν ὅκως διαφερόμενον ἑωυτῷ ξυμφέρεται·
παλίντονος ἁρμονίη ὅκωσπερ τόξου καὶ λύρης.

(Fr. 51)

["They do not understand how, though different, it agrees with
itself: there is a connection at work both ways, as with the bow
and lyre."]

or   τῷ οὖν τόξῳ ὄνομα βίος, ἔργον δὲ θάνατος.

(Fr. 48)

["For the bow the name is life, but its work is death."]

The paradox of man's fortunes, the irony of life stands fully revealed
to the reader.[29]

But Horace promptly sets forth his customary more positive attitude
in the last strophe, which begins with another aphorism. Here again there
appears a radical statement of the theme in the form of oxymoron. *Angustis*
(21) in its context means, 'difficult' or 'adverse' but its literal meaning is
'narrow' or 'confined' and, as we have pointed out, this notion of confine-
ment or restrictiveness connotes death for Horace.[30] On the other hand,
animosus (21), while it may in its context here mean 'spirited,' has a more
fundamental meaning 'full of life.'[31] *Angustis* and *animosus* form a tension

with each other on the connotative level. ~~Even in the midst of life we are never far from death.~~

Bravery is a necessary virtue in any man's life no matter what his circumstances may be and in *fortis* (22) Horace calls our attention once again to Aristotle.[32]

The last three lines of the poem recall us to the image of the journey at sea and to the addressee. In his use of *sapienter* (22) Horace shows that he confidently hopes that the lessons of his poem have not been lost on Murena. Murena should now begin to behave as the ideal wise man of the Stoics.

Notes

[1]W. C. McDermott, *TAPA* 72 (1941) pp. 255ff. R. Hanslick, *Rh. Mus.* 96 (1953), pp. 282ff. A. W. Verrall, *Studies Literary and Historical in the Odes of Horace*, Kinnikat Press Inc., New York: Port Washington, (1969), pp. 11ff.

[2]*EN* 106[b] 16–107[a] 27; cf. 106[b] 34 and the definition of virtue which follows 106[b] 36 καὶ διὰ ταῦτ' οὖν τῆς μὲν κακίας ἡ ὑπερβολὴ καὶ ἡ ἔλλειψις, τῆς δ' ἀρετῆς ἡ μεσότης· ...ἔστιν ἄρα ἡ ἀρετὴ ἕξις προαιρετική, ἐν μεσότητι οὖσα τῇ πρὸς ὑμᾶς ὡρισμένη λόγῳ καὶ ᾧ ἂν ὁ φρόνιμος ὁρίσειεν. ["For this cause, then, excess and defect belong to vice, but the mean to virtue... Virtue is the disposition of choice, which depends on our observing the mean, determined by reason and as a thoughtful man would define it."] For a general discussion of the relationship of the terms of the poem to Aristotle's terminology which will bear repeating here. Cf. D. N. Levin, 'Horace, Carm. 2.10: Stylistic Observations' *CJ* 54 (1959) pp. 169–171.

[3]E. J. Silk, 'On Theme and Design in the Poetry of Horace' *Venture* 7 (1967) p. 47.

[4]G. Nussbaum, 'Symbolism in Horace's Poetry,' *Latomus*, 24 (1965) pp. 133–143.

[5]H. C. Toll, 'Unity in the Odes of Horace,' *Phoenix*, 9 (1955) p. 160. The structure is: a b c b a a b b a.

[6]N. E. Collinge, *The Structure of Horace's Odes*, pp. 70–72. Cf. also Enk, 'De Symmetria horatiana,' *Mnemosyne* (1936–37), 171 and Kiessling-Heinze, *Oden und Epoden*.

[7]M. O. Lee, *Word, Sound and Image in the Odes of Horace* (Ann Arbor, University of Michigan Press, 1969), pp. 39–41.

[8]Dict., s.v.; Cic. *Off.* 1,8ff. Cf. Page, *Horace: Odes*, p. 253.

[9]*Ibid.*

[10]*Ibid.*

[11]Commager, *op. cit.*, p, 67.

[12]*Op. cit.*, n. 2.

[13]Commager, *The Odes of Horace* (New Haven, Yale University Press, 1962), p. 54; cf. also 55.

[14]Dict. s.v.

[15]Cf. Page, *op. cit.*, n. 3, D. N. Levin. *op. cit.*

[16]*Ibid.*

[17]*Ibid.*

[18]*Op. cit.*

[19]H. D. Naylor, *Horace: Odes and Epodes*. Cambridge, The University Press: 1922; *loc. cit.*

[20]*Horace* c. 4. 2.23.

[21]μέτρον ἄριστον D.L. 1. 6. 6.93 τὸν μέσον...βίον...βέλτιστον Arist. *Pol.* 4.11 mediocritas optima est. Cic. *Off.*1.131 mediocritatis regula optima est. *ibid.* 2.59.

[22]Dict. s.v.

[23]*Ibid.*

[24]*Ibid.*
[25]*Ibid.*
[26]*Ibid.*
[27]Cf. *Ode.* 1.4; 1.9.
[28]Dict. s.v.
[29]Leo Spitzer. *Classical and Christian Ideas of World Harmony,* Baltimore: Johns Hopkins Press, 1963.
[30]Dict. s.v.
[31]*Ibid.*
[32]*EN* 1115[b] 8–24.

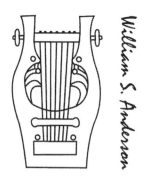

THE OCCASION OF HORACE'S CARM. 2.14

In this poem, Horace produces another memorable variation on his favorite theme of *carpe diem*. He concentrates almost exclusively on the inevitable death of his addressee, whose no doubt carefully chosen name, Postumus, helps to stress what comes "next" for him. Postumus is told of the miserable Underworld where he must go, and then reminded of what he must leave behind here. The estate, charming wife, trees, and tight-locked cellar of prize wine all add up to the pleasures of the present which Postumus should be enjoying. What is he doing? What is the situation or occasion of this poem? In my essay, I argue against Quinn's ingenious hypothesis that Postumus is hosting at a banquet a half-baked Epicurean, who, having imbibed too much, drunkenly thanks his host with absurdly gloomy advice. I suggest instead that the advice, consistent with other poems where *carpe diem* is seriously advanced, is the true theme here, that the speaker is quite sober, because neither he nor Postumus is enjoying cups at a banquet, but rather focusing on the religious confidence that Postumus is voicing (or even acting out in a sacrifice) that his *pietas* somehow guarantees his future. We don't control our futures, only some part of the present. (Ed.)

✧ ✧ ✧

In interpreting 2.14 Kenneth Quinn starts from an altogether acceptable hypothesis: that the ode, like many superior lyric poems including those of Horace himself, employs an imaginary situation and a speaker who need not be identified as Horace.[1] The problem he sets himself, then, is to define for us the particular situation and speaker which, as he sees it, Horace imaginatively created within the circumscribed world of this poem. Since any good poem works with great economy to introduce the audience to its private world within the space of a few opening lines, Quinn rightly concentrates first on the initial stanza of this ode. He has this to say about the situation: "The scene implied is a rather different sort of dinner party from those in i, 27 or iv, 13. The reader is once again called upon to fill in the semi-extraneous details for himself, and each reader will naturally fill them in differently. A speaker (whom we should be ingenuous in taking to be Horace himself) breaks in on a conversation to address his host, Postumus, with a gloomy earnestness that comes (we may suspect, taking up a hint in the last stanza) as much from what he has imbibed of his host's liquor as

---

from what he has imbibed of Epicurean philosophy."² Once he has distinguished this dramatic scene and the speaker's tone, Quinn contents himself with sweeping over the next four stanzas, enthusiastically described as "pure poetry" and poetry made out of a commonplace, in order to draw all our attention to the final two stanzas.

Perhaps, though, before we go to the sixth stanza, we should look more closely at the first, to see whether we can agree with the inferences which have been drawn about its dramatic scene. The earnest, gloomy speaker is there, I concede, although I see no reason as yet — nor will I when I come to the last stanza — to diagnose this gloom as the result of drink. The dinner party I see nowhere implied in the first stanza. I do not say that the party is excluded, if later portions of the poem seem to bring such a scene to the fore; I do say that the first stanza offers no evidence at all for a party. The earnest, gloomy speaker starts from a background that Horace does not choose to define. And if he implies anything, he does it by the words that he inserts in that stanza, not by ideas drawn from the last stanza. Thus, although *pietas* appears regularly in gloomy poems on the unavoidability of death, to emphasize the absolute inflexibility of the natural order,³ in this poem Horace stresses the point more than strictly necessary. Not only does the futile "battle" of *pietas* against the invading forces of age and death serve to make vivid the first statement of the poem about the "fleeing years," but also Horace continues the theme into the second stanza with an apparently hyperbolic reference to extravagant sacrifices designed vainly to buy off Pluto. Suppose we conclude that this cluster of material on *pietas* constitutes all that Horace wishes to imply of the dramatic scene at this point. What should we infer from it? I suggest that Postumus has been talking with some confidence about his right relations with god and man, possibly even claiming that the gods therefore will guard him in the future. The earnest, gloomy speaker, then, pitying the simple-mindedness of Postumus, tries to impress upon him a true grasp of his mortality. I do not insist on the necessity of my inferences; I do not believe, on the other hand, that, if we are looking for Horace's implications as to the dramatic scene, we are entitled to ignore the details of the opening stanza and rush to the last stanza to grasp a tenuous hypothesis.

At the end of the second stanza, Horace names two mighty giants of mythology, Geryon and Tityos, who have been overcome by death, then expands his net to include in the next three stanzas all mankind as victims, because mortal, of Pluto. It serves his purposes both of inclusiveness and of consolation to move from the second person singular (Postumus alone) to the first person plural by means of the relative clause (*quicumque...vescimur* 10) and the attached "universalizing doublet" (*sive reges / sive inopes erimus coloni* 11-12). The fourth stanza uses two main verbs in the first person plural, and the fifth stanza, although not specifying the agent of the gerundive *visendus*, presumably expects the audience to supply *nobis* rather than restrict the action as yet to *tibi* (Postumus). Only in the sixth stanza, in the inserted relative clause (*quas colis* 22), does Horace decisively break away from the generalizing form to concentrate once again on Postumus; in ret-rospect, the initial gerundive of that stanza acquires as its agent *tibi*. In its structure, therefore, this poem is quite typically Horatian. Its first two stan-zas are devoted to sketching as much of the situation involving Postumus as the poet cares to introduce; the end of the second stanza fades neatly into the dominant theme of the central stanzas (as the speaker both warns and consoles Postumus with the vision of all men's mortality); then the sixth stanza, starting as a mere continuation of the gerundive construc-tion in stanza five, cleverly transfers all attention back to Postumus, who obviously is expected to draw, with us, some conclusions for his personal situation from the generalizations. And Postumus' personal situation, as the final two stanzas reveal, obligates him to live a little more reasonably, to concentrate less on *pietas* and more on the blessings which he already possesses.

For Quinn, "the line of meaning remains relatively unimportant until we get to stanza 6" (p. 103). Then, according to him, the opening line brings us sharply back to Postumus' home.[4] As many commentators have been prone to observe, the phrasing of 20–21 is remarkably like a justly famous passage of Lucretius. In most cases, the editors have confined themselves to this safe observation. A few, however, have dared to draw a comparison between the two passages and remarked on the un-Lucretian qualities of Horace's poem.[5] Quinn makes a striking innovation by arguing that Horace *alludes* to Lucretius and, through that allusion, economically conveys the fact that the speaker in the Ode, like the speaker of the similar lines in Lucretius, utters words which we are not to accept. "Horace, we should re-peat, is writing for an audience that knows its Lucretius. An audience that can be relied on to catch the echo of a familiar quotation. And, more than that, to recall the context of a familiar quotation."[6]

Again, the hypothesis is an attractive one. Horace does like to allude to familiar poetry, and he surely referred to Lucretius on more than one occasion in his earlier Satires.[7] However, in my experience one of the most pernicious pursuits of classical philology is the tracking down of supposed reminiscences, whether it be for the purpose of identifying sources or positing allusions, and it is the task of a responsible critic to demonstrate conclusively by fact, not by rhetoric, that a putative allusion exists and functions. Just because Horace's audience "knows its Lucretius" is no reason to assume that the context of Lucretius controls that of Horace. To put it quite brutally, Horace's audience did indeed know its Lucretius, better than Quinn does, and I find it utterly impossible to believe that it could ever have distorted Lucretius into the shape required by Quinn. If that is so — and I shall demonstrate my assertion — then the supposed allu-sion vanishes like a bubble. We must return, then, to the safer comments of the traditional editors, that Horace's line is like Lucretius', possibly inspired by the unquestioned poetic power of Lucretius, possibly an affec-tive evocation of another commonplace (like *pietas*) of meditations, poetic and rhetorical, on death. In the second alternative, Lucretius' passage would function merely as a further witness to the existence of this quite likely "commonplace."

At first sight, Horace's passage, *linquenda tellus et domus et placens / uxor*, does have striking affinities with Lucretius' longer passage:

iam iam non domus accipiet te laeta, neque uxor
optima nec dulces occurrent oscula nati
praeripere et tacita pectus dulcedine tangent.

(Lucr. 3.894–896)

["Now no longer will your happy home welcome you, and your perfect wife and sweet children will not run out to snatch kisses from you and touch your heart with quiet delight."]

Both home and wife are mentioned, and Horace could be said in *placens* to vary the epithet *optima* of Lucretius to fit the Alcaic meter. We may be sorry that Horace has omitted the affective picture of the children and their welcoming kisses, but Latin *variatio* does operate in this free way in other instances. So far, then, Horace might be alluding to Lucretius. If it can be shown that the context of Lucretius fits closely that of Horace, then the possibility of allusion becomes more of a likelihood. As I have argued, the context of Horace is far from clear at this point, not patently the dinner party that Quinn affirms. Nevertheless, in these final two stanzas, Horace, with the help of Lucretian echoes, could intend to work out, in an ironic way not at all unusual for him, a surprising clarification of the dramatic scene. So we may legitimately investigate the context of Lucretius, if only with the hope that it may assist us.

Quinn says: "What is the context of these lines in Lucretius? They are given as typical of the talk of men at dinner parties when among their cups they start to lament the brevity of human life:

hoc etiam faciunt ubi discubuere tenentque
pocula saepe homines et inumbrant ora coronis,
ex animo ut dicant 'brevis hic est fructus homullis;
iam fuerit neque post umquam revocare licebit.'"[8]

["This is what men do when they have reclined and grasp their cups and shade their brows with garlands: they start saying passionately, 'How short is this enjoyment for poor little human beings; soon it will have passed and it will be impossible ever to call it back.'"]

To summarize the remainder of his argument, because Lucretius satirizes this dinner talk and because Horace's context seems to be another dinner with talk of a similar vein, it follows that Horace is also satirizing the speaker. But is Quinn right in his construction of the context in Lucretius 3.894–896; is the context in fact defined by a passage which in all manuscripts appears nearly twenty lines later, which seems not to refer back to 3.894 but forward to a *new* context and quite different statements?

Quinn reports that J. P. Postgate saw reason to transpose 3.912-918 to a point immediately before 894-899, but he does not explain why Postgate did so and whether in fact he agrees with that dubious authority. Having obscured the issue, though, he conveys the impression that his view of the context of 894-899 is certain. But no recent edition that I can discover even deigns to mention Postgate's transposition, let alone follow it. Editors and translators regularly agree that the manuscript order makes good logical and poetic sense, and they would willingly assent to the summary of the Lucretian scholar Cyril Bailey, who, introducing comments on 3.912-930, wrote: "Lucr. passes from the solemn mourners at the graveside" — he refers to 3.894-911 — "to the ordinary pleasure-loving man (the Epicurean in the popular sense) who cries 'let us eat, drink, and be merry, for to-morrow we die,'"[9] If Quinn had not made the mistake, I should have said that it was impossible to confuse Lucretius' meaning, for after moaning the three lines quoted by Quinn (3.894-896), the unidentified friends continue unambiguously: *misero misere...omnia ademit una dies infesta tibi tot praemia vitae* ["Poor wretch, one cruel day has wretchedly robbed you of all the prizes of life"], (898-899). In other words, the future tense of Lucretius' passage is not a warning uttered by a maudlin, half-drunk guest, but a lament voiced by a friend at the tomb or bier of the dead man who, now that he has died, will no longer enjoy life's blessings. A second speech is then assigned to mourners (904ff), again making clear the condition of the person being apostrophized (*leto sopitus* 904, *horrifico cinefactum te prope busto* 906): he is dead, they have been weeping (*deflevimus* 907) at his funeral rites. Therefore, when in 912 Lucretius starts with *hoc etiam faciunt*, we have every right to expect some additional details about the attitude toward death, but we certainly will not let the relative clause (*ubi discubuere* etc.) that qualifies this new group of people cancel the details which Lucretius has carefully introduced to define the previous group as mourners. The banqueters of 912ff have absolutely nothing to do with the statements of 3.894ff.[10]

Once the context of Lucretius is demonstrated to be other than what Quinn has argued, the particular Lucretian allusion which he finds in this Ode vanishes. Whatever the dramatic situation of Postumus, he surely is not dead, as is the person being addressed in the Lucretian passage supposedly echoed by Horace; nor is the speaker a mourner as in Lucretius. We must then inspect more closely the final two stanzas of Horace's Ode to see whether any of the conjectures of Quinn are in fact supported by the Latin. Horace tells us that Postumus possesses land (*tellus*), a presumably fine home (*domus*), and a charming wife (*placens uxor*). Without Lucretius to lean upon, we cannot draw any safe conclusions as to the location of these items. One certainly can have a *domus* either in the city or country; one's wife can be in either home at a set time; and *tellus*, a poetic word, although I suspect that it here refers to agricultural land, might merely denote the earth which all men must leave at death. When the speaker continues the list of Postumus' possessions by mentioning and pointing to some cultivated trees (*harum quas colis arborum* 22), Quinn infers crucial details for the hypothetical scene of the poem: "Not a rural scene, but a scene in a wealthy Roman's house in the city. The speaker is looking out from the *triclinium* into his host's formal garden in the *peristylium*."[11]

Now, most readers of this poem have inferred the opposite from these same trees: a rural scene, not an urban one. Without the Lucretian allusion, it is possible to determine the relative strength of each inference on its own merits. Does the speaker point to a formal garden in a peristyle, or does his gesture embrace a group of trees cultivated on a country estate? Horace did know of gardens within a peristyle, gardens which included some kinds of trees or shrubbery which could be qualified by the terms *silva* or *nemus*. In *Epist.* 1.10.22, he refers to such a garden, not without a certain irony that may well affect his choice of the word *silva*: *nempe inter varias nutritur silva columnas* ["a forest: why it is raised among vari-colored columns"]. It is generally assumed that a similar garden is evoked by a passage in *Carm.* 3.10.5–6: *nemus / inter pulchra satum tecta* ["a grove sown within a beautiful home"].[12] A *nemus*, however, does not suggest to the Roman mind a profusion of trees; it defines rather something like a forest glade, a grove. I take it that, in fact, there were few, if any, true trees in the garden of the usual peristyle, for the simple reason that they would be of the wrong scale. The *nemus* in such a case was the variegated growth of the clearing seen through the columns (which represented to the pastoral imagination the trees of the woods). Now, Horace goes to great pains to specify what he means when he is referring to the garden of the peristyle: he mentions *silva inter columnas* or *nemus inter tecta*. He does no such thing here. In a context not otherwise defined, cultivated trees would not, I believe, suggest to a sophisticated Roman audience, any more than it has to most readers of Horace today, a formal garden in the peristyle. Too many Romans of Horace's generation were familiar with Vergil's *Georgics* and the agricultural writings of Varro and the great Cato to interpret these trees as anything but the various kinds of useful *arbores*, for fruit, timber, shade, and the like, to be seen on a rural estate.

The decisive detail, it seems to me, is the set of cypress. The cypress is not a tree for a garden, and the Romans knew it well. Cato regarded it as an imported item, but attributed to it enough practical value to give careful directions as to its cultivation on the farm.[13] Varro described its use for supporting shoots and for marking off farm-boundaries.[14] Pliny, assimilating this and other information from his many sources, allowed little aesthetic merit to the cypress, except where it was allowed to grow in stands and then cut to represent a variety of forms, like the yew hedge of English country houses.[15] But the cut cypress hedge was a tall hedge, not suitable for the enclosed space of the peristyle but eminently appropriate to define a portion of a large estate under the open sky. The cypress itself is a tall tree, to which Catullus assigns the poetic epithet *aerea*;[16] and Vergil, comparing mighty Rome among the lesser cities of the world, thinks of cypress towering into the air among mere shrubs.[17] It is because of its height that

Varro used the cypress to mark off the boundaries of his farm, visible to everyone from a great distance. Therefore, if Postumus is the master of cypress trees, we are entitled to assume that these trees, notoriously tall, devoid of shade, unappealing to the eye, but useful for wood and providing supporting stakes for plants, formed part of a plantation in the country, not a formal garden in a peristyle.

The final stanza must also be approached without prejudice. We have found no evidence in any preceding line for a dinner scene or the conversation that usually accompanied Roman *convivia*. On the contrary, the details from which legitimate inferences may be drawn seem to point to a rural setting, probably a stroll among the trees of Postumus' plantation. When the speaker concludes his monologue by predicting the wasteful behavior of Postumus' heir with the hoarded wine in his cellar, there is no reason to follow Quinn and assume that a sly comparison is being made between two kinds of dinner, the present one with its lack of wine and various future ones where precious Caecuban is spilled on the *pavimentum*. The speaker does intend an implicit comparison, undoubtedly, between Postumus and his heir, but not in the sense Quinn suggests. On the one hand, we consider Postumus here and now; he has locked up his choice Caecuban, that is, cut himself and his friends off from the pleasures of the dinner party. The very last thing that Horace wants us to picture is a Postumus acting as host. On the other hand, the speaker invites us to imagine Postumus' heir who, once he becomes master of that cellar, will make extravagant use of the wine, probably in dinner parties. All the abstemious self-denial of Postumus will ironically result in the drunken spilling of his treasured bottles.

In rejecting Quinn's hypothesis of the dinner scene and the somewhat inebriated speaker spouting his maudlin commonplaces, I wish also to raise questions about the way Quinn presented the poem in general: as a dramatic monologue in which the focus of Horace, the sophisticated Roman audience, and intelligent modern readers rests upon the speaker. For Quinn, Postumus functions only as a host of the speaker; otherwise, we concentrate on the slowly revealed foolishness of the speaker, his guest. In order to establish this thesis, though, Quinn limits his careful reading to three stanzas only, as if the central portion of the ode could be eliminated from consideration. He is very flattering to Horace, of course, in that he praises those more or less ignored stanzas as "pure poetry." But if those stanzas are good poetry, unqualified in any way to awaken suspicions about their speaker; if their picture of death is to stir some kind of assent in our imaginations, how can we be expected suddenly to reject this impression and scorn the speaker as a drunken fool? By all the standards of poetic economy, we should have expected Horace to plant here and there words that occasioned doubts as to the speaker's reliability, precisely where Quinn senses "pure poetry." The result of Quinn's reading is a speaker who produces line after line of excellent poetry, then surprises us by his folly, and a Postumus who is virtually a cipher, in short a poem whose "meaning" resides in a highly original interpretation of three out of seven stanzas.

The traditional interpretation of this ode has devoted itself almost exclusively to Postumus. Whether or not the speaker is to be identified with Horace, nevertheless it has been assumed that the words he utters have authority and serve to reveal to the Roman and modern audience of Horace not the character of this speaker, but the true nature of Postumus' existence. I find this interpretation, *pace* Quinn, essentially unassailable. In what follows, then, I should like to bring out, perhaps a little more elaborately than is customary, the poetic art by which this ode operates. After all, it should be self-evident that with Horace we are far less interested in what he says than in how it is said. We should have little difficulty in locating a multitude of verbal and thematic parallels, to prove how trite — if that is what we seek to demonstrate — the idea of the ode is. Particularly in Book II Horace devoted attention to aging Roman nobles and politicians who miss the true enjoyments of existence. Postumus differs somewhat from Dellius of 2.3 and Quintius Hirpinus of 2.11, but there is little appreciable difference among the speakers of the three poems either in attitude or arguments. When we compare the three poems as to the manner in which the speaker makes his argument, it is immediately obvious that 2.3 and 11 consist of direct advice whereas 2.14 works obliquely, or, to use Heinze's terms, as indirect paraenesis.[18] Through this indirection, we gradually acquire an impression of Postumus and apply the details used to describe him to the familiar scheme of counsel utilized in such odes as 2.3 and 11.

As part of their direct method, both 2.3 and 2.11 start concretely from the present situation. In 2.3 the speaker uses an imperative *memento* that looks to the future (supported by the future perfects *vixeris* 5 and *bearis* 7), but it is quite evident that the advice being given applies to both present and future. Then, by pointing to the natural beauty surrounding Dellius, by the present imperative *iube* 14, and by the clause *dum...patiuntur* 15–16, the speaker makes it clear that he contrasts the future with the present, the only temporal period which Dellius can in any positive way affect. The following stanza fixes attention on the future (17ff), to warn Dellius that he will leave all his accumulated possessions; it is then reinforced by a generalization about all men and their mortality (*omnes eodem cogimur* 24). The whole poem has been explicitly constructed around the present, and the interrelation of tenses and moods helps to reinforce the imperative of the speaker: enjoy these things now. In 2.11 the speaker fuses present and future in a different manner, still concentrating on the imperative of now. Having revealed what Quintius is doing, anxiously inquiring into the intentions (for the future) of the distant Spaniard and Scyth, the speaker gives his advice (the subjunctive serving as a substitute for the imperative): *remittas quaerere* 3–4. Time flies (*fugit* 5); nature does not remain lovely forever, he warns. Then, he advances his positive alternative to the negative advice with which he began: with a series of questions and an imperative (*dic age ... maturet* 22–23), he indicates the natural setting of trees (*hac pinu* 13–14) and the physical blessings available to Quintius, but inserts the admonitory *dum licet* 16 to keep Quintius attentive to the transitory aspect of even those advantages which he can be said to control. Thus, 2.11 works explicitly in the present, implicitly in terms of the future's threat. Not one future tense occurs.

By contrast, 2.14 elaborates its themes almost exclusively in relation to the future. After the initial *labuntur* 2, every main clause employs either a future active verb or, what amounts to the same effect, a future passive participle. One relative clause, *quicumque ... vescimur* 10, in the present tense functions primarily to reinforce *omnibus* and the thought: "We all shall die." The second relative clause in the present tense, *quas colis* 22, possesses, as we have seen, major importance, for it restores our attention to Postumus and his present circumstances and encourages us to supply the personal pronoun *tibi* for the gerundive *linquenda* 21. Otherwise, the only verbal form which might be construed to refer to the present is the participle *servata* 26. In the future, the heir will waste the wine which has been locked up carefully; that implies that Postumus now locks up his Caecuban, that Postumus owns some wonderful wine and foolishly leaves it untasted. All this explicit emphasis on the future, a consistent aspect of the poem from first to last stanza, surely suggests less about the speaker than about Postumus. If he will open his eyes to a realistic picture of the future (in sharp contrast to his pious expectations), he may at least acquire an appreciation of the present and accept its implicit imperatives. By avoiding the present tense, though, by refraining from all imperatives, by sketching in the scene only through a seemingly incidental relative clause and a participial clause, the speaker keeps his advice indirect, and the poem becomes one of the most artful of these typically Horatian hortatory odes.

A regular element of these odes, as noted in 2.3 and 2.1 1, is the *dum*-clause. "Gather ye rosebuds *while* ye may," for the roses do not remain in their bloom forever; they are short-lived, and our span of life is short. Horace employs no *dum*-clause to interrupt the oblique methods of 2.14, and he handles the equally conventional appeal to *brevitas* (cf. 2.3.13, 1.4.25, 1.11.6) with great restraint. Of all the trees which Postumus cultivates on his estate, only the cypress will attend their short-lived master (*brevem dominum* 24) when he departs from life. Another common topic of these odes is the heir, regularly represented as an implicit enemy to the present owner of the estate, a warning to use what one has now (cf. 2.3.19-20, 4.7.19; *Epist.* 1.5.13, 2.2.190-191). Here, too, Horace employs the theme with much oblique economy, for he attaches to this unknown inheritor details which apply implicitly to the present condition of Postumus. From the perspective of the speaker, the heir earns the adjective *dignior*, because by comparison with Postumus' tenacious hoarding the younger man's wasteful spilling of choice vintages constitutes a more worthy occupation.[19] So the heir serves as a veiled threat in a specific sense: he reminds Postumus of all the wine which he is vainly leaving behind him untasted.

The artistry which Horace exhibits in this indirect paraenesis makes it intrinsically unlikely, it seems to me, that Franz Buecheler correctly appreciated this poem in pointing out a series of "infelicities " and assigning it to an early period of Horace's productivity.[20] On the contrary, I should assume that 2.14 was written after both 2.3 and 2.11, just as it is placed after them in the Book, because Horace knew he could rely on the audience's familiarity with the poem's implicit argument and so devoted his attention to his indirect presentation. Buecheler levels his attack in general at "the grossly mythological tone, the extensive reminiscences from Greek, the inclination toward exaggeration," and in particular at verbal awkwardness. Little need be said to counteract his criticism on the three general points. The references to the Underworld are not crude; they have been selected carefully. For example, Geryon (8) was chosen probably because his name connotes great herds of cattle. Postumus, who seems to think that huge sacrifices of bulls might save him from death, can well take that gigantic owner of bulls and cows as a pattern. Tityos also was a giant, but his name, juxtaposed to *tristi*, suggests the pain of death, the permanent *tristitia* which Postumus will be unable to alter. The Danaides and Sisyphus (18–20) emphasize another crucial aspect about the Afterlife to which Postumus is destined: it consists of protracted toil (*longi laboris* 20).[21] The allusions to Greek literature do not stand out in opposition to the rest of the poem. Thus, the supposed echo of Homer in 10, *quicumque terrae munere vescimur*, by its very Homeric associations would serve to validate the generalization about *omnibus*; it also acts as an implicit reminder to Postumus that he should enjoy the bounty of the earth while he can. Finally, if Buecheler meant by hyperbolical such numbers as *trecenis* 5 and *centum* 26, we may concede the fact of exaggeration without also condemning it; for the exaggeration serves rhetorically to bring home the unwise, excessive commitments of Postumus.

    In his list of verbal awkwardnesses, Buecheler specified *inlacrimabilem* (6), *enaviganda* (11), *carebimus* (13), and *mero...potiore cenis* (26–28). I do not share his judgment about Horace's innovation, *inlacrimabilem*, nor did Horace; for he reused the word in another late Alcaic poem, 4.9.26. Moreover, a little study will reveal how skillfully Horace fitted the sonorous word to the other vowels and consonants of the context. With *enaviganda*, Horace also behaved boldly, for he took what had been an intransitive verb of motion and made it transitive: this gerundive construction is particularly striking, in that Horace delays *enaviganda* and separates it from *unda* by a line and a half. But look at what this single word helps the poet to achieve. In the first place, he supports the grammar by a rhyme (*unda ... -anda*). He also inserts between the related words the Homeric reference, and thereby he juxtaposes the pictures of grim water and bounteous earth; *enaviganda* picks up the water image and insists on the absolute divorce between the two elements. Once dead, we all sail irredeemably across the Styx away from this lovely earth of ours. Finally, the gerundive initiates a procession of such constructions, whose cumulative effect in representing the unavoidable constraints of Postumus' future is undeniable. As for *carebimus*, Horace uses this word freely in his Odes, and here its choice is partially suggested by the sound-patterns of the context.

The last of Horace's supposed infelicities deserves special study, and it will bring us back to the question from which Quinn started: what is the situation of the poem in the first stanza? Buecheler considered juvenile the suppressed comparison in *mero...pontificum potiore cenis*, a comparison which all editors agree should be expanded and translated as follows: "wine better than that served at the banquets of the pontifices." I do not deny that such might be the correct translation. I suggest, however, that those who are tempted to belittle Horace's poetic maturity on the basis of such a translation might investigate the alternative rendering: "wine better than the banquets of the pontifices." It seems relatively obvious that Horace could easily have avoided "infelicity" by using *vinis* as his last word. If he indeed meant us to compare Caecuban with pontifical wine, the right word was at hand. Inasmuch as he chose *cenis*, not *vinis*, he invited his audience at least to try comparing Postumus' Caecuban wine, locked in his cellar originally but destined at last to be drunk, with proverbially lavish banquets of the pontifical colleges. Does this comparison make any sense? I think it does. Proverbial though such banquets were, they are also to be interpreted closely with the implied personality of Postumus. Buecheler inferred at this point that Postumus was a pontifex, but that is neither provable nor necessary. Banquets of pontifices do, however, represent what Postumus regards as important, for the lavish extravagance of such meals belongs to the same kind of superficial *pietas* as the munificent sacrifices referred to in the second stanza. The comparison, then, serves to remind us of the unwise scale of values cherished by Postumus, for that Caecuban wine, when properly enjoyed, symbolizes a way of life that is indeed better than formal paraphernalia of *pietas* like Postumus'. Indeed, it is no accident that the sound-patterns of 28 echo parts of the opening line. The repeated initial *po-* sound should remind us of the rare and affective anadiplosis: *Postume, Postume*; and of the letters of *fugaces* (1) only *g* and *a* fail to recur in 28. It seems as though Horace encourages us to link sound and sense of the opening and close of 2.14, to interpret the unwise Postumus as a man who puts all his confidence in formal religious *pietas* to guarantee his future, but completely fails to grasp the practical wisdom of his ultimate heir who will prefer the wine at hand to all that is symbolized by *cenae pontificum*, banquets of priests.

One final point needs to be made about the mature conception behind this poem. Although we can hardly be so presumptuous as to date its composition, it should be noted that Horace carefully placed it in immediate juxtaposition to an ode that deals in a strikingly different manner with many of the same themes, including the *pietas* which, I have argued, is so important in 2.14. The interaction of 2.13 and 2.14 is possibly more significant than that of any other pair in a Book which is, as is well known, almost entirely arranged according to paired poems.[22] *Carm.* 2.13 is a recognized masterpiece, and I have no doubt that Horace knew it in 23 B.C. If so, he would hardly have juxtaposed to it an effort that he knew was juvenile, knew that his audience would feel inartistic. He planned that two good poems should interact.

In 2.13, the speaker is Horace, and the poem deals with his own experiences and the manner in which he personally applies them. A tree, or
perhaps only a branch, has just fallen near him, almost killing him. Very
much alive, but feeling the closeness of death, he now interprets the accident.
First, he solemnly speaks of man's inevitable fate: try as we may to avoid
particular dangers, sudden death will sooner or later sweep us away (13ff).
The speaker in 2.14 made the same point, but in a significantly different
context, for, whereas Horace, breathing a sigh of relief, is commenting on
his recent near-death by accident, the speaker to Postumus is warning him
that death will seize him, *pietas* notwithstanding. How did Horace escape
this "tragic" demise? In line 12 he modestly calls himself *immerentis*; in line
23 he states that, had he died, he would have been assigned to a place
among the *pii*, together with Sappho and Alcaeus. The implication, sufficiently clear in this clever poem, is confirmed by 2.17.27ff and 3.4.27:
Horace's special *pietas* earned the miraculous protection of the gods.[23] Thus,
a poem, honoring with playful seriousness the beneficent aspects of
Horatian *pietas* is placed in immediate juxtaposition to 2.14, where *pietas* of
a more formal type, associated with vain sacrifices of bulls and lavish pontifical banquets, is treated as pathetically futile, not only to save Postumus
from death, but also to gain him any happiness after death.

Both poems devote considerable attention to the Afterlife, each in its
special manner. In 2.13 Horace professes to be speculating or imagining
what might have happened to him, had the tree killed him; in 2.14 the
speaker confidently predicts what will happen to Postumus. Thus, in addition to the contrast between certain future for Postumus and avoided
present (but probable future) of Horace, we feel the playfulness of Horace's
situation and the quite different destiny of Postumus. It is here in part that
Buecheler and others go wrong when they fix on the "crass mythological"
elements of 2.14, for the traditional, commonplace elements of the Underworld serve the purposes of the poem as nicely as the patently untraditional,
personal mythology of 2.13 contributes to its effects. If he had died, Horace
"modestly" claims, he would have experienced an Underworld defined
by the exquisite poetry of Sappho and Alcaeus. As they sing among the
dead and the monsters of that usually grim world, they transform everyone and everything. Not only are the shades of ordinary people affected,
as they gather around in hushed and marvelling silence, but Cerberus also
abandons his threatening stance (33ff), Prometheus and Tantalus under
the spell of the poetry can ignore their toil (*laborem* 38), and Orion abandons his wild *cura* to pursue lions and lynxes. Compare that picture of
Death, in which the "pious poets" transform everything for the better, with
the Death to be experienced by Postumus: all is unrelieved wretchedness.
Postumus will have only a sense of *tristitia* (with Tityos 8), blackness (*ater*
17), and permanent, unchanging toil (*longi laboris* 19–20). Postumus, the
speaker implies, has damned himself by the unwise way he has chosen to
live on earth and so will be among the Damned, utterly barred from the
Elysian Fields and the toil-relieving songs of an Alcaeus. But perhaps if he

reverses his ways, begins to enjoy his immediate blessings, he may attenuate both the *tristitia* and *laborem* of this life and that which otherwise surely lies in store for him after death. Thus, the ode on the *pius poeta* helps to comment on *pius Postumus* of 2.14 and to confirm, I think, the traditional interpretation vis-à-vis the clever hypothesis of Quinn.

Notes

❖ ❖ ❖

[1]Kiessling-Heinze, Q. *Horatius Flaccus: Oden und Epoden* (Berlin 1955, 8th edtion) 194: "Gegenstücke sind übrigens auch die allzu ungetreue Barine des vorigen und der allzu getreue Valgius dieses Gedichts."

[2]Quinn, *Latin Explorations: Critical Studies in Roman Literature* (London 1963) 100–101.

[3]Orellius cites a fragment from Aeschylus' *Niobe*; cf. also Euripides' *Alcestis* 962ff. Horace refers to *pietas* as a brief topos for similar circumstances in 1.24.11 and 4.7.24.

[4]In fact, we start to supply the opening line of the stanza with the pronoun *nobis* in accordance with the preceding context until in the following line the deictic *harum* and the relative clause *quas colis* make clear, as I have shown above, that the correct agent to understand is *tibi*.

[5]So Munro in his commentary on the passage of Lucretius and Commager, 287.

[6]Quinn, 105.

[7]E.g., *Serm.* 1.5.101ff and 2.4 passim. Cf. A. Weingärtner, *De Horatio Lucretii imitatore* (Halle 1874).

[8]Quinn, 104–105. He appends a note fixing the passage as Lucr. 3.912–915. Then, without directly facing the question of the remoteness of 3.894 from 3.912 or the apparently disjunctive use of *etiam* in 912, he seems to sweep away any objections with these two laconic sentences: "The order of the lines in this passage of Lucretius is disputed. Some editors follow Postgate in putting 912–918 immediately before 894–899." See my discussion infra.

[9]Bailey, *Lucretius* (Oxford 1947) II 1146.

[10]The same introductory words, *hoc etiam*, occur in 3.1024 and serve a similar purpose. There, Lucretius has completed one argument about death with 1023; he then announces that he is proceeding, as he indeed does, to a new way of consoling oneself for the inevitable extinction of death. The word *etiam* is clearly disjunctive in such usage.

[11]Quinn, 106.

[12]Cf. [Tibullus] 3.3.15, *nemora in domibus sacros imitantia lucos*.

[13]Cato *R.R.* 151.1.

[14]Varro *R.R.* 1.15 and 26.

[15]*N.H.* 16.60.139ff.

[16]See 64.291.

[17] *Ecl.* 1.25.

[18]Kiessling-Heinze, 216.

[19]It is probably significant that Horace does not include among the affective details in 21ff, where he lists what Postumus will lose by death, any son or children. In this, he differs markedly from Lucretius, who devoted two memorable lines to *dulces nati* running to snatch kisses from their beloved father. We do not, then, have to imagine the heir as a renegade son who frustrates the affection of his late father. On the contrary, Horace suggests that Postumus, childless, has left all his hoarded riches and wines to a dissolute nephew, a youth who never appreciated

the uncle except for his money. Postumus has thus failed to enjoy the pleasures of marriage, his *placens uxor*, or the parent's pride in children.

[20]*RhM* 37 (1882) 234.

[21] I suggest, too, that Horace resorted to the patronymic *Aeolides* 20 in part to enhance the alliteration of those carefully separated, pointedly disposed words *longi...laboris*.

[22]Cf. W. Port, "Die Anordnung in Gedichtbüchern augusteischer Zeit," *Philologus* 81 (1925) 300.

[23]On Horace's development of a private mythology on the basis of the traditional theme of *pius poeta*, cf. Commager, 126ff.

This article was submitted in May 1967, before the publication of the study by A. J. Woodman, "Eheu Fugaces," *Latomus* 26 (1967) 377–400, and hence it could not take note of his useful work. In brief, he also rejects Quinn's hypothesis on 2.14, gives a careful reading of the whole poem, and offers a special interpretation of the last stanza (with which I cannot fully agree), including an analysis of the comparison, *mero...potiore cenis* (28) that resembles mine.

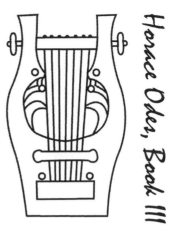

Horace Odes, Book III

Charles Witke

HORACE AND THE ROMAN ODES

Horace begins Book 3 of his Odes with six successive poems in Alcaic stanzas, all serious and focused on Roman political themes; and scholars have grown accustomed to grouping these poems under the term "Roman Odes." This selection deals only with the first of these poems, in which Horace announces a grander tone and a role as "priest of the Muses" singing songs never heard before (1–4). After discussing some background to the cycle, Witke offers a close reading of 3.1, with attention to the speaker and his announced audience, the structure and themes he uses, and the alteration of his self-presentation between first and final stanzas. He rightly argues against reducing the contents of these forty-eight lines to: "What is the point of personal ambition?" Rather, the poem is the collection of unpredictable images and contrasts that Horace composes. Although he seems to talk about a kind of impartial Fate (*Necessitas* 14) which disposes of high and low, rich and poor, his emphasis falls on the doom of high and rich. The poor obviously fall victim to the savage wars that the great wage against each other, and the simple farmer suffers from the same storms that destroy the crops of estate-owners; but the poet chooses the more memorable picture. Death and fate strike all alike, but contented sleep is a precious gift to few. It can come to farmers (21 ff.), it is true, but not because they live in the country so much as because they represent an attitude: *desiderantem quod satis est* (25). It is a version of the Golden Mean of 2.10. In the shorter final section (33–48), the poet reviews in more specifically Epicurean terms the vain efforts of the materialistic rich to gain happiness by accumulation of possessions. He evokes through *dolentem* (41) the opposite of the ideal in 25, the unhappy fool steeped in unhappiness amid all his things; and he opts for the Sabine Farm, the Horatian symbol of moral contentment. Our poet is both the priest of the Muses and the man who has achieved moral understanding and satisfaction in the retirement of the Sabine countryside. (Ed.)

✧ ✧ ✧

The idea of civic poetry in lyric form is foreign if not repugnant to a modern Western audience. For us, the lyric is essentially private, even an overheard statement made by the poet in relation or reaction to some vision or experience of his world to which his words give us access. For the ancient world, such a conception of lyric poetry would have been embarrassing or even incomprehensible, as were certain aspects of Catullus' highly personal and unironic verse for Horace. Classical Greek usage had

Published by Brill, Leiden, The Netherlands (1983). This material first appeared in Mnemosyne Supplementband 77 (1983) 2–5 and 19–27.

restricted *melé* to poems sung to musical accompaniment, in distinction to iambic and elegiac verse, and in contrast to non-narrative and non-dramatic poetry. Horace's poems, which open up Latin lyric to the wealth of Greek meter and subject, were indeed lyrics but not designed for singing,[1] rather they are lyrical by virtue of their meters, subjects and forms. The term lyric as modernly used is non-generic and descriptive, denoting poetry presenting the artist's image in relationship to himself, fusing concept and image in sound. For the Greeks as for the Romans, the lyric poet, in varying ways and with increasingly complex developments, spoke not only for and to himself, but for all who could hear him and heed him. There was a clear place for the lyricist in Greek literature; one need only think of the political statements of the Aeolian poets reflecting tension between the received oligarchic traditions and newer ideas. The Roman audience for Horace's three books of *Odes*, published as a unit in 23 B.C., would have been prepared through awareness of Greek antecedents to understand that lyric poetry addressed to public concerns existed as a recognizable form. Further, their own literature had provided, through Ennius' *Annales* and Lucilius' books of satires, to name but two of many, the examples of poets who addressed civic concerns, if not in lyric, at any rate in verse. An Augustan audience would experience increasing manipulation of its attention also by means of political statements made on coins, and in civic art. Finally, an attentive reader of the first two books of odes preceding Book III would have noticed recurring expressions of civic concern as early as the second poem of the first book. Here at the outset of his lyric corpus Horace presents the city, indeed the state, lashed by civil strife, attacked by the gods, and imploring heaven for the fulfillment of the rôle Augustus is to play in resolving conflict. This second poem of the collection follows one wherein the poet presents himself and his life in contrast to others engaged in diverse pursuits: in other words a forecast of III.1 and 2, the poet's self representation (but without reference to a patron) and the exultation of civic *virtus*.

Other themes occur in common between the preceding odes and III.1–6, the Roman Odes.[2] The reader of Horace's *Odes* has received through reading other lyric in Greek, and more specifically the poems preceding the Roman Odes themselves a quantity of data enabling him to deal effectively with both civic lyric and with the complex themes and manifold levels of interpretation found in the cycle. Instead of approaching the Roman Odes through this preceding aggregation, however, it is purposed to study them directly after a brief look at the political scene of around 23 B.C. It is not the intention of this study to attempt a reconstruction of the perceptions and expectations of an "original audience," since such an effort is doomed to fall short of its hoped-for goal inasmuch as each act of reading a literary text is a fresh creative act. Nevertheless, some awareness of the milieu of this poem cycle, both in the process of reading through the *Odes* to reach it and in the historical world of poet and audience, is desirable.

Horace's political and intellectual stances have been long and well charted through means of his *Epodes*, *Satires* and *Odes*, as well as through the *Epistles* and fourth book of *Odes* subsequent to *Odes* I–III. His relationship and attitudes in regard to Augustus, who figures so largely in the Roman Odes, may be taken as indicative of his complex evolution of ideas about the new Roman state coming into being after a century of civil war.[3]

It seems clear that Horace gave Augustus his full support only for a relatively short time, and that the time of publication of *Odes* I–III, 23 B.C., marked a time when the tide of commitment began to ebb away. Horace's youthful feelings of social and political concern can be seen in his fighting in the army of Brutus and Cassius as a tribune: a commitment referred to with pride several times in his poetry and once in the Roman Odes themselves.[4] Further, Horace's aristocratic rather than democratic bias appears often: e.g., *Odes* III.1.1 ff. alone show his distrust of the masses. After the wreck of his world at the end of the civil war, Horace buys the post of *scriba quaestoris* and works in Rome, meeting Octavian's minister of internal affairs, Maecenas, in the early 30's, when Octavian was struggling to end the Roman revolution and reestablish a structured society for Rome. From probably late 38 B.C. on, Horace had Maecenas' support and encouragement as well as a limited access to Octavian. As his success through the 30's and early 20's grew and order was restored to the Roman state, Horace's gratitude and support for Octavian's program (the success of which resulted in Octavian taking in 27 B.C. the name Augustus) can be seen in the first three books of *Odes*, including specifically the Roman Odes.[5] Later the ever-present shadows of doubt and pessimism grow deeper; Horace turns increasingly to philosophy, especially Stoicism, and enunciates, principally in his *Epistles*, growing concern for the tone of contemporary society.

The pessimism about the Roman order at the end of the Roman Odes, III.6.46–48, and the prominent attack on materialism there and the use of the term *libero* in III.5.22,[6] show that Horace's aristocratic contacts and biases, and his complicated character, increasingly content to assign to Augustus mere conventional flattery unlike his deep and authentic expressions of sincerity in *Odes* I–III, did not allow him to continue for long to present Augustus and the state's well-being as coterminous.

The context of the Roman Odes is no longer solely that of 23 B.C., however. There is an interaction of text and reader, both contemporary to the poet and contemporary to ourselves, that must be examined. The modern reader is not interchangeable with an ancient, nor can he imaginatively or scientifically recreate and animate his ancient counterpart's text. Rather, the modern reader is handicapped, in respect to the ancient audience, by not being able to read many Greek lyrics and many works of Roman literature now lost that no doubt had a bearing on Horace's Roman Odes, and helped create a context for reading them. To counterbalance this deficiency the modern reader has (potentially at any rate) the experience of more lyrics in other non-classical languages, a radically different idea of civic poetry (often bad political oratory made worse by pretensions of meter) and a lot of critical baggage that probably had no counterpart in the ancient reader's mind.

THE FIRST ROMAN ODE

The competent reader of Horace's first Roman Ode may be relied upon to make certain observations and to establish certain connections as he re-reads this poem. Let us examine some of these as they occur in the ongoing process of reading this text.

The first four lines of the third book of *Odes* economically establish three operational categories: the speaker, the spoken and those spoken to (or not spoken to). Building on the exultation of II.20 and its authentication, II.19, the poet's self is revealed as occupying a privileged state: distinct from the non-initiates, and about to convey in the silence prescribed by ritual and demanded by his utterance of the formula "favete linguis," *carmina*, texts of great virtue and importance. It is the young to whom the poet speaks, those capable of implementing the vision which he mediates. A kind of ritual space is created by these four lines.[7] Its axis runs from the person of the *sacerdos* to those of the chosen audience, and the space excludes those not free enough from the yoke of time (their age, or the age itself) to heed the divinely qualified poet. No longer content as one of many to hymn the goddess Fortune of Anzio, the poet rises above the undifferentiated masses and appeals to a select audience: those who have acknowledged the supremacy of *Fortuna* go on to see in her a sign of God's greatest dimension: the ordering power of the divine. Spoken earlier but not heeded (*non audita*), these texts of high cultural, civic and religious import will create a new audience capable of heeding. Silence can betoken either negative qualities, silence resulting from its potential violators, the deniers, who are at a distance (*arceo*); or positive effects: silence maintained out of pious consent. (Originally Roman ritual called for silence in order to forestall any ill-omened words, a combination of these two functions.) It is up to the audience to choose one of these two rôles: to draw near in silence, or to withdraw in silence of another sort altogether.

The three verbs of this first strophe are in the first person singular; the poet who despises and repels also sings; it is the same person, this hierophant and poet; are the activities the same? That is, is the god-sent vision and the god-inspired sacred text coterminous with estrangement from the undifferentiated *volgus* and its unprofound concerns? Possibly so. Sacred space must be cleared or defined for sacred acts; the setting up of the space, excluding as well as encapsulating, is indeed the first sacred action of a religious ritual. Within this *templum* the *profanum volgus* is hardly forgotten; rather, many references to it occur, as III.1 itself amply demonstrates. But it is the young, the pliable, those upon whom the performance of sacred text may make its deepest and longest-standing effect, that are addressed in the enclosure of the Roman Odes. To forget this is to forget that one element of the cycle that gives it what unity it has. The poems with themes previously enunci-ated and not precisely heeded are here renewed; the poet, charged with the divine, turns his message into art (*musarum sacerdos*) and selects a special addressee for his messages.

He begins in a most unRoman way, by presenting, in line five, undifferentiated, unRoman masses, *greges*, who are the property of very unRoman kings, *reges*: a departure from the status quo, a violation of audience expectation, inasmuch as it is a presentation of the world not from the viewpoint of the *greges* or of the *reges* but from Jupiter's: for him, kings and peoples are unspecified, unindividuated, the neuter plural *cuncta* of line eight. What lies behind this sweeping opening is the hymn to Zeus of Cleanthes, theologian of the early Stoa;[8] *ab Iove principium* is a very Roman way of expressing this idea of the dependency of all upon God, but it is usually presented from the perspective of the lower looking upward rather than the way Horace manages it here, from above, at a great distance (the after-effects of *arceo*) looking down on the great collectives of *reges* and their *greges*.

The principle of undifferentiation may even extend to the mention of the Giants in line seven; for it is usually the Titans, not the Giants, who are named in connection with Jupiter's great power, and to confuse them with the Giants may signal blurring or lack of identification because of disinterest and hence distance, like that associated with *odi* and *arceo*, line one.

The specificity of lines one through four, at least in regard to poet, audience and message, broken off by the sweeping generalizations of lines five through eight, may also suggest the prologue quality of verses one through four. However, lines nine following introduce a distillation of the particular, which obtains until *turba*, line thirteen, that undifferentiated *grex* of clients, which in turn leads back to the supernatural level and the force of *Necessitas*. If the *reges* have their *greges*, and Jupiter has both in sway, so too the individual has property, station, character, repute, and a following of clients, to greater or lesser degree in comparison with his fellows. As Jove rules rulers and peoples, so *Necessitas*, in that aspect of her akin to the *Fortuna* of I.35, and not as death,[9] is in control of high and low alike. Lines nine through sixteen repeat on the level of human affairs and from a more human perspective the points made in lines five through eight. However, Jupiter has become *Necessitas*, and the divine figure, far from perceiving undifferentiated masses of people, now knows your name: *cuncta* the neuter plural, of line eight becomes *omne nomen* in line sixteen. This degree of particular awareness on the part of *Necessitas* is ominous, and may bode ill. Differentiation in degree of status on earth is levelled by the *aequa lex* of collectivization; the personal individualities represented by *est ut vir* are flattened by the gnomic quality of the utterance about the equal law. Property, ancestry, character, repute, political following, all the factors by which we distinguish social rôles and individuals, for *Necessitas* all are *nomen*.

If it be granted that *Necessitas* here is not death but adamantine fate sealing one's lot, then the impending terror of lines seventeen through twenty-four is terror of loss, of discovery: sleeplessness, worry, fears that dog the *cervix impia* do so not because of wealth only, but because they are tied to a particular station in life, for the *ensis* of line seventeen is quite clearly associated with not just any rich man, but with the tyrant of Sicily, Dionysius, whose dinner-guest, Damocles, sees the sword suspended over his host's head and draws conclusions about his vulnerability.[10] The rich tyrant is soon contrasted with men of low station, eking out a living in the country.

At the center of the poem, a second gnomic utterance occurs: *desiderantem quod satis est*, line twenty-five; this person, in contrast to *cui* of line seventeen, is not evidently a merchant dependent on the weather signs for late sailings, about to be mentioned, nor a farmer, who is likewise dependent. In fact it is impossible, in the terms provided by the text, to assign the man who desires what is enough any specific rôle or station. By implication he, like the *viri agrestes* of lines twenty-two following, through contrast with the *impia cervix* of line seventeen, is *pius*, and obviously *desiderat quod satis est*. But if he were a small farmer, one with a *humilis domus*, line twenty-two, he would be ruined by such weather as is described in lines twenty-nine following. Clearly Horace has shifted to the problem of attitude, away from the problem of social categories. Otherwise, if one were to regard the *viri agrestes* as still in the network of communication, as it were, after the gnomic *desiderantem quod satis est*, one would be compelled to judge Horace inconsistent, unrealistic, and even unfair to farmers. Commentators, by characterizing the recipient of the bad weather as a great property owner, do but read into the text a solution to a problem they do not read out of the text.[11] A small farm suffers total loss, their reasoning may be supposed to run, so the poet must be concerning himself with a large farmer greedy for more than his due. But obviously the point is made in regard to *quod satis est* as the object of desire. Attitude is superordinate here just as in preceding strophes; one has to be aware of the hanging sword, or of the troubles it symbolizes, before being so worried as to be insomniac. Farmers know no sword, and work hard too, and therefore sleep: so would run the logic of the "real" world if imported to the poem. But the poet is not dealing with psychological commonplaces or truisms, but with a special vision of the world and himself in it. Those who work for subsistence, for maintenance, for *quod satis est*, sleep; those who want more do not rest easily; and over all is the *imperium* of heaven, containing all is the vessel of fate. Awareness of the sword, or sound sleep or its absence, are meaningless distinctions in a world where natural process is so altered as to admit trees that put blame for low yield on flood, drought, and cold, and fish that feel constrained by marine architectural ventures (lines thirty following).[12] Rather, it is the striving for elaboration (line nineteen, *elaborabunt*; cf. *moliar*, line forty-six), the crossing of natural barriers symbolized by building over and in water[13] that is held up for question. The farmer is no more aware of *Necessitas* or the god than is the rich man; perhaps even less so. He is merely free of worry because he has less to lose: only *quod satis est*. He does not work harder than is needed to achieve *quod satis est*: but by whose criterion? Surely in the end, in the *capax urna*, it does not matter.

Those who, like Gordon Williams,[14] try to make this poem into a connected discursive statement are obliged to treat it roughly. The poem rather exhibits various layers susceptible to various interpretations and an endless range of significance, as has just been demonstrated. To confine observation solely to interpretations: Williams avers that "the thought in the poet's mind, was basically: 'What is the point of personal ambition?'"[15] and relates this to wealth on the one hand, and quiet country living on the other. It apparently occasions no surprise that a text prepared for so lavishly and sacrally as III.1 can be reduced to "Live an unambitious life." Yet if one remains shackled to the literal, to the discursive, to the text isolated from its context of other poems in the cycle, this is the kind of interpretation that must result. The fault lies not in the logic of such a superb critic as Williams but in not having a critical method that does more than examine "the relationship of the great generalization" (5-8) to the rest, which is this critic's diagnosis of "the problem in this poem."[16] Poems need not be or exhibit problems. The reader is always the problem, usually because he is reading the text in the wrong context, or sometimes the wrong text. Here enough has been said about the solemn preparation for III.1 to show that it is very likely not simply an enunciation of a basic moral which "function[s] simply as an underlying principle."[17] Williams is right when he draws attention to the unpredictable contrasting pictures presented in the sweep of III.1, and he does well to stress their dominant quality. But it is these "pictures" alone that constitute the text, not any underlying moral which may well be a cultural pre-text, or a post-textual extrapolation, and as such should be carefully demarcated from the text by any responsible critical operation. Let us turn to a somewhat detailed examination of the text itself in hopes of recovering grounds for an interpretation on the text's own terms.

I have above suggested that the poem forms halves. The first half has the *viri agrestes* (plural) for a foil to the *impia cervix* (singular) of the very singular tyrant of Sicily; a gentle breeze refreshes these humble country dwellers. In the second half a similar armature can easily be discerned: the *pisces* (plural) form a foil for the excesses of the *redemptor / dominus* (singular) whom a violent desire to alter the natural landscape assails. Other elements that suggest a mirroring effect in the two reaches of the poem include a sound pattern *desiderantem quod satis est* (25) and *quodsi dolentem* (41) in the first and second halves respectively. Further, note how *desiderantem quod satis est* is followed by the connectives *neque, nec, aut* (25ff.); its phonic kin, *quodsi dolentem*, is followed by *nec, nec, nec* (41ff.), the densest array of connectives in the poem. The two passages reinforce each other; the man who desires what is enough and the sick man are closely parallel (if not identical). The text seeks to level syntactically and phonically the very distinctions it lexically and semantically advances.

Further evidence of similarities between the beginning and end of this message can easily be found. The first person singular occurs only in the first and last strophes. Future passive participles occur only in line five (*timendorum regum*) and line forty-five (*invidendis postibus*). In contrast, personifications are confined to a central area, *fundus mendax* (30), *Timor, Minae* (37), *Cura* (40). Perfect passive participles abound everywhere, e.g., 3, 17, 24, 29, 33, 34, 39. Present active participles in the genitive are (*Iovis*) *moventis*, 8, (*Arcturi*) *cadentis*, 27, and (*Haedi*) *orientis*, 28, all celestial, a suggestive array. Lexically, (*non*) *fastidit*, 23, and the prominently placed *fastidiosus*, 37, are the mainsprings of the poem. Sleep does not scorn humble lodgings (but does evade the worried tyrant); the rich man disdains the land (but not the wrong element, the water) yet worry catches up with him at sea or on land. The man who is *fastidiosus* is not *impius* (nor does he explicitly undergo the experience of the *impius* in this poem) but neither does he desire *quod satis est*. There is land enough for man, but he goes to build on the alien sea. Yet in the world of this poem, if there be any consistency the land is also *mendax*[18] when it comes to providing man with sustenance.

A pattern of equivalency, latent in these examples, may now be set forth. Poem III.1, the first Roman Ode, is a declarative poem; there is no subjunctive in it except for the *est ut* construction, 9ff. (Contrast should be made by the reader later with III.2 and its initial jussive subjunctives, III.2.3ff.) This poem establishes a context, a world, makes distinctions, and orders its reality. It uses the interrogative form only twice, both in the last strophe: the two questions contain in their formulation two words that provide their answers: *sublime* and *operosiores*. Aspirations are sure to elicit hostile reactions from others; the city brings worries along with riches; why change? But what one should bear in mind is that the poet is left not in respectable rural shabbiness but clothed with the importance of the first strophe. His Sabine valley is the retreat of the Muses, a setting for his art, not merely for his humble historical social self. The poet is not engaged in differentiating two selves in the first and last strophes of this poem any more than he is distinguishing between kings that must be feared and despots sure to be envied: both are operations resulting from the perspective of the world from which the poet is seeking to free others, as he himself has been freed by the authenticating vision he proclaims. The *aequa lex Necessitatis* brings all to one end; things cannot help the human condition, be it *desiderans* or *dolens*; they are much the same, for even if one is *desiderans quod satis est*, the same awaits. God rules, kings reign, and man is either ill at ease or at home in the world; but the world's things, beyond mere subsistence, are useless in making a difference to man. Much depends on rulers and on heaven; but even with benevolent rule and good weather, the same end awaits.

Those who see the Roman Odes ending, with III.6, in an unforeseen pessimism should bear in mind that III.1 is not exactly optimistic in tone, but rather is solemnly dark and resignedly passive in the face of *Necessitas*, Jupiter and, in the background *Fortuna* herself. Far from issuing didactic calls to take attitudes or actions, the poet here advances brilliant pictures of the futility of personal drive, personal power, personal possessions. The next ode will introduce a new term in this lexicon of possibilities: the state.

Several elements common to the Roman Odes as a whole are introduced in III.1. Among these are the interplay of abstract personifications such as *Necessitas, Timor, Minae, Cura,* and vivid concrete details, such as *Siculae dapes, Phrygius lapis,* etc. Further, the incipient tension between the personal rôle or aspect of the poet as contrasted with his public side might also be raised as a question. In the terms of III.1, is the *vallis Sabina* not only the stronghold of art, as here suggested, but also that comfortable fastness of private cultivation, and are *divitiae operosiores* public and civic pronouncements and responsibilities? In the dynamics of III.1, the question can be asked but not answered. Further interpretation of the Roman Odes may, however, suggest an avenue for approaching this question.

If the poet's outburst about *quod si dolentem* (41f) is made up of sounds similar to *desiderantem quod satis est* (25) and if an assimilation of even the non-ambitious to the sick at heart — sick with the illness of human existence — can be made, so too parallelism or assimilation can be seen elsewhere knitting the text into a comprehensive assertion of this vision of the world. First, both Roman examples (strophes 3 and 4, and 7ff) and non-Roman examples (strophes 2 and 5) show the universality of this poet's visionary scope. Next, one may observe how the text passes from vast concerns (eastern kings and their peoples) to the Roman merchant and farmer, thus preparing the way for the poet to re-appear in civic guise at the end. He is the same poet as in strophe 1, but functions as *cives* and not as *vates*. Finally, the superordinate rule of Jupiter and the underlying control of *Necessitas* are transformed into a sword suspended over a neck, and the weather (about which indeed nothing can be done) becomes a local manifestation of *Necessitas*. The grand and universal continually shade into the particular and the everyday, but of course not presented in everyday language or tone. The personifications of 37ff. do much to elevate the tone, and to show that it is to the powerful and prominent man that the poet wishes to draw final attention before breaking off his pictures of cosmic ruler and leveller contrasted with their mundane means of operation.[19]

Far from being a text enjoining contentment with one's lot and discouraging personal ambition, the first Roman Ode is a psychological model of a social state: God's control, capable of being articulated on a grand scale, shades off into the everyday where it is no longer perceived except in social terms: *quod satis est, dominus terrae fastidiosus,* etc. Yet the outriders of divine permeation of the world's fabric, *Timor, Minae, Cura,* objectify the interior state of the man who is *dolens,* in spite of his success, wealth and power, economic and hence social. Artistic retreat breaks their power and suffuses it with the right perspective: all is in the sway of God, *Necessitas* knows all our names.

Perhaps Friedrich Solmsen was right for a reason he did not advance when he observed[20] that *Odes* III.1 may urge young Romans to seek individual happiness, rather than to help build up the new Rome of Augustus. When all levels, social, economic and political, are illusions before the great power of God and the levelling law of *Necessitas,* one must realize the futility of aspirations that well up from individual or collective man. A higher power must support, strengthen and validate any such efforts; having dismantled, in III.1, the world bereft of this direct intervention of heaven and its concomitant social organ, the state, and having shown its vanity, the poet goes on in III.2 to show a rudimentary evolution of civic awareness built upon the absolute zero, the chilling denials and hard realities of III.1.

This theory of reading applied to III.1 obliges us to postulate as well a theory of taste, an interpretation or set of interpretations (one of many possibilities) for the text just discussed. We have moved from the phenomenology of the writer's consciousness to our framework of understanding, but not without a suspicion that Horace's poem (here as well as elsewhere in his corpus) resists the, or even a, final meaning, and goes on proliferating interpretations endlessly: no unusual result for a text as shifting, dynamic and vivid as III.1 can easily be discerned to be.

Notes

¹*Pace* A. Bonavia Hunt, *Horace the Minstrel* (Kineton, Warwick England, 1969), an idiosyncratic work devoted to this thesis. It is the contention of E. Poehlmann, "Marius Victorinus zum Odengesang bei Horaz," *Philologus* 109 (1965), pp. 133ff., that the Odes were to be recited, not sung. On Horace's Alcaic meter see J. P. M. Blackett, "A Note on the Alcaic Stanza," *Greece and Rome*, second series 3 (1956), pp. 83f.; J. Hellegouarc'h, "Observations stylistiques et métriques sur les vers lyriques d'Horace," *L'Information littéraire* 18 (1966), pp. 66ff., especially p. 74. For rhyme in Horace, see O. Skutsch's remarks in the *Bulletin of the Institute of Classical Studies* of the University of London 11 (1964), pp. 73–78.

²E.g., *Odes* I.12, 14, 35, 37, and II.1. See also H. C. Toll, "Unity in the Odes of Horace," *Phoenix* 9 (1955), pp. 153ff., especially pp. 156ff. F. Fontaine, *Enchainement et groupements des poèmes dans l'oeuvre lyrique d'Horace*, Liège, 1941–42; Mémoire de licence; H. Haffter, "Zur Komposition horazischer Oden," *Wiener Studien*, N. F. 10 (1976), pp. 199ff.

³For what follows on Horace and Augustus, see Chester G. Starr, "Horace and Augustus," *American Journal of Philology* 90 (1969), pp. 58–64. See also his "Virgil's Acceptance of Octavian," *American Journal of Philology* 76 (1955), pp. 34–46; see also M. Bourgeois, "Horace, Serious Reformer," *Classical Bulletin* 31 (1955), pp. 62ff.; A. La Penna, "La lirica civile di Orazio e l'ideologia del principato," *Maia* 13 (1961), pp. 831–23, 209–245, 257–283; A. La Penna, *Orazio e l'Ideologia del Principato*, (Torino, 1963); G. Williams, "Poetry in the Moral Climate of Augustan Rome," *Journal of Roman Studies* 52 (1962), pp. 28–46 on the *Odes*; and P. Grimal, "Les Odes romains d'Horace et les causes de la guerre civile," *Revue des Etudes Latines* 53 (1975), pp. 135–156.

⁴*Odes* II.7; *Satires* 1.6 and 7; *Epistles* I.20, 23 and II.2, 46ff.; *Odes* III.4.26.

⁵E.g., see Eduard Fraenkel, *Horace* (Oxford, Oxford University Press, 1957), pp. 260ff.; Laura O. Sangiacomo, *Le "Odi Romane"* (Rome, 1942). For the religious dimension of Horace's friendship with Maecenas, see K. Eckert, "O et praesidium et dulce decus meum," *Wiener Studien* 74 (1961), pp. 61–95.

⁶The adjective *libero* in III.5.22 is not used in connection with materialism, to be sure; words like *liber, libertas* and their derivatives appear only once again in *Odes* I–III: see III.24.12, this time on materialism; their frequency mounts from the first book of *Epistles* on; see Starr, "Horace and Augustus" (supra n. 3) p. 63.

✧ ✧ ✧

[7]The use of "ritual space" in this connection is an extension of the idea of Frank E. Brown, *Roman Architecture* (New York, 1967), pp. 9–11. For Horace and religion, see R. Hanslik, "Die Religiosität des Horaz," *Altertum* I (1955), pp. 230–240, and T. Oksala, *Religion und Mythologie bei Horaz* (Helsinki, 1973).

[8]Cf. also Callimachus' *Hymn to Zeus*, line 79. See as well V. Pöschl, "Horaz," *L'Influence grecque sur la poésie latine de Catulle à Ovide, Entretiens sur l'antiquité* II, pp. 93–130, Fondation Hardt, (Genève, 1956).

[9]It is often assumed that *Necessitas* in III.1.14 is Death, e.g., Gordon Williams, *The Third Book of Horace's Odes* (Oxford: Oxford University Press, 1969), *ad loc.* and p. 125. However, the work of E. T. Silk has convincingly shown that this need not be the case: "Towards a Fresh Interpretation of Horace Carm. III.1," *Yale Classical Studies* 23 (1973), pp. 139–145. On III.1, see also Eduard Fraenkel, *Horace* (Oxford: Oxford University Press, 1957), pp. 261ff., and Steele Commager, *The Odes of Horace* (New Haven: Yale University Press, 1962), p. 16, and V. Pöschl, "Die Einheit der ersten Römerode," *Harvard Studies in Classical Philology* 63 (1958), pp. 333–346, and especially his *Horazische Lyrik: Interpretationen* (Heidelberg, 1970), pp. 144–164, the only Roman Ode treated in this valuable book. See also E. T. Silk, "The God and the Searchers for Happiness: Notes on Horace's Repetition and Variation of a Favorite Topos," *Yale Classical Studies* 19 (1966), pp. 241–244 on III.1 (and I.35 and III.3 in contrast).

[10]G. Williams, *op. cit. supra*, n. 9, *ad loc.* gives the argument.

[11]This is the approach of standard commentators, e.g., *Q. Horatius Flaccus Oden und Epoden*[9] ed. Adolf Kiessling and Richard Heinze (Berlin, 1958), *ad loc.*, hereafter referred to as Kiessling-Heinze.

[12]This is not the hyperbole that Kiessling-Heinze, *ad loc.*, assert.

[13]Building programs over the water at Anzio were carried out; the most renowned were those of Nero, revealed in Allied bombardment of Anzio during World War II. Cf. also J. E. G. Whitehorne, "The Ambitious Builder," *Journal of the Australian Universities Languages and Literature Association* 31 (1969), pp. 28–39, and L. Alfonsi, "Notes de lecture," *Latomus* 20 (1961), pp. 845–846 on III.I. 33f.

[14]G. Williams, *op. cit. supra*, n. 9, *ad loc.* See also Hendrik Wagenvoort, *De Horatii quae dicuntur Odis Romanis* (Groningen, 1911), pp. 18–47 (on III.1 and 2). This work is also useful on all the Roman Odes.

[15]G. Williams, *ibid.*, and p. 32.

[16]G. Williams, *ibid.*

[17]G. Williams, *ibid.*

[18] Note the context of *mendax* here, and cf. Petronius, *Satyricon* 117.

[19] A word about *Timor, Minae* and the armor-plated trireme may be useful. Almost all commentators, ancient, medieval, Renaissance and modern, suggest the context of civilian life. However, the presence of *Timor* and *Minae*, twin companions of Mars (like *Phobos* and *Deimos* of Ares) suggests that a warlike setting is not to be ruled out. If so, there is a slight anticipation here of the subsequent ode's preoccupation at its outset with war.

[20]Friedrich Solmsen, "Horace's First Roman Ode," *American Journal of Philology* 68 (1943), p. 338.

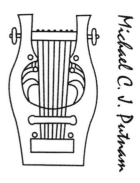

Michael C. J. Putnam

HORACE ODES 3.9:
THE DIALECTICS OF DESIRE

Horace has constructed this appealing poem as a dialogue — three exchanges by each speaker, four lines in each — which dramatizes the temporary reconciliation of two lovers. The male, unnamed, initiates things by recalling their happiness together in the old days. She agrees, naming herself ostentatiously as Lydia. He, then she makes a big point of the new arrangement with other mates. But after all his proud boasting, the male proposes that they get together again, and she, pretending some reluctance, assents with evident passion. Putnam's essay examines the personalities that Horace gives to the speakers by the words he assigns them and their way of expressing their feelings. Lydia takes every advantage of being the second speaker, topping the man again and again. She reminds him of how he was more interested in Chloe (6), as if he alone were to blame for the separation; she claims to be twice as loyal to her Calais as he is to Chloe (15-16); and even at the end she implies that he is less handsome than Calais (21-22). He, on the other hand, talks of love as power (2), like that of Persian kings (4), affects to admire Chloe for her musical as well as amatory talents, and romantically describes their love in almost Valentine (or elegiac) terms as *prisca Venus* (17) and now a re-yoking (18). In his opening of negotiations, he offers to toss Chloe out (19). In the following line, he makes a second suggestion, the sense of which depends on the syntax: is *reiectae Lydiae* dative or genitive? Putnam and many scholars opt for the dative; and so he proposes opening his door to Lydia. Another interpretation, assuming the genitive, would have her opening her door to him, which she shut after he had spurned her. Thus, the man would propose a re-sponse from her that would match his giving up Chloe and assure them both of being unattached for a while. I find it quite attractive and suggestive of greater equality in the resumed love (Ed.)

✧ ✧ ✧

Though its antiphonal form is unique in the remains of ancient literature for such a lyric theme, Horace's delightful dialogue between two lovers has aroused little critical comment.[1] One reason is not far to seek. A simple directness of structure, nearly anomalous in a collection of otherwise complex poetic statements, fosters in the reader an equally easy reaction. Content and style are at one. In the course of six exactingly balanced strophes we learn that boy and girl once loved each other. There was a falling out as new arrangements with new partners were adopted. Yet what if former Venus returns? he asks. Though my new lover is an attractive sort, she

Reprinted by permission of The Regents of the University of Michigan. This essay first appeared in *Ancient and Modern Essays in Honor of Gerald F. Else*, ed. D'Arms and Eadie (Institute for Ancient & Modern Studies, University of Michigan, 1977) 139-57.

responds, and you addicted to fickleness and cursed with a hot temper, I would still like to be yours—and forever. Happy, straightforward stuff, turned out with suitably engaging facility, the relieved critic concludes. But such a plot summary remains puzzlingly insufficient. Though the lovers seem bent on returning to each other, the poem is based as much on change and experimentation as on continuity. And though the way she caps his words is a regular feature of any amoeboean interchange, and betokens allegiance as much as idiosyncratic challenge, there are subtle tonal and psychological distinctions between the two protagonists that argue for their autonomy as well as their unity. To analyze this verbal play is my present purpose.

Seen as a cycle, the lyric stretches from past to future, from unity then, to other dalliances for each in the poem's present, to potential renewal of old love in the hereafter. It is also a debate, a mimesis of lovers' verbal play, an intellectual game leading in a brilliantly modulated crescendo to her final affirmation of a shared desire his opening words already betray. Yet in the course of this little interplay, as argument vies with agreement, evolution challenges stability, and individuality is at odds with imitation, there never occurs the possibility of total collusion between rhetoric and emotion. The antiphony serves as much to differentiate as to equate the protagonists while the poet's sharp structuring of this give and take offers reason enough to approve the presence of a brazen yoke, however lightly worn, to hold them together. Three words against two, odd against even, to keep on edge the reader's expectations of a balanced amatory order reached through spoken word. The meter, with its alternating short and long lines, seems at first to favor unity. It repeats in miniature the patterned interchange of male and female in six stanzas, he beginning and leading, she following and concluding. Yet its lines suggest inequality as much as balance, while the uneven triadic grouping around three time periods arouses suspicion that disenchantment might well set in again, as it had before, in the lives of this strangely matched pair.[2]

Though he initiates the colloquy, the male protagonist forthwith announces his dependence on her and sees their former relationship in terms of the *gratia* in which she held him.[3] The reader assumes from *tibi* what might be a plausible outcome of the poem, one which the speaker may even be anticipating. Whatever the case, his reaction to her former devotion is also seen in subjective terms—a Persian king's wealth metaphorized into a state of *beatitas*. Analogy to regal stance also proves that power, whether active or passive, is much in his thoughts. Aesthetic considerations combine with notions of physical potency in his extraordinary sketch of her putative young lover. He savors the exquisite beauty of her neck, yet *candidae* is the central feature of a chiastic deployment of words which catches this whiteness between *bracchia* and *cervici*, *potior* and *iuvenis*, even *quisquam* and *dabat*. His language displays the erotic force he holds in value.[4]

She by contrast lives more for surfaces. In exchanging his *beatior* for *clarior*, she chooses bright fame and public acknowledgement over inner riches and personal strength. She finds a likeness for herself not in some anonymous exotic king, devoted no doubt to a life of delicate abundance. Instead she opts for a more immediate Roman Ilia whom all would know. Titles fascinate her. Where we never learn his name, she narcissistically thrusts hers upon us twice, and in the very act calls attention to the *nomen* that results from her repute.[5] The very sounds which run from *alia* to *Lydia*, *Lydia*, and *Ilia* feed on each other.[6] Naturally she thinks first of her rival and sees their interconnection as one of rank in the eyes of their common lover. Naturally, too, she exploits *arsisti*, an image of glittering presence as well as sensuality to describe his emotion.

In his reply, which initiates their differing views of the present, he seems not to have heard her. He announces, what we already knew, that Chloe is his new love. True to his fashion he chooses someone of non-Roman extraction, and sees their relationship in terms of power. She now rules him whereas in the earlier liaison there existed mutual interdependence: he was *gratus* to her and *rex* as well in his own thinking. More pointedly than before he prizes the life of the mind. Chloe's learning (twice noted) and the artistic form it takes appeal to him.[7] His proclamation of a *liebestod* is couched in terms of not fearing—an internal reaction—and, aptly enough, it is her *anima* his death would save. He values Chloe for her spiritual side, of itself but surely also for the inspiriting effect it exerts on his own mental impulses.[8]

Lydia's riposte holds true to form. She is direct where he was oblique. We learn not only her new lover's name but his father's and that of his natal town. Since Calais, apparently, means turquoise, the dazzling object again lures her eye.[9] We are also ready for the double metaphor of burning and the protests of mutuality (no gradations here) with which she introduces her new amour.[10] In capping *non metuam* with *bis patiar* she hyperbolically rejects fear imagined in favor of torture felt. And in replacing *animae* with *puero* she yet again chooses the physical over the metaphysical, immediate literal sexuality instead of some deeper more intellectual design.

If his previous lines had betokened a certain inner-directedness by not addressing her face to face, he now withdraws still more completely into analysis of his own intellectual processes by presenting two neatly balanced hypotheses. Alternatives are his to manufacture out of life's possibilities. His language is riddled with conceits. *Venus* is a metonymy, *ianua* a synecdoche. *Iugo, diductos* and *excutitur* are richly metaphoric. Chloe is "shaken off" or "out" like a disease or a mental attitude. Lydia's reacceptance is the opening of a door.[11] This energetic world of going and coming, expelling and receiving, rejecting and accepting, separation and compulsion, is reflected in the careful, calculated pattern his thoughts receive. He still deals in positions of strength and, as in previous stanzas, wavers between active and passive. We have both a Venus who commands and a lover who opens the door. He is the controller and the controlled, the verbal leader who at times is also the emotional follower.[12] It is appropriate that the first person to hint at the restoration of prior affections should draw on symbols of stability and force centralized, as well as of sexuality, such as the yoke and the door.[13] The very posture he had imagined and dismissed for her new lover in the opening lines is in fact a yoking. It is likewise appropriate that such strength of purpose be displayed in the steady ordering of the conditions on which he meditates, apparently to himself in spite of her assumed presence.

If he lays down conditions, she makes concessions, and by the act of answering his question suggests through grammatical enjambement that reestablishment of intimacy he adumbrates. But even in this dialectic of proposal and disposal, suggestion and submission, she remains herself, direct where he is oblique, passionate where he is contemplative. Her analogies are brisk and revelatory. She sees her present suitor as *sidere pulchrior*, a stable object of attention, physically attractive, tailored to her interests. For her former lover and present interlocutor, she finds two similes, dedicated appropriately to psychic, not physical characteristics: his fickleness (at least in her view) and his changeable temper. The final comparison — *improbo iracundior Hadria* — gains special prominence. By breaking the chiastic balance she had created between *ille* and *tu*, it offers animated proof of the infidelity we assume she now forgives, as well as further contrast to the stately rigor of his preceding sentiments.

Yet her last line with its intense intertwinings is a bow to his propensity for order — ABC, ABC in terms of idea; nearly ABC, ABC in terms of grammar.[14] His final lines, it would appear, aim for unity of the whole by taking to themselves the structuring echoes and reechoes of the previous four stanzas. But her replies, after all, made these very resonances possible, and it is reasonable that her last lines should draw strands from both their worlds together at the end. Her three comparatives, *pulchrior, levior, iracundior*, renew in the reader's attention the related juxtapositions of the opening lines (*potior, beatior, clarior*). Likewise her concluding wish to live or die with her old amour corresponds to their earlier individual protestations of altruistic suicide in the middle segments of the poem. All of which would lead the reader to believe that she sees the poem as a cycle of reunification from *tibi gratus* to *tecum lubens*, and the dialogue that is its form, as a means of working out (and into) a relationship toward a final rapprochement.

But her terminal play on *amem* — "like" instead of "love," desire in the place of fruition — proves the dialectic still inconclusive.[15] Instead of tragic collapse or comic fruition the poem concludes only with a redoubled affirmation of her yearning. At the same time her words provoke the theory that any rhetorical exchange among personages so disparate is Venus' way of utilizing language itself as a brazen yoke to govern competitive energies. The only other lyric where Horace uses the image of the *iugum aeneum*, *Odes* 1.33, is equally concerned with the all-too-regular mating of opposites. There the poet as abstracted commentator on the human scene to the constantly committed, constantly hurt elegist Tibullus, uses oxymoron, aptly enough, to figure his insight: "sweet" Glycera is harsh to him, the freedwoman Myrtale holds him in thrall — all part of Venus' "harsh joke."

A "better Venus" is regularly displaced by someone less apt. In *Odes* 3.9 words alone are sufficient indication of dissimilarity. Horace's humorous self-distance grants that for each individual, including himself, there is always a *melior Venus,* a more appropriate, kindred attachment, which could replace one's present antonymy, but such perfection one is rarely allowed to choose, not to say maintain.

Odes 3.9 presents an evolving documentation both of the "better Venuses" each lover at present possesses and of the once and future mate with whom each now converses. We have seen something of the disparity of the one set and the natural attraction of the other. The male protagonist, with his feeling for love as power and penchant for the aesthetics of grace and happiness, would naturally enough be magnetized by the spiritual rule of musical Chloe. Physical Lydia, attracted by externals and a name, should no doubt find fulfillment in shining Calais, more alluring than a star, who is equally enthralled by her. Instead, Horace, not unexpectedly, binds his speakers together with a verbal chain that would have to be firm indeed.[16]

Their personality differences have been easy enough to trace. It could be said that each uses language apposite enough to individual characteristics. His language is obsessional, as befits the subjective, solipsistic contemplative, hers compulsively directed to externals, reacting, not proposing.[17] Over and above these differentials the poet establishes his own principle of orderly disorder as comment on their union. I refer to the striking manner in which she chooses to parallel or fails to mimic his utterances.

The first two stanzas, with the repetition of *donec* and *vigui,* the reverberation of *eram* in *erat* and the corresponding comparatives, betrays a certain linguistic conformity, and hence erotic intimacy, which the two parties have disturbed but have not replaced. The third and fourth stanzas, however, are paradoxical. Close reiteration advises that his manner of expression is hers, that an expanding mode of familiarity has been achieved in a fabric of words that still conveys appropriate personality differentiations. To reproduce as closely as she does the architectonics of his stanzaic construction postulates a certain kindred imaginative ordering and spiritual interdependence. Her selfhood is defined most clearly as an expansion of his proclivities. Her attempt at greatest freedom is framed in terms that refer as much to him as to herself.

Yet the message of the words themselves speaks of an emotional break, of committed affections elsewhere. At the same time, ironically but suitably, the iterated appeal to suicide, though the height of devotion, is likewise the height of the non-erotic. It presupposes the death of one's closest partner—an intellectual, fabricated posture, a quasi-romantic pose that exchanges masochism for reciprocity. One need scarcely add that the humor Horace elicits from such overstated seriousness does much to undercut the very protestations themselves.

The interrelationship between the last stanzas is even more problematical. The linguistic enjambement provided the answered question would seem to recreate amatory harmony, but its total restoration is cast in doubt by her hesitant use of "like" for "love," as if her willingness did not quite match his stipulations. If syntax offers reason for dialectical unity, extreme verbal disjunction intimates a contrary course. In the development of the most rational, calculated stanza in the poem he relinquishes his former preference for artistic Chloe and opts for passionate, self-projecting Lydia. Reason and sexuality are at odds. And her response, which releases her from his framings, with equal irony presents the greatest distinction of verbal play, the strongest divagation from previous structures, and hence the most patent self-assertion in the poem. These final lines, for example, contain the greatest number of liquids of any stanza in the poem (twenty-five in contrast to eight in his preceding verses). She voices the only two and seven word lines in the poem — its extremes of brevity and length — and *iracundior* is its longest word. His last stanza was noteworthy for its regularity. Each line is self-contained. Nowhere else in the poem are balanced meter and balanced sense so tightly merged. She, on the contrary, in the course of indulging in broken chiasmus, strange emphases, patterns worked and unworked at the end, presents one of the two stanzas in the poem with three lines that cannot stand alone (her way, perhaps, of pointing up *pulchrior* and *iracundior*, the distinction between her two lovers, as well as of proving her excitability).

Verbally, then, she manifests aspects of disorder that she finds patent in his character. Yet there is also a reductive humor to this realistic appraisal of her turned-about lover. His character is partitioned between the cork, that trivializes, and the Adriatic, which presses toward hyperbole. Such earthy analogies, distinguished from his careful calculations, assess facts. No theories here, merely the straight truth, dispelling any illusions, yet not, however, without an element of surprise, since the reader waits in suspense for the main clause until the last line and within that clause every word is given due weight.

Briefly, in the finale, as old love is almost renewed, his controlled pondering of alternatives, his balanced weighing of possibilities is directly challenged by her sharp excitement and intricate likenings. Where we most expect congruence in language we find variance, just as in the previous pair of stanzas close imitation complements the proclamation of extreme erotic distinction.[18] There are no verbal echoes at the moment when greatest intimacy should be espoused. There is most individuality at the instant where reinforced allegiance would be in order. Which is to say that in the complex amalgam of unity and differentiation by which he defines amatory coupling, Horace sees patterns of sexuality constantly challenged by patterns of language. The poem's dialectic is the actual working out of an oxymoron, proving how opposites attract — a favorite Horatian principle. But Horace is wiser than to end even here. In their highly idiosyncratic ways, as we have seen, both protagonists complete the poem as a cycle of their own return to each other. At the same time they intimate through structure as well as content that the dissolution of such a verbal bond is

equally plausible. In the case of Lydia and her lover the pattern may be a
frictional alternation of fidelity and faithlessness. One suspects, however,
that Horace, learned in the nature of human foibles, would have put little
trust in the permanence of such a tenuous bond, and that the very conflicts
between erotic unity and verbal discord are his sympathetic way of telling
us so.

Here, as often, Horace exploited Catullus as inspiration and measure
of originality:

> Acmen Septimius suos amores
> tenens in gremio 'mea' inquit 'Acme,
> ni te perdite amo atque amare porro
> omnes sum assidue paratus annos,
> quantum qui pote plurimum perire,
> solus in Libya Indiaque tosta
> caesio ueniam obuius leoni.'
> hoc ut dixit, Amor sinistra ut ante
> dextra sternuit approbationem.
>
>   at Acme leuiter caput reflectens
> et dulcis pueri ebrios ocellos
> illo purpureo ore suauiata,
> 'sic,' inquit 'mea uita Septimille,
> huic uni domino usque seruiamus,
> ut multo mihi maior acriorque
> ignis mollibus ardet in medullis.'
> hoc ut dixit, Amor sinistra ut ante
> dextra sternuit approbationem.
>
>   nunc ab auspicio bono profecti
> mutuis animis amant amantur.
> unam Septimius misellus Acmen
> mauult quam Syrias Britanniasque:
> uno in Septimio fidelis Acme
> facit delicias libidinesque.
> quis ullos homines beatiores
> uidit, quis Venerem auspicatiorem?

Septimius, holding his love Acme in his lap, says "My Acme,
unless I love you overwhelmingly and am further prepared to
love you unceasingly for all time, as madly as any man can be in
love, may I meet face to face a green-eyed lion, alone in Lybia or
sunburnt India." When he said this, Love, although before on the
left, sneezed approval on the right.

But Acme, lightly bending her head and kissing with her
purple lips the drunken eyes of the sweet boy, says "So let us serve

this one master, my little Septimius, my life, as a much greater
and sharper fire burns within my soft marrow." When she said
this, Love, although before on the left, sneezed approval on the
right.

Now, having set out from a good auspice, they love and are
loved with mutual response. Love-sick Septimius prefers Acme
alone to Syrias and Britains, in Septimius alone faithful Acme takes
her pleasure and delight. Who has seen any happier creatures,
who has seen a more auspicious love?

The Acme and Septimius of Catullus' forty-fifth poem may also have had a
period of separation and the poet joins them together again, quoting their
protestations of utter devotion and giving his own carefully arranged seal of
approval at the end. There are essential formulations in the discrimination
between the two characters that must have caught Horace's ear. To support
his claims of total allegiance in the future Septimius prays (6–7):

> solus in Libya Indiaque tosta
> caesio veniam obvius leoni.

Catullus bolsters the impression of someone attracted by the distant and
exotic, as public servant, perhaps, or traveler, in his final summary of the
youth's behavior (21–22):

> unam Septimius misellus Acmen
> mauult quam Syrias Britanniasque; ...

Unique exposure to green-eyed lions (in Septimius' quoted words) and
many looks at a variety of Syrias and Britains (in the poet's configuration)
form a unified portrait.

While Septimius holds her, Acme bends her head and kisses his
drunken eyes. If his interests in the faraway betray a bravado of sorts, hers
are unabashedly sexual.[19] In her own voice she urges them both to serve
love the master (15–16):

> ut multo mihi maior acriorque
> ignis mollibus ardet in medullis.

Catullus again confirms the picture in his authorial summary (23–24):

> uno in Septimio fidelis Acme
> facit delicias libidinesque ...

Horace fancied this creature addicted to love's fires and pleasures as literary ancestress for his Lydia. He also clearly draws on the interaction of
infidelity and faithfulness seen against a backdrop of time passing. One

clear way to explain the overwrought hyperbole in each statement of future
constancy is to accept it as token of a once opposite frame of mind – in
Septimius' case revealed by an inclination for foreign wanderings (whether
literal or figurative), in Acme's by a series of lustings elsewhere. This is
born out by the implication of the refrain subsequent to each speech: if
love now sneezes endorsement on the right he had previously demonstrated disapproval on the left. Catullus twice confirms as much in his
envoi to the two suitors.[20] He begins (19–20):

> nunc ab auspicio bono profecti,
> mutuis animis amant amantur. –

as if to suggest that this dedicated mutuality (which the asyndeton enhances) had not always been the case, that in fact once in the past they had
set out with an inauspicious omen.[21] Such a context forces the reader to
take the full measure of the final questions (25–26):

> quis ullos homines beatiores
> vidit, quis venerem auspicatiorem?

Is this love only more auspicious by comparison to former times? To be
more cynical, what if in reality we have seen lovers setting out more happily
matched?

But the differences between the two poems are more telling than their
similarities. Catullus, as we have seen, devotes himself to an intense "now,"
a crucial moment in the romance of his protagonists with only hints that
there was a former history potentially ready to repeat itself. Horace devotes equal time to past, present and future, with no illusions about love's
permanence. He allows his *dramatis personae* total freedom in the verbal
evolution of their emotions. Catullus by contrast quotes directly for only
ten lines out of twenty-six.[22] The burden of the poem is the working out of
setting – the posture of the two lovers, the refrain exactly repeated, the final
pronouncement of a bright departure into love. Their individual outbursts
are embedded in a poetic framing that is both descriptive and incantatory.
Catullus positions his characters, offers a ritual chant of love's enticing
approval and concludes with eight lines where exacting verbal arrangements
are worked out in a trio of pairings (*amant, amantur; unam, uno; beatiores,
auspicatiorem*) extending over four sets of lines. The magical repetition of
the refrain is elaborated in the iterative techniques used to describe the
final leave-taking.

In sum, Horace allows his characters to speak for themselves, as they
unfold their own peculiar parallelisms in a verbal dance of love-making.
Their inner life seems ours to behold; their ironies self-made. Catullus, on
the contrary, feels the need for a narrative of framings. He is a *coniugator
amoris*, the third-party observer who as poet designs a controlling pattern
for their outbursts of affection.

Perfect as this all may appear, there is nevertheless something disquieting in the tension between a poet's orderings and his creations' passionate hyperboles. The finale is a bit too neat, too obtrusively made, as if Catullus had deliberately adopted a clinical detachment or, better, as if the logic in his own arrangements was both requisite and somehow quixotic at the same time. It is requisite if we trust the poem as an idealized vision of love perfected at last. It is quixotic if we realize how fallible such a patterning is elsewhere for Catullus. Such richness of intonation allows the reader to run the emotional gamut between humor and sorrow, seeing the poet either serious or amused over his protagonists' intensities.[23] But the final reaction, surely, is one of irony toward them and toward the possibility of their, or any, happy union. We need only observe other instances of Catullus' change from past to present to realize the vulnerability of his design in poem 45. Once bright suns shone for Lesbia and himself, he intones in poem 8; now life is miserable self-torture. In poem 58 we hear that once Catullus loved Lesbia more than himself and all his own; now she satisfies the descendants of Remus in the alleys and crossroads of Rome. If we read poem 45 "straight," it offers an ideal vision of love to be preserved by all the poet's devices, or a witty parody of amatory manners. But if we ponder its inner tonal variations between quotation and setting with Catullus' own constant emotional problematics in mind, we are forced to see the poet ironizing against himself as well as his creatures.[24]

Another level of irony is raised by comparison with the Horatian ode. We find the ordinarily direct, impassioned Catullus imagining other lovers' avowals of fidelity and capsulating them as if only thus could a uniquely ideal situation be preserved. Antithetically Horace, by nature more aloof and contemplative, more concerned than Catullus with grander problems of man and his destiny, gives his duo free rein to work out their situation. Each poet, however, is actually very much himself. Horace, by allowing Lydia and friend apparent independence from a shaping voice, reveals more bluntly the cyclic vagaries of emotion between two people in the counterpointing rhetoric they use. Catullus, tracing the ardent outbursts of his lovers and touching gently on their past, takes refuge in the role of authorial match-maker but in so doing betrays as well his own deep involvement by imposing a pattern of disciplined enclosure not of their manufacture. Perhaps only a poet's artifice can capture and preserve such attitudes as Septimius and Acme proclaim. Left to themselves, as Catullus well knew, they become easy prey to wind and water.

Immediate Catullus, so fond of determined self-questioning, seems here the contriver of an ideal; more distant Horace appears the realist. Catullus, *auspex* of happy departure, attempts to abort change by freezing the status quo and to maintain its earnest immediacy. Horace urges that process in human relationships is both reasonable and predictable. Catullus, playing the third party external to their situation, yokes Acme and Septimius by his own ceremony of words. As excited raconteur he intones the echoes and balances that conjoin. Horace, the more remote craftsman and tolerant as always of man's caprices, allows his disparate subjects, with Venus' help, to enmesh themselves in their own verbal toils. They create and dissolve linguistic unities of their own making, markedly in the last two stanzas where the male takes Catullus' artful correlations to himself and the female exerts her words both for and against them.

Catullus is extreme, either in the attempt to capture the ideal present or in the bitter cynicism that must lie behind knowledge of an inevitable failure. At the end of his poem we question his tone, as if it bordered on self-parody, and worry through his inner response toward such a topic. With Horace, more relaxed, more cosmopolitan, less personally tortured, aware that a poet's power need not always be direct, the human condition develops easily of itself with kindly irony from within the dialogue, avoiding any need for the author's further probing presence.

Finally, we may glance at Propertius' treatment of a similar theme. Separation and the emotions it provokes are a constant topic in the *Monobiblos*, and in its twelfth poem the elegist ruefully counterpoises his eternal constancy to Cynthia's changeableness. After commenting on the literal and spiritual distances between them, he looks at time past (1.12.7–8):

> olim gratus eram; non illo tempore cuiquam
>   contigit ut simili posset amare fide.

> Once I was pleasing to her: at that time it happened to no one
>   that he was able to love with equal fidelity.

We are not so far verbally from *donec gratus eram tibi / nec quisquam ...* , but philosophic difference is firm in the distinction between *olim* and *donec*. Each poet is observing time past but through diverse lenses. For the elegist the past was rewarding, the present desolate. For Horace's protagonist alteration is already implicit even in the heretofore. To the lyric poet *fides* is a virtue more mobile than enduring in any relationship. Propertius' last lines, however, prove that firmness and stability are as essential for the poet as they are needless or impossible for his mistress (1.12.19–20):

> mi neque amare aliam neque ab hac desistere fas est:
>   Cynthia prima fuit, Cynthia finis erit.

> It is right for me neither to love another nor to cease loving
>   her: Cynthia was the first, Cynthia will be the end.

Cynthia, though caught between the extremes of "was" and "will be," beginning and end, remains doubly invariable to her lover.

We may compare these doublets with the pairings in Horace's final line:

> tecum vivere amem, tecum obeam lubens.

Lydia equates love with existence (Catullus' *vivamus... atque amemus*), with living and dying together. Propertius equates Cynthia with love's extent, a process in the abstract defined by a name and lived out in hopeless yearning. For Horace's Lydia living, dying and loving are bundled into a concrete, sensory, emotional plea for unity. Propertius' stance teeters indulgently on the edge of self-pity, conserving with true elegiac fixity an ill-matedness he cannot or is unwilling to cure.

Wise Horace proves acutely aware of the futility of such steadfastness in his poem to Tibullus who espouses the same backward glance as his elegiac colleague—*Albi, ne doleas plus nimio....* Better a brazen yoke for the unmatched, Horace appears to say, than no partner at all. Better a dialogue, noteworthy for its openendedness as much as for its closure, than a soliloquy turning in on itself. Better, finally, a sense of humor instead of either Propertian elegiac despair or Catullan ironic idealism, in coping with the pitfalls Venus and Amor proffer to their hapless prey.

Notes

[1]The most sensitive, percipient discussions of *Odes* 3.9 are by S. Commager, *The Odes of Horace* (New Haven 1962) 57ff., and M. Owen Lee, *Word, Sound and Image in the Odes of Horace* (Ann Arbor 1969) 103ff. My debt to each will be patent. The novelty of the dialogue form in *Odes* 3.9 and Catullus 62 is considered by C. Williams, *Tradition and Originality in Roman Poetry* (Oxford 1968) 210f., who also summarizes the poem in *The Third Book of Horace's Odes* (Oxford 1969) 75–6. N. E. Collinge (*The Structure of Horace's Odes* [London 1961] 58ff.) analyzes the highly patterned (for Horace) strophic arrangement in an ode to whose thought processes he allots the term "progressive."

The notion of the poem as dance is developed by W. Wili, *Horaz* (Basel 1948) 184, who feels that Horace couches his poem "in einem...volksliedartigen Ton." ["in the manner of a folk song."] This idea was hinted at in their commentary by A. Kiessling and R. Heinze (*Q. Horatius Flaccus, Oden und Epoden* [Berlin 1958] 301) who speak of "Die Form des volkstümlichen Streit- und Neckgesprächs..." ["The form of popular arguments and insults in dialogue."] and has been elaborated by H.-P. Syndikus *Die Lyrik des Horaz II* (=*Impulse der Forschung* VII) (Darmstadt 1973) 112f.

I am particularly happy to offer this small token of appreciation to the honorand of the present volume who has been an unfailing source of encouragement for many years. I also owe thanks, once again, to professors K. Geffcken and K. Reckford for their gentle tutelage.

[2]We can, of course, think in terms of twos or threes when dealing with the initial pair of lovers and their later liaisons. We can also view the triadic structure in terms of amatory thesis, antithesis and synthesis which presses for unity.

[3]Many commentators assume the male voice to be that of Horace himself. The present authoritative text (ed. F. Klingner [Leipzig 1959]) even sets off stanzas 2, 4 and 6 in quotation marks, implying that her words are quotations and not his. Kiessling-Heinze (above, note 1), *ad loc.*, reason as follows: "...denn er will sich selbst unter dem Sprechenden verstanden wissen, der darum von den vier beteiligten Personen allein namenlos bleibt...." ["For he [Horace] wishes himself to be understood among the speakers; he is the only one of the four people involved who remains nameless."] The reasons usually given for such an equation are

Horace's own revelation of his inclination toward the very faults Lydia observes in her lover, fickleness and a quick temper (cf. *Sat.* 2.3.323 and *Epis.* 1.20.25).

[4]The phrase *bracchia dabat* is ambiguous. One gives one's arms as a gesture of embrace (and hence physical control) or surrender. For the former re. Vir. *Aen.* 2.792 (= 6.700); for the latter Prop. 4.3.12.

[5]The unexpected use of *multi* for *magni* with *nominis* may arise from the nearness of *magis*. It may, however, also be another means for Horace to insist on her propensity for quantifying and qualifying.

[6]There is a certain deliberate shock value in someone named (and from?) Lydia drawing to herself not an eastern but a Roman Ilia. With what gesture could she grow more clearly in the public eye (or climb higher on the social ladder) than by proclaiming herself consort of Mars and mother of Rome's founding twins? He ventures east in search of an abstraction. She fixes on Rome and reality.

[7]*Modos* is, of course, ambiguous and could be seen referring as much to sexual as to musical forms of activity. In the sense of "postures," Pichon (*Index verborum amatoriorum* [repr. Hildesheim 1966]) lists Tib. 2.6.52; Ovid *Am.* 3.7.64, 2.14.24; *A.A.* 2.680, 3.771, 787. Horace nears the meaning "wiles" at *Odes* 3.7.12 but the large majority of his uses, some fifteen instances, concern the measuring rhythm and sound, "sweet" though this be and doubtless alluring.

The combination of *Thressa* and *cithara*, of Thrace and lute, recalls Orpheus to our attention, surely the highest compliment our male protagonist could pay to Chloe (cf., e.g. Vir. *Aen.* 6.119-20).

[8]For the interconnection between the *gratia* that he prizes and song, re. *Odes* 1.15.14-15, 3.4.23-24, 4.13.21-22. In the end, of course, he veers toward Lydia's physicality.

[9]For *cal(l)ais* meaning "turquoise" or "topaz" see Pliny *H.N.* 37.151: "Callais sappirum imitatur candidior et litoroso mari similis." ["Callais imitates the sapphire, but whiter and like the sea near the shore."] (The only other use of the word in classical Latin is in the catalogue of the same book, 1.37.56.) The Greek spelling varies between κάλαις and κάλλαις, though Liddell and Scott put the former first. A listing of its usage as a slave's name, particularly at Rome, is given in TLL onomasticos *s.v.*

For further possible plays on the names in his pedigree see I. Düring, "Thurini Calais filius Ornyti: A Note on Horace, *Carm.* III.9," *Eranos* 50 (1952) 91-97.

[10]The slight alliteration in *me torret face mutuo* may itself betoken mutuality.

[11]His control of the housedoor is noteworthy. Door and house are common enough symbols of the female, and his authority over them implies a reversal of the regular Roman amatory posture of the *exclusus amator* and the *domina* who exerts power over the door, its keeper and the lover beyond. The implications, literal and generic, are that the man has taken over for a moment even the woman's position of authority.

[12]Yet there are anomalies in his presentation. He uses the present tense instead of an expected future (she at least makes a gesture in that direction with the concluding subjunctives). It is as if generalization, not assurance, were his policy. And in his reliance on passives he seems as well to shirk the responsibility of direct action.

[13]The ancient commentators concluded that Horace chose brass for his yoke because something literally metallic would be of long duration: "ad perpetuitatem revertentis gratiae iugum aeneum posuit; aes enim non sicut ferrum robigine consumitur" ["He made the yoke bronze to imply the permanence of the restored favor. Unlike iron, bronze is not eaten away by rust."] (Pseudo-Acron *ad loc.*); "Si rursus, inquit, nos Venus iungit ac firmat perpetua coniunctione. Hoc enim per iugum aeneum dicit. Aeris namque materia non sicut ferrum robigine consumitur" ["If, he says, Venus joins us again and confirms us in a permanent union. That is

what he means by a bronze yoke. For the material of bronze, unlike that of iron, does not rust away."](Porphyrion *ad loc.*). Endurance under particular emotional stress was not in their mind.

[14]Nearly but not totally, because *vivere* and *libens* are not parallel. On this curious and important line see further Lee (above, note 1) 105.

[15]The play on *amem*, extended by *libens* as well, is clarified by comparison with Catullus' *vivamus, mea Lesbia, atque amemus* (5.1), where the verbs are equal and coordinate. The verb *obeam* is an important replacement for *mori* here. It is possible that the fourth line of Catullus 5 influenced Horace's word choice: *soles occidere et redire possunt*. Since *obire* is used for the setting of celestial bodies as well as for the death of humans, Horace and Lydia may be telling the male protagonist that he has a certain kinship with a *sidus* after all.

[16]For further discussion of the differentiation between the two characters see Lee (above, note 1) *loc. cit.* and H.-P. Syndikus (above, note 1) 115, and, as part of a larger panorama, R. W. Minadeo, "Sexual Symbolism in Horace's Love Odes," *Latomus* 34 (1975) 411ff.

[17]Linguistic differentiation between obsessional and hysterical speech is made in an interesting article by L. Irigarey, "Approche d'une grammaire d'énonciation de l'hysterique et de l'obsessionnel," *Languages* 5 (1967) 99–109, a reference I owe to professor Eugene Vance. I am not concerned here with any putative difference in the use of language between male and female as such, a subject of growing interest among scholars. See, e.g., M. R. Key, *Male/Female Language* (Metuchen 1975), esp. ch. 8 ("Subjects, not objects: Linguistic structures"), and *ibid.* "Linguistic Behavior of Male and Female," *Linguistics* 88 (1972) 15–31.

[18]Yet the compliment she pays him of close imitation and exaggerated capping may indicate an allegiance of sorts to his mental processes which could lead as well into a restoration of their previous relationship. The very parallelism of language may prefigure renewed interest in spite of the diversity of the actual statements. Language may anticipate felt, not to say expressed, desire. And one of the results of this language, of course, is that they kill each other off and in the killing end any other inchoate relationships!

[19]Even her protestation of constant fidelity must be placed in an erotic context.

[20]The military and political overtones of Catullus' language here are discussed by H. Dietz "Zu Catulls Gedicht von Acme und Septimius," *SO* 44 (1969) 42–47.

[21]This is in my view still the most plausible way to explain *sinistra ut ante* in the refrain. Love had once sneezed inauspiciously on the left.

[22]Another important difference is that in Catullus' meter, hendecasyllabic, all lines are the same whereas in Horace's fourth Asclepiadean long lines (*versus Asclepiadeus*) follow alternately upon short (*Glyconeus*). Rigidity therefore contrasts with limited variability.

It has been trying for critics of both poems to remain non-partisan in their judgments. In treating their interconnection J. Ferguson ("Catullus and Horace," *AJP* 77 [1956] 12f.) finds Catullus' the more sympathetic effort (p. 13: "Horace produces the tidier poem, Catullus is more deeply affecting. Horace moves the mind, Catullus the heart. Horace's verses are the product of wit, Catullus' of the romantic imagination.") Many would agree. To offer one general example, the gist of Ezra Pound's famous essay is to dispraise Horace ("less poetic than any other great master of literature") by comparison with Catullus and Ovid (*The Criterion* 9 [1930] 217–27). For further comparisons see Commager (above, note 1) 141, and G. Williams, *Tradition and Originality* 210, 524 ("....the excellence of poem 45 lies in the formality and precision of the description, the unemotional realization of emotion").

Sunt qui Horatium malint, among them L. P. Wilkinson, *Horace and His Lyric Poetry* (Cambridge 1945) 49 and, more pointedly, Lucian Mueller (*Q. Horatius Flaccus, Oden und Epoden* (Leipzig 1900] 231): "Schmeichler des Catull haben sein 45. Gedicht mit unserer Ode verglichen. Was ich darüber denke, brauche ich wohl nicht zu sagen."

Critics who still see Horace throwing down some intellectual gauntlet to the shade of Catullus should review E. K. Rand, "Catullus and the Augustans," *HSCP* 17 (1906) 15–30.

[23]For appraisals of the ironic aspects of Catullus 45 see S. Baker, "The Irony of Catullus' 'Septimius and Acme,'" *CP* 53 (1958) 110–12; D. O. Ross, Jr., "Style and Content in Catullus 45," *CP* 60 (1965) 256–59; H. Akbar Khan, "Catullus 45: What Sort of Irony," *Latomus* 27 (1968) 3–12.

[24]Catullus, in a manner different from Horace, also raises many questions he fails to answer. When we have finished reading the poem the distinction between the lovers, which their hyperbolic, mock-political language only vivifies, remains as clear as their fusion. And how is the final question to be answered?

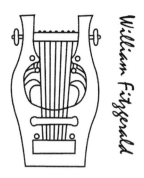

William Fitzgerald

HORACE, PLEASURE AND THE TEXT (PART 2)

Fitzgerald, who writes here on pleasure and the text, has earlier been cited in connection with 1.38. This is a more complex poem, addressed as both prayer and hymn to the spring, it is thought, that gushed out from beneath a tree on the Sabine Farm. Such religious gestures were regularly accompanied with offerings, and the offering that seems to have been given springs was wine and flowers (2). Horace has shocked writers ancient and modern by promising the spring in line 3 a young goat and specifying in the second stanza first the lively activities of which the kid will be deprived, then describing how the life blood of this playful animal will dye the cool waters red. Horace's pleasure with the spring has expressed itself in a murderous act of worship. He then goes on in the next two stanzas to apostrophize the spring with the familiar gesture of the repeated pronoun *te...tu...tu* (9, 10, 13), which would normally function in a list of the magnificent attributes of a deity. Here, the poet instead tells of the comforting coolness in the vicinity of the water, which is somehow untouched by and impervious to the summer's heat. The herds find pleasure in such a cool, wet spot, and so does the poet, who, in vowing to make the humble spring the proud equal of the famous springs of Greek poetry, speaks of the oak tree that shades and cools its waters as it wells forth from stones at its roots. The poet, then, takes the familiar stance of one who creates glory for men and things, only to have Horace in the last two lines admit that somehow the eloquent liquid (like our poetic "babbling brook") has given voice to his verse. The reciprocal effects of taking pleasure and giving honors that seem to border on the negation of humanity in the act of blood sacrifice touch in a special way the Horatian limits of pleasure. (Ed.)

❖ ❖ ❖

I turn now to another of Horace's most pleasurable poems, which is also a text about pleasure in the context of a particular, though rather more elusive relationship:

O fons Bandusiae splendidior vitro
dulci digne mero non sine floribus,
    cras donaberis haedo,
      cui frons turgida cornibus

This essay is reprinted from *Arethusa* 22 (1989) 93–102, with permission of the Johns Hopkins University Press.

primis et venerem et proelia destinat;
frustra: nam gelidos inficiet tibi
   rubro sanguine rivos
      lascivi suboles gregis.
te flagrantis atrox hora Caniculae
nescit tangere, tu frigus amabile
   fessis vomere tauris
      praebes et pecori vago.
fies nobilium tu quoque fontium,
me dicente cavis impositam ilicem
   saxis, unde loquaces
      lymphae desiliunt tuae.

(C. 3.13)

✧ ✧ ✧

This is a dedication poem, though in his characteristic manner Horace compli-
cates its generic status by making the very slightness of the poem into a potentially grandiose statement on the nature of his own art: the humble spring will
be raised to the status of one of the great springs of poetic inspiration (Castalia,
Hippocrene, Peirene, etc.) by virtue of having been described by Horace, just
as the humble dedication poem can now lay claim to major status.[1] This, at any
rate, is the primary utterance of the final stanza, and Wordsworth seems to
have missed it:

> Give *me* the humblest note of those sad strains,
> Drawn forth by pressure of his gilded chains,
> As a chance sunbeam from his memory fell
> Upon the Sabine farm he loved so well;
> Or when the prattle of Bandusia's spring
> Haunted his ear — he only listening.[2]

Commager quotes these lines as an example of the "sentimental echoes" that
have obscured a true hearing of this poem, and his objection focuses on the
words "he only listening." Now, of course, the last stanza begins with Horace
taking a much more active role in relation to the spring than "only listening,"
but what he actually says is that the spring will achieve fame through his description of the oak crowning the hollow rock, *from which* the prattling waters
descend. The prattling waters take over from Horace's speech (*me dicente ...
loquaces lymphae tuae*) and it is with the sound of their falling, which in the ears of
the poet become a kind of speech, that the poem ends.[3] Has Horace really *in-
verted* the traditional association of springs with poetic inspiration, as Commager
argues?[4] Surely the relation between spring and poetry is more complex than he
allows when he states: "The waters of the spring do not create his poetry; rather

his poetry gives new life to nature." The effect of this stanza, its pleasure, comes from the conflict between proud boast and humble listening, between speaking for the spring and letting it speak for itself. In effect, there is a Barthesian dialectic here, for the *doxa* that the spring must be glorified by the poet in order to be promoted to classic status is met by the *paradoxa* that this glorification will be no more than the stepping down of the poet in favor of the spring, for which the poet merely provides the conditions under which we can hear its prattling.[5] "Is that all?" we ask. "I have a *right* merely to listen." We can find something of this dialectic in Wordsworth also, I think. The word "listening" in "he only listening" is usually pronounced as a disyllable, which gives the whole line ("Haunted his ear — he only listening") a foreshortened effect compatible with "only;" and yet the word's terminal position and the pentameter scheme serve to counterpoint that reading with one that draws out the listening

/ X / X / X
("he only listening")

so that "only listening" insists on itself as an intensely active experience (being all ears).

The final stanza of Horace's ode, then, is not just a claim that the power of his poetry can raise a humble spring to classic status; the spring *is* a source of inspiration to the poet, as the listening with which the poem ends indicates. Horace's claim is rather to the right to be inspired by nothing more, or less, than the prattling of this insignificant spring; that is the *paradoxa* that constitutes the claim to a poetry of pleasure. We should note, though, that Horace also claims that the spring truly comes to be heard through his poetry: it is his *telling* of the oak placed on the hollow rock that allows the waters that fall from the rock to *prattle*. The rather complicated dynamics of the relationship between spring and poet will be examined later. In this final stanza we have an oscillation between liquid and solid, with the various analogues of that opposition (speech and prattle, standing and falling, pride and humility), that may remind us of Nietzsche's mosaic effect. The mosaic can be seen either as a set of individual pieces strategically placed or as a shimmer of light and color, the *flow* of strength that Nietzsche describes as the result of the *placing* of each word. Horace seems to have been there before his commentators, for in this stanza he shows that the shimmer and prattle of the waters emerges as an effect of the solid structure of the lines: the enjambement between lines 13 and 14 creates an icon of the structure built out of blocks placed on top of each other, while that between lines 14 and 15 allows the falling of liquid to appear: the structure of the spring is homologous with that of the poetry, which in turn is the structure of the double physiology of pleasure.

If this is a poem of pleasure we should be disturbed by the presence of the blood sacrifice, which is a crucial element of Horace's relation to the spring. Commentators have observed, often with shock, that the traditional offering of flowers associated with the Fontinalia is set aside in favor of a blood sacrifice; the description of the kid about to be cut off in the prime of life, his warm blood staining the chilly spring, has also given offense.[6] Where is the much vaunted *humanitas* of Horace in all this? There have been various responses to this problem: the occasion of the poem is not the *Fontinalia*; there is at least one ancient precedent for blood sacrifice to a spring; the ancients were not as sentimental as us about animals and their sacrifice.[7] The last statement is undoubtedly true, but the fact remains that in this passage Horace deliberately provokes empathy for the animal that he has destined for death. Williams characterizes the tone of the pathos that Horace arouses as a "detached, slightly callous irony,"[8] and I think he is right to see something disturbing in the character of the pathos, a pathos that is hard to miss in this particular passage whatever one may know about the general attitude of the ancients to animal sacrifice. Commager retrieves the passage by finding in it a comforting *cliché*: "the 'offspring of the wanton flock' epitomizes life's comprehensive vitality, and as the warm blood mingles with the lucid waters it is easy to sense a suggestion of the transformation of life into art."[9] Yes, but the ease with which we trot out this formula should make us uneasy! In what follows I am not going to approach the problem of the blood sacrifice from the standpoint of ancient cultural norms, nor am I going to try to characterize the precise tone of Horace's words on the kid; instead I will consider the rhetorical, or figural, function of the sacrifice in the context of the developing relationship between speaker and addressee. What is at stake in this relationship is something akin to Commager's formula: the production of aesthetic pleasure; but if we consider this issue in terms of the poem's rhetorical action, rather than treating the poem as an emblem, we will find Horace a more challenging exponent of the mechanism of pleasure.

In order to approach the poem as a rhetorical action we will have to take seriously the fact that it is cast as an address. I will therefore avoid the strategy by which the poem is treated as a dramatic monologue that merely *conforms* to the ancient habit of addressing a lyric poem to a person or thing.[10] Many commentators have pointed out that the poem is in hymn form, but this recognition of its apostrophic nature goes no further than highlighting certain formal properties of the ancient hymn that would seem to have a merely decorative function. If the poem apostrophizes the spring, then the spring must become an object capable of response, and it is the development of the responsive structure of the relation between speaker and addressee, culminating in the continuity between Horace's constructing speech (*dicente*) and the spring's fluid prattle (*loquaces*), that I will now pursue.

The poem begins by setting up a relation between speaker and spring that is not so much responsive as reflecting: by addressing the spring as *splendidior vitro*, "more brilliant (not 'translucent') than glass," the speaker constitutes the spring as an object that throws back his own voice just as it does the light, so that the final syllable of *vitro* echoes the "O" of the apostrophe and the two polysyllabic choriambs in the middle of the line fill out the mirroring ABBA structure.[11] The encounter with the spring, itself the reflecting brilliance of pure surface, reveals what one might call the structure of delight, in which the "O" that is the pure voice of encounter is thrown back at the speaker.[12] To anticipate a little, the movement of the poem will take us from the reflecting structure of delight to the dialectical structure of pleasure with its two sets of terms and its reciprocity between the speaking of the poet and the prattling of the spring.

The reflecting surface of the spring, and of the relation between speaker and addressee, is disturbed by the promise of blood-sacrifice. Although the spring is *worthy* (*digne*) of the customary sacrifice of wine and flowers, an offering that would reflect its beauty, this is not what the spring will get. By promising to sacrifice a kid, rather than the customary wine and flowers, the speaker unbalances the relation with the spring insofar as he is not content merely to reflect the worthiness of the spring as the spring had reflected his delight at its presence. This unbalancing paves the way for the statement in the final stanza that this ordinary spring (*tu quoque*, 13) will become one of the *nobiles*.

The promise of the blood-sacrifice and the narrative of the potential life of the kid cut short by this sacrifice is a shock not only to the relation between speaker and spring but also to the expression of delight with which the poem begins. Critics have been right to feel that this element of the poem creates a dissonance, though wrong to argue that it is either a result of miscalculation or that it manifests a fault of sensibility. The dissonance puts something at stake, and this is crucial for the transformation of the immediate surface of delight into the dialectic of pleasure with its ideological operations. The dissonance created by the passage on the kid is resolved on another level of the text: the disturbing mixture of pathos and ironic callousness in the narrative of the kid's career is neutralized on the aesthetic level as the kid's career is resolved into the economy of poetic energy, released over the enjambement between the two stanzas, dammed up in the premature caesura of the second line after *frustra*, and then set flowing again in the long, sinuous phrase that completes the second stanza. In this way the rupture of the kid's life and the disturbances in the tone on the narrative level are mediated by the various flow of poetic energy that is impervious to the emotional charge of the narrative it carries. The possibility of absorbing the final and definitive rupture of death into a continuous but varied flow of energy is set up primarily by the word *turgida*, which brings the promise of the kid's life, the swelling of horns that presages love and war, into the metaphorical field of the spring's waters (for *turgidus* used of swollen waters, see *C.* 4.12.4), so that the kid's death becomes merely a nodal point in the passage of energy, poetic or aquatic, and in this new context we may feel the tension of the swelling horns released in the flow of its blood into the spring.

In the third stanza, the hymnic listing of qualities (*aretalogia*) presents the spring as a source of comfort to the flock. But the causal relation between the fact that the spring is untouched by summer's heat and that it provides cool to the flock is disguised beneath the hymnic anaphora and asyndeton (*te ... tu ...*). The second line of the stanza, which juxtaposes the untouchable spring with the supremely tactile *frigus amabile*, reveals the functioning of the spring's comfort, which depends on the neutrality that allows it to provide discontinuity in the environment. So the hymnic distance between speaker and spring in this stanza, which avoids the attribution of any purposefulness to the spring, is itself a factor in the constitution of the spring as an agent of pleasure. The spring's discontinuous otherness with respect to the speaker, to the animate and narrative implications of the kid's warm blood, and to the heat of the dog star, its ability not to be touched (*tangere* in Latin has the same range, emotional and physical, as English "touch"), all this is a prerequisite for the spring's being used for the mechanism of pleasure.

But, if the spring is to serve the purposes of pleasure it cannot exist in a total state of otherness with respect to the human world that invokes it as its other side. Looking at the structure of the poem as a whole, we can now see that it repeats the same action twice: the hymnic *vis à vis* that constitutes the spring as the reflecting but untouchable Other is twice disturbed by an excess on the part of the poet. In the first case, the substitution of the blood-sacrifice for what is customarily appropriate brings the flowing energy of the spring's waters into a determinate relation to the swelling energy of the kid's life and to the pathos of its truncated narrative; in the second case, the prospective promotion of the cool, untouchable spring to one of the famous sources of poetic inspiration brings the sound of the waters into a determinate relation with the speech of the poet. These two modifications of the hymnic confrontation draw the otherness of the spring into the purposes of the poet of pleasure. In the final stanza, the sound of the spring's waters becomes that other side of articulate speech that is identified with one aspect of the Horatian poetic text, its fluid energy, and as this takes over from the solid, articulate construction against which it becomes visible, the pleasure of pure listening is claimed from a speech that is obliged to *account* for itself (in this case, to make a claim for a certain status). But this relieving of articulate speech does not quite work, for the spring carries traces of a pathetic narrative as it leaps down the rocks, and that is because the condition of its becoming a comforting and relieving other side to a burdened animate life is that it should become complicit in the sacrifice, which in this case means that there is a reciprocity between the spring's metaphorizing of the kid's death as a redistribution of liquid energy and the kid's narrativizing of the spring's liquidity. It is the sacrifice that draws the spring into the operation of pleasure, putting at stake the cruel irreversibility of death, smudging it in the pleasurable oscillation between narrative, with its irreversible sequence of discrete blocks, and the fluid energy of metaphor. But the spring, as the Other necessary to the dialectic of pleasure, is always either too far or too close: too far inasmuch as the untouchable spring that provides cool to the wandering flock is the indifferent spring that is untouched by the kid's death, and too near inasmuch as any contamination of the rhythm of the waters with a story (and how else can this rhythm be made perceptible?) will turn its pleasurable prattle into a disturbing reminder of the kid that would have leapt down the rocks just as the waters do (*desiliunt*, 16).

Clearly the relationship within which Horace locates the question of pleasure in this poem is rather different from the more tangible master-slave relationship of 1.38. It is not a social relationship, but rather an aesthetic one, as we see from the fact that the spring is throughout associated with poetic factors, and from the homology between the structure of the spring and that of Horace's poetry in the final stanza. We cannot say that the spring *represents* any particular thing; its function is to let Horace explore the nature of the relationship with various forms of otherness in which pleasure is implicated, and most particularly with that poetic otherness that appears against the solidity of constructed statement and narrative. But this is not a bloodlessly aesthetic treatment or pleasure, for the shock of the blood-sacrifice alerts us to what is at stake and to the limits of what can be achieved.

The pleasure I have been describing is certainly a stable, classic pleasure compared with Barthes's *jouissance*. In a time when criticism is claiming for the reading experience a kind of dizzy heroism, Horace does not seem to provide the right kind of challenge. Because there always has to be a straight-man against whom to measure the true poet and the dangerous pleasure to which we aspire, the poets who are traditionally associated with Barthes's classical pleasure will no doubt continue to be described in negative terms by the progressive and cherished as an exclusive bastion of civilization by the conservative. The character in Meredith's *The Tragic Comedians* who identifies Horace's "small crow and croon" as "the chanted philosophy of comfortable stipendiaries" has been echoed more recently.[13] The *Arion* questionnaire of 1970 produced responses that are probably typical of the attitude of nonclassicists (and many classicists) today. Northrop Frye there says that Horace "represents the authority of the humanist tradition, the incorporating of all its values in a lifestyle,"[14] and, though he does not say so, this lifestyle, what Barthes witheringly refers to as the "art of life," is the lifestyle of "comfortable stipendiaries." Henri Peyre, who sees Horace as an average, second-rate and uninspired poet, comments that "Horace's gentle Epicureanism has charmed hundreds of retired magistrates and army officers who have tried to turn him into French."[15] I have already referred to Brigid Brophy's response: she finds that her reaction to Horace as a "literary strategist" is cold admiration because he won't "commit himself to a *poem's* being a baroque extravagant gesture."[16] It is interesting to note that both Brophy and Peyre compare Horace unfavorably with Lucretius, who has been decidedly passed over in the process of establishing an authoritative humanist tradition, probably because it would be difficult to use Lucretius to advocate a particular lifestyle, and certainly because he does not serve the purposes of authority. I hope to have shown that we may read Horace not simply as the author and advocate of the litany of classical pleasures that may quite legitimately be opposed to other more disruptive pleasures not incorporated into the humanist tradition, but as an analyst of the mechanisms, purposes and contexts of that pleasure. It is the tradition that uses Horace for its authority that has reduced pleasure to the litany that Barthes parodies. Horace himself offers us the opportunity to do more than recite it.

Looking back on our two poems, we can certainly see why the pleasures that they represent have recommended themselves to comfortable stipendiaries, retired magistrates and army officers: they are the pleasures of retirement. But it is not just the vicarious enjoyment of pleasures that these poems offer us. Horace allows us to penetrate the rhetorical structures through which pleasure is claimed, to see the discourses against which it is constituted and, particularly in 3.13, to understand it as the utopian, and problematic, projection of an other side of dominant discursive structures. In other words, Horace does not see it as a simple quality that can be *represented*. Both of these poems make an issue of textuality and are important documents in Horace's self-definition as a poet: 1.38 is a particularly interesting act of situating aesthetic pleasure and the work that produces it against the work of the most important agent of ancient pleasure, the slave; 3.13 is a brilliant exploration of the mechanics and implications of what Nietzsche identified as the pleasure of the Horatian text (what 3.13 does for Nietzsche, 1.38 does for Petronius' *curiosa felicitas*). In this context, the two addressees, slave and spring, mark the outer limits within which, and by means of which, Horace situates the pleasure of his text: on the one hand, the slave whose sedulous preparations would reify pleasure, and on the other hand the brittle sparkle of the spring that would dehumanize it (like Barthes's *jouissance*). Horace situates pleasure in the interaction with these agents, in the dialectic of textual with servile work, and in the responsive oscillation between constructed human speech and liquid sound.

Notes

[1]The spring, raised from insignificance to the heights of fame, is like Horace himself, *ex humili potens* (C.3.30.12). Wilson 1968.295–96 makes much of this comparison, which is certainly viable, but he goes too far in saying that "in praising the spring he is almost praising himself." It has been argued that the spring is to be thought of as being on the Sabine farm and that he has transferred the name of a spring near Venusia to one in the neighborhood of his farm (Fraenkel 1957.203); this would strengthen the association of the spring's elevation to Horace's own.

[2]Quoted by Commager 1962.323.

[3]"But in this poem it is Bandusia, and not the poet that dominates to the end" Fraenkel 1957.203.

[4]Commager 1962.323. Wilson 1968.295 cites a number of passages in which Horace presents nature as a source of inspiration to him; however, like Commager, he believes that here the relationship is reversed because the spring is identified with Horace.

[5]Commager 1962.323 disapproves of Wordsworth's "stock epithet 'prattling'" and Quinn 1980.269 sees "*loquaces*" as a more daring figure than our "babbling

brook," claiming that the spring is fully articulate. I have retained Wordsworth's "prattling" because it is crucial to make a distinction between *dicente* (fully articulate speech) and *loquaces*, which, as I will show, has to refer to something just below the threshold of human speech. The *OLD* has two sections on the word, the first of which groups together uses that refer to an excess of words (loquaciousness, gossiping) that become inarticulate by virtue of overload, and the other uses that elevate something that cannot speak to figurative powers of articulation (speaking looks, etc.). *Loquax* seems never to refer to fully articulate speech.

[6]See the objections of Campbell cited by West 1967.129. West urges us to shed our local prejudices in dealing with this passage, but would Horace have recognized his words in West's paraphrase: "the blood spurting from an animal's jugular, an ancient religious observance of your race ..."? (130). Here one modern attitude (Campbell's squeamishness) is shed for another.

[7]The festival of the *Fontinalia* was celebrated, as Varro tells us (*Ling. Lat.* 6.22), on October 13 by throwing flowers into springs and putting garlands on wells, with the usual libations of wine in addition; Williams 1968.89 has some good comments on the unorthodoxy of Horace's sacrifice. Quinn 1980.269 argues that the dramatic moment of the poem must be mid-summer because of the reference to the Dog-star in the third stanza, but concedes that *cras* (3) would seem to indicate the imminence of a particular event, such as the festival. Syndikus 1972.149–51 has some good observations on the festive character of sacrifice for the ancients and also on ancient *Naturgefühl*, but while he may be right in castigating modern sentimentality in regard to sacrifice, this particular poem does evoke sympathy for the kid, though of course that is not the whole story. As for parallel literary sacrifices to a spring, Quinn 1963.77 cites Ovid *F.* 3.300 and *Iliad* 23.147: in the first case king Numa, trying to capture Faunus and Picus, sacrifices a sheep to a fountain at which they drink, and in the second Achilles, at the funeral of Patroclus, reminds the river Spercheios that his father vowed a sacrifice of fifty rams for his return home. Neither of these passages is at all close to the Horatian context. Horace makes no deal with the spring, and he is not a king (kings naturally do things big).

[8]Williams 1968.89.

[9]Commager 1962.323–24.

[10]This is the approach of Quinn 1963.76–9, who translates the poem into a dramatic monologue and argues that the "monologue" is what in a modern poem would be an "inner meditation," but that the ancient conventions demanded that Horace use some form of address as an "excuse for a serious poem." As will be clear, I regard this complete elimination of the poem's rhetorical structure as a serious mistake. See the excellent treatment of the rhetoric of apostrophe in Culler 1981.135-54.

[11]It is interesting to see that Ronsard accentuates the mirroring effect of this opening in his imitation of this poem (*Odes* 2.9):

> O fontaine Bellerie,
> Belle fontaine, chérie...

[12]The "O" fulfills what Jakobson 1963.217 calls the phatic function of language, which is that function of a communication that accentuates the establishing of contact. Culler (1981) has a very good treatment of the way in which apostrophe locates the entities apostrophized in relation to the act by which the poetic voice constitutes itself; as we shall see, Horace's apostrophe to the spring will constitute it as what I will call the other side of his own speech, which comes out most clearly in the final stanza with its dialectic between *dicente* and *loquaces*. Although the poem is cast in hymn form, it is important to observe that Horace here addresses the spring, and not some deity in addition to or instead of the spring, which as Syndikus 1972.138 points out, distinguishes it from comparable Greek poems. This means that the

spring comes to be responsive in the framework set up by the apostrophizing poet; it is not an independently existing subject, which would be more true in the case of a hymn to a deity.

[13]Meredith 1893.199.
[14]Frye in *Arion* (1970.132).
[15]Peyre in *Arion* (1970.130).
[16]Brophy in *Arion* (1970.129-30).

BIBLIOGRAPHY

Anderson, W. S. 1974. "Autobiography and Art in Horace," in *Perspectives of Roman Poetry* ed. G. K. Galinsky. Texas.

Arion. 1970. Issue on Horace, vol. 9, nos. 2 & 3.

Barthes, Roland. 1953 and 1957. *Le dégré zéro de l'écriture*. Paris.

———. 1973. *Le plaisir du texte*. Paris.

———. 1975. *The Pleasure of The Text*, trans. Richard Miller. New York.

Commager, Steele. 1962. *The Odes of Horace*. New Haven.

Culler, Jonathan. 1981. *The Pursuit of Signs*. Ithaca.

Fraenkel, Eduard. 1957. *Horace*. Oxford.

Gold, Barbara K. 1982. *Literary and Artistic Patronage at Rome*. Austin.

Jakobson, Roman. 1963. *Essais de linguistique générale*. Paris.

Leishman, J. B. 1956. *Translating Horace*. Oxford.

Meredith, George. 1893. *The Tragic Comedians*. London.

Nietzsche, Friedrich. 1967-77. *Sämtliche Werke*, vol. 6. Berlin.

Nisbet, R. G. M. and Margaret Hubbard. 1970. *A Commentary on Horace: Odes Book I*. Oxford.

Nussbaum, G. B. 1971. "A Study of Odes 1.37 and 1.38: The Psychology of Conflict and Horace's *Humanitas*," *Arethusa* 4.91-97.

Quinn, Kenneth. 1963. *Latin Explorations*. London.

———. 1980. *Horace: The Odes*. London.

Ross, David. 1975. *Backgrounds to Augustan Poetry*. Cambridge.

Syndikus, H. P. 1972. *Horaz: Eine Interpretation der Oden*. Darmstadt.

West, D. A. 1967. *Reading Horace*. Edinburgh.

White, Peter. 1979. "*Amicitia* and the Profession of Poetry in Early Imperial Rome," *JRS* 69.74-92.

Williams, Gordon. 1968. *The Third Book of Horace's Odes*. Oxford.

———. 1970. *The Nature of Roman Poetry*. Oxford.

Wilson, J. 1968. "*O Fons Bandusiae*," *CJ* 63, 7.289-296.

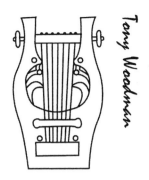

EXEGI MONUMENTUM
HORACE, ODES 3.30

In a meter which uniquely matches 1.1, the opening poem of this published collection of three books, Horace reaches a resounding conclusion, combining the autobiographical elements of the traditional closure with the Roman tradition of tomb inscriptions couched in the first person, as if the dead address the living. As Woodman nicely demonstrates in this essay, however, Horace's combination makes of this "funeral monument" an eternal commemoration of his deathlessness, his immortality. He has recounted his miraculous escapes from death threatened by the wolf of 1.22 and from the enemy swords at Philippi in 2.7; and he will have another escape to recount to us in Satire 1.9. He escaped because he was a poet, and the gods wanted to preserve him to produce poetry. Now that he has written these odes, he claims permanent escape from death, because what seemed like a funeral monument, composed of perishable, though tough, materials, is in fact the poems that have no tactile matter: they consist of images and verbal constructs that are timeless and invulnerable. So the personal "I" of the poet subtly turns into the voice of the poetry itself, which Horace boasts will last as long as Rome, little realizing that it would survive ancient Rome by more than 1500 years (already). He predicts that future generations, as though again reading his inscription and recalling his human fame, will in fact compare him to a triumphant general, perhaps even to the Princeps (13) Augustus, and record how he "colonized" Italy with Greek meters. These are proud words, but Horace evades the charge of pride by subtly bidding his Muse herself to take just pride in his work and to crown him with Apollo's laurel. He has ended in prayer. (Ed.)

❖   ❖   ❖

THE CONTEXT OF THE POEM

We have been made aware, especially in recent years, that an analysis of a Latin or Greek poem should take into account the category to which the poem belongs.[1] Does the poem have the form of a hymn, for example, and if so what kind of hymn? The category of poem to which *Exegi monumentum* belongs would seem to be clear from its position in the collection of *Odes* which Horace published in 23 B.C. It is the very last poem in the last book, an epilogue, occupying as important a position as the very first poem in Book I. Now a particularly favourite method of concluding a book of poetry in the ancient world was known as the 'seal' or *sphragis* (as

This essay first appeared in *Quality and Pleasure in Latin Poetry*, ed. Tony Woodman and David West (Cambridge University Press, 1974) 115–28.

it is technically called).[2] This would be a number of lines, or perhaps a complete poem, added at the end of a book of poetry and including some personal details of the poet's life or background, together with a mention of the poet's name. In this way a kind of 'copyright' was established. The last eight lines of Virgil's *Georgics* are an excellent illustration. Here in *Odes* 3. 30 we are admittedly given no reference to Horace's own name; but since we are given three lines dealing with his local territory and a hint of his successful career (*qua...ex humili potens*, 10–12), we may conclude that in this last ode of all Horace intended there to be some similarity to the *sphragis*-motif.[3]

These same three lines, however, have recently been subjected to a rather different interpretation. Epitaphs as found on tombstones conventionally mentioned the place of a person's origin and details of his career,[4] exactly as we see in lines 10–12; and it has been argued that this ode belongs to the category of epitaph poems, composed (as it were) for Horace's own grave.[5] A good case can be made for this thesis. It was also conventional for epitaphs to refer to the *merita* a man had performed during his life,[6] and these too we are given in line 15 (see below, p. 126). Yet such features on their own would not be conclusive in deciding whether this poem is indebted to the epitaph form; the opening of the poem is decisive. Horace calls his poetry a *monumentum*, more everlasting than bronze and higher than the pyramids. The two objects with which the *monumentum* is compared are both memorials to the dead: bronze plaques adorned the tombs of the dead in Italy, while the pyramids are of course the tombs of the Egyptian kings. It is thus likely that the *monumentum* is itself a memorial to the dead, especially since we know that one of the commonest meanings of the word is 'tombstone.' By means of a strong and vivid metaphor Horace sees his lyric poetry as the tombstone which will cause him to be remembered by future generations. Moreover, the first two words of the poem, *Exegi monumentum*, bear a striking resemblance to inscriptions commonly found on Roman tombstones, such as *hoc monumentum feci* or *hoc monumentum apsolui*.[7] Horace's *Odes* are his tombstone, and this final ode, the epilogue, is the epitaph inscribed upon them.

That Horace decided to write his epilogue in the form of an epitaph is not unexpected. On the one hand writers had long expressed a desire for literary immortality,[8] and this might occur naturally in an epilogue (thus in the epilogue to Book 2 of the *Odes*); on the other hand tombstone inscriptions conventionally proclaimed either that the tombstone was itself immortal[9] or that the words inscribed thereon would live for ever.[10] It was therefore inevitable that sooner or later poets would combine literary immortality and the writing of epitaphs, and this is exactly what we see in one or two poems in the Greek Anthology[11] and in Ennius' epitaph:[12]

> Nemo me lacrimis decoret nec funera fletu
>   faxit. cur? uolito uiuus per ora uirum.

["Let nobody honor me with tears or conduct my funeral with weeping. Why? I am flitting alive on the lips of mankind."]

But Horace is always full of invention and surprises, and this ode is no exception. In visualizing his poetry as his *monumentum* and the present poem as its inscription he has invented not only a new image but a completely new context for his claim to immortality.[13] We may also care to observe how, in his fusion of the epilogue and epitaph forms, Horace has produced a characteristic shock for his readers. Although we would be wrong to brand Horace a strict Epicurean, nevertheless one of the distinctive qualities of his poetry, and one which has appealed so much to generations of readers, is his popular Epicureanism. We might well have expected a hint of his philosophy to reappear in this epilogue, a natural place in which to sum up those aspects which have marked the poet's work as a whole. Instead, however, we are given five glorious opening lines describing Horace's pride in his *monumentum*, his metaphorical tombstone; this was the exact opposite of Epicurean doctrine, which held that the wise man will be indifferent to statues and will not concern himself with his tomb![14]

The ode concludes with a prayer to the Muse (lines 14–16), making this the third poetic form (along with those of the epilogue and epitaph) to be considered in an analysis of *Exegi monumentum*.[15] But our awareness of the form or category of a poem should not blind us (as it blinds some scholars) to even more important considerations, the words and imagery of which a poem consists.

THE POEM ITSELF

In the long and impressive first sentence, which stretches into the second stanza through the medium of an ascending tricolon,[16] Horace says that his *monumentum* is

> aere perennius
> regalique situ pyramidum altius.

What does *situ* mean? The noun *situs* can mean either 'site' or 'decay.' Here the word is usually taken to mean 'site.' The commentators admit that the usage is unusual, but the expression can be defended on two counts. There would be little point if Horace compared his *monumentum* to a decayed ruin, and besides he may have wanted the unusual noun *situs* = 'site' to stick in our minds and evoke thoughts of the common sepulchral inscription *hic situs est*.[17] Such a suggestion would be in harmony with the epitaph form discussed above. Some critics, however, have maintained that *situ* means 'decay.'[18] Horace would be using the word in a proleptic sense, 'higher than the pyramids which themselves must soon decay'; and the adjective *regali* provides a pleasing oxymoron 'royal decay.' If 'decay' is the right meaning, Horace's lines gain added lustre by recalling Simonides' famous poem on the dead at Thermopylae (lines 2–5):[19]

εὐκλεὴς μὲν ἁ τύχα, καλὸς δ' ὁ πότμος,
βωμὸς δ' ὁ τάφος, πρὸ γόων δὲ μνᾶστις, ὁ δ'

οἶκτος ἔπαινος·
ἐντάφιον δὲ τοιοῦτον τις εὑρώς
οὔθ' ὁ πανδαμάτωρ ἀμαυρώσει χρόνος.

Theirs is a glorious fortune and a noble lot:
for grave they have an altar, for mourning remembrance,
for pity praise. Such a burial decay shall not darken,
nor time the all-conquerer.

Simonides contrasts the heroes' metaphorical burial (ἐντάφιον) with physical decay (εὑρώς) in much the same way as Horace contrasts his metaphorical *monumentum* (his poetry) with physical decay. Scholars have long debated which meaning *situ* must have in Horace's poem;[20] but surely the truth is that the word's meaning changes as our reading of the poem progresses. We initially take it to mean 'site,' for the reasons given above; but as we remember Simonides and see the references to destruction in lines 3–5, the meaning 'decay' is activated.[21] Horace's lyric poetry is full of such ambiguities, this ode more than most.

In lines 3ff. Horace proceeds to prophesy the future of his *monumentum*: it will survive rain and wind. An American critic, writing on the Pindaric style of Horace, has said that here he 'undoubtedly had in mind' Pindar, *Pythian Odes* 6. 7–14:[22]

ὕμνων θησαυρός...
τὸν οὔτε χειμέριος ὄμβρος ἐπακτὸς ἐλθών,
ἐριβρόμου νεφέλας
στρατὸς ἀμείλιχος, οὔτ' ἄνεμος ἐς μυχοὺς
ἁλὸς ἄξοισι παμφόρῳ χεράδει
τυπτόμενον.

A treasure-house of songs....,
which neither the rain-storm from abroad,
that relentless army of shrieking cloud,
nor the wind with its swirls of dust will strike
and drive into the corners of the sea.

In Pindar both rain and wind are depicted in terms of violence: his adjectives (ἐριβρόμου, ἀμείλιχος, παμφόρῳ, 'shrieking,' 'relentless,' 'carrying-everything-along-with-it') provide the background to this idea, an idea which is pictured most vividly in his verbs (τυπτόμενον, ἄξοισι, 'struck,' 'drive'). In Pindar these actions are common to both the wind and the rain—by their sheer force they will attempt to sweep away the treasure-house of songs into the sea. Horace, however, is different. His verb, *diruere*, like Pindar's ἄξοισι, refers to both wind and rain; but whereas Pindar's ἄξοισι is a precise action ('drive'), Horace's *diruere* ('destroy') is not. We are left to discover from elsewhere in Horace's sentence the *manner* in which his wind and rain attempt their destruction. The clue lies in his use of adjectives. Horace's wind is violent (*impotens*), like Pindar's; but his rain is *edax*, an adjective which implies the gradual gnawing-away of the rain, not its violence. When the ancient commentator on Horace's poem, the third-century Porphyrio, remarks 'conrumpens *ui* tempestatis,' he has not looked closely at the words used by the poet. Gnawing rain is the potential destroyer of bronze memorials and the pyramids; to appreciate the full force of Horace's poetry, we must examine the interaction of these three elements more closely.

What happens when *imber edax* gets to work on the pyramids? Over a long period of time (the *innumerabilis | annorum series* of 4–5) it gnaws gradually at the stone. Now the wearing away of stone by water is an extremely common motif with a long heritage in classical literature, but as far as we can judge, no writer before Horace had used this particular image to illustrate mortality or immortality.[23] The first readers of this poem must have been struck by what was a novel application of a familiar idea. Next, what happens when 'gnawing rain' gets to work on bronze? When water comes into contact with *iron*, the iron rusts away. Propertius uses the image of water on stone to illustrate the way he wears down his loved one, and to it he joins the image of iron which eventually rusts; forty years later Ovid also linked the two ideas to describe his exile at Tomi on the shores of the Black Sea.[24] Now bronze, of course, is not the same as iron and does not actually rust; but it does decay in much the same way, and such technical writers as Columella and the elder Pliny use the word *robigo* ('rust') of bronze as well as of iron.[25]

Horace thus has two precise ideas before his mind, quite different from anything in Pindar: water wearing away a stone memorial and 'rusting' a bronze memorial. His own *monumentum*, however, will be able to withstand both these fates. The idea appealed to Ovid, who years later coupled two similar images to contrast with the immortality of his poetry (*Amores* I.15.31–2, 41–2):[26]

> ergo cum silices, cum dens patientis aratri
>   depereant aeuo, carmina morte carent...
> ergo etiam cum me supremus adederit ignis,
>   uiuam, parsque mei multa superstes erit.

["Therefore, although flints and the tooth of the long-suffering plow may waste away in time, poems are deathless... So even when the final funeral fire has consumed me [my body], I shall live and a large part of me will survive."]

Also *Ex Ponto* 4.8.47–51:

> carmine fit uiuax uirtus, expersque sepulcri
>   notitiam serae posteritatis habet.
> tabida consumit ferrum lapidemque uetustas,
>   nullaque res maius tempore robur habet.
> scripta ferunt annos...

["Through poetry virtue becomes long-lived, and, exempt from the tomb, it occupies the attention of posterity. Old age wastes and consumes iron and stone, and no material thing has strength to withstand time. But writings survive the years..."]

But in Ovid water is not mentioned specifically: it is *aeuum* or *uetustas* (admittedly *tabida*) doing the damage. Horace is superior for his immediacy and vividness, a point to which we shall return below (pp. 216–7).

The reason why Horace's *monumentum* will not be destroyed by the violence of the wind or the rusting of the rain is that the *monumentum* is only metaphorical: the *monumentum is his poetry*, which in literal terms can clearly neither rust nor be blown away. But we must remember that rust and the blowing wind have metaphorical applications too. Catullus and Ovid use the metaphor of 'rust' to describe something which has fallen into disuse,[27] while Tacitus uses it to describe an obsolete style.[28] Horace is perhaps indicating that his verses will never 'rust' in as much as they will be continually read and their style will appear forever fresh. We see this idea repeated later in the poem with the words *usque ego postera | crescam laude recens* (7–8), where the adverb *usque* (as some, but not all, of the commentators remark) qualifies *recens* as well as *crescam*. Similarly when Horace refers to the wind attempting to destroy the *monumentum* which is his poetry, he perhaps had in mind the motif of a person's words being scattered on the wind. The motif is extremely common in ancient literature to express the idea of 'speaking in vain'; but this will not be the fate of Horace's poetry.[29] With lines 6–14 we move into the second section of the poem, which is again formed around an ascending tricolon (balancing that in lines 1–5): (a) *non...moriar...uitabit Libitinam* (1½ lines), (b) *usque...pontifex* (2½ lines), (c) *dicar...modos* (4½ lines). Within this second section, lines 6–9 are important in forging a link between the first five lines and the latter portion of the ode. For the sequence of thought in these fourteen lines is as follows: 1–5 I have completed a *monumentum* which will be indestructible; 6– 9 however (a contrast, since the building of a *monumentum* implies death), I shall not all die (*non omnis moriar*, a negative statement) but rather I shall grow in acclaim (*crescam*, a very positive assertion); 10–14 my claim is one of originality.[30] It will be noticed how in lines 1–5 Horace is talking about his poetry, but in line 6 says *multaque pars mei* and in line 7 *ego* (placed in an emphatic position). Almost imperceptibly Horace has changed ground to become identified with his own poetry. The change is intentional. A tombstone, however durable, carries only the name of its dedicatee:[31]

sepulcri similis nil nisi nomen retineo.

["Like the tomb, I keep nothing except a name."]

But in Horace's poetry it is the essence of the poet himself which lives on.[32] The sequence of thought analysed in the previous paragraph calls to mind a similar progression of ideas in the fifth book of Lucretius, lines 306–37. In the first part of this section Lucretius is discussing the mortality of monuments and, if any reliance can be placed on the notoriously corrupt line 312, is comparing their mortality to the mortality of man (306–7, 311–12):[33]

denique non lapides quoque uinci cernis ab aeuo,
non altas turris ruere et putrescere saxa...?
denique non monumenta uirum dilapsa uidemus,
quaerere proporro sibi sene senescere credas?

["Finally, don't you see that stones are overcome by age, that tall towers collapse and rocks rot?... Lastly, don't we see the tombs of men fall apart; do you believe that they seek for themselves an old age like human beings?"]

Both monuments and man, he concludes, are equally susceptible to decay and death. He then attempts to prove that the world is in fact still young, and he introduces events which preceded the Trojan Wars but which had no poet to immortalize them (328–9):

quo tot facta uirum totiens cecidere neque usquam
aeternis famae monumentis insita florent?

["Where all men's deeds have utterly perished and nowhere, grafted into monuments of eternal fame, do they flower."]

The process of culture and civilization, says Lucretius, is still developing; the nature and system of the world have only recently been discovered, and he himself is the first to describe them in Latin (335–7):

denique natura haec rerum ratioque repertast
nuper, et hanc primus cum primis ipse repertus
nunc ego sum in patrias qui possim uertere uoces.

["Finally this understanding and explanation of things has only recently been discovered, and I am the very first to be able to translate it into our native Latin."]

When Horace wrote *Odes* 3.30 he may well have had in mind this passage of thirty lines from Lucretius.[34] The similarities are unmistakable, but Horace, as so often, tempers and alters the rigid doctrine of Lucretius to suit his own more realistic view of the world. Whereas Lucretius, if we may trust line 312, compares the mortality of monuments to the mortality of man,[35] Horace compares the mortality of monuments to his own immortality. Horace's claim gains added weight if we allow for a 'corrective' allusion to Lucretius. Lucretius picks up the literal use of *monumenta* in 311 by a metaphorical use of the word in 329, *aeternis famae monumentis*. His subject now is poetry and its power to make men immortal, and we may wonder whether the coincidence of this particular metaphor and idea here provided the germ of Horace's first few lines—although Lucretius' metaphor lacks the immediate impact and brilliantly original context of Horace's confident claim *Exegi monumentum*.[36] It is true that when Lucretius moves on to talk of his own originality (336-7) he is simply repeating a claim often heard elsewhere in ancient poetry,[37] and we have no need to assume that Horace in lines 10-14 is alluding to Lucretius; yet the sequence of thought in both poets is so similar that we may like to think that when Horace wrote his claim to originality he had an eye on Lucretius also.

In lines 10-14, the third section of the poem, Horace defines his claim to immortality. He begins by stating the locale where he expects his claim will be remembered (10-12):

> dicer, qua uiolens obstrepit Aufidus
> et qua pauper aquae Daunus agrestium
> regnauit populorum…

> *I shall be spoken of where the violent Aufidus roars*
> *and where Daunus, poor in water,*
> *reigned over his wild people…*

He is referring to the territory of Apulia, where he was born, through which the River Aufidus runs, and which in ancient legend was ruled over by king Daunus. The king is called 'poor in water' because Apulia was famous for its poor water-supply: Horace calls the region *siticulosa* ('thirsty') at *Epodes* 3.16. But why does Horace stress the aridity of Apulia in this way when he has already pointed out that the territory is blessed by a river which is both violent (*uiolens*) and noisy (*obstrepit*, in counterpoise to *tacita* in line 9)? These two features of Horace's native landscape seem at first sight paradoxical, but the paradox is there to stimulate our imagination. Horace intends to emphasize the river, to make it stand out: it is a force of nature to be compared with the forces of nature in line 3. There the gnawing water and violent wind were attemptive destroyers of his *monumentum*, whereas here the violent rush of water in the Aufidus symbolizes the locale where above all Horace and his poetry will be preserved. The contrast is helped by the echo of *impotens* (3) in *uiolens* (10): the violence of nature in the second half of line 3 is destructive, in 10 it is preservative. And we may also like to see in *regnauit* (12) an echo of *regali* (2):[38] the lofty royal pyramids will eventually crumble, but Horace will live on in a place which has its own proud royal heritage, preserved in legend and in Horace's own poetry.

In the previous paragraph we translated the repeated *qua*-clauses as if they qualified *dicar* ('my reputation in Apulia will be to have introduced Greek poetry into Italy'); but most of the commentators take these clauses with *deduxisse* in line 14 ('my reputation will be to have introduced Greek poetry into Italy from my homeland Apulia'). If we translate this latter way, Horace is describing not his proposed fame but his actual achievement, which must be seen in terms of his humble birthplace. There is a very similar idea to this in the first stanza of a later ode, 4.9 (and compare too *Epistles* I.20.20-1, quoted below, p. 215):

> Ne forte credas interitura quae
> longe sonantem natus ad Aufidum
>   non ante uolgatas per artis
>   uerba loquor socianda chordis.

["Do not believe that those words will perish which I, born by the far-sounding Aufidus river, by arts which have not yet been trivialized, speak to the accompaniment of the lyre."]

But how, on this interpretation, do we explain the paradox of lines 10-11 which seemed to throw so much emphasis on the river? We must remember that in the ancient world water was frequently a symbol of literary inspiration: the Greeks had their fountains of Hippocrene and Castalia, while Horace himself could address his Muse as one 'quae *fontibus integris* | gaudes' (*Odes* I.26.6-7).[39] Horace appears to be saying that he took his inspiration from the river which ran through his native territory. King Daunus, despite the region's natural resources, was helpless (11-12): he could not utilize the river and himself remained *pauper aquae* (a metaphorical way of saying that he lacked poetical inspiration), while his people remained uncultured (*agrestium*). Horace, on the other hand, was able to draw inspiration from his local river. As a result he is now *potens* (12) — and here we may see another echo of *impotens* in line 3. In its immediate context the wind is 'violent' (like the wind in Pindar's ode and like the Aufidus itself); but now it comes to have its other meaning of 'impotent' (as in *Odes* 2.1.26). Horace has become *potens*, *and* the forces of nature are 'powerless' to resist him.

Thus we can no more settle upon a definite, static meaning of *impotens* in line 3 than we could of *situ* in line 2 (above, pp. 207f.); nor can we be conclusive as to the exact reference of the *qua*-clauses in lines 10-12. We must just assume that Horace knew what he was doing and intended these ambiguities to give his compact ode a wealth of extra meaning lying beneath the surface.[40]

In the last three lines of this third section (12-14) Horace eventually speci-
fies his poetic claim, although the language which he has used to express
himself simply confirms the pervasive equivocalness of the whole poem:

> ex humili potens
> princeps Aeolium carmen ad Italos
> deduxisse modos.

What does *deduxisse* mean? Is it a metaphor from founding colonies, from
a victorious general celebrating a triumph, or from the spinning of fine
thread? Each of these possibilities has been canvassed by scholars,[41] but
one of them seems immediately attractive. In the last two lines of the poem
Horace appears to see himself as a victorious general being crowned by
the Muse (see below, pp. 215-6). The technical term for taking to Rome for
a triumph is *deducere,* as in *Odes* 1.37.31-2 '*deduci superbo* | non humilis
mulier *triumpho.*'[42] Horace would be saying: 'the first to have brought
Aeolian song (that is, the lyric poetry of Sappho and Alcaeus, who both
wrote in the Aeolic dialect) to Italian music in triumph.'[43] We are thereby
neatly prepared for the more explicit triumph-image in lines 15-16. At the
same time it is impossible for us to forget that Horace, like the so-called
'new poets' of the previous generation (of whom Catullus was one) and
like his famous contemporaries Virgil and Propertius, was strongly influenced by the early third-century Greek poet Callimachus, who had insisted
that poetic style should be λεπτός (the Latin equivalent is *tenuis*).[44] This
style was achieved only through a continual process of perfecting and refinement, and a metaphor which came into fashion with Callimachus' Latin
followers to describe this process is *deducere* = 'spin,' found in Virgil's
Eclogues, Propertius, and elsewhere in Horace's own work.[45] In the context
of the poem itself we take *deduxisse to* be part of the triumph-image, but
our knowledge of the literary background to which Horace belonged means
that we cannot exclude the notion of 'spinning' (that is, producing finely
wrought work) from our minds.

The Callimachean language of *deduxisse,* if we accept it, confirms other
hints of Callimachean technique elsewhere in the poem. We agreed (above,
p. 206) that the opening words *Exegi monumentum* strongly resemble tombstone inscriptions, but the verb *exigere* also became fashionable with the
Augustan poets to describe the same process of poetic refinement as
deducere: the usage *is* found in Propertius, Horace's *Epistles,* and in Ovid.[46]
We can now also see the phrase *ex humili potens* (12), about which a little
has already been said (above, p. 206), in sharper focus, with the help of
another famous ode, 2.16. In the fourth stanza of that poem Horace describes a characteristically simple outlook on life, saying that frugal living
is essential for inner happiness:

> uiuitur paruo bene cui paternum
> splendet in mensa tenui salinum.

He lives well on little whose family salt-cellar
gleams on a sparely laid table.

The following stanzas elaborate this theme by contrast and example in a typically Horatian manner until we reach the final stanza of the ode, where Horace claims to be content with his own small lot because he has his poetic powers:

> mihi parua rura et
> spiritum Graiae tenuem Camenae
> Parca non mendax dedit et malignum
>   spernere uolgus.

> *But to me Fate is consistent,*
> *in giving me a little farm, the spare spirit*
> *of the Greek Muse, and a taste*
> *for rejecting the common crowd.*

The adjectives *parua* and *tenuem* in the final stanza clearly echo *paruo* and *tenui* in the fourth: Horace is drawing an analogy between his mode of living (which is *tenuis*) and his poetic principles (which are also *tenues*). Horace regularly portrays himself as a devotee of the simple life, and the *tenuitas* of Callimachean style is practiced throughout his work:[47] here in *Odes* 2.16 the two themes have become fused into one, his way of life is mirrored in his poetic technique. This fusion of ideas is found elsewhere in the *Odes*,[48] and we may like to see it also in the phrase *ex humili potens*. Horace, though *potens*, is still *humilis* (or *tenuis*) in both his life and poetic technique.[49] This is a note we might well expect to be sounded in an epilogue poem, comparing the last poem in the first book of Horace's own *Epistles* (lines 20–1):

> me libertino natum patre et in tenui re
> maiores pennas nido extendisse loqueris.

["You will say that I, son of an ex-slave, in modest situation, have spread from my nest larger wings."]

The final section of the poem (lines 14–16) is a prayer to Horace's Muse, the function of which can only be understood if we appreciate the climactic tone of the section just ended: *princeps Aeolium carmen ad Italos | deduxisse modos*. Knowing that many other poets had claimed their work to be original (see above, p. 212 and n. 37), we may tend to dismiss Horace's claim as merely conventional, especially since in some respects his *Odes* had been anticipated by earlier Latin poetry such as that of Catullus. But we must remember that there is one respect at least in which Horace's *Odes* are almost completely original, their metres.[50] Modern poetry tends to disregard the importance of formal versification, but to the ancients regular metre was an essential feature of poetic craftsmanship. The difficulty of adapting the heavier vocabulary of the Latin language to the lighter metres of Greek lyric poetry must have been a supreme test of sustained effort and poetic competence, and for this one achievement alone Horace could feel justifiably proud at the result.[51]

Now that Horace has come to the end of his three books of lyric poetry and they are about to be published, his pride shows itself (14–15): *superbiam | quaesitam meritis,* 'the pride which has been won by my own merits.' The commentators differ as to whose *merita* are being referred to, Horace's or the Muse's, but the whole tone of the poem indicates that these are Horace's *merita,* nor must we forget that epitaphs commonly referred to the *merita* of the dead person (see above, p. 206). Since this poem is Horace's epitaph, there would seem to be no question that these are his *merita.* If, on this interpretation, we sense that Horace's attitude is overbearing, he tempers it by offering his newly won pride to the Muse: *sume superbiam.* The verb contains the notions of 'putting on' (a crown or cloak, for example) and 'taking for one's own.'[52] The Muse must assume Horace's *superbia* and make it her own; in return, meanwhile, she must garland Horace's head with a Delphic laurel (*cinge,* 16, activates the latent sense of 'putting on' in *sume*). The crowning of the poet's head with laurel recalls the procedure of Roman triumphs;[53] Propertius too was soon to see himself as a victorious general (3.1, especially lines 19–20 for crowning).[54] The image is grand and majestic, but here again Horace does not permit extravagance to creep in: he addresses the Muse as *uolens* (16), a word which, as the commentators point out, belongs to the respectful language of prayer-ritual. Indeed the prayer as a whole is 'a perfect antidote to the expression of personal pride' and 'seems formally to close a whole period of the poet's work.'[55]

THE FAME OF THE POEM

When Horace published his first three books of *Odes* in 23 B.C., *Exegi monumentum* had an immediate impact. Propertius concluded the second elegy of his third book with a passage which is clearly influenced by, and probably written in rivalry of, Horace's poem (lines 17–26).[56] Later there was Ovid too (see below), then Seneca, St Jerome, Shakespeare possibly, Ronsard, Herrick, the eighteenth-century writers Klopstock and Derzhavin, Pushkin, and a whole host of others.[57] We may briefly consider the case of Ovid to emphasize by comparison the quality of Horace's ode.

Ovid's most well known aspirations to poetic immortality occur in the epilogue to his *Metamorphoses,* where the language is clearly borrowed from this ode of Horace (15. 871–9):[58]

> iamque opus exegi, quod nec Iouis ire nec ignis
> nec poterit ferrum nec edax abolere uetustas.
> cum uolet, illa dies, quae nil nisi corporis huius
> ius habet, incerti spatium mihi finiat aeui;

parte tamen meliore mei super alta perennis
astra ferar, nomenque erit indelebile nostrum,
quaque patet domitis Romana potentia terris,
ore legar populi, perque omnia saecula fama,
siquid habent ueri uatum praesagia, uiuam.

["Now I have completed a work which cannot be destroyed by the
anger or lightning of Jupiter or sword or the rust of time. When it
wants, that day, which has the power only over this body, can put
an end to my uncertain life; still, with a better part of myself, eternal, I shall be lifted above the high stars, and my name will be inde-
structible. Wherever Roman power extends its domination on earth,
I shall be read by the lips of people and through all the ages, if
poets' predictions have any validity, in fame I shall live."]

Ovid does not specify what he imagines his immortal construction to be,
opus being a weak word commonly used of any literary composition. This
lack of precision is not improved by the assortment of objects which might
attempt to destroy the *opus*. *Iouis ira* (presumably 'lightning') and *ignis* are
consistent enough, but what about *ferrum* and *edax uetustas*? It is hardly a
compliment to himself if Ovid says that a mere sword (*ferrum*) will not
destroy his *opus*.[59] And in describing age as *edax* Ovid is returning to a
metaphor he had used several hundred lines earlier in this book of the
Metamorphoses (234-6):

tempus edax rerum, tuque, inuidiosa uetustas,
omnia destruitis uitiataque dentibus aeui
paulatim lenta consumitis omnia morte.

["Time that eats away at things and you, envious old age, you
destroy everything, and, when you have weakened them with
time's teeth, you gradually devour all things in a slow death."]

He looks at time and old age in human terms (he even addresses them), as if
they were a man with sharp teeth who attacks monuments and the like.[60]
Horace, on the other hand, has chosen from the start a single metaphor,
monumentum, which he imagines as being attacked by the immediate, natural
forces we should expect, rain and wind. It is only when we have reached this
stage of the image that Horace predicates the metaphors *edax* and *impotens*.
Cecil Day Lewis once wrote that in his opinion 'image-patterns must in fact *be*
patterns and not random assemblages of word pictures.'[61] The consistency of
detail in Horace's opening metaphor presents a much more imaginative and
compelling picture than the imagistic fragmentation of Ovid.
      Horace was proud of his lyric poetry, and rightly so. He saw fit to end
Odes 1–3 with a poem about his poetry which in its depth, grandeur, delicacy and suggestiveness surpasses even the finest odes he had already

written. When in the latest standard commentary on the *Odes* we read,
'Poetry is not the best subject for poetry and Horace's greatest odes are not
written simply about themselves,' *Exegi monumentum* will refute this judgement every time.[62]

Notes

The most recent full discussion of this poem is that of Pöschl (1970), 248–62; earlier
there was Fraenkel (1957), 302–7. Individual aspects of the ode are treated by
Korzeniewski (1968 and 1972) and Hulton (1972). I have also consulted a large number of Horatian commentaries, although references to them in the notes are severely
restricted. I think it only fair to say that I had completed a final draft of this essay
before I saw the extremely thorough work of Suerbaum (1968), especially 325–9.

It is a pleasure to acknowledge friendly criticism I have received on various
points from Mr R. G. G. Coleman, Mr A. G. Lee and Professor D. A. West.

[1] G. Williams (1968 and 1969), Nisbet-Hubbard (1970) and Cairns (1972) are
especially concerned with the categories into which Horace's lyric poems fall.

[2] Cf. Kranz (1961), and Curtius (1953), 515. With reference to Horace cf. Fraenkel
(1957), 362–3.

[3] This is also the conclusion of Paratore (1959), 181–2.

[4] For place of origin cf., e.g., *CLE* 1318.2 *uixi Lucrinis,* ["I lived at the Lucrine
Lake."] 856.1 *Tibur mihi patria* ["my native land is Tibur"]. For details of career cf.,
e.g., 372.1 *natus sum summa in pauperie, merui post classicus miles* ["I was born in the
worst possible poverty, but later I served as a soldier in the fleet"], and see especially how Trimalchio demands that on his tombstone there be inscribed the motto
ex paruo creuit (Petronius, *Cena* 71.12): this is very close to Horace's *ex humili potens.*
Further examples in Korzeniewski (1968), 33–4, (1972), 386.

[5] Pasquali (1920), 320–4, saw that this ode is an epitaph poem but his discussion is only of the most generalized nature; Korzeniewski (1968 and 1972) pointed
out just how many details Horace's ode shares with epitaphs proper. Neither scholar,
however, seems to have appreciated fully the metaphorical terms in which Horace
is talking.

[6] E.g. *CLE* 1103. 5–6 *dicite qui legitis solito de more sepulto:* | *pro meritis, Pylades, sit
tibi terra levis* ["You readers, say in customary manner to the buried: as you de-
serve, Pylades, may the earth lie softly on you"]. Also *IG* 4.800; Korzeniewski (1968),
34, (1972), 387.

[7] Cf. Kiessling-Heinze (1964) ad loc., Korzeniewski (1968), 32, (1972), 384.

[8] E.g. Sappho 55 and 193 Lobel-Page; Plato, *Symposium* 209D; cf. Curtius (1953), 476.

[9] E.g. *CIL* 1².1319 *haec est domus aeterna...hoc est monumentum nostrum* ["This is
my eternal home...this is my tomb"], *IG* 12.9.285. Further examples in Korzeniewski
(1968), 32, (1972), 385, and also Lattimore (1942), 167 n.78, whose work is a rich
mine for those interested in epitaph poetry.

[10] E.g. *CLE* 1278 *quodque meam retinet uocem data littera saxo,* | *uoce tua uiuet
quisque leges titulos,* ["because the letter inscribed on the stone preserves my voice,
it will live by your voice, whoever reads this inscription"] *CIL* 8.7156 *hic ego qui
taceo uersibus mea uita demonstro* ["I who am silent here give information about my
life in verse"].

[11] *Anthologia Palatina* 7.715 = lines 2535–40 Gow-Page: 'Far from the land of
Italy do I lie... but the name of Leonidas has not been forgotten; the Muses' gifts
proclaim it till the end of time.' Two other poems are similar in theme but not
strictly epitaphs: 7.12 'The fine work of your poetry, Erinna, cries out that you are
not dead but join in the Muses' dance'; 7.713 = lines 560–7 Gow-Page: 'Erinna has

written few verses and her songs have few themes, but she has been assigned this brief epic by the Muses. Therefore is she remembered and is not confined by the shadowy wing of black night.'
[12]Ennius, *Varia* 17–18 Vahlen. See again Pasquali (1920), 320–4.
[13]No poet before Horace has used the metaphor of a tombstone to describe his poetry, and the only certain example I have found after Horace is the fourth-century A.D. writer Themistius (*Orationes* 4.59d ἠρία τῶν ψυχῶν τὰς βίβλους, 'books are the tombs of the spirit'). Horace's vocabulary is of course quite different from such expressions as *litterarum monumenta* (Cicero, *De Inuentione* 1.1, *De Officiis* 1.156 etc.) or *annalium monumenta* (*Pro Sestio* 102, Livy, 7.21.6 etc.), where *monumenta* has its commonest meaning of simply 'monuments.' For *monumentum* used without qualification of literary productions cf. Catullus 95.9, Cicero, *Ad Atticum* 12.18.1, *Ad Familiares* 5.12.1. For less sceptical remarks than mine on the word *monumentum* see Suerbaum (1968), 327–8.
[14]Cf. De Witt (1939), 129, who rightly sees a 'pointed interpretation' of the opening of this ode. Hulton (1972), 501–2, even observes that for true Epicureans poets were people *in quibus nulla solida utilitas omnisque puerilis est delectatio* ["in whom there is no definite usefulness and all delight is childish"](Cicero, *De Finibus* 1.72).
[15]For a *sphragis*-poem ending with a prayer see the 'seal' of Posidippus in Lloyd-Jones (1963), 80–1, 92–3, 96.
[16]The ascending tricolon is (a) *aere perennius*, (b) *regalique...altius*, (c) *quod...temporum.* ◇ ◇ ◇
[17]G. Williams (1969), 150, following Kiessling-Heinze (1964) ad loc., goes so far as to translate *situs* here as 'grave.'
[18]The usual parallel is Martial 8.3.5–7 'et cum *rupta situ* Messalae saxa iacebunt | altaque cum Licini marmora puluis erunt, | me tamen ore legent.'
[19]Simonides 531 Page. In line 4 I have adopted an emendation by M. L. West (1967), 133. The exact meaning of Simonides' verb ἀμαυρώσει is doubtful (cf. Lloyd-Jones (1965), 243n.) but is used frequently of time (cf. Pfeiffer (1949) on Callimachus, *Iambus* 12.67, Borthwick (1971), 431 n. 2). On the question of whether Simonides' ἐντάφιον is metaphorical or not compare M. L. West (1970), 210–11, and Page (1971), 317–18.
[20]For a survey of scholarly opinion cf. Pöschl (1970), 251–3, who himself strongly favours 'decay.' Korzeniewski (1968), 31–2, strongly favours 'site.'
[21]This is also the view of Plessis (1924) ad loc.: 'Ici, malgré la plupart des commentateurs, n'écartons pas l'idée de ruine: la dégradation est justement un témoignage d'antiquité; et ne négligeons pas la suite des idées: grammaticalement, *situ pyramidum* ne dépend que de *altius*; mais, dans la pensée du poète, il dépend aussi de *perennius*. ...*situ* doit donc, de toute manière, faire allusion à la fois à la longue stabilité des pyramides et à leur commencement de décrépitude.' ["Here, in spite of most commentators, let us not set aside the idea of ruin: decay is indeed evidence of antiquity; and let us not ignore the consequence of the idea: grammatically, *situ pyramidum* depends only on *altius*; but in the thought of the poet it also depends on *perennius*. ...Thus, *situ* should unquestionably allude at the same time to the prolonged stability of the pyramids and to the beginning of their disintegration."]
[22]Highbarger (1935), 251. This is the usual tradition, cf., e.g., Macleane (1853) ad loc., 'What follows seems to be imitated from Pindar.' To his credit Pöschl (1970), 253–4, notices the differences between Horace and Pindar but does not even begin to consider their implications and does not go into any detail.
[23]The motif is at least as old as Aristotle, *Physics* 8.3 (253b). Some, but by no means all, of its occurrences are listed by Smith (1971) on Tibullus 1.4.18, a passage which is an instance of the image's commonest function, illustrating the way a lover gradually wears down the loved one. For the image used to illustrate mortality

or immortality *after* Horace cf. Ovid, *Ex Ponto* 4.10.1–7, Sulpicius Lupercus, *PLM* 4.107.7.

[24]Propertius 2.25.15–17 *sed tamen obsistam. teritur robigine mucro | ferreus et paruo saepe liquore silex: | at nullo dominae teritur sub limine amor...* ["Nevertheless, I shall persist. The blade is worn down by rust and the flint often by a little water: but love is worn down at no mistress' door"]; Ovid, *Ex Ponto* 1.1.67ff. *non igitur mirum, si mens mea tabida facta | de niue manantis more liquescit aquae. | ... aequorei scopulos ut cauat unda salis, | roditur ut scabra positum robigine ferrum* ["So it is no wonder if my mind pines away, melting like water running off snow... as the wave of the salt sea hollows out cliffs, as buried iron is rotted by scaly rust"].

[25]Columella, *De Re Rustica* 7.5.12 *aeris robigine*, Pliny, *Natural History* 7.64 *aes etiam ac ferrum robigo protinus corripit* ["Rust quickly consumes bronze as well as iron"], 34.99 *aera extersa robiginem celerius trahunt quam neglecta* ["Polished bronze contracts rust more quickly than when it is neglected"] (Pliny here also tells us that bronze was used on *monumenta* to make them more durable).

[26]Compare also *Amores* 1.10.61–2 *gemmae frangentur et aurum; | carmina quam tribuent fama perennis erit* ["Gems and gold can be broken; the fame which poetry provides will be eternal"].

[27]Catullus 68.149–52 *hoc tibi, quod potui, confectum carmine munus | pro multis, Alli, redditur officiis, | ne uestrum scabra tangat robigine nomen | haec atque illa dies atque alia atque alia* ["This gift composed in such poetry as I could compose is given to you, Allius, in return for your kindness, that no day, now or any time in the future, may touch your name with scaly rust"]; Ovid, *Tristia* 5.12.21–2 *adde quod ingenium longa rubigine laesum | torpet et est multo quam fuit ante minus* ["In addition, my talent injured by long rusting is dulled and much less effective than it once was"].

[28]Tacitus, *Dialogus* 22.5 *nullum sit uerbum uelut rubigine infectum* ["Let there be no word that is so to speak rotted by rust"]. Compare also Quintilian 10.1.30; and Curtius (1953), 411.

[29]For words being scattered on the wind cf. Nisbet-Hubbard (1970) on *Odes* 1.26.2. It is possible that we are meant to understand *altius* (line 2) metaphorically too. *altus* is a familiar term for describing the kind of poetry, with elevated themes, which Horace believes many of his *Odes* to be. He might be declaring a belief in the seriousness of his poetry; it is not simply a collection of *nugae*. Such a belief would sound natural in a poem of this type, although on other occasions of course Horace can look upon his poetry as light and even trivial: for this apparent paradox see Hulton (1972).

[30]Lines 1–14 thus form a climax, followed by a concluding prayer. For a different, rather eccentric, view, cf. Collinge (1961), 69–70, who sees these lines as a three-part *anti*-climax, and the final prayer as a return to the 'opening bravado' of lines 1–5.

[31]Laberius, *Prologue* 124 Ribbeck. For further exs. of this idea cf. Suerbaum (1968), 326, adding *CIL* 6.9604.

[32]This notion is thus not exclusively 'the conceit of a later age,' as Hulton (1972), 499, says.

[33]The reading of line 312 here adopted is that of Munro (1873). The line has caused a great deal of discussion, e.g. D. A. West (1965).

[34]But Lucretius 5.306–37 is quoted by none of the Horatian commentators I have seen, nor by Merrill (1905). It is, however, quoted by Suerbaum (1968), 328.

[35]An idea which became quite common, e.g. Florus 1.6.11, Lucian, *Charon* 23, Ausonius, *Epigrams* 35.9–10, Rutilius Namatianus, *De Reditu* 1.409–14.

[36]For a discussion of Lucretius' metaphor see D. West (1969), 2–3.

[37]For poets' claims to originality see Nisbet-Hubbard (1970) on *Odes* 1.26.10.

[38]So too Huber (1970), 126 n. 3.

[39]See Nisbet-Hubbard (1970) ad loc., with further references.

[40] A reading of *Exegi monumentum* should make us sceptical of the remark that 'The mature poet of the *Odes* was in the habit of producing unambiguous constructions' (Fraenkel (1957), 251 n. 6). On pp. 304–5 Fraenkel discusses the repeated *qua*-clauses and unhesitatingly takes them with *dicar*; more realistic, it seems to me, is the comment of Quinn (1960), 40: 'It is most unlikely that Horace was unaware of the perils of an ambiguously related relative clause, or inadvertently committed one in a poem written with such obvious care for so prominent a place in the collection.'

[41] For a brief survey of this debate see Pöschl (1970), 257–9, who himself favours spinning.

[42] See Nisbet-Hubbard (1970) ad loc.

[43] The best parallel is Virgil, *Georgics* 3.10–11 'primus ego in patriam ... | Aonio rediens *deducam* uertice Musas.' Cf. also Horace, *Epistles* 2.1.156 'Graecia capta ferum uictorem cepit,' Greece taking Italy captive. In Horace's ode I take the word *modos* to mean 'music,' or 'rhythms,' or more generally 'poetry,' as at *Odes* 2.1.40 *quaere modos leuiore plectro*, 2.9.9–10 *urges flebilibus modis* | *Mysten ademptum*, 2.12.3–4 *mollibus* | *aptari citharae modis*, 3.3.72 *magna modis tenuare paruis*, 3.9.10 *dulcis docta modos*, 4.6.43–4 *reddidi carmen docilis modorum* | *uatis Horati*, *Epistles* 1.3.12–13 *fidibusne Latinis* | *Thebanos aptare modos studet*. I do not think that Horace here uses the word = 'metres' (as he does on some occasions, e.g. *Epistles* 1.19.27) since his *metres* could in no sense be called 'Italian'; but this is not to deny that Horace's debt to the Greek lyric poets was above all a metrical debt: see above, p. 215–6 and nn. 50–1. A rather different interpretation is given by G. Williams (1969), 151.

[44] ❖ ❖ ❖ For Callimachus and Horace cf. Wehrli (1944), Wilkinson (1968), 118ff., Brink (1963), 288 (index), and Newman (1967), 303ff.

[45] Virgil, *Eclogues* 6.5 *deductum dicere carmen*, Propertius 1.16.41 *at tibi saepe nouo deduxi carmina uersu*, Horace, *Epistles* 2.1.225 *tenui deducta poemata filo*. Further instances in Pöschl (1970), 258.

[46] Propertius 3.1.8 *exactus tenui pumice uersus eat* ["Let the verse go forth finished off with light pumice"], Horace, Epistles 2.1.71–2 *sed emendata uideri* | *pulchraque et exactis minimum distantia miror* ["But I am surprised that they [verses] seem emended and handsome and little short of finished"], Ovid, *Metamorphoses* 15.871 *iamque opus exegi* ["Now I have finished a work"].

[47] There is a further Callimachean feature in the final stanza of *Odes* 2.16, that of rejecting the common crowd. See Callimachus, *Epigrams* 28.4 Pfeiffer, Nisbet-Hubbard (1970) on *Odes* 1.1.32.

[48] See Mette (1961), 138 'Wahl des Bios und Wahl der Gattung fallen für Horaz in eins. Gattung und Bios sind aufeinander zu stilisiert.' ["Choice of life and choice of genre unite into one for Horace. Genre and life are stylized mutually on each other."]

[49] The paradox between *potens* and *humilis* (or *tenuis*) is only superficial: see Hulton (1972), 499, 'In the last analysis we are confronted...by simply another example of the well-known Horatian "dualism" or "ambivalence ."'

[50] Of *Odes* 1–3 71.5% are written in the two Aeolian metres, the Sapphic stanza (26 poems) and the Alcaic stanza (37 poems). A glance at the statistics in Raven (1965), Appendix B, will show that in composing lyric poetry in Aeolian metres Horace had virtually no rival. No one, so far as we know, had written Latin Alcaics before, and there were no Latin Sapphics before Horace with the exceptions of Catullus 11 and 51. But scholars have usually decided (e.g. Williams (1969), 151) that Catullus' two poems hardly impair the justice of Horace's claim. Even so, when he came to write *Epistles* 1.19, Horace narrowed his claim to exclude any originality as far as the Sapphic stanza was concerned (lines 32–3).

[51] So too Wilkinson (1968), 13, 'His pride at having introduced Aeolian lyric to Italy is very likely due, not to the phrases or ideas, nor even to the small amount of

spirit, which he derived from Alcaeus and Sappho, but to his success at mastering and adapting their metres.' It is quite wrong to say that 'Horace is not primarily interested in metre as such,' as does Newman (1967), 343.

[52]The opposite phrase is *ponere superbiam*, as at *Odes* 3.10.9; for *ponere* and *sumere* as opposites cf. *Odes* 3.2.19.

[53]Cf. Versnel (1970), 57.

[54]For the contemporary popularity of the *triumphator* motif see Galinsky (1969), who discusses Propertius 3.1 at pp. 88–9.

[55]G. Williams (1969), 152 and (1968), 153.

[56]Cf. Solmsen (1948), especially 106. Also Flach (1967), 97ff.

[57]Seneca, *Epigrams* 27 and 28; Jerome, *Epistles* 108.33 *exegi monumentum aere perennius quod nulla destruere possit uetustas*; for possible influences upon Shakespeare see Leishman (1961), 27–91; Ronsard, *A sa Muse* in Laumonier (1914), 2.152; Herrick, *Pillar of Fame* and stanzas 5 and 6 of *His Poetrie his Pillar*; Klopstock, *An Freund und Feind*, last three stanzas, in Schleiden (1954), 110; for Derzhavin and Pushkin see Bayley (1971), 302ff. I am very grateful to Cesca Thompson for the reference to Klopstock and to Professor J. Gwyn Griffiths for the references to Derzhavin and Pushkin.

[58]Correspondences of language are conveniently set out in parallel tables by Bauer (1962), 17–18, but he regrettably uses Ovid in an attempt to disparage Horace.

[59]It is interesting to note that Shakespeare (*Sonnet* 55), in his allusion to the Ovidian passage, tried to strengthen this weakness but in so doing fell into loose writing elsewhere in his couplet: "Nor Mars his sword nor war's quick fire shall burn | The living record of your memory."

[60]For the teeth of time see Simonides 75 Diehl; Shakespeare, *Measure for Measure* 5.1; Phineas Fletcher, *Purple Island* 1.15 in Boas (1909), 2.15; W. B. Yeats, *The New Faces*. For the teeth of death cf. Lucretius 1.852; Seneca, *Hercules Furens* 555. For other personifications of time and age cf. Leishman (1961), 134–42.

[61]Day Lewis (1947), 74.

[62]Nisbet-Hubbard (1970), on *Odes* 1.26, introductory note.

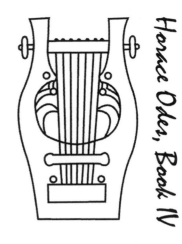

Horace Odes, Book IV

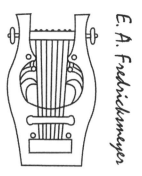

HORACE, ODES 4.7: "THE MOST BEAUTIFUL POEM IN ANCIENT LITERATURE"?

This poem, a favorite with many, has also struck some sober audiences as an unconvincing series of trite Horatian sentiments on death, into which the thought of *carpe diem* has been briefly and tepidly planted. Fredricksmeyer, who clearly favors the lovers of Horace such as the poet-classicist A. E. Housman, shows some of the ways this ode works for himself. We may compare it with the ode to Postumus (2.14), who trusting that his piety guaranteed him long life, needed to be reminded that he was all too mortal and therefore should enjoy his present opportunities for pleasure in this life. Here, Horace starts from the hopeful feelings inspired by Spring. However, far from encouraging us to relax and seek love in this season (as in 1.9), the poet involves us in the remorseless passing of the year's stages. The nymphs may dance to greet Spring, but the poet turns to his audience and urges us to abandon all hope for immortality, to be warned by the passing seasons, which all too soon (emphatic *mox* at the end of the hexameter of 11) will end up again in winter, the symbol of nature's and our death in its whiteness and stillness. Though we resemble the seasons in our mutability, we, alas, do not have the capacity to recoup our losses and repeat regularly the cycle of youth to old age. We live but once, as all human beings (= mortals) have done, from the great Aeneas commemorated by Vergil down to today. We cannot even know whether we shall be alive tomorrow (17–18). Now, in one short couplet (19–20), come the words that elliptically imply *carpe diem*. You can frustrate your greedy heir by being friendly to yourself while alive. With that, Horace resumes the pounding emphasis on the inevitability of death, even for the noble addressee Torquatus, whom he finally names in 23. As Fredricksmeyer suggests, it is wrong to infer tepidity from the brevity of the *carpe diem* passage: on the contrary, the very brevity enhances the poetic stress on our mutability and the preciously short opportunities for pleasure as mortals. (Ed.)

Ulrich von Wilamowitz-Moellendorff dismissed this poem as an "insignificant spring-song."[1] A. E. Housman called it the "most beautiful poem in ancient literature."[2] How can two great scholars, profound students of classical literature, so disagree? Is it possible that there are, after all, no objective criteria by which the merit of poetry can be assessed? Surely no classicist, or any critic worth the name, would accept such a proposition. It is more plausible to assume that in this instance, at least, one of these two men was mistaken. The issue is intriguing enough to invite another close reading of the poem.[3]

Reprinted from *Hypatia: Essays in Classics, Comparative Literature, and Philosophy Presented to Hazel E. Barnes*, ed. W. Calder, U. K. Goldsmith, and P. B. Kenevan (University of Colorado, Boulder, 1985) 16–26.

Diffugere nives.... Winter has gone, spring is here. The poem opens with the picture of various patches of snow, last holdouts of winter, fleeing in different directions, like a routed enemy, at the onset of the spring sun. They are now gone and, as if in triumph, grass is returning to the fields and foliage to the trees. And as the earth changes in appearance,[4] so the rivers, no longer overflowing from the thaw, are subsiding and peacefully flowing along their banks. The picture then rises from the natural to the mythological level.[5] If we can make here a distinction between Graces and Nymphs, the Nymphs represent the element of nature, while the Graces represent the qualities and activities which bestow beauty and grace on the life of man. Together now, led by one of the Graces, these lovely and joyful creatures venture forth, naked, to dance in the open, to welcome spring and celebrate life. Their example can inspire in us, too, a *joie de vivre*. What follows, however, is unexpected, a bit of a jolt.

> Immortalia ne speres, monet annus et almum
> quae rapit hora diem!

Abruptly the poet has introduced a *memento mori*. It is not that under the influence of what we have witnessed we have conceived the hope that, perhaps like the Nymphs and Graces, we ourselves might be immortal. We simply have not thought, one way or the other, of the ephemeral nature of spring and of our own mortality. But what can help us to be mindful of it is to consider spring not by itself, without its larger context, as we did at first, but as merely one in the sequence of the seasons (*annus*, 7) and to remember that the hours (*hora*, 8) in their quick succession soon "snatch away" (*rapit*, 8) the day, another beautiful spring day (*almum diem*, 7-8). Soon spring is gone, and the next season follows. If we turn back for a moment to the initial picture of spring, we can see what at first we did not, that there are all along subtle warnings of the transitory nature of spring. The remark *mutat terra vices* (3) now assumes its full force of "the earth changes with the alteration of the seasons." All verbs in the depiction of spring denote not a state or condition but movement and change: *diffugere, redeunt, mutat, decrescentia, praetereunt.* And even *Gratia audet...*suggests that this condition is only temporary.[6]

To illustrate more precisely how the sequence of time is related to our life, the poet then makes a fresh start, and now runs through the entire cycle of the seasons (9-12). The cold of winter becomes mild through the balmy breezes of spring, spring promptly summer "crushes" — the *proterit* (9) suggesting the abruptness, even violence (of the heat) with which summer finishes spring; — then summer is not described but characterized only by the necessity that it perish, *interitura simul* (10) — the moment's pause at the end of the line suggesting a moment longer for summer to last; and then, in the next line (11), autumn is here, described by its fruit bearing bounty for man, but we note that its arrival and its imminent end are presented as virtually simultaneous (*aestas interitura simul autumnus fruges effuderit* [future perfect], 9-11); and soon (*mox*, 11) — the monosyllable at the end of the line suggesting that it is very "soon" indeed, the brief pause at the end of the line suggesting just one more moment for autumn to last, and then—sluggish winter comes running back (11). Winter is agile, quick to return and finish autumn, but once here, it is sluggish, listless, lifeless (iners, 11).[7]

The cycle has opened and closed not with spring, the season of hope and of life, but with winter, the "sad and death-portending season."[8] Again, and now conspicuously, the verbs denote persistent movement and change: mitescunt, proterit, interitura, effuderit, recurrit. The picture of the rapidly passing seasons is an effective indicator of our own quickly passing life and imminent death, but the analogy may yet give us a bit of comfort. A fate which we share with nature, a universal fate, is less hard to bear. This thought, however, is only an illusion, and the poet promptly takes it away from us (13–16).

The heavenly bodies, which determine and control the seasons, though swift to pass, experience damage, losses, not really death, and these losses they forever recover.[9] Or, if we do apply the word "death" to nature, there is an eternal succession of life, death, and rebirth. But we, once we have died, are dead and gone forever. The poetic formulation of the thought is more significant. We (nos, 14), in contrast to the heavenly bodies (lunae, 13), when we have "fallen down" —as if we lived on a trapdoor, and once it is dropped, suddenly, abruptly, we drop down below—where even such worthies as rich, powerful Tullus and Ancus and, most tellingly, the founding father himself, Aeneas, have gone, never to return, then surely we like all others are dead, nothing, "dust and shadow" (16).[10]

The image of decidimus (14), and the present tense of sumus (16), as if the fate were upon us already, have brought out the uncertainty of life, and the suddenness and even violence with which we may die. This notion the poet now elaborates further (17–18). Who knows whether the gods above, whoever makes the decision, are adding— are they deciding at this very moment (adiciant, 17)?—to the sum of today the time of tomorrow? If we live to see the end of today, tomorrow we may not be so lucky (summae/tempora, 17–18). Tomorrow we may die.

Let us briefly take stock. After presenting a charming picture of spring to arouse our pleasure in it, and a joie de vivre, the poet has voiced a memento mori and then reinforced it by comparing our transitory life with the swiftly passing seasons, of which spring is only one. Then, however, he has isolated us from the seasons, from nature, by stressing that unlike them we alone must truly die, and that death, moreover, may come suddenly, abruptly, and even violently. What then is left for us? Despair?

At this critical juncture, in the very jaws of death, as it were, Horace voices his invitation to life.

Cuncta manus avidas fugient heredis amico
    quae dederis animo!

The fortune hunter (heredis, 19) was at this time becoming a notorious character in Roman society.[11] Pretending to be your friend (amicus), he really hoped for your early demise, so that he could inherit your wealth and possessions and enjoy them himself. But you should be your own best friend (*amicus*), and to allow this to happen, if it could be avoided, would be foolish, even perverse.[12] "Everything will escape the greedy grasp of the heir which you have given to your own beloved spirit, or soul" (*amico animo*, 19–20). That is, everything will be truly your own which you have given to your own dear self. Thus in a pungent statement the poet exhorts us to live life fully, physically as well as spiritually, while we can. *Carpe diem!*[13]

Indeed, we have only a brief time to heed the advice. With the next statement the poet returns to the theme of death, as if to punctuate the need immediately to act on the advice. *Cum semel occideris* (21).... When once we have died and Minos, the proverbial judge of the underworld, has passed his final judgment on you, absolutely nothing will ever bring you back. The judgment is called *splendida* (21). It may be the only thing bright and shining in that pervasive infernal gloom. It is here called *splendida*, I suggest, because it is not dark and enigmatic but decisively, brilliantly clear, in that it consigns us, without ambiguity or chance of appeal or reprieve, to everlasting death.[14] And once this judgment has been passed, none of the qualities or arrangements which in life could secure for you special privileges and dispensations will bring you back, not an illustrious lineage, not eloquence and intelligence, and not even the cardinal virtue *pietas* (24). The thrice-repeated *non* punctuates the warning. *Pietas* recalls the earlier mention of Aeneas, the man of *pietas* par excellence (15). If even the founder of the Roman race and the Roman empire (*pater*, 15), despite his supreme *pietas* and, we readily add, despite his reputed divine ancestry, could not return from death, nothing will restore you, *Torquatus* (23).[15] Here the poet for the first time names the addressee of the poem. We have not missed him. Torquatus may or may not have had *genus*, *facundia*, *pietas*.[16] It does not matter. Horace addresses us, and the human condition.[17] We all should make the best use of our gifts and qualities while we can, for soon they will avail us nothing.

For his conclusion, the poet turns again to mythology (25–28). The truth that nothing will restore us from death is illustrated by the assertion that neither Diana can free chaste Hippolytus from the infernal shades, nor Theseus break the bonds of hell from his beloved Perithous. Thus the poem ends on a note of tender pathos. A goddess's desire to restore her devoted favorite, and a hero's attempt to rescue a beloved friend, are equally futile. There is also a bit of comfort, perhaps, in the thought that we share our mortal lot with all the heroes of the past. But there is irony here, as well. According to one old tradition, Diana *did* secure Hippolytus' release from death, and even Perithous, according to a minor tradition at least as old as Euripides, was returned to life, although not by Theseus, but by Heracles.[18] Thus Horace concludes the poem by appealing to mythological traditions which are true, about the nature of life and death.[19] The truth is, we all must die, and death is eternal.

According to Eduard Fraenkel, the theme of the poem is death, the *carpe diem* is only a "passing remark," and one does not believe that "the poet's heart is in it."[20] I cannot agree. The poet is careful to point up the importance of *carpe diem*. The meter with its quickly moving dactyls in alternating lines of hexameters and half-pentameters gives a sense of the quick rhythm of nature, of life and death, and in this rhythm there is not much time for us. The voicing of *carpe diem* in only one distich is not a "passing remark" but an indication that, since our life is only a passing moment, we must seize quickly the chances we have to enjoy it. The poem's structure has a similar effect. The two *gnomai*, *memento mori* (7–8) and *carpe diem* (19–20), are strategically positioned in the first and second parts of the poem, respectively. The *memento mori* points toward and gives urgency to the *carpe diem* appeal. The statements on death which precede and follow the appeal say essentially the same thing: tomorrow you may die, to be dead forever, and once you are dead you will never come back. Thus the two statements can be seen, not as presenting a sequence of thoughts about death in which *carpe diem* is only a passing remark, but as focusing and enhancing the appeal. Patently a sense of melancholy pervades the poem at the thought of death. Yet Horace dwells on it not just for its own sake, in a mood of melancholy resignation, but as a means to point up, as well, the value of life. He exploits the psychological fact that what is valuable becomes more dear to us, more precious and important, if it becomes threatened and jeopardized.

And the formulation of the appeal itself is striking and memorable. The key word *amico* (19) is emphatically positioned at the end of the line where we have expected, rather, an adjective to modify *heredis* (19). With the ending of *amico* we realize that the word will qualify, or be explained by, something yet to come. It remains suspended for a moment at the end of the line to make its mark on the reader's consciousness, and then, at the end of the next line it comes, surprisingly and pointedly, to qualify *animo* (20). The antithesis of (*amico*) *animo* to (*avidas*, by metathesis) *heredis*, as if it were another person (similar to the *genius*), communicates the notion that instead of leaving your wealth to someone unworthy (*avidas*) to enjoy after your death, you ought to bestow it on someone worthy (*amico*) to enjoy while you are alive — yourself (*animo* being the concluding word of the statement).

Now, phrases to express the notion of indulging one's *animus* may have been common enough in Latin. Witness Plaut. *Amph.* 131: *suo animo morem gerit; Mil.* 677: *es, bibe, animo obsequere*. And in Greek, there is the epitaph of Bacchidas at Athen. 8.336d: πιεν φαγεν και παντα τη ψυχα δομεν ["drink, eat, and give everything to the soul"]; Theocr. 16.24: το μεν ψυχα...δουναι ["give to the soul"]; Aesch. *Pers.* 841: ψυχη διδοντες ηδονην ["giving pleasure to the soul"]; Simon. Frg. 97 (Edmonds): βιοτου ποτι τερμα ψυχη των αγαθων τληθι χαριζομενος ["Endure to the end of life gracing the soul with good things"]; Eurip. *Cycl.* 340: την δ' εμην ψυχην εγω ου παυσομαι δρων ευ ["I shall never cease doing well by my soul"]. What makes the word *animo* remarkable in Horace's poem, however, is its qualification by *amico*. The phrase is unparalleled in Latin literature. In Homer, there is the familiar φιλον ητορ (e.g., *Il.* 3.31; 5.250, 364, 670; 9.705; 13.84; 19.307; 21.201; *Od.* 16.92; 17.514). But Horace's *amicus animus* means much more than the formulaic Homeric expression. Behind it lies Horace's philosophical conception of friendship with oneself, *amicus sibi*, as a positive virtue. See, for example, *Sat*. 1.2.17–22: *"maxime" quis non // "Iuppiter!" exclamat simul atque audivit? "at in se // pro quaestu sumptum facit?" hic? vix credere possis, // quam sibi non sit amicus, ita ut pater ille, Terenti // fabula quem miserum gnato vixisse fugato // inducit, non se peius cruciaverit atque hic.* ["Almighty Jupiter! Who does not exclaim as soon as he has heard this? 'But he spends on himself in proportion to his profit.' He does? You would hardly believe what an enemy he is to himself; why, that famous father, whom the comedy of Terence represents as having lived in wretchedness after he drove his son away, did not torment himself worse than this man."] Compare *Ep*. 1.18.101; *Sat*. 2.2.97 (*te tibi iniquum = tibi inimicum*); *Ep*. 1.18.107–8; 1.3.29. In a recent study K. Gautar has shown that the idea meant for Horace "einen veredelten Egoismus, dessen sich der Dichter nicht zu schämen braucht, den er, im Gegenteil, sowohl sich selbst als auch den anderen als ein Lebensideal empfehlen kann"[21] ["An enlightened egoism of which the poet need not be ashamed, which he, on the contrary may adopt as an ideal for himeslf as well as others"]. Gautar shows that the notion occurs very seldom in Latin and Greek literature, and that Horace apparently derived it from Aristotle, who argued for it on philosophical grounds against Plato who condemned it (Pl. *Lg.* 731D–732A2; Arist. *EN* 1168a27–1169b2; cf. *EE* 1240a9–1240b36; *MM* 1211a16–1211b3, 1212a28–1212b23). Gautar does not adduce our passage, but it is clear that the phrase *amicus animus* assumes its full significance only in light of Horace's particular conception of φιλαυτια as an ethical good.

Thus the expression adds to the *carpe diem* appeal moral authority, and because of its novelty it arrests the reader's attention. As *topoi*, both the *carpe diem* and the *memento mori* of course are most familiar in both Greek and Latin literature. They express ancient wisdom. But we still can profit from being reminded of it, and Horace has given voice to it in a poem that is, altogether, original, masterful, and affecting.[22]

In our evaluation of the poem we may thus incline toward Housman. But it would be rash to conclude that, therefore, Wilamowitz was wrong. Fortunately, the assessment of poetry can never be, like an exact science, entirely objective. To the objective level, which is accessible to rational analysis, is added a subjective level. For the meaning of a poem to be realized, its communication to be effected, the reader cannot be a passive recipient but must bring to it, in addition to objective analysis, his personal, subjective sensibilities and values. Thus a poem will never mean the same thing to every person. If we consider this fact, we can understand, even though we will not, I hope, share, Wilamowitz's indifference. It was Ulrich van Wilamowitz-Moellendorff who stated, in the best tradition of his caste and his profession, like a true Stoic: "Der Mensch ist . . . nicht dazu da, glücklich zu sein, sondern der Pflicht zu gehorchen."[23] ["Man does not exist to be happy, but to obey duty."]

On the other hand, we can understand Housman's love for the poem even better if we appreciate that he was not only a scholar but a poet of considerable affinity with Horace.

Loveliest of trees, the cherry now
Is hung with bloom along the bough,
And stands about the woodland ride
Wearing white for Eastertide.

Now, of my threescore years and ten,
Twenty will not come again,
And take from seventy springs a score,
It only leaves me fifty more.

And since to look at things in bloom
Fifty springs are little room,
About the woodlands I will go
To see the cherry hung with snow.

A Shropshire Lad, II.[24]

Notes

[1]*Sappho und Simonides* (Berlin, 1913), p. 321: "Die beiden unbedeutenden Frühlingslieder 7 und 12 nehmen ältere Weisen auf und mahnen nur, wie der alte Goethe 'und wenn die Zeit verrauschend flieht, Jahreszeiten kehren wieder.' Ungleich schöner klingt die Mahnung an die verrauschende Zeit in den beiden Mädchenliedern" (4.11: *Est mihi nonum;* 13: *Audivere Lyce!*). Subsequently, there have been other detractors, notably Woodman, Collinge, and Becker. See n. 20 below.

[2]The quotation is given by Mrs. T. W. Pym in a letter to the *Times* published in a column under the heading "Prof. Housman: Appreciations," May 5, 1936, reprinted at Grant Richards, *Housman 1897–1936* (Oxford, 1942), p. 289: "Your obituary notice of Professor Housman has vividly recalled one of the rare occasions when he 'betrayed passionate emotion in public.' During my time at Cambridge I attended his lectures for two years.... One morning in May, 1914, when the trees in Cambridge were covered with blossom, he reached in his lecture Ode 7 in Horace's Fourth Book, 'Diffugere nives, redeunt iam gramina campis.' This ode he dissected with the usual display of brilliance, wit, and sarcasm. Then for the first time in two years he looked up at us, and in quite a different voice said: 'I should like to spend the last few minutes considering this ode simply as poetry.' . . . He read the ode aloud with deep emotion, first in Latin and then in an English translation of his own. 'That,' he said hurriedly, almost like a man betraying a secret, 'I regard as the most beautiful poem in ancient literature,' and walked quickly out of the room."

There are those who agree. L. P. Wilkinson, *Horace and His Lyric Poetry*[2] (Cambridge, 1951), p. 40: "[*Odes* 4.7] is, as Housman once said, the most perfect poem in the Latin language." A. Y. Campbell, *Horace* (London, 1924), p. 224: "It seems to me quite one of the supremely beautiful among the *Odes.*" Jacques Perret, *Horace* (Paris, 1959), p. 171: "Une des plus belles, assurément, qu' Horace ait jamais écrites." For Housman's translation of the ode see n. 13 *below.*

[3]4.7 has most often been discussed by comparison with 1.4. I shall refrain from it. See Helen Gardner, *The Business of Criticism* (Oxford, 1959), p. 7: "The critic's function then is to assist his readers to find the value which he believes the work to have. To attempt to measure the amount of value, to declare or attempt to demonstrate that this poem is more valuable than that, or to range writers in order of

merit does not seem to me to be the true purpose of criticism. Such attempts ignore the nature of taste and the nature of values."

[4]*Mutat is* probably intransitive, and *vices* the cognate or inner object.

[5]Or perhaps, rather, reality and mythology meet on equal terms. See Gordon Williams, *Tradition and Originality in Roman Poetry* (Oxford, 1968), p. 636 f.

[6]Cf. H. P. Syndikus, *Die Lyrik des Horaz*, vol. 2 (Darmstadt, 1973), p. 357; C. Becker, *Das Spätwerk des Horaz* (Göttingen, 1963), p. 149.

[7]R. Heinze, *Komm. ad loc.*: "meisterhaft auch [die] Verwendung der Klangmittel: denn *ver proterit aestas* veranschaulicht das brutale Zertreten der Frühlingspracht so gut wie *bruma recurrit iners* den Schauder der Winterkälte, und die weiche Frühlingsluft malt *mitescunt zephyris* ebenso wie die Gestaltung des v. 11 den strömenden und plötzlich abgebrochenen Überschwang des Herbstes." ["Also masterful [the] use of sound devices: *ver proterit aestas* makes vivid the brutal destruction of Spring's beauty, just as *bruma recurrit iners* epitomizes the shivering cold of Winter, and the gentle breeze of Spring is painted by *mitescunt zephyris*, even as the composition of verse 11 suggests the teeming and suddenly terminated mastery of Autumn."]

[8]I have taken the phrase from A. J. Woodman, "Horace's Odes *Diffugere nives* and *Solvitur acris hiems*," *Latomus* 31 (1972): 759.

[9]Specifically, the poet thinks of the changing phases of the moon, that after the night of the full moon it diminishes each day and yet soon regains its former shape.

[10]On *decidimus*, cf. Ov. *Met.* 10.18, where, similarly, the suggestion is that we "fall" (*recidimus*) into a pit or chasm. As for *pater* (*Aeneas*) (15), *pius* is attested equally well. For the preference of *pater*, see Heinze, *Komm. ad loc.* In drawing the contrast between nature's eternity and our mortality, Horace was influenced patently by Cat. 5. The vivid image *pulvis et umbra* is anticipated at Asclepiades, *AP* 5.85.4: οστεα και σποδιη, and Soph. *El.* 1159: σποδον τε και σκιαν.

[11]See, e.g., H. Last, *CAH* 10 (1934): 437 f.

[12]Cf. *Od.* 2.3.17–20; 2.14.25–28; 3.24.61–62; *Sat.* 2.3.122–23, 151; *Ep.* 1.5.12–14 2.2.191–92.

[13]Housman translates: "Feast then thy heart, for what thy heart has had // the fingers of no heir will ever hold" (*More Poems*, 5). Housman here actually improves on the original in that he moves the *carpe diem* from a subordinate relative clause (*amico quae dederis animo*) to the main clause ("feast then thy heart"). It may be noted that 4.7 is the only poem of Horace which Housman ever ventured to translate.

[14]Niall Rudd notes: "Most of the line's power undoubtedly resides in *splendida*" ("Patterns in Horatian Lyric," *AJP* 81 [1960]: 382). N. E. Collinge criticizes it as "purely ornamental" (*The Structure of Horace's Odes* [London and New York, 1961], p. 111).

[15]The reference to Vergil's *Aeneid* is unmistakable.

[16]*Ep.* 1.5 is addressed to Torquatus. He appears to have been an orator of some distinction. Perhaps he belonged to the illustrious *Manlii Torquati*. Cf. Kenneth Quinn, *Comm. ad Od.* 4.7.23.

[17]Cf. Becker (n. 6 above, p. 156): "[Es geht] nicht allein um Torquatus; daher steht nicht *tuum genus, tua facundia* usw."

[18]See, also for references, Sauer (no first name), *Roschers Ausführliches Lexikon der Griechischen und Römischen Mythologie*, vol. 1 (1886–90), p. 2682 f.; S. Eitrem, *RE* 8 (1913): 1866, 1869; J. E. Fontenrose, *RE* 19 (1938): 125 f.

[19]The same applies, more indirectly, to *pater Aeneas*. Aeneas had been identified, probably as early as the second century B.C., with *pater Indigens* (CIL 10.8348) or *deus Indiges* (Tib. 2.5.44), and according to the *Aen.* 1.259 was transported to heaven. Collinge remarks that the variants of the myths about Hippolytus and Perithous "nullify the whole point of [the] allusion" (n. 14 above, p. 19 n. 2), and that therefore Horace's use of mythology in this poem is "maladroit" (n. 14 above, p. 111). Similarly Woodman

(n. 8 above, p. 765). Both scholars have quite missed the point. For a sensitive and intelligent review of Collinge's book, of which his treatment of 4.7 is typical, see Kenneth Reckford, "Wretched Percival," *Arion* 2 (1963): 137–49.
    [20]*Horace* (Oxford, 157), p. 421. Others have found fault. Collinge (n. 14 above, p. 111): "Fraenkel's comment that 'one does not believe that the poet's heart is in it' is a far milder stricture than it deserves." Becker (n. 6 above, pp. 149–58) regards vv. 17–20 as an interpolation, primarily on the grounds that (he believes) they are superfluous. One scholar agrees: O. A. W. Dilke, *Gnomon* 35 (1963): 584 (review of Becker). The most extreme view is that of Woodman (n. 8 above, p. 778), who considers the whole poem a failure and vastly inferior to 1.4. On vv. 17–20 he writes (766): "The structure [of the poem] is utterly ruined by stanza 5, which not only has nothing to do with the consistent theme which surrounds it on both sides (death is once and for all), but has nothing to do with anything else in the poem either . . . [and] the two constituent couplets are trite in the extreme." He considers the poem's technique "crude" (778) and its structure totally devoid of imagination (760). *Habeat sibi.* Uneasiness about the lines was also expressed, more prudently, by K. Quinn, *Latin Explorations* (London, 1963), p. 25 f., and N. Rudd (n. 14 above, p. 383).
    On the other hand, H. P. Syndikus asks pointedly (n. 6 above, p. 361 n. 26): "Sollte Horaz Torquatus nur darum angesprochen haben, um ihm zu sagen, dass er bald sterben wird?" ["Would Horace have addressed Torquatus merely to tell him that he must soon die?"] Wolfgang Schmid writes (*RAC* 5 [1962]: 723): "Die horazische Verbindung des 'carpe diem' – Motivs mit der Vergänglichkeitsreflexion ist genuin epikureisch. Das zeigt mit besonderer Deutlichkeit die Ode 4,7, welche die der kosmischen reparatio gegenüberstehende Einmaligkeit der flüchtigen Ich-Existenz gerade deshalb vergegenwärtigt, um aus diesem Gedanken das Recht, nein, die Notwendigkeit abzuleiten, der im Heute enthaltenen Lebenswonne innezuwerden." ["Horace's linking of the *carpe diem* motif with the reflection on mortality is genuinely Epicurean. Ode 4.7 shows this with particular clarity: it emphasizes the uniqueness of the fleeting human existence in contrast to the renewal of the cosmos precisely so as to derive the right, no, the necessity to take advantage of the pleasure of life contained in the present day."] (Cf. p. 767. But see also M. Erler, "Horaz über den Wandel der Jahreszeiten," *RM* 123 [1980]: 333–36.) Similarly R. R. Dyer, "*Diffugere Nives*: Horace and the Augustan Spring," *G&R* 12 (1965): 84: "The *summa hodierna* is a thing for joy. We must enjoy today, for *quis scit an adiciant hodiernae crastina summae // tempora di superi*? His mind is running on the *carpe diem* theme." Cf. D. N. Levin, "Concerning Two Odes of Horace: 1.4 and 4.7," *CJ* 54 (1959): 357.
    [21]K. Gautar, "Horazens 'Amicus Sibi'," *AAntHung* 12 (1964): 129–35.
    [22]On the subject of originality and tradition, note the salutary remarks of H. Bardon, "*Carpe diem*," *REA* 46 (1944): 354 f.: "Chez Horace, tout nous ramène à Horace. Certes, importants sont les rapprochements que permet la recherche des sources, et tel texte d'Alcée, telle épigramme de l'*Anth. Pal.* facilitent parfois la compréhension des *carmina*. Mais ces rapprochements risquent d'induire en erreur, si l'on croit que des analogies de thèmes ou même des similitudes si nettes que l'imitation par Horace d'un modèle grec est indiscutable, autorisent à affirmer que telle idée, tel sentiment sont d'emprunt. Un grand artiste n'imite autrui que pour mieux s'exprimer." ["In Horace, everything takes us back to Horace. Granted, the connections suggested by research into the sources are important, and this text of Alcaeus or that epigram from the *Anth. Pal.* often helps us understand the Odes. But these connections threaten to mislead us, if we believe that thematic analogies or similarities so patent that Horace's imitation of a Greek model is indiscussible, authorize us to claim that a particular idea or sentiment has been borrowed. A great artist imitates others only to express himself better."]

On the literary antecedents of 4.7, see, conveniently, Woodman (n. 8 above, p. 752 ff.)
[23] *Erinnerungen 1848–1914,* 2nd ed. (Leipzig, 1929), p. 239. I wish to thank William M. Calder III for this reference.
[24] Or consider:

> With rue my heart is laden
>   For golden friends I had,
> For many a rose-lipt maiden
>   And many a lightfoot lad.

> By brooks too broad for leaping
>   The lightfoot boys are laid;
> The rose-lipt girls are sleeping
>   In fields where roses fade.

A Shropshire Lad, 54.

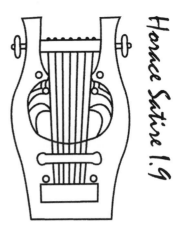

Horace Satire 1.9

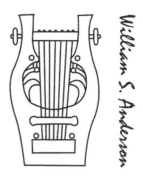

HORACE, THE UNWILLING WARRIOR: SATIRE 1.9

The Odes from Books 1–3 were mostly written between 30 and 23 B.C. This Satire was included in a Book that Horace published in 35, his first publication. Roman satire exploits the meter of epic poets, so we are dealing here with hexameter, not the lyric meters on which Horace bestowed so much ingenuity. It narrates an amusing incident that occurred to the poet as he was strolling through the Forum in Rome, where he encounters a brash social climber, who hounds him, talking his ear off, and trying to use Horace to secure an introduction to Maecenas and to the halls of power around Octavian (not yet Augustus). In this period, when Octavian spent so much time away from the city, trying to keep and restore order, Maecenas served as his trusted adviser and regent in Rome. Horace had been introduced to Maecenas a few years earlier by Vergil and was now one of his regular companions at moments of leisure. Suspecting that all Maecenas' friends were ambitious and unscrupulous like himself, this brash pursuer of Horace through the Forum reveals his crass goals even while mouthing words which he hopes sound friendly. The art of the Satire consists in the ironic picture of Horace being tormented as he struggles as politely as possible to extricate himself from the clutches of this obnoxious fellow; it also consists, I suggest, in the implicit comparison developed by Horace between his struggle and the familiar encounters between enemy heroes in epic warfare. We are charmed by this comic version of the peace-loving poet, apparently doomed to "death" at the hands (or words) of this pushy fellow. In the nick of time, though, a legal summons, to which Horace eagerly serves as witness, drags the man off; at which the poet remarks, like a character from the *Iliad:* "Thus Apollo rescued me" (78), leaving us to perceive that this "epic" salvation comes to him as a poet, as it did at Philippi (2.7), not as a warrior. (Ed.)

In his monumental study of the influence of Lucilius upon Horace, G. C. Fiske brought the question as close to a definite answer as the fragmentary nature of Lucilius would permit. Considering these few remnants and the well-known scruples of Horace against extended verbal imitation, one must admit that Fiske emerged with an impressive list of similar motifs and expressions between the two satirists.[1] To be sure, similarities in detail are not always an exact indication of the individual method of treatment,[2] and the latitude, which a poet might require, was never denied Horace.[3] When he came to consider *S.*, I, 9, Fiske inherited a theory first advanced by Iltgen,[4] but ignored by subsequent scholars,[5] that the Satire was largely

This essay is reprinted from *American Journal of Philology* 77 (1956) 148–66, with permission of the Johns Hopkins University Press.

influenced by an earlier work of Lucilius. Careful study of Horace and an imaginative reconstruction of the fragments of Book VI of Lucilius convinced Fiske that Horace was indebted, not merely for lines, but for the general plan of his poem. "We may conclude, therefore, that the sixth book of Lucilius contained a satire upon the bore, which was the direct model for Horace's ninth satire of the first book."[6]

Of approximately fifteen lines in Lucilius which confirmed Fiske in his opinion, perhaps those which are most generally accepted as influencing Horace's poem are 231–2 (Marx):

(nil) ut discrepat ac 'τὸν δὲ ἐξήρπαξεν 'Απόλλων' /fiat.[7]

["It is just like Apollo snatched him away."]

The Greek phrase resembles so closely Horace, I, 9, 78: *sic me servavit Apollo*, that, even without the authority of Porphyrio,[8] a connection between the two passages would ultimately have been observed. The question next arises: In what sense and why is Horace imitating Lucilius? The answers proposed fall into three main groups:

1. Horace, like Lucilius, is referring to the ultimate source of the allusion, Homer. He thus, like Lucilius, acquires the advantages of epic parody and ends his description on a humorous note appropriate to the ironic character that he here most successfully achieves.

2. Horace is implicitly criticizing Lucilius for citing the original Greek.[9] He therefore carefully translates the Greek, places the line in a significant position, and still has the advantages of parody.

3. Horace is implicitly criticizing Lucilius' uneconomic use of the parody and demonstrating his own technical superiority. It appears that Lucilius inserted the Greek phrase, as was frequently his custom, to serve as a witty contrast, as a neat, exaggerated reference to an incident entirely alien to his context.[10] On the other hand, when Horace adopts this phrase as his conclusion, he cleverly makes it relevant to his dramatic development. Here, the focus of economy is *Apollo*. As the god who watches over poets and concerns himself with principles of justice, Apollo can be regarded, on the supernatural level, as the agent effecting Horace's release from the *garrulus*. In human terms, the bore's legal opponent appeared when Horace was desperate, dragged the fool off to justice, and thus left Horace a free man. It is, however, the genius of Horace to transform this experience into an amusing drama, to picture Apollo as a *deus ex machina*, and to give the scene a finished form by recalling the opening reference to his poetic concerns (line 2).

It is evident that none of these explanations of 9, 78 is exclusively correct; in fact, the most adequate interpretation would — as Lejay did[11] — synthesize these apparent alternatives into a coherent whole. Accordingly, the understanding of Horace's conclusion generally agrees with the words of Ritter: "clam se inde discessisse poetice significavit" ["He secretly meant that he escaped in the poetic manner"],[12] where "poetice" is applied to the wealth of allusion which Lucilius' successor ingeniously develops from a line used by Lucilius in his typically witty and extravagant manner.

Synthesis of these three interpretations does not necessarily exhaust the potential allusions in Horace's line. Since economy is characteristic of Horace, it is tempting to speculate on other applications of his words, which would extend the scope of his poetic parody. Recently, E. T. Salmon, without denying the validity of the literary explanations hitherto advanced, has proposed an additional reference for the *Apollo*.[13] He believes that the Satire has consistent topographical allusions indicating various stages in Horace's progress towards Caesar's Gardens, the destination announced in 18. As we are told in the first line, Horace was walking along the Via Sacra when he was accosted by the *garrulus*. Later, he mentions arriving at the Temple of Vesta (line 35). Apart from these two specific references to sites in the Forum, Horace gives no further direct indication of the scene of action. Salmon, assuming quite plausibly that there are indirect indications, has suggested an attractive solution to the difficulty usually sensed in *tricesima sabbata* (l. 69)[14] by interpreting the phrase as a subtle allusion to the Jewish Quarter near the Forum Boarium. Horace, in this view, has moved out of the Forum Romanum, down the Vicus Tuscus, and into the Jewish residential area. Further, it was near here that the *garrulus* unexpectedly met his legal opponent. In the ensuing confusion, Horace escaped, to take refuge in the sanctuary of the patron of poets, as Salmon infers from the conclusion. *Apollo*, who signifies the god of justice and poetry, can also be considered topographically relevant, as applying to the Temple of Apollo Medicus, newly re-built by Sosius in the late Thirties B.C.[15] In this type of interpretation, there is an opportunity to check against the facts. For this reason, Salmon has been challenged by the Roman topographer F. Castagnoli, who denies the allusions suggested and attempts to return to the limited interpretations listed above. *Apollo*, in fact, he restricts to its Homeric relevance, while he seems to regard the Lucilian parallel as coincidental. Accordingly, he states: "L'acceno ad Apollo non ha bisogno di un riferimento topographico, ma, come commenta Porfirione, e semplicemente una reminiscenza omerica (*Il.* XX, 443) citata anche de Lucilio." ["The reference to Apollo has no need to be considered a topographic allusion, but, as Porphyrio notes, it is simply a Homeric reminiscence which Lucilius also used."][16] The present writer takes no position in this controversy; yet it is significant that the disagreement springs from the relevance or irrelevance of an admittedly allusive line.

Castagnoli's phrase "reminiscenza omerica" suggests still another method of interpreting *sic me servavit Apollo* and of defining the limits of Lucilius' influence upon this poem. In the first place, Horace translates Homer freely, whereas Lucilius cited him verbatim. When, then, Lucilius used the phrase, he was obliged to attach the Greek line to a Latin context; he was, we may say, aiming at the conflict between the Greek and Latin, between the epic and satiric, the supernatural and the real. As if to mark the opposition clearly, Lucilius connected the Homeric words to his context in the form of a negative simile (*nil ut discrepat ac*).[17] The effect is to imply the inapplicability of the Homeric context to Lucilius' story, and, in my opinion, Fiske rightly concludes that the satirist was humorously referring to a frivolous situation, quite possibly the unwelcome presence of a bore.[18] Such an inference would be consistent with what is known of Lucilius' treatment of Greek: his tendency to extravagance, but also his achievement of witty statements.[19] By contrast, Horace assimilates the line of Homer to his context, makes himself the object instead of the non-personal τὸν, and alters ἐξήρπαξεν to the more emotional *servavit*. These changes enable Horace to use *Apollo* more fully. In particular, the rejection of the simile as a method of using the reminiscence frees Horace from the necessity of a mechanical citation of Homer merely for purposes of witty contrast, permits him instead to adapt Homer with subtlety to his dramatic account.

The indirect method of citation, I suggest, makes Homer more relevant to Horace than to Lucilius. It is, therefore, necessary secondly to return to the context in Homer upon which Horace's phrase is based, to see what possible bearing it can have upon Horace's hypothetical experience with the bore.[20] At this point in Book XX of the *Iliad*, the epic poet describes the brief encounter between Hector and Achilles. Hector's efforts to wound Achilles are checked by Athena. As Achilles is rushing in for the kill, Apollo intervenes and carries the Trojan off in a cloud to safety. These details fit the traditional interpretation of Horace previously mentioned, namely, that the intervention of Apollo in the *Iliad* is humorously appropriate to his imagined rescue of the poet Horace. One factor, however, has been ignored: the original context is a battle scene. Apollo saves his favorite, who is a warrior, not a poet. On the surface, the basic martial context seems to have no bearing upon the drama here enacted, which plainly presents anything but warfare. But Horace has employed throughout *S.*, I, 9 a number of similar expressions, epic and martial, which can be related to the Homeric battle; when related, they assume form as a new level of meaning based on the significance of battle in this Satire, of Horace as a warrior. Further developed, this new pattern explains more specifically certain portions of the drama which have been viewed simply as humorous exaggerations. It can be shown, I believe, that Horace has treated the dramatic situation in a different manner from Lucilius, so as to utilize extensively the martial overtones of his Homeric original.

As Heinze noted, the first obvious statement of a military word occurs in 42-3, where Horace visualizes the bore as a conqueror (*victore*). If, however, this passage is patent, reinforced as it is by *contendere*, it is also anticipated at several earlier points, as Horace intimates his attitude towards his companion in terms applicable also to war. When the bore rushes up and seizes his hand, Horace implies that the act is an affront to him. The man does not sense the unfriendliness in Horace's over-polite reply to his own effusive greeting; he persists. Horace, therefore, determines to end the conversation immediately and bluntly says goodbye (6). The word suggesting bluntness, *occupo*, is more commonly employed in other senses. In its root meaning, it is a word of war: to seize, take possession of, and, by derivation, to begin the attack.[21] By itself, the word might be simply humorous. Supported in the context by *arrepta*, which regularly has violent associations,[22] it hints at a battle theme which will gradually become clearer. In this sense, the opening lines could be visualized as the first stages of a personal combat between Horace and the bore. The man's attitude is aggressive (*arrepta*) and offensive to Horace, so, in desperation, Horace determines to fight (*occupo*). It is a strange type of battle. Longing only to escape, Horace tries every device he can invent to frighten or discourage the *garrulus*. No matter what he does or says, he is beaten; while, the *garrulus*, merely by forcing his company on the unfortunate poet, is regarded as an enemy in pursuit. In each passage of arms — an intolerable effusion from the *garrulus* followed by a desperate, though polite, reply from Horace — the bore emerges victorious, because he is completely obtuse to Horace's feelings and irresistibly persistent in his own crude designs. This nightmare battle,[23] perceived in the conflict of personalities, is fought by words. As the drama proceeds, it becomes more and more evident that the satirist treats the situation as a real combat between himself and his objectionable companion.

Part of the irony of the Satire depends upon the fact that the bore does not realize how offensive he is. When he praises himself as *doctus* (7), it is a painful wound (*misere*, 8) to a real poet. No longer willing to fight bravely face-to-face, Horace tries to break off the battle (*discedere*, 8).[24] The engagement becomes a running conflict, in which Horace periodically makes a futile gesture of resistance and attempts to discourage his pursuer. First, he tries to outdistance the man (*ire ocius*, 9); then, he stops to fight, makes a stand (*consistere*).[25] The martial sense of *consistere* and the normally poetic connotations of *ocius* are then combined with the context implied by *sudor* (10). On the dramatic level, Horace's sweating is an amusing exaggeration; an unpleasant conversation does make one perspire, but one is hardly bathed in sweat. In the *Iliad*, however, men sweat (ἱδρώς) under the strain of combat when they are defeated and flee in terror, as Lycaon (XXI, 51); when they have been wounded;[26] and when they fight well, but against greater numbers.[27] The passage concerning Ajax and his battlesweat (XVI, 109) is a prototype for the description of Turnus, when he is hard-pressed within the encampment of the Trojans; and ἱδρώς is the basis of *sudor* in Vergil.[28] After this, other intolerable remarks from the *garrulus* provoke the unspoken thought in Horace: *o te, Bolane, cerebri / felicem* (11-12). Horace wishes that he were choleric, that his temper frightened company; his exaggerated emotion, however, continues the overtone of epic warfare. Frequently, the epic hero cries out in a moment of crisis, envying the fortune of another, particularly his happy death in battle.[29] Similarly, Horace envies Bolanus, because a bad temper has always permitted the latter to escape from such predicaments as that which the poet faces.

Even the obtuse bore eventually perceives that Horace is trying to get away (14). Rather than permit this, he blatantly insists on accompanying his victim. As he puts it, Horace is helpless (*nil agis*, 15); he, the bore, will hold on to his man (*usque tenebo*); he will continue his pursuit (*persequar*, 16) wherever Horace goes. The militant overtone of *persequar* is unmistakable, and it tinges the other verbs. Confident of capturing Horace, the bore boasts that he will pursue him indefinitely. Still, Horace tries some strategy. He invents a friend far across the Tiber, a sick friend, whom he must visit (17-18). This ruse makes not the slightest impression on the dull wit of the fool. Instead of being discouraged by the prospective walk, he boasts of his energy and repeats his threat of constant pursuit: *non sum piger: usque sequar te* (19). The choice of *piger* is designed, for to be *piger* is to be unheroic.[30] When, however, the bore denies that he is *piger*, Horace is making him reveal his basic fault. A definite relation exists between his energetic eagerness and his offensiveness, to the extent that, concentrated on his own antipathetic purposes, the *garrulus* is blind to the reactions of others. With ill-concealed distaste, Horace resigns himself to the pursuit: he compares himself to an overburdened ass (20-1).[31] Then, his companion sets out to ingratiate himself with the poet. Naturally, he chooses the most offensive approach, comparing himself to Hermogenes, the most obnoxious of poetasters in Horace's opinion (22-5). The stage directions are suggestive: *incipit ille* (21). As a verb of speech, *incipere* is generally associated with epic.[32] Moreover, when the verb precedes its subject, the form resembles the emphatic technique of formal poetry. Implicitly, then, 22 ff. is introduced as an epic speech. At the end of 22, where it will receive stress, Horace has placed *amicum*, a word which is markedly ironic as applied to this person who antagonizes Horace with every word he speaks. Rather, the boasts uttered by this man render him *inimicum, hostem*. To me, there is a suggestion here of another aspect of battle. About to come to blows at last, our epic heroes praise themselves and threaten the enemy with reports of their fearsomeness. Horace interrupts the offensive chatter of the *garrulus* with his rejoinder (26-7). It is intended to use the sick friend as a threat. As it is put, though, the satirist seems to be reminding the bore of his fond relatives, warning him of the folly of attacking so mightly a hero as himself.[33] Thus, *salvo* (27) connotes not merely preservation from sickness, but safety in war.[34]

Unfortunately, the bore frustrates Horace's fearsome threat. He has buried all his family, and there are no relatives to worry about his health. Horace can only envy the dead as *felices* (28), people who have died and fortunately escaped the fate he is undergoing (cf. 12). Now at last the hero realizes that he is doomed. Fatalistically he enters combat, requesting a quick finish (*confice*, 29).[35] Then begins the oracle which, as others have noted, is an epic parody.[36] To describe a passage as epic parody, however, does not reach the heart of the question, as this paper is attempting to demonstrate; while implying the humorous effect, it does not explain the function of the parody in its context. From acquaintance with Horatian economy, it would be reasonable to assume that the poet has used epic parody here because it is thematically functional, not merely for its witty

impression. It is accordingly necessary to determine the epic context specifically relevant to this Satire. We have seen that the satirist regards his
unwelcome companion, to a certain extent, as an enemy and therefore pictures himself as a warrior fighting a losing battle with him. Now, a situation
suggests itself in which the satirist describes himself as the hero who suddenly remembers the prophecy of his death in battle at the moment of
fulfilment. There are analogues in Homer. Ritter pointed to the oracle which
Polyphemus recalled after being blinded.[37] On the whole, the context is
not so appropriate as the more common use of oracles in the battle scenes
of the *Iliad*. The phrase of introduction seems conclusive; yet, to my knowledge, no commentator has observed that the words *instat fatum me triste*
(29) are a good translation of *Il.*, XXII, 303: νῦν αὖτέ με μοῖρα κιχάνει ["Now
at last fate finds me"]. The Greek acts as one of the formulaic phrases of
Homer, in which any personal pronoun can be substituted, providing it is
metrically equivalent.[38] Its context is always the death of a warrior. In the
single instance where the personal pronoun is με and the parallel with the
Latin is exact, Hector is the speaker. The hero realizes that he has been
overcome by the gods and his own weakness; after speaking, he turns to
face Achilles and meet the inevitable death. On the other hand, Hector
does not mention a prophecy in his moment of realization; he is, so to
speak, his own prophet. We must look to other portions of the *Iliad*, where
the death of a warrior is foretold, but the formulaic phrase not used. For
example, Polyidus foresaw the death of his own son;[39] Achilles hears his
doom prophesied;[40] Aeneas is threatened with death by the supreme
prophet, Apollo;[41] and Achilles acts the prophet.[42] Because of the negative
manner of prophecy here exhibited and not illustrated in Homer, a different
ancient analogue has been suggested.[43] Diogenes Laertius reports an epigram
recited about Zeno the Stoic which has a similarly negative form.[44] Although
the context of the epigram involves neither battle nor death, it is not impossible that Horace parodies the epigram as well as the epic. Curiously
enough, Shakespeare provides the closest parallel of all in *Macbeth*. Deceived
up to the last moment by the speciously convincing oracles, Macbeth sees
one after the other fulfilled; finally, he meets Macduff and hears the nature
of his enemy's birth. It is at this moment (Act V, Scene VII, line 59) that,
certain of his death, he faces Macduff with those famous words: "Lay on,
Macduff . . ." (cf. *confice*). Whatever may have been the exact source of
Horace's passage — if there is a single source — epic gives the tone to the
language. The circumstances in which the oracle was uttered (*cecinit*, 30)
suggest epic grandeur. Moreover, the first line (31), containing the poetic
dira and the archaic *hosticus* and concerned with the type of destiny associated
with epic or tragedy, fits the mood of an oracle or formal, grand poetry. It
is the irony of the prophecy to descend from tragic deaths, which it denies
our hero, through more prosaic fates to the most ridiculous of all ends.
Horace must perish ignobly at the hands of a *garrulus* (33). Still, suffering
the fool's aggressiveness, while an ignominious fate, is significantly placed
in the same context of hostility as a death in real battle would be. In fact,

the anticlimactic end of the prophecy, with its mock-epic tmesis *quando ...cumque* (33), reveals the weapon which, above all others, is deadly to Horace: meaningless verbosity. Accordingly, he criticizes Lucilius for talkativeness in *S.*, I, 4 and 10; he attacks Hermogenes for his lack of literary discipline in I, 2 and 3; and he sets up as his own great artistic ideal *brevitas*.[45] There is, then, no alternative: Horace is irrevocably doomed.

In terms of epic battle, the remainder of the Satire determines the fate of the doomed poet. Conquered now, he is granted his life and made a helpless prisoner. Possibilities of escape occur, are hopefully grasped, but as quickly forestalled by captor or fate. The first chance arises as a result of the lawsuit impending against the bore (33 ff.). On the basis of their mutual friendship, the fool asks Horace to stop a moment and give him support. Since this "friendship" (38) is viewed by the poet as enmity, he swears that he cannot and will not stop (*inteream*, 38). Villeneuve found problems in the traditional interpretation of the phrase *valeo stare* (39).[46] He rejected construing *stare* as equivalent to *adstare*[47] and, pointing to a common theory about Horace's delicate health, treated *stare* as a properly simple verb. According to this interpretation, Horace has not the strength to stand; there is no other implication. Limitations on the relevance of Horace's language, as 78 and the systematic connotations present in this Satire imply, generally result in the error which comes from eliminating important meanings. Quite probably, Horace has used the simple verb as a simple verb *and* for its compound.[48] Such usage would be consistent with economy, since the simple verb, not specifying the preposition in the compound, allows a moderate freedom of application. For instance, the legal context here suggests the prepositions *ad-* or *prae-*; but Horace's unhappy condition might well support *con-* or *prae-*, with their thematic relevance. The military metaphor, that is, cannot be totally disregarded. At any rate, Horace has no fight left; he certainly can no longer fight the presence of the bore. For a hopeful moment, the man hesitates as to whether to face his lost cause in court or retain Horace captive. The latter alternative seems preferable and, captor that he is, he leads off his victim (*praecedere*, 40). The poet cannot resist (*contendere*); he resigns himself and meekly follows the triumphant *garrulus* (*victore*, 41).

For the next fifteen lines, the dreadful predicament of the captive seems to be ignored. The two men converse about Maecenas, and the bore expresses his desire to be admitted into his select circle. If, however, the military theme is applied, it is not out of place. As Horace looks back upon this period, he compares it to supreme torture; he has been under the knife, he says (*sub cultro*, 74). With the poet in hand, the *garrulus* is considering a more valuable conquest, that of the great Maecenas himself. As an instrument of his campaign, he will employ Horace. Therefore, he keeps threatening the poet, in order to make him pliable to his designs. When the man reveals his plot upon Maecenas, he also discloses an aspect of his character which has so far only been implicit: he is not only antagonistic because of his chatter; he is also highly aggressive, in fact unscrupulous in the pursuit of his ambitions. These two qualities are complementary in his personality, to be sure, but aggressiveness does not necessarily follow from talkativeness. Impelled as he is by ambition, the fool makes the egregious error of attributing the same aggressive traits to Horace, and, under this illusion, he appeals to the poet by the crude motives influencing his own manner. Since Horace is a good friend of Maecenas, he assumes that Horace has consciously seized opportunities (*fortuna*, 45)[49] to pretend the sort of friendship which makes use of a powerful political figure. So begins Horace's torture. Fortune governs the military sphere as well as the political, at least when one is crudely ambitious. In as much, then, as the poet already has the advantages of Fortune, the *garrulus* devises a campaign which will depend on Horace's Fortune and will have as its object the capture of similar Fortune. To begin with, he speaks of himself as a potential *adiutor* (46) of Horace's ambition. The metaphor in *adiutor*, ambiguous in its clause, quickly acquires a precise meaning as a result of the definite stage metaphor in *ferre secundas*. Since, however, it precedes the specific dramatic image, it might also possess momentarily a valid military significance. If so, the *garrulus* first proposes himself as Horace's aide-de-camp,[50] then requests a supporting role in the play where Horace takes the lead. The plan of operations is simple: the poet will introduce the *garrulus* to Maecenas.[51] The word used for "introduce," *tradere* (47), is the equivalent of *commendare*.[52] It is not unlikely, however, that the word betrays the aggressive nature of the speaker by suggesting also a military overtone. By this interpretation, a scene could be imagined where, introduced into the fortified city, the enemy overcomes all resistance (*summosses*, 48)[53] and treacherously seizes power from within. At this point, thoroughly antagonized by such shameless effrontery, Horace protests at the schemer's misconceptions. There is no truth in the belief that Maecenas' circle has political importance; rather, it is opposed to unscrupulous climbing: *his aliena malis* (50).[54] Just as the fool's ways arouse the antagonism of Horace, so his ambition only earns the hostility of the artistic circle to which the poet belongs.

Horace's protests only fire the man's desire to win the favor of Maecenas. When the fool applies to himself the metaphor *accendis* (53), Horace immediately construes it in its military sense and completes the ellipsis mentally to read: "you fire my courage." Carrying on in the same vein, the satirist now openly uses the military metaphor as proper to his companion's manner. As he ironically puts it, nothing could withstand the persistence of such a person; the man will take Maecenas by storm (*expugnabis*, 55) in an easy victory (*vinci*). In this metaphorical context, *virtus* (54) also reverts to its original meaning of manliness, fitness for war. Once again, by its striking incongruity, the image stresses the moral significance of the Satire. The bore is aggressive and offensive: that constitutes his *virtus*. Because, however, his aggressiveness springs from crude personal ambition, devoid of any trace of honor, his virtue must fall far short of the epic ideal. Therefore, too, the military theme will always be an ironic suggestion of the schemer's ignobility. With this implication, Horace continues: there are strategic approaches (*aditus*, 56), he says, to Maecenas' city, but difficult and well-guarded. Completely missing Horace's irony and taking his cue from the military metaphor, the schemer openly parades his methods and his scale of values: he will use bribery on the guards (*corrumpam*, 57). If the gates are shut on him and, like a lover, he is ignored (*exclusus*, 58), he will remain true to his character: he will not give up. Awaiting his opportunity, he will attack his man in the street (*occurram*, 59),[55] force a meeting. He will impose himself on Maecenas as an escort; he will, in other words, lead Maecenas captive just as he is now leading Horace (*deducam*).[56] Then, as if to summarize his energetic character, he recites the noble truism, which he has perverted to his own purposes:

> nil sine magno
> vita labore dedit mortalibus. (59-60)

As Heinze noted, the saying originated in the dignified Greek oracular proverb:

οὐδὲν ἄνευ καμάτου πέλει ἀνδράσιν εὐπετὲς ἔργον.

["No task is easy for human beings without effort."]

It is perhaps significant that the unscrupulous *garrulus* has perverted the neat hexameter unit as well as the moral basis of the original.

The greater offensive of the schemer has now been exposed; Horace remains in his predicament. At this juncture, Fuscus Aristius comes up — as Horace hopefully believes — to the attack (*occurrit*, 61; cf. 59). The warriors, prepared for battle, make a stand (*consistimus*, 62; cf. 9). By every means in his power, Horace tries to show his longing for rescue (*eriperet*, 65), gesticulating, nudging, going through a series of facial contortions. Aristius pretends obtuseness. Furious yet helpless, Horace describes his desperation in physical terms: *meum iecur urere bilis* (66). Though by no means an exact parallel, there is a possible reminiscence here, I suggest, of Homeric phrases used to denote deep feeling, such as χόλον θυμαλγέα ["Anger that pains the soul"].[57] When subtle methods bring no result, Horace is obliged to speak out. He reminds Aristius of an important message which requires privacy (67-8). It is amusing to tease, and Aristius refuses to co-operate, alleging a flimsy excuse (68-71). With a cry of frustration, the intensity of which suggests epic emotionality, the poor satirist curses his evil day: *solem / tam nigrum* (72-3). After Aristius has fled from battle with the bore (*fugit*, 73), he is doomed. The phrase *sub cultro*, according to Porphyrio, is a well-known proverb. Unfortunately, this proverb is used once in extant Latin literature, in this passage.[58] Most commentators gloss the phrase: "as a sacrificial victim." It seems likely that this interpretation should be accepted, for the *culter* was most commonly used as a sacrificial knife and victims were put under the knife.[59] In Ovid's time, though, the *culter* could be spoken of as weapon also; and by 50 A.D. the short sword of the gladiator was sometimes called *culter*. There is, then, considerable justification for interpreting the victim under the knife as human and accepting Heinze's ingenious gloss: "wie ein wehrloses *Schlachtopfer*, bereit den Todesstoss zu empfangen" ["Like a helpless battle-victim, ready to receive the death stroke"].[60] At this point, Horace's predicament seems desperate indeed.

Suddenly, another warrior (*adversarius*, 75) arrives on the scene, to contest the way (*obvius*, 74). As he recognizes his enemy, the newcomer hails the *garrulus* with a curse, takes the willing Horace as witness, and drags his man violently off to trial. In this final scene, the description is very allusive, and the poet uses his economic device of ellipsis to advantage (77-7). Although specifically he is depicting the uproar occasioned by the cursing *adversarius*, the resisting *garrulus*, and the crowd of spectators, he also succeeds in suggesting a scene of battle. Possibly, one might think of an episode such as that in the *Iliad*, when the Greeks and Trojans fight over the body of Patroclus. Wherever the battle is hottest, the most men are involved, and reinforcements are continually pouring in. The *garrulus*, by nature antagonistic, must be the center of battle, and when he is dragged off, his victim Horace, a naturally peaceful individual, is left in tranquility. The uproar (*clamor utrimque*, 77) is similar to the thunder of battle in the *Iliad* (ὀρυμάγδος). When the curious onlookers run up (*concursus*, 78),[61] there is a general confusion like that of a violent engagement. Rescued from battle at last, free of the intolerable aggressiveness of the *garrulus*, Horace thinks of Apollo as his protector. Apollo has saved him, indeed, from a struggle as ominous for him as the hopeless combat between Achilles and Hector. Unlike Hector, the satirist is not snatched away (ἐξήρπαξεν = *eriperet*, 65); instead, his enemy is carried off (*rapit*), and he himself remains safe.

None of this elaboration of battle and war symbolism in I, 9 negates the validity of the factual interpretations or the perceptive comments made by previous scholars in regard to this poem. At most, it questions what should always be questioned in the criticism of poetry: dogmatic, absolute assertions of a single specific interpretation, limiting Horace at points where he appears to have been deliberately unspecific and suggestive. On the positive side, it serves to explain some of the intricacy of Horace's technique. The observation has long since been made, for instance, that the satirist frequently uses military metaphors.[62] In S., I, 9, this practice can be explained as systematic and economic development of the moral insight of the poet. In an ordinary situation, a meeting between a typically contented, unambitious, sensitively artistic writer and an unwelcome, pushing poetaster, the satirist perceives, through his controlled irony, the elements of epic battle. The point of contact between the described event and the imagined overtones of war is the personality of the *garrulus*, which, being thoroughly objectionable, motivates the action of the drama. The man is *aggressive*; he makes himself *offensive*; he arouses *antagonism* in Horace. These metaphorical terms epitomize the relation between drama and battle, the relation which Horace is subtly stressing in his account. At no time does it appear that the action is sacrificed to the symbol. Where the symbol pushes forward, as in the exaggerated descriptions of Horace's feelings (10, 12, 28, 66, 72), the oracle (29–34), or the unambiguous metaphors (42, 55, 73), it is always nicely blended in the attractive irony of the satirist. But humor in Horace is not usually uneconomical or un-moral. It is his genius to suggest much without asserting and without ever distorting his dramatic setting. In *S.,* I, 9, accordingly, he has expressed his insight into the character of a typical man by ironically identifying an aggressive personality with the heroic standards of epic. The incongruity is subtly controlled, maintained throughout the poem. To fit it neatly to his drama, the satirist depicts himself as the unfortunate warrior, fatally inferior to the aggressor, whose doom, long since prophesied, is now at last brought almost to fulfilment before our eyes. Only the providential intervention of Apollo saves him. It is perhaps doubtful that *Apollo* can be identified with a specific Roman monument of Apollo. It does, however, appear certain that Horace is speaking of the Apollo of mythology and literature, the god of poetry and justice, the character in Lucilius' clever, but limited, parody, and the deity whom Homer originally described as intervening to save Hector. Only Horace could devise a poem in which he subtly condemned Lucilius' use of Greek words and uneconomic parody by taking a specific line borrowed by his predecessor from Homer and using it more dexterously. The martial context of the *Iliad*, admirably adapted to the ordinary incident here dramatized, extends the significance of the Satire and reveals the maturity of Horace at this relatively early stage in his poetic career.

Notes

[1]G. C. Fiske, *Lucilius and Horace: a Study in the Classical Theory of Imitation* (Madison, 1920).

[2]Vergil offers the best example of controlled imitation. In his important book, V. Pöschl, *Die Dichtkunst Virgils* (Wiesbaden, 1950), studies Vergil's use of Homeric similes and reaches striking conclusions about the former's methods of imitation.

[3]E. g., Fiske, pp. 46, 134.

[4]J. J. Iltgen, *De Horatio Lucilii Aemulo* (Montbauer, 1872), pp. 18 and 19.

[5]None of the following editions regard the influence of Lucilius upon *S.,* I, 9 as significant beyond lines 1 and 78: L. Mueller (Wien, 1891); J. Orellius, 4th ed. (Berlin, 1892); J. H. Kirkland (Boston, 1894); P. Lejay (Paris, 1911); E. P. Morris (New York, 1909); Kiessling-Heinze, 5th ed. (Berlin, 1921).

[6]*Op. cit,* p. 335.

[7]*Op. cit.,* p. 335: "The closing line of the Horatian satire was directly modelled on that of Lucilius, as is proved by Porphyrio's quotation of line 231."

[8]Porphyr.: "Hoc de illo sensu Homerico sumpsit, quem et Lucilius in sexto Satirarum repraesentavit sic dicens...."

[9]Cf. Horace's attacks on Lucilius' use of Greek words in *S.,* I, 10, 23 ff.

[10]Cf. the reconstruction of Lucilius' argument by Fiske, *op. cit.,* pp. 335 ff.

[11]*Op. cit.* in his excellent notes on line 78.

[12]F. Ritter, in his edition of the *Satires* (Leipzig, 1857), note on line 78.

[13]E. T. Salmon, "Horace's Ninth Satire in its Setting," *Studies in Honor of Gilbert Norwood* (Toronto, 1952), pp. 184–93.

[14]Cf. the efforts of interpretation in Orellius, *op. cit.*, and Lejay, *op. cit.* Because of the difficulty and the absence of any definite indications as to the significance of the phrase, Kiessling-Heinze, *op. cit.*, regard the words as devoid of factual application.

[15]There is a potential difficulty in dating the Satire as late as the building of Sosius' Temple, since the date of construction is often assigned to the year of Sosius' consulship. Salmon argues plausibly that the temple was erected in 33 B.C., as Shipley had already suggested. If so, there is no necessary conflict, since Book II of the *Satires* was written in the years 33–30 B.C.

[16]F. Castagnoli, "Note di Topografia Romana," *Bull. Comm. Arch. Com.* LXXIV (1952), p. 53.

[17]The negative *nil*, not in Porphyrio, is added by Marx. Subsequent editors, however, have accepted the emendation: so Warmington and Terzaghi; and Fiske reads *nil*.

[18]Fiske, *op. cit.*, p. 335 rejects Marx's interpretation of the line. Marx imagined a situation in which somebody is badly beaten up and prays that he may be saved in the miraculous manner of Hector: "ita enim pugnis et fustibus erat male mulcatus." I doubt that Lucilius' use of Greek words was that subtle.

[19]On the use of Hellenisms in Lucilius, cf. W. C. Korfmacher, "'Grecizing' in Lucilian Satire," *C.J.*, XXX (1935), pp. 453–62; also, M. Puelma Piwonka, *Lucilius und Kallimachos: zur Geschichte einer Gattung der hellenistisch-römische Poesie* (Frankfurt, 1949), pp. 13 ff.

[20]I agree with the majority of scholars, who regard this Satire as based on an imaginary experience.

[21]For *occupare* with a personal object in a martial context, cf. *Aen.*, X, 699: *Latagum saxo atque ingenti fragmine montis / occupat os faciemque adversam*. Horace uses this word in *Epist.*, I, 7, 66 to signify abrupt address, though without any suggestion of the military theme.

[22]There are four usages of *arripere* in Horace, all of them indicating violent activity. Three of them suggest the ferocity of animals. Cf. *A.P.*, 475, where *arripuit* is associated by simile with *ursus*. In *S.*, II, 1, 69 and 3, 224, the verb is characteristic of the satirist's invective. Only *Epist.*, I, 7, 89 does not fit the metaphor. As for the phrase *arrepta manu*, it is quite possible that Horace is thinking of a line in Plautus and its violent associations: cf. *Curc.*, 597: *manum arripuit mordicus*. That the line is well-known is indicated by the fact that it is imitated by Turpilius (*Com.*, 108) and by Apuleius (*Met.*, VIII, 23). In short, the first view we have of the *garrulus* is carefully influenced by *arrepta*, so as to suggest his aggressiveness.

[23]I should like to have found support for my first impression, that the whole scene resembles Achilles' pursuit around the walls of Ilium in *Il.*, XXII; I do not now believe, however, that Horace justifies the connection.

[24]Horace uses *discedere* three times in this same military sense. Cf. *Epist.*, I, 7, 17: *victor violens discessit ab hoste*; also, *Epist.*, II, 2, 99, where he is describing the rivalry of critics, and *S.*, I, 7, 17, where he comments on the famous meeting of Glaucus and Diomedes in the *Iliad*. For the military meaning in general, cf. *T.L.L.*, *s.v.*, § C. It appears in Caesar, e.g., *B.C.*, III, 112, 7, and Livy, e.g., IX, 44, 8.

[25]Cf. *Aen.*, IX, 789: *agmine denso / consistunt*. For the military meaning in general, cf. *T.L.L.*, *s.v.*, § I 2b. The word appears in Caesar, e.g., *B.G.*, II, 21, 6, and Livy, e.g., I, 27, 5.

[26]Cf. *Il.*, V, 796; XI, 811.

[27]Cf. *Il.*, XIII, 711; XVI, 109.

[28]*Aen.*, IX, 812.

[29]Cf. *Aen.*, XI, 159: *felix morte tua*. It is in a similar context that Aeneas voices his emotions: *o terque quaterque beati . . .* (I, 94).

[30]Cf. *Epist.*, II, 1, 124: *militiae quamquam piger et malus*. In fact, *piger* regularly denotes him who is unfit for military exploits. Cf. Cicero, *Fam.*, VII, 17, 1; Livy, XXI,

25, 6; Juvenal, 8, 248. By contrast, *impiger* connotes the zeal and energy necessary for war. Cf. *Carm.*, IV, 14, 22: *impiger hostium / vexare turmas*.

[31]Tempting though it may be, the simile should not be taken as analogous to the epic simile in *Il.*, XI, 558 ff., describing Ajax in terms of an ass.

[32]Cf. *Aen.*, VI, 103: *ut primum cessit furor et rabida ora quierunt, / incipit Aeneas heros*.

[35]Cf. the speech of Achilles to Aeneas in *Il.*, XX, 196.

[34]In two other cases, Horace uses *salvus* to apply to circumstances of war: cf. *Epist.*, I, 2, 10 and 16, 27.

[35]It will be noticed that Horace is practicing ellipsis regularly and has here omitted the direct object of *confice*. The conventional object would probably have been something like *negotium*, as it is interpreted in *T.L.L.*, *s.v.* § I A 2b. However, the ellipsis permits a personal subject, specifically *me*. To fit such a construction, there is a sense of *conficere* related to killing: cf. *T.L.L.*, *s.v.*, § III E 1. Cf. Livy, VI, 13, 5: *iusta caede conficere hostem posset*.

[36]Cf. Orellius, Kirkland, Lejay, Morris, Fiske, Kiessling-Heinze, and others.

[37]*Od.*, IX, 507 ff.

[38]Cf. *Il.*, XVII, 478 and 672; XXII, 436.

[39]*Il.*, XIII, 666.

[40]*Il.*, XIX, 409.

[41]*Il.*, XX, 332.

[42]*Il.*, XXI, 110.

[43]The credit for suggesting this new analogue, as Lejay notes, goes to Kiessling.

[44]*Lives*, VII, 27. The epigram is fully cited in Orellius, Kirkland, and Lejay.

[45]Cf. *S.*, I, 10, 9: *est brevitate opus*.

[46]F. Villeneuve, *Horace: Satires* (Paris, 1932), *loc. cit.*

[47]One might assume *adstare* on the basis of *ades* (36).

[48] The exact implication conveyed when a simple word is used for its compound varies according to the context. Frequently, abbreviation of this type has informal connotations and is congenial to satire. Cf. E Wölfflin, "Bemerkungen über das Vulgärlatein," *Philol.*, XXXIV (1876), pp. 149 ff.; F. Ruckdeschel, *Archaismen and Vulgarismen in der Sprache des Horaz* (Diss. Munich, 1910), pp. 25 ff.; A. Engel, *De Q. Horati Flacci Sermone Metro Accomodato* (Diss. Breslau, 1914), pp. 68 ff.

[49]I interpret the ellipsis, with most editors, as implying *te*, not *illo*.

[50]Cf. Livy, X, 26, 2: *adiutorem belli sociumque imperii darent*.

[51]Though it would be convenient for the image to have *hunc hominem* refer to Maecenas, one must interpret the phrase, following Porphyrio, as a familiar expression probably accompanied by a gesture, as the *garrulus* points to himself.

[52]Cf. *Epist.*, I, 18, 76–8, where Horace uses *commendare* and *tradere* in the same sense.

[53]Cf. Caesar, *B.G.*, I, 25: *victis ac summotis resisterent*; also, *B.G.*, VIII, 10.

[54]Lejay glosses *aliena*: "hostile, contraire." For the meaning "hostile," cf. *T.L.L.*, *s.v.*, § II A 2.

[55]For the use of *occurrere* in a military sense, cf. Lucretius, III, 524: *falsae rationi vera videtur / res occurrere et effugium praecludere*, also Lucretius, VI, 32. In Caesar, cf. B.C., I, 40 and III, 92: *ipsi immissis telis occurrissent*. Cf. also *Aen.*, X, 734.

[56]Prof. H. T. Rowell has pointed out to me a second Horatian usage of *deducere* in this meaning of leading in triumph: *Carm.*, I, 37, 31: *scilicet invidens / privata deduci superbo / non humilis mulier triumpho*. For the general military sense, cf. *T.L.L.*, *s.v.*, § I A 2f. With this significance, it is used in Caesar, e.g., *B.G.*, III, 38, and Livy, e.g., XXVIII, 32, 7.

[57]Cf. *Il.*, IX, 260.

[58]Cf. A. Otto, *Die Sprichwörter und sprichwörtlichen Redensarten der Römer* (Leipzig, 1890), p. 100; also, the article on *culter* in *T.L.L.*

[59] Cf. *Aen.*, VI, 248: *supponunt alii cultros tepidumque cruorem / suscipiunt pateris*; also *Georg.*, III, 492.

[60] Cf. *Trist.*, V, 7, 19: *dextera non segnis fixo dare vulnera cultro*. Seneca mentions the use of the *cultor* by gladiators in *Epist.*, 87, 9. In his note on the passage, Heinze associates the phrase with the obvious military metaphor of 43, *victore*.

[61] For the military application of *concursus*, cf. *T.L.L.*, *s.v.*, § I 2. There is a curious parallel to *clamor utrimque, / undique concursus* in Cicero, *Tusc.*, II, 37: *quid? exercitatio legionum, quid? ille cursus, concursus, clamor, quanti laboris est?* Cf. also Livy, XXII, 19, 12: *pertinaci certamine et concursu*.

[62] F. Bäker, *Die Metaphern in den Satiren des Horaz* (Stralsund, 1883), p. 20.

BIBLIOGRAPHY OF HORACE

Ancona, Ronnie. *Time and the Erotic in Horace's Odes*. Duke University Press, 1994.

Armstrong, David. *Horace*. New Haven, 1989.

Bailey, D. R. S. *Profile of Horace*. Harvard University Press, 1982.

Cairns, Francis. *Generic Composition in Greek and Roman Poetry*. Edinburgh, 1972.

Campbell, A. Y. *Horace, a New Interpretation*. London, 1924.

Cody, J. V. *Horace and Callimachean Aesthetics*. Collection Latomus, no. 147. Brussels, 1976.

Collinge, N. E. *The Structure of Horace's Odes*. Oxford University Press, 1961.

Commager, Steele. *The Odes of Horace*. New Haven, 1962.

Connor, Peter. *Horace's Lyric Poetry: The Force of Humour*. Aureal Publications, 1987.

Davis, Gregson. *Polyhymnia: The Rhetoric of Horatian Lyric Discourse*. University of California Press, 1991.

Dettmer, Helen. *Horace: A Study in Structure*. Hildesheim, 1983.

Edmunds, Lowell. *From a Sabine Jar. Reading Horace, Odes 1.9*. Chapel Hill, 1992.

Fraenkel, E. *Horace*. Oxford University Press, 1957.

Garrison, D. H. *Horace: Epodes and Odes*. University of Oklahoma Press, 1991.

Gold, B. K., ed. *Literary and Artistic Patronage in Ancient Rome*. Austin, 1982.

Highet, Gilbert. *Poets in a Landscape*. New York, 1957.

Johnson, W. R. *The Idea of Lyric. Lyric Modes in Ancient and Modern Poetry*. University of California Press, 1982.

Lee, M. Owen. *Word, Sound, and Image in the Odes of Horace*. Ann Arbor, 1969.

Lyne, R. O. A. M. *The Latin Love Poets. From Catullus to Horace.* Oxford, 1980.

———. *Horace: Behind the Public Poetry.* New Haven, 1995.

McDermott, E. A. "Horatius callidus." *American Journal of Philology* 98 (1977) 168–77.

Minadeo, R. *The Golden Plectrum. Sexual Symbolism in Horace's Odes.* Amsterdam 1982.

Murray, O. "Symposium and Genre in the Poetry of Horace." *Journal of Roman Studies* 75 (1985) 39–50.

Musurillo, H. "The Poet's Apotheosis: Horace, Odes 1.1." *Transactions of the American Philological Association* 93 (1962) 230–39.

Nisbet, R. G. M. and M. Hubbard, eds. *A Commentary on Horace: Odes, Book I.* Oxford University Press, 1970.

———. *A Commentary on Horace: Odes, Book II.* Oxford University Press, 1978.

Nussbaum, G. B. "A Study of Odes 1.37 and 38: The Psychology of Conflict and Horace's Humanitas." *Arethusa* 4 (1971) 91–97.

Pasquali, G. *Orazio lirico: Studi.* Florence, 1920.

Peradotto, J., ed. *Horace: 2000 Years. Arethusa* 28: 2 and 3 (1995).

Perret, J. *Horace.* English translation by B. Humez. New York, 1964.

Pöschl, V. *Horazische Lyrik: Interpretationen.* Heidelberg, 1970.

Porter, , D. H. *Horace's Poetic Journey. A Reading of Odes 1–3.* Princeton, 1987.

Putnam, M. C. J. *Essays on Latin Lyric, Elegy, and Epic.* Princeton, 1982.

———. *Artifices of Eternity: Horace's Fourth Book of Odes.* Ithaca, N.Y. 1986.

Quinn, K. *Latin Explorations: Critical Studies in Roman Literature.* London, 1963.

Race, W. *The Classical Priamel from Homer to Boethius.* Mnemosyne Supplement, no. 74. Leiden, 1982.

Reckford, K. *Horace*. Twayne World Author Series, No. 73. New York, 1969.

Santirocco, M. *Unity and Design in Horace's Odes*. Chapel Hill, 1986.

Shey, H. J. "The Poet's Progress: Horace Odes I, 1." *Arethusa* 4 (1971) 185–96.

Shorey, P. and G. J. Laing, eds. *Horace: Odes and Epodes*. Chicago, 1919.

Silk, E. T. "Towards a Fresh Interpretation of Horace Carm. III.1." *Yale Classical Studies* 25 (1973) 131–45.

Syndikus, H.-P. *Die Lyrik des Horaz: Eine Interpretation der Oden*. 2 vols. Impulse der Forschung, no. 7. Darmstadt, 1972–73.

Verrall, A. W. *Studies Literary and Historical in the Odes of Horace*. London, 1884. Reprint, Port Washington, N.Y.: Kennikat Press, 1969.

Vessey, D. W. T. "From Mountain to Lover's Tryst: Horace's Soracte Ode." *Journal of Roman Studies* 75 (1985) 26–38.

West, D. *Reading Horace*. Edinburgh, 1967.

Wili, W. *Horaz und die augusteische Kultur*. Basel , 1948.

Wilkinson, L. P. *Horace and his Lyric Poetry*. 2d ed. Cambridge University Press, 1951.

Williams, G. *Tradition and Originality in Roman Poetry*. Oxford University Press, 1968.

―――. *The Third Book of Horace's Odes*. Oxford University Press, 1969.

―――. *Horace*. Greece and Rome New Surveys in the Classics, no. 6. Oxford University Press, 1972.

Woodman, T. and D. West, eds. *Quality and Pleasure in Latin Poetry*. Cambridge University Press, 1974.

Other Titles of Interest

Why Vergil?
A Collection of Interpretations
by Stephanie Quinn

Forty-four distinguished selections; foreword by
Michael C. J. Putnam; introduction and
afterword: "Why Vergil?" by Stephanie Quinn

*We lack automatic and simple answers to the question
"Why Vergil?"...Yet even after 2,000 years, the voice
of Vergil still resonates with the universal human cry.*
— **From the Introduction**

(1999) Paperback, ISBN 0-86516-418-5
(1999) Hardbound, ISBN 0-86516-435-5

Horace Satire I.9
THE BOOR
by Margaret A. Brucia & Madeleine M. Henry

*Horace is simple and complex, witty and serious, proud
and humble...If a student were to read but one satire of
Horace, 1.9, The Boor would be the one to choose.*
— **from the Preface**

Student Text: Illus., 45 pp., (1998) 6 x 9, Paperback, ISBN 0-86516-413-4
Teacher's Guide: 20 pp., (1998) Paperback, ISBN 0-86516-429-0

Horace
Selected Odes and Satire I.9
by Ronnie Ancona

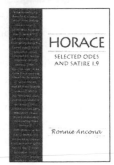

Student Text: Introduction, Latin text, notes,
vocabulary, section on meters and figures of speech,
bibliography. Contains *Odes* 1.1; 1.5; 1.9; 1.11;
1.13; 1.22; 1.23; 1.24; 1.25; 1.37; 1.38; 2.3; 2.7;
2.10; 2.14; 3.1; 3.9; 3.13; 3.30; 4.7; *Satire* 1.9

Teacher's Guide: large format Latin text, literal
translation, sample tests, bibliography.

Student Text: (1999) Paperback, ISBN 0-86516-416-9
Teacher's Edition: (1999) Paperback, ISBN 0-86516-430-4

Bolchazy-Carducci Publishers, Inc. ✦ http://www.bolchazy.com